مـختارات من الأم باللغة العربية
مع النصوص الإنجليزية الأصلية

Anthology from the Mother in Arabic
– Bilingual Edition

Printed in the United states of America
Distributed by: Amazon CreateSpace
Copyright © 2015, Golden Bridge Publications -- a department of Auromere Inc.

Lotus Photo on Cover: courtesy of Jim Page, www.jimpagephotography.com

ISBN: 0-69254-743-6

Table of Contents

شـكـر وتـقديــــر

كمصنف ومترجم لنصوص هذا الكتاب، أود أتوجه بأصدق مشاعر التقدير إلى السيد مانوج داس جوبتـــا Sri Manoj Das Gupta، القـــائم بأعمـــال أشـــرام* شـــري أوروبينـــدو فـــي بودوشري، جنوب الهند، على السماح بنشر نصوص هذا الكتاب،

د. زكريا ممدوح مرسي

sriaurobindotranslations@gmail.com

Acknowledgement

As comp ler and translator of this book, I would like to express my sincere thanks to Sri Manoj Das Gupta, Managing Trustee of the Sri Aurobindo Ashram, Puducherry, South India, for permission to publish the texts of this book.

Zackaria Moursi, Ph.D.

sriaurobindotranslations@gmail.com

The Mother الأم
Around 1955

Sri Aurobindo   شري أوروبيندو
1950

Introduction

Mirra Alfassa, known to many as The Mother, was born in Paris (in 1878) to an Egyptian mother and a Turkish father. She joined, at the age of forty-two, the great revolutionary, poet, seer and modernizer of spirituality Sri Aurobindo in India and became his co-worker and the realizer of his visions.

Early in the 20th Century, in India, Sri Aurobindo had major experiences that crystallized in a new vision for the future of humanity. At about the same time, the Mother, then living in Paris, had independently the same vision. They both foresaw, unknown to each other, the dawn of a new consciousness of Oneness unifying humans with the entire existence, and changing them into happier, nobler and higher beings, endowed with more knowledge and self-mastery, and showing them a way for gradually transforming earthly life into the "Life Divine" [title of Sri Aurobindo's major philosophical work]. We can witness today this new consciousness of Oneness penetrating, at an ever accelerating pace, the entire globe. The signs of unification are unmistakable: in politics and trade, in technology and science, on the web and other media, in culture and sports, and even in fashion and entertainment. Unexpected ways of living and modes of interaction are dramatically improving the quality of life in many countries of the world. The spreading of such a consciousness to encompass all humanity is considered by many the only hope and foundation for saving a world besieged by war, environmental degradation, social inequality, famine, fundamentalism and sectarianism.

Sri Aurobindo and the Mother, referred to their teachings as the Integral Yoga. For them Yoga was, to use Sri Aurobindo's well-known phrase, "nothing but practical psychology." The spirituality they stood for has nothing to do with religious ideologies or with world renunciation or with occultism and so-called supra-normal phenomena. They held rather that man is a transitional being evolving to a "Supramental Being", a being that will be to man what man is to the animal" They firmly believed that humans have reached a stage of progress that enables them to consciously participate in and speed up their own evolution, and that this speeding up can be carried out methodically and without recourse to occult powers or artificial "miracles". In the same way as science discovers the laws governing the outer working of Nature, yoga discovers the laws that govern the its inner workings and utilizes them to effect the spiritual transformation of mankind. Sri Aurobindo and the Mother did not conceal the difficulty of their yoga. Although the transformation of human nature has been considered impossible by most spiritual seekers in the past, they maintained it can be done, at least partially, and concrete results attained within one human life-span.

مقدمــــة

ولدت ميــرا ألفاصــا، المعروفــة لكثيرين باسم **الأم**، في باريس عـام 1878 لأم مصرية وأب تركــي. التحقت فــي عامهــا الثاني والأربعين بشــري أوروبينــدو ، الثـائر المناضل فــي كفـاح التحريــر فــي الهنــد، الشاعر المفكـر، المبتكـر فـي مجـال التطـور، والمتصوف المجـدد فـي الروحيات وأصبحت زميلة عمله ومحققة رؤيته. منذ ذلك الحين صارت تعرف **بالأم.**

في أوائـل القرن الماضي مــرَّ شـري أوروبينـدو في الهنـد بتجـارب روحيـة حاسـمة مهدت لـه الطريــق إلــى رؤيـة شـاملة لمصيـر الإنسـانية. في حـوالي نفـس الوقت توصلـت **الأم،** وكانـت آنـذاك مـا تـزال تعيـش في باريـس، إلى نفس الرؤيـة. رأى كلاهمـا فجر وعـي وحدائـي جديد يوحد البشـر ويربطهم بالوجـود كلـه، ويُحَـوِّل الإنسـان تدريجيـاً إلى كـائن أسـمى وأسـعد وأنبـل وأبعـد فـي المعرفـة والتحكم في النفس وقـادراً علـى تغييـر الحيـاة الأرضية ممـا هـي عليـه الآن إلــى "الحيـاة الإلهيـة" [عنـوان أهـم الأعمـال الفلسـفية لشـري أوروبينـدو]. نعاصـر اليـوم وعـي الوحدانيـة هـذا وهـو ينتشـر فـي الأرض كلهـا، ونـرى آثـاره جليـة فـي مجـالات السياسـة والاقتصـاد، والتقنيـات والعلـوم والاتصـالات، وفـي الإبـداع الثقـافي والرياضـة، وحتـى فـي مجـالات الأزيـاء والترفيـه. كـذلك نشـهد في بلـدان كثيـرة ظهـور أنمـاط وطرائـق جديـدةً للتعايـش والتفاعـل ترتقـي كثيـراً بنوعيـة الحيـاة علـى الأرض. يـرى الكثيـرون أن تعميـم هـذا الـوعي الجديد بحيث يتملك من البشـر جميعـاً، أو علـى الأقل من غالبيتهم، هو الأمل الوحيد فـي إنقـاذ عالمنا المهدد بأخطار الحروب وتدهور البيئة وعدم المساواة والجوع والجهل والأصولية.

أطلـق شـري أوروبينـدو والأم علـى تعاليمهم اسـم "اليوغـا المتكاملـة." كانـا يريـان، علـى حـد تعبيـر شـهير لشـري أوروبينـدو، "أن اليوغـا مـا هـي إلا سـيكولوجيا عمليـة". وكانـت الروحيـة بعيـدة كل البعـد عـن الأيـدلوجيات الدينيـة وعـن التخلـي عـن العـالم وعـن التـداول في الغيبيـات والظواهر الفائقـة للطبيعة. آمنـا بأن الإنسـان كائـن انتقالي يتطور إلـى كـائن أرقـى أطلقـا عليه "كـائن مـا بعد العقل" سـيكون في سـياق التطـور بالنسـبة إلـى الإنسـان مـا كانـه الإنسـان بالنسـبة للحيوان. اعتقدا اعتقاداً راسـخاً أن البشـر بلغـوا مرحلـة من التقـدم تمكنهم من مسـاندة تطـورهم الطبيعـي بحيـث يحتاجون إلى وقت أقصـر لبلـوغ المرحلـة التاليـة في تطـورهم الطبيعي، ورأيـا أن إسـراع التطـور بهذه الطريقـة يمكن أن يـتم منهجيـاً وبـدون أي حاجـة إلـى قـوى غيبيـة أو "معجـزات" مصطنعـة. وكمـا أن العلـوم الفزيائيـة تكتشـف قوانين **الطبيعـة** الظاهربـة، فـإن اليوغـا تكتشـف قوانيـن الطبيعـة الباطنيـة وتسـتغل هـذه القوانين فـي تهـذيب وتحويـل طبائـع البشـر. لـم ينكـر شـري أوروبينـدو والأم صعوبة مثـل هـذه اليوغـا، ولكنهمـا رأيـا أن هـذا التحويـل، الـذي كـان يعتبـر مسـتحيلاً فـي الماضـي، ممكن، وأن الممـارس المجـد يمكـز أن يغير طبيعتـه بصـورة ملموسـة في مدى حياة أرضية واحدة.

The crucial requirement in the Integral Yoga for the individual is to surrender fully to the Divine, who then takes up the guidance and effects the transformation Himself. To achieve this surrender and union, individual practitioners have to go through a shorter or longer preparation (depending on where they stand) and to fulfill some preliminary requirements such as sincerity, faith, fortitude and one-pointed determination. It is evident that the high goal of transforming one's nature cannot be attained effortlessly or overnight. Fortunately, the difficulty of the path applies only to the early stages of practice. Many of those who have practiced the Integral Yoga long enough, have testified that the more they advanced, the path became more and more a happy and spontaneous progression from "light to light", and from "joy to joy". The Integral Yoga does not expect all practitioners to follow any one prescribed path, it rather shows each individual how to discover and develop their own path guided by the Divine immanent in each of them

The readers who will appreciate and benefit the most from the visions and teachings of Sri Aurobindo and the Mother are those who are able to see that Truth has many facets, and who are thus open to accept the validity of views other than their own. This does not necessarily mean though that one abandons the views one has, whose truth one has verified for oneself. It is a matter of enriching and widening the consciousness, and not necessarily of replacing one truth by another. This wider view often requires a mind flexible enough to recognize that the same words can mean different things in different contexts to different people. This in turn requires a developed intuition capable of reading the truth of a statement and not stop short at literal interpretations of its words

Those who follow this path experience a noticeable change in their own consciousness, and as a result, a many positive changes in their lives. They find themselves pursuing their inner quest and journey free from fear and doubt. By slowly discovering the true value of things, they become able to look with a smile upon many of the life problems that had hitherto seemed intractable to them. They learn to work with greater energy and to find joy in whatever work they may be doing and to derive happiness from things they did not even notice before. They discover that with fewer material things, they are better able to surround themselves with abundance, beauty, serenity and meaning. They also discover that the joy of giving and self-offering far outweighs the joys of taking and exacting. They experience how the growing peace within themselves reflects positively on their health, and learn how to avoid and even heal many of the ailments that used formerly to trouble them. And finally, they become far more capable of overcoming their own weaknesses and resistances, of discerning the meaning of things that happens to them, and perceiving the Grace that is guiding every step of their lives.

المُتَطَلَّب الحاسم في اليوغا المتكاملة هو أن يُسَلِّم الممارس نفسه ، ومسئولية إرشاده وتوجيهه وتغيير طبيعته تسليماً تاماً **للواحد-الكل**. لتحقيق هذا التسليم يحتاج الممارس عادة إلى فترة إعداد قد تطول وقد تقصر (تبعاً لنقطة البدء الذي يبدأ منها الممارس)، كذلك ينبغي أن يتحلى الممارس ببعض الفضائل الأساسية مثل الصدق والإيمان والعزم الثابت. غني عن الذكر أن مسعى شامخ مثل تحويل الطبيعة البشرية لا يمكن إنجازه بدون جهد أو بين عشية وضحاها، ولكن صعوبة المسعى تتضاءل كلما تقدم الممارس على الطريق. وقد شهد كثيرون من الذين مارسوا اليوغا المتكاملة وقتاً كافياً أن نموهم في مراحل لممارسة المتقدمة أصبح مسيرة سلسة "من نور إلى نور أسطع" ومن "بهجة إلى بهجة أعظم". جدير بالذكر هنا أن اليوغا المتكاملة لا تفرض أي مسار محدد ومقرر للجميع، بل إنها بالأحرى تساعد كل فرد على اكتشاف وتطوير مساره الخاص تحت هداية الروح الإلهي الذي يقطن في هذا الفرد.

القراء سيحققون أعظم النفع من آراء شري أوروبيندو والأم لو تقبلوا أن **الحقيقة الالهية** لها أوجه عديدة وكانوا متفتحين لتقبل مفاهيم جديدة. هذا التقبل لا يعني بالطبع أنهم يجب أن يتخلوا عن الحقائق التي كانوا يؤمنون بها من قبل والتي سبق أن تحققوا من صدقها في أنفسهم. هدف اليوغا هو توسيع الوعي وإثراؤه وليس بالضرورة إحلال حقيقة محل أخرى. هذه النظرة الأشمل تتطلب ذهناً بلغ من التهذيب والمرونة درجة تمكنه من التحرر من الدلالات الحرفية للكلمات ومن رؤية أن نفس الكلمات قد تكون لها معاني مختلفة حسب السياق الذي تذكر فيه. وهذا بدوره يتطلب حدساً نامياً يسمح للقارئ باستشفاف المعاني من خلال النصوص، بدلاً من التشبث بدلالتها الحرفية

الذين يمارسون اليوغا المتكاملة يشهدون كيف ينعكس التغير الواضح في وعيهم بصورة إيجابية على حياتهم. ويستطيعون متابعة سعيهم ورحلة حياتهم متحررين من الخوف والشك. كما أنهم يكتشفون بالتدريج القيم الحقيقية للأشياء، ويصبحون قادرين على النظر بابتسامة إلى مشاكل الحياة التي كانت تعضلهم من قبل. أضف إلى ذلك أنهم ينشطون إلى العمل بطاقة أكبر ويجدون متعة أعظم في كل عمل يقومون به، ويستمدون السعادة والبهجة من أشياء لم يكادوا يلحظونها من قبل. وعلى الرغم من أن الأشياء المادية التي يحتاجونها تناقص كثيراً، يظلون قادرين على إحاطة أنفسهم بالوفرة والجمال والبهجة وبكل ما له معنى وقيمة حقيقية في الحياة. كما أنهم يكتشفون بدهشة أن متعة العطاء ووهب النفس تفوق كثيراً متعة الأخذ والمطالبة. وفي ظل السلام النامي بداخلهم تتحسن صحتهم ويتعلمون كيف يتجنبون الأمراض، بل وكيف يشفون أنفسهم الكثير من الاضطرابات الصحية التي كانت تزعجهم من قبل. وأخيراً تزداد كثيراً قدراتهم على التغلب على ما فيهم من نقاط ضعف، وعلى فهم أسباب ما يصادفهم من أحداث، وعلى إدراك **النعمة الإلهية** لتي تسدد كل خطوة من خطواتهم في الحياة.

When we follow sincerely our own calling and persevere on our chosen path; we arrive one day at the highest truth: that all beings are but different modes and manifestations of the One and Multiple Supreme, and that we are, therefore, entitled to and capable of realizing Him in ourselves and manifesting Him in our lives.

A few remarks about the texts compiled in this book:

The majority of the texts included in this book are records of informal classes given in French by the Mother to the students of the "Sri Aurobindo International Center of Education in Puducherry, India." Out of consideration for the age of the younger students, the Mother formulated her answers to the questions put to her in a very simple language. The talks were either tape recorded or noted in shorthand; they were later translated into English and published in several volumes under the title "Questions and Answers". In translating these texts from English into Arabic, I took the liberty of leaving out some of the repetitions, since my translations target mainly adult readers. I have also used English equivalents for the Sanskrit terms which the Mother could assume her listeners to be familiar with, but would probably be unknown to Arabic readers. Occasionally I have inserted between square brackets [ ] concise explanations for the benefit of the first-time readers of the Mother.

The words of the Mother do not disclose themselves fully on a first or a hasty reading. One has often to reread them and to allow oneself enough time for truly understanding and assimilating. The texts compiled in this book date from a time span extending over almost sixty years (1912-1970). Some are taken from the personal entries of the Mother in her diary, some were addressed to highly dedicated early residents of the Ashram who chose to live a life of celibacy and total consecration, and some were meant for all spiritual seekers leading normal lives. Just one advice to the reader: not to jump to final and sweeping conclusions from any one text, but to try to relate consider the context of that particular text.

May the words and teachings of the Mother bring the Arabic reader as much peace, strength and happiness as they have brought me, and much more...

Compiler and translator:
Zackaria M Moursi, Ph. D.
October 2105
sriaurobindotranslations@gmail.com

عندما نتبع بإخلاص الدعوة التي تلقيناها ونثابر على الطريق، نتوصل يوماً ما إلى الحقيقة الأسمى، ألا وهي أن جميع الكائنات ما هي إلا أنماط وأشكال من **الواحد-الكل**، وأننا لذلك أحقاء وجديرون بتحقيقه في أنفسنا وفي حياتنا.

بعض الملحوظات بخصوص النصوص:

معظم نصوص هذا الكتاب مأخوذة من تسجيلات لدروس وأحاديث مرتجلة ألقتها الأم باللغة الفرنسية على تلاميذ وطلبة "مركز شري أوروبيندو الدولي للتربية" في بودوشري، الهند. كانت هذه الأحاديث تسجل إلكترونياً أو اختزالاً ثم تُتَرجَم إلى الإنجليزية. جُمِعَت النصوص فيما بعد ونشرت بعنوان "أسئلة وأجوبة". كانت الأم تحاول دائماً، مراعاة لصغر سن التلاميذ، أن ترد على الأسئلة بلغة مبسطة وتلجأ كثيراً إلى الشرح والتكرار. في ترجمة هذه النصوص من الإنجليزية إلى العربية رأيت من الأنسب أن أدع جانباً كثيراً من التكرار واستبدلت المصطلحات السانسكريتية بمصطلحات إنجليزية مقابلة تسهيلاً على القراء والقارئات. وأخيراً أضفت في مواضع قليلة [بين أقواس مربعة] شروح قصيرة لبعض المضامين التي قد تغمض على قارئ الأم للمرة الأولى.

مقتطفات هذا الكتاب نشأت على مدى فترة زمنية امتدت حوالى ستين عاماً (1912-1970). بعضها أخذ من مذكرات الأم الشخصية، وفي حين كان بعضها موجهاً إلى باحثين روحانيين كرسوا أنفسهم كلياً لحياة العزلة وخدمة الغير، كان البعض الآخر يخاطب الباحث الروحي على الإطلاق. لهذا من الضروري فهم كل من هذه النصوص في سياقه الخاص مع تجنب القفز إلى استنتاجات قطعية وشاملة من أي نص واحد.

عسى أن يجد قراء العربية وقارئاتها في كلمات الأم وتعاليمها من السلام والقوة والسعادة مثل ما وجدت، وأكثر من ذلك بكثير...

مصنف ومترجم
د. زكريا ممدوح مرسي
أكتوبر 2015
sriaurobindotranslations@gmail.com

The Divine — الواحد-الكل

God, the Divine — الرب، الواحد-الكل

All depends on the meaning of the Word

All depends on the meaning you give to the Word.

It all depends on what meaning you put into the word "God". It is a word (I have told you this at least four or five times) to express "something" you do not know but are trying to attain. Well, if you have received a religious education, you are accustomed to call this "God". If you have received a more positivist and also a more philosophical education, you are accustomed to call this by all sorts of names, and you may at the same time have the idea that it is the supreme truth.

If one wants to speak of God and describe him, one is obliged to make use of things which are the most inaccessible to our consciousness, and to call God what is beyond anything we know and can grasp and be — all that is too far for us to be able to understand, we call God. Only some religions (there are some) give a precise form to the godhead; and sometimes they give several forms and they have several gods; sometimes they give one form and have only one God; but all this is human fabrication.

There is "something", there is a reality which is beyond all our expressions, but which we can succeed in contacting by practicing a discipline. We can identify ourselves with it. Once one is identified with it one knows what it is, but one cannot express it, for words cannot say it. So, if you use one kind of vocabulary, if you have a particular mental conviction, you will use the vocabulary corresponding to that conviction. If you belong to another group which has another way of speaking, you will call it or even think about it in that way. I am telling you this to give you the true impression, that there is something there which cannot be grasped — grasped by thought — but which exists. But the name you give it matters little, that's of no importance, *it exists*.

And so the only thing to do is to enter into contact with it — not to give it a name or describe it. In fact, there is hardly any use giving it a name or describing it. One must try to enter into contact, to concentrate upon it, live it, live that reality, and whatever the name you give it is not at all important once you have the experience. The experience alone counts.

The D:vine — الواحد-الكل

God, the Divine — الرب، الواحد-الكل

كل شيء يتوقف على معنى الكلمة

كل شيء يتوقف على المعنى الذي تضفيه على كلمة "الرب". أكرر مرة أخرى إنها مصطلح يعبر عن "شيء" [أو كيان أو مضمون] نسعى إلى بلوغه ولكننا لا نعرفه. لو كنت تربيت تربية دينية، فإنك تطلق عادة على هذا الشيء اسم "الرب". أما لو كنت تربيت تربية تنحو نحو الفلسفة الوضعية* أو الفلسفة عموماً، فالأغلب أنك ستلجأ إلى مصطلح آخر،\ مثل "الحقيقة العظمى"، على سبيل المثال.

عندما نرغب في التحدث عن الرب ووصفه، نكتشف سريعاً أننا نتحدث عن شيء يتخطى وعينا وأننا لا نستطيع أن نقول أكثر من أن الرب هو كل ما يتخطى علمنا وفهمنا وقدرتنا على الإدراك. ولكن هناك أديان تعطي الإله هيئة محددة، وبعضها يعطيه أكثر من هيئة ويعبد آلهة متعددة؛ وهناك أديان تؤمن بإله واحد له هيئة واحدة؛ ولكن كل ذلك من صنع الإنسان.

مع أن هذه الحقيقة العظمى تتخطى كل قدراتنا على التعبير، إلا إننا نستطيع الاتصال بها باتباع نظم معينة، ولا نتصل بها فحسب، بل نستطيع أن نتطابق معها [كما تتطابق قطرة المطر مع المحيط الشاسع]. عندما نتطابق مع هذه الحقيقة نعلم ما هي، على الرغم من إننا لا نستطيع أن نعبر عنها بكلمات، فالكلمات تعجز عن وصفها. طبيعي عندما تتكلم لغة معينة وتفكر بطريقة معينة، يكون طبيعياً أن تُعَبِّر عن هذه الحقيقة بلغتك وبالطريقة التي تناسب طريقة تفكيرك. وبديهي أنك لو كنت تنتمي إلى جماعة لهم لغة أخرى وطريقة تفكير مخالفة، أن تستخدم لغة وطريقة تفكير تلك الجماعة. أقول لكم ذلك لأوحي لكم بأن هناك حقيقة واقعة تتخطى الفكر وأن الاسم الذي نطلقه على هذه الحقيقة لا يهم كثيراً، الشيء المهم هو أنها موجودة بالفعل.

ما ينبغي أن نفعله هو أن نحقق الصلة بهذه الحقيقة — ذلك أفضل من تسميتها ووصفها. الأسماء والأوصاف لا طائل منها. يجب أن نحاول الاتصال بهذه الحقيقة والتركيز عليها ومعيشتها، ومتى توصلنا إلى التجربة والخبرة، لن يهم إطلاقاً الاسم الذي نطلقه عليها. التجربة والخبرة هما الشيء يعتد به.

The Divine — الواحد-الكل

And when people associate the experience with a particular expression – and in so narrow a way, so closed up in itself that apart from this formula one can find nothing – that is an inferiority. One must be able to *live* that reality through all possible paths, all occasions, all formations; one must live it, for that indeed is true, for that is supremely good, that is all-powerful, that knows all, that... Yes, one can live that, but one cannot speak about it. And if one does speak, all that one says about it has no great importance. It is only one way of speaking that is all.

There is an entire line of philosophers and people who have replaced the notion of God by the notion of an impersonal Absolute or by a notion of Truth or a notion of justice or even by a notion of progress –of something eternally progressive; but for one who has within him the capacity of identifying himself with that, what has been said about it hasn't much importance. Sometimes one may read a whole book of philosophy and not progress a step farther. Sometimes one may be quite a fervent devotee of a religion and not progress. There are people who have spent entire lifetimes seated in contemplation and attained nothing. There are people (we have well-known examples) who used to do the most modest of manual works, like a cobbler mending old shoes, and who had an experience. It is altogether beyond what one thinks and says of it. It is some gift that's there, that is all. And all that is needed is to be that – to succeed in identifying oneself with it and live it. At times you read one sentence in a book and that leads you there. Sometimes you read entire books of philosophy or religion and they get you nowhere. There are people, however, whom the reading of philosophy books helps to go ahead. But all these things are secondary.

There is only one thing that's important: that is a sincere and persistent will, for these things don't happen in a twinkling. So one must persevere. When someone feels that he is not advancing, he must not get discouraged; he must try to find out what it is in the nature that is opposing, and then make the necessary progress. And suddenly one goes forward. And when you reach the end you have an experience. And what is remarkable is that people who have followed altogether different paths, with altogether different mental constructions, from the greatest believer to the most unbelieving, even materialists, have arrived at that experience, it is the same for everyone. Because it is true – because it is real, because it is the sole reality. And it is quite simply that. I do not say anything more. This is of no importance, the way one speaks about it, what is important is to follow the path, your path, no matter which – yes, to go there. 17 February 1954

The Divine — الواحد-الكل

عندما نربط تجربتنا بتعبير معين وبنظرة محدودة ومقفلة على ذاتها — يكون ذلك نقصاً وقصوراً. ينبغي أن نكون قادرين على أن نعيش هذه **الحقيقة العظمى** على جميع الطرق التي تؤدي إليها وفي جميع الظروف، فهي بالفعل الحق والخير المطلق والقدرة الشاملة المُلِّمة بكل شيء... نعم، نستطيع حقاً أن نعيش هذه الحقيقة ولكننا سنظل أبداً عاجزين عن وصفها. وعندما نتكلم عنها، لا يكون لكلامنا إلا قيمة ضئيلة ونسبية.

استبدلت سلسلة من الفلاسفة والمفكرين مفهوم **الرب** بمفاهيم مثل "**المطلق الوضعي**" أو "**الحق**" أو "**العدالة**" أو حتى "**التقدم الأبدي المضطرد**"، ولكن بالنسبة لمن ينجحون في التطابق مع هذه الحقيقة، كل ما قيل عنها لا يهم كثيراً. قد يقرأ المرء كتاباً كاملاً في الفلسفة دون أن يحرز أي تقدم [روحي]. وقد ينتمي المرء بحماس إلى دين معين دون أن يتقدم. وهناك قوم أمضوا حياتهم جالسين في تأمل، ولكنهم لم يحققوا أي شيء على الرغم من ذلك. في حين أن بعض الأفراد [منهم أمثلة معروفة] كانوا يمارسون عملاً يدوياً متواضعاً، على سبيل المثال، كإسكافيين يصلحون الأحذية البالية، توصلوا إلى تجربة هذه **الحقيقة**. فهي حقيقة تتخطى كلياً كل ما نفكره أو نقوله عنها. الوصول إليها نعمة أو هبة تمنح للبعض. كل ما هو مطلوب هو أن ننجح في التطابق معها وأن نعيشها بالفعل. أحياناً تكفي جملة واحدة نقرأها في كتاب لكي نصل إليها. وأحياناً نقرأ كتباً بأكملها في الدين أو الفلسفة بلا طائل. هذا لا يمنع من أن قراءة الفلسفة قد تنفع بعض الناس. ولكن هذه كلها أشياء ثانوية.

الشرط الأساسي للتحقيق هو الإرادة الصادقة، ثم المثابرة لأن التحقيق لا يحدث في غمضة عين. يجب أن نثابر وحتى لو شعرنا أننا لا نتقدم، ألا نفقد عزيمتنا. بل نحاول أن نكتشف العقبة في طبيعتنا التي تحول دون تقدمنا ونزيل هذه العقبة. فجأة نكتشف أننا نتقدم مرة أخرى. وعندما نبلغ نهاية الطريق، ستكون التجربة الحاسمة في انتظارنا. من الملفت للنظر أن أشتاتاً من الناس الذين سلكوا سبلاً مختلفة — بتراكيب ذهنية متباينة، منهم مؤمنون ومنهم كافرون وحتى ماديون — توصلوا جميعاً في النهاية إلى نفس التجربة، فهي متماثلة بالنسبة إلى الجميع لأنها تجربة حقة، أو بالأصح لأنها التجربة الوحيدة الحقة. لن أقول عنها أكثر من ذلك، لأن الكلام لا يفيد، المهم هو أن يتبع كل فرد طريقه الشخصي، لا يهم أي طريق هو، فكل الطرق تؤدي إلى نفس الهدف.
17 فبراير 1954

The Divine — الواحد-الكل

Religion and Spirituality — الدين والروحية

The need for Religion

"Religion's real business is to prepare man's mind, life and bodily existence for the spiritual consciousness to take it up; it has to lead him to that point where the inner spiritual light begins fully to emerge. It is at this point that religion must learn to subordinate itself, not to insist on its outer characters, but give full scope to the inner spirit itself to develop its own truth and reality. In the meanwhile it has to take up as much of man's mentality, vitality, physicality as it can and give all his activities a turn towards the spiritual direction, the revelation of a spiritual meaning in them, the imprint of a spiritual refinement, the beginning of a spiritual character. It is in this attempt that the errors of religion come in, for they are caused by the very nature of the matter with which it is dealing, — that inferior stuff invades the very forms that are meant to serve as intermediaries between the spiritual and the mental, vital or physical consciousness, and often it diminishes, degrades and corrupts them: but it is in this attempt that lies religion's greatest utility as an intercessor between spirit and nature. Truth and error live always together in the human evolution and the truth is not to be rejected because of its accompanying errors, though these have to be eliminated, — often a difficult business and, if crudely done, resulting in surgical harm inflicted on the body of religion; for what we see as error is very frequently the symbol or a disguise or a corruption or malformation of a truth which is lost in the brutal radicality of the operation, — the truth is cut out along with the error. Nature herself very commonly permits the good corn and the tares and weeds to grow together for a long time, because only so is her own growth, her free evolution possible."
Sri Aurobindo, The Life Divine

Sweet Mother, is religion a necessity in the life of the ordinary man?

In the life of societies it is a necessity, for it serves as a corrective to collective egoism which, without this control, could take on excessive proportions.

The level of collective consciousness is always lower than the individual level. It is very noticeable, for example, that when men gather in a group or collect in great numbers, the level of consciousness falls a great deal. The consciousness of crowds is much lower than individual consciousness, and the collective consciousness of society is certainly lower than the consciousness of the individuals constituting it.

Religion and Spirituality — الدين والروحية

الحاجة إلى الدين

"وظيفة الدين الحقيقية هي اعداد الكيان البشري، في نواحيه الذهنية والحيوية والبدنية، اعداداً يسمح للوعي الروحي بأن يتملكها ويتكفل بها، ومهمة الدين هي قيادة الإنسان إلى النقطة التي يبدأ عندها النور الروحي بداخله في البزوغ بصورة شاملة. متى بلغ الإنسان هذه النقطة ينبغي أن يقبل الدين التراجع إلى المكانة الثانية وأن يكف عن التصميم على تعاليمه الخارجية، وأن يسمح لحقيقة الروح الباطني بأن تتطور في حرية. واجب الدين إلى ذلك الحين هو أن يأخذ أكبر قدر من عقلية الإنسان وحيويته وبدنيته ويوجهها نحو الروحية ويدمغها بالطابع والسمو الروحي. أخطاء الدين تظهر أثناء محاولة تهذيب الطبيعة البشرية وتنبع من صميم عمل الدين حيث ن النواحي البشرية الأدنى تتدخل في مساعي الدين وكثيراً ما تضعفها وتحط من قدرها وتفسدها. الدين يهدف إلى التوسط بين الروح وبين الوعي البشري، في مجالاته الثلاثة: الذهنية والحيوية والبدنية، وهو يسدي أعظم النفع كوسيط بين الروح والطبيعة. لازم الخطأ الحقيقة دائماً على مدى تطور الإنسان وارتقائه، ولكن لا يصح، في سعينا لإزالة الخطأ، أن نطرح معه الحقيقة أيضاً — كثيراً ما يكون استئصال الخطأ عملية صعبة ودقيقة، لو أسيئت تأديتها تضر بالدين كثيراً، وما ذلك إلا لأن ما نعتبره خطأ كثيراً ما يكون رمزاً أو تمويهاً أو صورة لحقيقة شوهتها همجية التطرف في الاستئصال نفسه الذي لا يستأصل الخطأ وحده، بل يستأصل الحقيقة أيضاً معه. الطبيعة نفسها تصبر مع الأعشاب الضارة مدئ طويلاً وتسمح لها بالنمو مع البذور الطيبة، لأن هذه هي الطريقة الوحيدة التي تكفل للبذور النمو والتطور في حرية."

شري أوروبيندو، الحياة الإلهية

أيتها الأم الحنون، هل الدين ضروري في حياة الفرد العادي؟

الدين ضروري لحياة المجتمعات لأنه يكبح الأنانية الجماعية، وبدونه تنمو هذه الأنانية وتتخطى الحدود المقبولة.

مستوى الوعي الجماعي أقل دائماً من مستوى الوعي الفردي، والوعي الكلي لمجتمع يكون دائماً أدنى من وعي الأفراد الذين يُكوّنون هذا المجتمع. هذا شيء نستطيع أن نلاحظه بسهولة من هبوط مستوى الوعي عندما يتجمع الناس أو يتجمهرون في حشود ضخمة.

The Divine — الواحد-الكل

There it is a necessity. In ordinary life, an individual, whether he knows it or not, always has a religion but the object of his religion is sometimes of a very inferior kind....The god he worships may be the god of success or the god of money or the god of power, or simply a family god: the god of children, the god of the family, the god of the ancestors. There is always a religion. The quality of the religion is very different according to the individual, but it is difficult for a human being to live and to go on living, to survive in life without having something like a rudiment of an ideal which serves as the centre for his existence. Most of the time he doesn't know it and if he were asked what his ideal is, he would be unable to formulate it; but he has one, vaguely, something that seems to him the most precious thing in life. For most people, it is security, for instance: living in security, being in conditions where one is sure of being able to go on existing. That is one of the great "aims", one might say, one of the great motives of human effort. There are people for whom comfort is the important thing; for others it is pleasure, amusement. All that is very low and one would not be inclined to give it the name of an ideal, but it is truly a form of religion, something which may seem to be worth consecrating one's life to....There are many influences which seek to impose themselves on human beings by using that as a basis. The feeling of insecurity, uncertainty, is a kind of tool, a means used by political or religious groups to influence individuals. They play on these ideas.

Every political or social idea is a sort of lower expression of an ideal which is a rudimentary religion. As soon as there is a faculty of thought, there is necessarily an aspiration for something higher than the most brutal daily existence from minute to minute, and this is what gives the energy and possibility of living.

Of course, one could say that it is the same thing for individuals as for collectivities, that their value is exactly proportionate to the value of their ideal, their religion, that is, of the thing they make the summit of their existence.

Of course, when we speak of religion, if we mean the recognised religions, truly, everyone has his own religion, whether he knows it or not, even when he belongs to the great religions that have a name and a history. It is certain that even if one learns the dogmas by heart and complies with a prescribed ritual, everybody understands and acts in his own way, and only the name of the religion is the same, but this same religion is not the same for all the individuals who think they are practising it.

The Divine — الواحد-الكل

الـدين ضـرورة بالنسبة للمجتمعـات. فـي الحياة العاديـة، كـل فـرد لـه ديـن خـاص بـه، سـواء أكـان يـدري ذلـك أم لا، وأحيانـا يكـون مضمـون هـذا الـدين خفيضـاً للغايـة. فقـد يتخـذ الفـرد النجـاح أو المـال أو السـلطة إلهـاً، بـل أنـه قـد يتخـذ لنفسـه إلهـاً عائليـاً كـان يعبـد أطفالـه أو أسـلافه أو عشـيرته. فـي حياة كـل فـرد ديـن دائمـاً؛ ونوعيـة هـذا الـدين تتوقـف علـى نوعيـة الفـرد. الإنسـان يجـد صعوبـة فـي أن يعيـش ويبقـى علـى قيـد الحيـاة بـدون صـورة مبسـطة لمثـل أعلـى تتمحـور حولـه حياتـه. الإنسـان نـادراً مـا يكـون واعيـاً بذلـك، بحيـث أنـه لـو سـئل عـن مثلـه الأعلـى يعجـز عـن الإجابـة، ولكـن هـذا لمثـل الأعلـى موجـود مـع ذلـك، وهـو بالتحديـد الشـيء الـذي يعتبـره الفـرد أثمـن مـا فـي حياتـه. الأمـان هـو لهـدف الـي يبتغيـه معظـم النـاس، فهـم يتوقـون إلـى ظـروف تهيـئ لهـم حيـاة آمنـة علـى الـدوام. الأمـان هـو أحـد أهـم الأهـداف التـي يسـعى إليهـا النـاس. ولذلـك نـرى أن الجماعـات السياسـية والدينيـة عندمـا تريـد التحكـم فـي النـاس واسـتغلالهم فـي تحقيـق أهدافهـا تبـث فيهـم مشـاعر الخـوف وعـدم الأمـان. بعـض النـاس يريـدون قبـل أي شـيء آخـر حيـاة مريحـة، والبعـض الآخـر يلهثـون وراء المسـرات والتسـلية. هاتـه أهـداف تافهـة لا تسـتحق أن نسـميها مثـلاً عليـا، ولكنهـا مـع ذلـك صـور مـن ديـن يـراه البعـض جديـراً بـأن يُكـرّسوا حياتهـم لـه...

جميـع المبـادئ السياسـية والاجتماعيـة مـا هـي إلا تعبيـر مخفـض عـن مثـل أعلـى يمكـن اعتبـاره صـورة مبسـطة وتقريبيـة لـدين. أينمـا وجـد الفكـر، يكـون هنـاك تـوق إلـى شـيء يتسـامى علـى ضعـة الحيـاة اليوميـة التـي لا تهتـم إلا باللحظـة الحاضـرة. هـذا التـوق هـو منبـع الطاقـة التـي تحركنـا وتمكّننـا مـن أن نحيـا حيـاة كريمـة.

وبـالطبع، مـا يسـري علـى الأفـراد يسـري أيضـاً علـى الجماعـات بمعنـى أن منزلـة أي جماعـة تتناسـب مـع سـمو المثـال الأعلـى الـذي يحـرك أفرادهـا ونوعيـة ديانتهـم أي مـا يعتبرونـه أهـم شـيء فـي الوجـود.

وحتـى فـي نطـاق الأديـان العظمـى ذات المكانـة والشـأن والتاريـخ، نجـد أن كـل مـن أتبـاع هـذه الأديـان لـه دينـه الخـاص، وحتـى عندمـا يتبـع الفـرد تعاليـم دينـه بحـذافيرها، نـراه يفسـرها ويطبقهـا بطريقتـه الخاصـة، ونجـد أن مفهـوم الديـن الواحـد يختلـف مـن فـرد إلـى فـرد بيـن الأتبـاع الذيـن يؤمنـون جهـرة بـه.

The Divine — الواحد-الكل

We can say that without some expression of this aspiration for the Unknown and the highest, human existence would be very difficult. If there were not at the heart of every being the hope of something better – of whatever kind – he would have difficulty in finding the energy needed to go on living.

(Silence)

But as very few individuals are capable of thinking freely, it is much easier to join a religion, accept it, adopt it and become a part of that religious collectivity than to formulate one's own cult for oneself. So, apparently, one is this or that, but in fact it is only an appearance.
16 July 1958

الواحد-الكل — The Divine

نستطيع أن نقول أن حياة الإنسان تصير في غاية الصعوبة لو لم يكن فيها نوع ما من التوق والتشوق نحو **المجهول** ونحو السمو. ولو لم يكن هناك في صميم كل إنسان الأمل في شيء أفضل، أياً كان هذا الشيء، لأصبح من العسير على الإنسان أن يجد الطاقة الكافية للاستمرار في الحياة.

(صمت)

التفكير المتحرر موهبة لا يتميز بها إلا أقلية ضئيلة من الناس، ولذلك تؤمن أغلبية الناس بدين معين يقبلونه كلياً ويندمجون في جماعته، فذلك أيسر بكثير من أن يكوِّنوا لأنفسهم ديناً خاصاً. وبذلك حتى عندما ينتمي الناس لدين أو لآخر، يكون هذا الانتماء ظاهرياً فقط.
16 يوليو 1958

The Divine — الواحد-الكل

Materialism and Spirituality — المادية والروحية

Joining the two Extremes

Throughout this teaching [the teaching of the Buddha] there is one thing to be noticed; it is this: you are never told that to live well, to think well, is the result of a struggle or of a sacrifice; on the contrary it is a delightful state which cures all suffering. At that time, the time of the Buddha, to live a spiritual life was a joy, a beatitude, the happiest state, which freed you from all the troubles of the world, all the sufferings, all the cares, making you happy, satisfied, contented. It is the materialism of modern times that has turned spiritual effort into a hard struggle and a sacrifice, a painful renunciation of all the so-called joys of life.

This insistence on the exclusive reality of the physical world, of physical pleasures, physical joys, physical possessions, is the result of the whole materialistic tendency of human civilisation. It was unthinkable in ancient times. On the contrary, withdrawal, concentration, liberation from all material cares, consecration to the spiritual joy, that was happiness indeed. From this point of view it is quite evident that humanity is far from having progressed; and those who were born into the world in the centres of materialistic civilisation have in their subconscient this horrible notion that only material realities are real and that to be concerned with things that are not material represents a wonderful spirit of sacrifice, an almost sublime effort. Not to be preoccupied from dawn to dusk and from dusk to dawn with all the little physical satisfactions, physical pleasures, physical sensations, physical preoccupations, is to bear evidence of a remarkable spirit. One is not aware of it, but the whole of modern civilisation is built on this conception: "Ah, what you can touch, you are sure that is true; what you can see, you are sure that is true; what you have eaten, you are sure of having eaten it; but all the rest--pooh! We are not sure whether they are not vain dreams and whether we are not giving up the real for the unreal, the substance for the shadow. After all, what are you going to gain? A few dreams! But when you have some coins in your pocket, you are sure that they are there!"

And that is everywhere, underneath everything. Scratch the appearances just a little, it is there, within your consciousness; and from time to time you hear this thing whispering within you, "Take care, don't be taken in." Indeed, it is lamentable.

The Divine — الواحد-الكل

Materialism and Spirituality — المادية والروحية

لقاء الطرفين

تعاليم بوذا لا تنادي أبداً بأننا يجب، لكي نعيش جيداً ونفكر جيداً، أن نكافح ونضحي كثيراً، بل هي، على العكس، تعلمنا أن الروحية هناء ودواء لكل معاناة. في وقت بوذا، كان ينظر إلى الحياة الروحية على أنها بهجة وهناء وأنها أسعد حالة يمكن للإنسان أن يكون فيها لأنها تحرره من مشاكل الحياة وشقائها وهمومها وتجعله راضياً وسعيداً. ما حَوَّل الحياة الروحية إلى كفاح شاق وتضحية ورفض لكل متع الحياة هو مادية العصور الحديثة.

الاتجاه السائد في المدنية الحديثة هو التصميم على أن العالم الفيزيائي والمسرات والممتلكات المادية هي وحدها حقيقية. هذه نظرة بعيدة كل البعد عن نظرة العصور القديمة عندما كان البشر يؤمنون بأن السعادة والبهجة الروحية يأتيان بالانسحاب من العالم والتركيز [على الروحيات] والتحرر من المشاغل المادية. من وجهة النظر الروحية، واضح أن الإنسان لم يتقدم منذ ذلك الحين، إذ نجد اليوم أن الذين يولدون في مراكز المدنية المادية الحديثة يؤمنون في وعيهم الباطن بأن الماديات وحدها حقيقية وأن الانشغال بما هو غير مادي يتطلب تضحية كبيرة وعناء عظيم، ويرون أن التحرر من المسرات والأحاسيس والاهتمامات المادية الصغيرة بحيث لا تكون شاغل الإنسان الأول من الفجر إلى المساء ومن المساء إلى الفجر، يتطلب ضلاعة كبيرة في الروحية. قد لا نكون دائماً واعيين بذلك، ولكن المدنية الحديثة تنبني على مفهوم أن ما نستطيع أن نلمسه أو نراه أو نأكله حقيقة أكيدة، وأن الدراهم في جيوبنا شيء يمكننا الاعتماد عليه والرجوع إليه، أما ما هو غير مادي فهو وهم أو حلم، وأن الانشغال به يكون بمثابة أن نستبدل الحقيقي بما هو غير حقيقي وأن نكتفي من الشيء بظله..

هذا المفهوم شائع في كل مكان، ومتخفي وراء جميع الأشياء، وبمجرد أن نخدش السطح قليلاً نكتشفه كامناً في وعينا الباطن، ومن آن لآخر نستطيع أن نسمعه هامساً لنا بأن نكون حذرين وأن نتجنب "الوقوع في شراك" ما هو غير مادي. يا له من شيء مؤسف بالفعل.

The Divine — الواحد-الكل

We have been told that evolution is progressive and that it follows a spiral of ascending progression. I do not doubt that what one calls comfort in modern cities is a much higher degree of evolution than the comfort of the cave-man. But in ancient narratives, they always spoke of a power of foresight, of the prophetic spirit, the announcement of future events through visions, life's intimacy with something more subtle that had for the simple people of that age a more concrete reality.

Now, in those beautiful cities that are so comfortable, when one wants to condemn anything, what does one say? – "It's a dream, it is imagination." And precisely, if a person lives in an inner perception, people look at him slightly askance and wonder whether he is altogether mentally sound. One who does not pass his time in striving for wealth or in trying to increase his comforts and well-being, to secure a good position and become an important person, a man who is not like that is mistrusted, people wonder whether he is in his right mind. And all that is so much the stuff of the atmosphere, the content of the air you breathe, the orientation of the thoughts received from others that it seems absolutely natural. You do not feel that it is a grotesque monstrosity.

To become a little more conscious of oneself, to enter into relation with the life behind the appearances, does not seem to you to be the greatest good. When you sit in a comfortable chair, in front of a lavish meal, when you fill your stomach with delicious dishes, that certainly appears to you much more concrete and much more interesting. And if you look at the day that has passed, if you take stock of your day, if you have had some material advantage, some pleasure, a physical satisfaction, you mark it as a good day; but if you have received a good lesson from life, if it has given you a knock on your nose to tell you that you are a stupid fellow, you do not give thanks to the Grace, you say, "Oh, life is not always fun!"

When I read these ancient texts, I really have the impression that from the inner point of view, from the point of view of the true life, we have fallen back terribly and that for the acquisition of a few ingenious mechanisms, a few encouragements to physical laziness, the acquisition of instruments and gadgets that lessen the effort of living, we have renounced the reality of the inner life. It is that sense which has been lost and it needs an effort for you to think of learning the meaning of life, the purpose of existence, the goal towards which we must advance, towards which all life advances, whether you want it or not. One step towards the goal, oh! it needs so much effort to do that. And generally one thinks of it only when the outer circumstances are not pleasant.

The Divine — الواحد-الكل

قيل لنا أن النشوء والارتقاء تطور مستمر وأن مساره يشبه حلزوناً صاعداً يتوسع باطراد. لا أنكر أن المدن الحديثة بما تحتويه من وسائل الراحة تمثل تقدماً في التطور بالمقارنة بحياة سكان الكهوف. ولكن القصص القديمة كانت مع ذلك تتحدث دائماً عن قدرات مثل الاستبصار وقراءة المستقبل والتنبؤ بالأحداث المقبلة، ومن هذه القصص نستطيع أن نستشف إلى أي مدى كان إنسان هذه الأزمان السحيقة في بساطته على علاقة حميمة ودقيقة بالأشياء غير المادية.

في عصرنا هذا، عندما يريد سكان المدن "المريحة" إظهار ازدرائهم لشيء ما، يصفونه بأنه "حلم وخيال"! وإذا وجد بينهم شخص يعيش حياة داخلية، ينظرون إليه باستهزاء ويتساءلون إن كان بكامل عقله. وهم لا يثقون إلا بالذين يمضون جل يومهم في الاستكثار من وسائل الرفاهية والراحة وفي الطموح نحو المراكز التي تجلب لهم إعجاب الآخرين. هذه النظرة المادية تخللت كل شيء حتى الهواء الذي نتنفسه و الأفكار التي نتلقاها لدرجة أنها أصبحت تبدو لنا طبيعية للغية وبحيث أننا تعودنا عليها وأصبحنا لا نندهش من غرابتها المذهلة.

أن تكون أكثر وعياً بذاتك وقادراً على الحياة وراء المظاهر، لا يبدو لشخص يعيش في الوعي المادي تحقيقاً رائعاً. ما يبدو له أحسن من ذلك بكثير هو أن يجلس على كرسي مريح أمام مائدة حافلة ليتخم نفسه بأصناف الطعام الشهية. وإذا نظر في المساء إلى حصيلة يومه الذي انقضى، ووجد أنه قد حقق نفعاً مادياً أو متعة بدنية، يعتبر أنه يومه كان ناجحاً؛ أما إذا علمته الحياة في يومه درساً جيداً وتلقى ضربة بسيطة تنبهه إلى حماقاته، فإنه يجحد **النعمة الإلهية** ويزدري يومه.

عندما أقرأ هذه النصوص القديمة [مثل تعاليم بوذا] يكون انطباعي إننا قد تدهورنا كثيرٌ من وجهة نظر الحياة الداخلية الحقة، وأننا لم نكتسب في مقابل ذلك سوى آليات وابتكارات تشجعنا على الكسل البدني بالإضافة إلى بعض الأدوات والأجهزة التي تسهل حياتنا. والآن وقد طرحنا جانباً حياتنا الداخلية، أصبح لزاماً علينا أن نبذل الجهد لنتعلم مرة أخرى معنى الحياة وأن نتعرف على الهدف الحق الذي نسعى إليه، ويسعى إليه الجميع، سواء رغبناه أم لا. ثم أننا أصبحنا لا نفكر في هذا الهدف إلا تحت ضغط ظروف غير سارة، وكم يبدو لنا عظيماً الجهد المطلوب لكي نتقدم خطوة واحدة!

The Divine — الواحد-الكل

How far we are from the times when the shepherd, who did not go to school and kept watch over his flock at night under the stars, could read in the stars what was going to happen, commune with something which expressed itself through Nature, and had the sense of the profound beauty and that peace which a simple life gives!

It is very unfortunate that one has to give up one thing in order to gain another. When I speak of the inner life, I am far from opposing any modern inventions, far from it, but how much these inventions have made us artificial and stupid! How much we have lost the sense of true beauty, how much we burden ourselves with useless needs!

Perhaps the time has come to continue the ascent in the curve of the spiral and now with all that this knowledge of matter has brought us, we shall be able to give to our spiritual progress a more solid basis. Strong with what we have learnt of the secrets of material Nature, we shall be able to join the two extremes and rediscover the supreme Reality in the very heart of the atom.
January 24, 1958

The Divine — الواحد-الكل

كـم بعـدنا عـن الأوقـات التـي كـان فيهـا راعـي الغنـم الأمـي يتأمـل النجـوم فـي الليـل ويستشـف منهـا المسـتقبل ويتواصـل مـع الأمـور التـي تجـد تعبيرهـا فـي **الطبيعـة** مـن حولـه، وينعـم بحـس وعمـق الجمـال والسـلام الذيـن يسـودان فـي حياتـه البسـيطة.

مـن المؤسـف إننـا كثيـراً مـا نفكـر علـى نمـط ازدواجـي: "إمـا هـذا وإمـا ذاك". مـع إنـي أحـث علـى تطويـر الحيـاة الداخليـة، فأنـا بعيـدة كـل البعـد عـن رفـض المخترعـات الحديثـة، علـى الرغـم مـن قولـي إن هـذه المخترعـات قـد جعلتنـا متصنعيـن وحمقـاء وثلمـت إحساسـنا بالجمـال الحقيقـي وزادتنـا عبئـاً بمـا أدخلتـه فـي حياتنـا مـن "حاجات" لا نفـع منهـا.

ربمـا قـد آن الأوان لكـي نواصـل تسـلق حلـزون النشـوء والارتقـاء، مـزوديـن بكـل المعرفـة التـي اكتسـبناها مـن العلـوم الفيزيائيـة، تلـك المعرفـة التـي سـتمكننا مـن ترسـيخ نمونـا الروحـي علـى أسـاس أمتـن يمكننـا أخيـراً مـن وصـل الطرفيـن والتوفيـق بيـن الماديـة والروحيـة ومـن اكتشـاف **الحقيقـة الأسـمى** فـي صميـم الـذرة نفسـها.

24 ينايـر، 1958

Bases of the Integral Yoga — أسس اليوغا المتكاملة

Sri Aurobindo's Yoga — يوغا شري أوروبيندو

What does it mean to do Sri Aurobindo's Yoga

To do Sri Aurobindo's yoga is to want to transform oneself integrally, it is to have a single aim in life, such that nothing else exists any longer, that a one exists. And so one feels it clearly in oneself whether one wants or not; but if one doesn't, one can still have a life of goodwill, a life of service, of understanding; one can labour for the Work to be accomplished more easily — all that — one can do many things. But between this and doing yoga there is a great difference.

And to do you yoga you must want it consciously, you must know what it is, to begin with. You must know what it is, you must take a resolution about it; but once you have taken the resolution, you must no longer flinch. That is why you must take it in full knowledge of the thing. You must know what you are deciding upon when you say, "I want to do yoga"; and that is why I don't think that I have ever pressed you from this point of view. I can speak to you about the thing. Oh! I tell you a lot about it, you are here for me to speak to you about it; but individually it is only to those who have come saying, "Yes, in any case I have my idea about the yoga and want to do it"; it is good. And then for them it is something different, and the conditions of life are different, specially inwardly. Specially within, things change.

There is always a consciousness there acting constantly to rectify the situation, which puts you all the time in the presence of obstacles which prevent you from advancing, makes you bump against your own errors and your own blindnesses. And this acts only for those who have decided to do the yoga. For others the Consciousness acts like a light, a knowledge, a protection, a force of progress, so that they may reach their maximum capacities and be able to develop as far as possible in an atmosphere as favourable as possible — but leaving them completely free in their choice.

The decision must come from within. Those who come consciously for the yoga, knowing what yoga is, their conditions of living here are…. outwardly there is no difference but inwardly there is a very great difference. There is a kind of absoluteness in the consciousness, which does not let them deviate from the path: the errors one commits become immediately visible with consequences strong enough for one to be able to make any mistake about it, and things become very serious. But it is not often like that.

Bases of the Integral Yoga — أسس اليوغا المتكاملة

Sri Aurobindo's Yoga — يوغا شري أوروبيندو

ماذا تعني ممارسة يوغا شري أوروبيندو

عندما نقول إننا نمارس يوغا شري أوروبيندو، نعني بذلك أننا نرغب في تحويّل أنفسنا بصورة متكاملة، وأن هذا التحوُّل قد أصبح هدفنا الأوحد في الحياة وأنه لم يعد في الحياة شيء يهمنا غير الهدف. نحن نشعر في أنفسنا بوضوح ما إذا كنا نرغب في تحقيق هذا الهدف أم لا. فلو كنا لا نرغب، ما يزال في وسعنا أن نعيش حياة تسود فيها النية الطيبة والرغبة في التعلم والفهم والخدمة والنفع والسعي في تسهيل **العمل الإلهي**: أي أن الفرصة ستكون متاحة لنا لتحقيق أشياء كثيرة. ولكن هناك فارق كبير بين ذلك وبين ممارسة يوغا شري أوروبيندو.

لكي تمارس اليوغا، يجب، قبل كل شيء، أن تمارسها واعياً، أي أنك يجب أن تعرف ما هي هذه اليوغا. ينبغي أن تعرف ما تنطوي عليه الممارسة وأن تتخذ قرارك بناءً على ذلك، ولكن متى اتخذت قرارك، يجب ألا تتراجع فيه. ينبغي ألا تتخذ القرار إلا عندما تكون على معرفة تامة بهذه اليوغا وأن تكون على علم بما أنت مقبل عليه عندما تقول: "أريد ممارسة هذه اليوغا." هذا هو السبب في أنني لم أضغط على أي منكم ليتخذ هذا القرار. ما أفعله هو أن أتحدث معكم عن اليوغا بصفة عامة وأخبركم الكثير عنها حيث أنكم موجودون هنا لكي تسمعوا مني ذلك [الأم تخاطب هنا طلبة وتلاميذ مركز شري أوروبيندو الدولي للتربية في بونديشري بالهند]. ولكني لا أحث على هذه اليوغا إلا الذين يأتون هنا معلنين أنهم " قد كوّنوا رأيهم عن هذه اليوغا، وأنهم يرغبون ممارستها على أي حال." هؤلاء سيكونون هنا في المكان المناسب والأمور ستختلف قليلاً بالنسبة لهم، كما أن ظروف الحياة ستكون مختلفة أيضاً، خاصة حياتهم الداخلية.

هناك وعي يعمل دائماً على إصلاح ما يَعوّج من الأمور بأن يضع عقبات في طريقك تمنعك من التقدم وتجعلك تتعثر كالأعمى في أخطائك. ولكن ذلك لا يسري إلا على الذين عقدوا النية على ممارسة اليوغا. أما بالنسبة للآخرين، فإن هذا الوعي يعمل كضوء، كمعرفة، كحماية، أو كقوة تقدم ويمكنهم من تحقيق أقصى طاقاتهم وبلوغ أقصى مداهم في النمو في أحسن الظروف ملاءمة — وإلى جانب كل ذلك، يمنحهم هذا الوعي الحرية التامة في الاختيار.

القرار يجب أن يأتي من الداخل. هؤلاء الذين يأتون بإرادتهم وعلى علم بماهية اليوغا، تكون ظروف حياتهم هنا مخالفة تماماً في الداخل وإن كانت ظاهرياً هي نفس الظروف. فنجد وعيهم حاسماً لا يسمح لهم بالانحراف عن الصراط، لأنهم عندما يخطئون، تصبح أخطاؤهم على الفور مرئية لا يمكن تجاهلها وذات عواقب على درجة كبيرة من الجدية. ولكن ذلك لا يحدث كثيراً.

Bases of the Integral Yoga — أسس اليوغا المتكاملة

All of you, my children — I may tell you this, I have repeated it to you and still repeat it — live in an exceptional liberty. Outwardly there are a few limitations, because, as there are many of us and we don't have the whole earth to our disposal, we are obliged to submit to a certain discipline to a certain extent, so that there may not be too great a disorder; but inwardly you live in a marvelous liberty: no social constraint, no moral constraint, no intellectual constraint, no rule, nothing, nothing but a light which is there. If you want to profit by it, you profit by it; if you don't want to, you are free not to.

But the day you make a choice — when you have done it in all sincerity and have felt within yourself a radical decision — the thing is different. There is the light and the path to be followed, quite straight, and you must not deviate from it. It fools no one, you know; yoga is not a joke. You must know what you are doing when you choose it. But when you choose it, you must hold on to it. You have no longer the right to vacillate. You must go straight ahead. There!

All what I ask for is a will to do well, an effort for progress and the wish to be a little better in life than ordinary human beings. You have grown up, developed under certain conditions which are exceptionally luminous, conscious, harmonious, and full of goodwill; and in response to these conditions you should be in the world an expression of this light, this harmony, this goodwill. This would already be very good, very good.

To do the yoga, this yoga of transformation which, of all things is the most arduous — it is only if one feels that one has come here for that (I mean here upon earth) and that one has to do nothing else but that, and that it is the only reason of one's existence — even if one has to toil hard, suffer, struggle — it is of no importance — "This is what I want, and nothing else" — then it is different. Otherwise I shall say, "Be happy and good, and that's all that is asked of you. Be good, in the sense of being understanding, knowing that the conditions in which you have lived are exceptional, and try to live a higher, more noble, more true life than the ordinary one, so as to allow a little of this consciousness, this light and its goodness to express itself in the world. It would be very good." There we are.

But once you have set foot on the path of yoga, you must have a resolution of steel and walk straight on to the goal, whatever the cost…
Questions and Answers, June, 8th, 1955

Bases of the Integral Yoga — أسس اليوغا المتكاملة

أنتم جميعاً يا أطفالي — أقول لكم ذلك وأكرره، وقد سبق أن كررته من قبل — تعيشون في حرية استثنائية. صحيح أنكم خارجياً مطالبون بالالتزام ببعض القواعد، فأعدادنا وفيرة، ونحن لا نستطيع أن نتصرف كما لو كنا نملك الأرض بما عليها، أي أننا ملزمون إلى حد ما بتباع نظام معين لو أردنا تجنب الفوضى المطلقة. إلا أنكم داخلياً تعيشون في حرية رائعة بدون أن تفرض عليكم أي قواعد أو قيود سواء أكانت اجتماعية أم أخلاقية أم ثقافية، لا شيء من كلّ ذلك، بل تتركون لتعيشوا في ضوء يغمركم وتمنحون الحرية في الانتفاع أو عدم الانتفاع من هذا الضوء.

أكرر: متى اخترتم اليوغا بكل صدق وإخلاص وأحسستم بداخلكم أنه قرار حاسم — فإن الأمر يختلف. عندئذ ترون أمامكم الضوء والطريق المرسوم، الطريق المستقيم الذي يجب ألا تحيدوا عنه. لا مجال للخداع هنا، فاليوغا، كما تعلمون، ليست عبثاً أو هزلاً، ويجب أن تكونوا على علم بما تفعلون عندما تختارونها. متى اخترتم اليوغا يجب أن تتمسكوا بها ولا ينبغي أن تتبذبوا، بل يجب أن تمضوا أماماً على الطريق. هذا هو كل ما في الأمر!

كل ما أطلبه منكم هو أن تعقدوا النية على أن تحسنوا عملكم وتبذلوا الجهد اللازم للتقدم وأن ترغبوا في تحقيق حياة أسمى قليلاً من الحياة البشرية العادية. لقد كبرتم ونموتم تحت ظروف خاصة وترعرعتم في النور والوعي والاتساق والنية الطيبة؛ وينبغي أن يكون رد فعلكم على هذه الظروف أن تصبحوا في العالم تعبيراً عن هذا الضوء وهذا الاتساق وهذه النية الطيبة. لو فعلتم ذلك، فإن ذلك يكون حسناً للغاية، حسناً بالفعل.

لكي تمارسوا اليوغا، يوغا التحول التي هي أصعب الأمور إطلاقاً، يجب أن تشعروا أنها السبب في أنكم أتيتم إلى هنا (أعني هنا على الأرض)، وأنكم لا تريدون أي شيء سواها وأنها السبب الوحيد في وجودكم. وحتى لو اقتضى الأمر أن تكدحوا كثيراً وتعانوا وتكافحوا، لا تكترثوا ولا تبدلوا موقفكم: "هذه اليوغا هي ما أريد ولا أريد أي شيء سواها." عندئذ يختلف الأمر. وإلا فإني سوف أقول لكم: "كونوا سعداء وصالحين، صالحين بمعنى أن تفهموا أن الظروف التي تعيشون فيها ظروف استثنائية، وأن تحاولوا أن تعيشوا حياة أكثر سمواً ونبلاً وصدقاً من الحياة العادية، لكي تسمحوا لنصيب من هذا الوعي وهذا النور وهذا الصلاح بأن يتجلى في الحياة." ذلك يكون حسناً وطيباً للغاية. هذا هو ما أردت أن أقول.

ولكن متى شرعتم في طريق اليوغا، يجب أن تتحلوا بإرادة حديدية وأن تمشوا بدون انحراف إلى الهدف، مهما تكلفتم في سبيل ذلك...
أسئلة وأجوبة، 8 يونيو، 1955

Bases of the Integral Yoga — أسس اليوغا المتكاملة

The Gradations of Existence — درجات الوجود

The Origin of Individuality

Who will tell me what constitutes an individual? What is it that gives you the impression that you are a person existing in himself?

One can say with Descartes: "I think, therefore I am."

Ah, no! that does not prove that you are individualized.

What is it that gives you the impression that you are an individual?... When you were ten, you were very different from what you were when you were born, and now you are very different from what you were at ten, aren't you? The form grows within certain limits and there is a similarity, but even so, it is quite different from what it was at your birth; you may almost say, "It was not I." So much for the physical. Now, take your inner consciousness when you were five and now. Nobody would say it is the same person. And your thoughts, at five and now? All are different. But in spite of everything, what is it that gives you the impression that it is the *same person* who is thinking?

Let us take the example of a river following its course: it is never the same water which flows. What is a river? There is not a drop that ever is the same, no stability is there, then where is the river? (Some take this example to prove that there is no personality — they are very anxious to prove that there is no personality.) For beings it is the same thing: the consciousness changes, ideas change, sensations change, what then is the being? Some say that individuality is based upon memory, remembrance: you remember therefore you are an individual being. This is absolutely wrong, for even if you had no memory you would still be an individual being.

The river's bed constitutes the river.

The bed localizes the river, but the bed also changes much; which means all is inconstant, all is fugitive, and this is true. But it is only one part of the truth, it is not the whole. You feel quite clearly that there is something "stable" in you, don't you, but where does this sensation of stability come from?

If I were to place it physically, I would say it is somewhere in the chest. When I say "I am going to do something", it is not the true "I" which speaks. When I say "I think", it is not the true "I" which thinks —the true "I" looks at the thinking, it looks at the thoughts coming. Naturally this is a way of speaking.

The Gradations of Existence — درجات الوجود

أصل الشخصية الفردية

مـن يسـتطيع أن يخبرنـي عـن الشخصـية الفرديـة: مـا أصـلها وكيـف تنشـأ؟ مـا ذا يعطيـك الإحسـاس بأنـك شخص أو كيان قائم بذاته؟

ربما تسعفنا هنا عبارة ديكارت الشهيرة: "أنا أفكر، إذاً أنا موجود."

كـلا، مجـرد أنـك تفكـر لا يجعلـك شخصـاً مميـزاً. مـا ذا يعطيـك الانطبـاع أنـك فـرد يتميـز عـن الآخرين؟...

عندما كنت في العاشـرة مـن عمـرك كنـت تختلـف كثيـراً عمـا كنـت عليـه عندما ولـدت، وأنـت الآن تختلـف كثيـراً عمـا كنـت عليـه في العاشـرة، ألـيس كـذلك؟ صـحيح أن الهيئـة الخارجيـة نمـت إلى حـد مـا وأنـه مـا زال هنـاك تشـابه، ولكـن هيئتـك الآن تختلـف عـن هيئتـك عنـد ولادتـك إلى درجـة تسـمح بالقـول بأنكمـا شخصـان مختلفـان. هـذا مـن الناحيـة البدنيـة؛ دعنـا ننظـر إلى الأمـر مـن ناحيـة الـوعي ونقـارن بـين وعيـك الحـالي ووعيـك عندمـا كنـت في الخامسـة. الفـارق كبـير لدرجـة يصـعب معهـا أن نقـول أنكمـا نفـس الشـخص. ثم انظـر إلى أفكـارك عندمـا كنـت في الخامسـة وأفكـارك الآن. الاخـتلاف شاسـع هنـا أيضـاً. ولكـن علـى الـرغم مـن كـل هـذا الاخـتلاف، أنـت نفـس الشـخص، فمـا هـو الشـيء الـذي يجمـع كل هذه الأحوال وينسقها في شخص واحد؟

دعنـا الآن نأخـذ كمثـال حالـة نهـر يتابـع مجـراه: المـاء يتـدفق في النهـر ويتغيـر باسـتمرار. ولكـن مـا هـو بالتحديـد هـذا النهـر؟ النهـر يتكـون مـن قطـرات مـاء لا تظـل قطـرة واحـدة منهـا علـى حالهـا، فـأين هـو النهـر مـع كـل هـذه الحركـة الدائمـة بـدون اسـتقرار؟ (الـذين يحرصـون علـى إثبـات انعـدام الشخصـية، يأخـذون هـذا المثـال برهانـاً علـى أن الشخصـية لا وجـود لهـا). دعنـا نعـود إذاً ونسـأل سـؤالاً شـبيهاً في حالـة البشـر: وعـي الإنسـان يختلـف باسـتمرار، وآراؤه تتغيـر، وأحاسيسـه تتبـدل، فمـا هـو الشـيء الثابـت في الكيـان البشـري؟ قـد يقـول الـبعض أن الشخصـية الفرديـة أساسـها الذاكـرة: "أنـا أتـذكر، ولـذلك أنـا إنسـان ذو شخصـية متميـزة." هـذا غيـر صـحيح علـى الإطـلاق، لأننـا حتـى بـدون ذاكـرة، نظـل كائنات متميزة.

حوض النهر هو ما يُكوّن النهر.

ربمـا كـان ذلـك جـزءاً مـن الحقيقـة ولكنـه لـيس الحقيقـة كلهـا. صـحيح أن الحـوض يحـدد مكـان النهـر، ولكـن الحـوض نفسـه يتغيـر كثيـراً. ومـع ذلـك، أنـت تشـعر بوضـوح أن هنـاك شـيء "ثابـت" فيـك، فمـن أين لك هذا الإحساس بالثبات؟

لـو أردت أن أحـدد مكـان هـذا الشـيء الثابـت في البـدن، لقلـت أنـه في مكـان مـا في الصـدر. ولكنـي عندمـا أقـول "سـأفعل شـيئاً"، فمـن يتحـدث هنـا لـيس "أنـا" الحقيقـي. وعنـدما أقـول "أنـا أفكـر"، فلـيس "أنـا" الحقيقـي هـو الـذي يفكـر — بـل إن الـ "أنـا" الحقيقـي شـيء يراقـب التفكير ويرى الأفكار مقبلة. هذه بالطبع طريقة واحدة من طرائق كثيرة لشرح الأمور.

Bases of the Integral Yoga — أسس اليوغا المتكاملة

When the vast majority of people say "I", it is a part of them, of their feeling, their body, their thought, indifferently, which speaks: it is something that always changes. Therefore, their "I" is innumerable or the "I" always varies. What is the constant thing therein?... The psychic being* evidently. For, to be constant a thing must first be immortal. Otherwise it cannot be constant. Then, it must also be independent from the experiences themselves. Hence, it is certainly not the bed of the river which constitutes the river; the bed is only a circumstance. If the comparison is carried a little farther (besides, comparisons are worthless, people find in them whatever they want), it can be said that the river is a good symbol for life, that what is constant in the river is the species "water". It is not always the same drop of water, but it is always water — without water there would be no river. And what endures in the human being is the species "consciousness". It is because it has a consciousness that it endures. It is not the forms which last, it is the consciousness, the power of binding together all these forms, of passing through all these things, not only keeping a memory of them (memory is something very external), but keeping the same vibration of consciousness.

And that is the great mystery of creation, for it is the same consciousness, the Consciousness is one. But the very moment the Consciousness manifests itself, exteriorizes itself, deploys itself, it divides itself into innumerable fragments for the need of expansion, and each one of these fragmentations has been the beginning, the origin of an individual being. The origin of every individual form is the law of this form or the truth of this form. If there were no law, no truth of each form, there would be no possibility of individualization. It would be something extending indefinitely, there would perhaps be points of concentration, assemblages, but no individual consciousness. Each form then represents one element in the changing of the One into the many. This multiplicity implies an innumerable quantity of laws, elements of consciousness, truths which spread out into the universe and finally become separate individualities. So the individual being seems constantly to go farther and farther away from its origin by the very necessity of individualization. But once this individualization, that is, this awareness of the inner truth is complete, it becomes possible, by an inner identification, to re-establish in the multiplicity the original unity; that is the *raison d'être* of the universe as we perceive it. The universe has been made so that this phenomenon may take place. The Supreme has manifested Himself to Himself so as to become aware of Himself.

In any case, that is the rationale of *this* creation. Let us be satisfied with our universe, let us make the best possible use of our life upon earth and the rest will come in time.

Bases of the Integral Yoga — أسس اليوغا المتكاملة

عندما يقول الغالبية العظمى من الناس "أنا"، فإن ما يتكلم فيهم أحياناً جزءاً من بدنهم وأحياناً صوت مشاعرهم وأحياناً أفكاراً في ذهنهم، أي أن هذا "الأنا" شيء متعدد ودائم التغير. ما هو الشيء الثابت إذاً؟... إنه الكيان السيكي* بالطبع. لكي يكون أي شيء ثابتاً على الدوام يجب بالضرورة أن يكون أزلياً ولا يعتمد على التجارب التي يمر بها. من هذا المنظور، حوض النهر لا يمثل النهر كله، بل هو مجرد "ظرف طارئ" ملحق به. نستطيع أن نرى في النهر رمزاً جيداً للحياة، ولو دفعنا بالمقارنة أبعد قليلاً (وإن كانت المقارنات عديمة القيمة في الحقيقة، لأن المرء يستطيع أن يفسرها كيفما شاء)، نستطيع أن نقول إن الشيء الثابت في النهر هو عنصر "الماء". صحيح أن النهر يتكون من قطرات تتغير أبداً، إلا أنه يتكون من ماء في جميع الأحوال — بدون ماء لا يكون هناك نهر. كذلك فإن ما يدوم في الكائن البشري هو "الوعي"، إذ أن بدونه لا دوام للإنسان. الأشكال والهيئات لا تدوم، ما يدوم هو الوعي وهو الذي يربط كل هذه الأشكال والهيئات بعضها بالبعض ويُكوّن ذاكرتها و ينسقها جميعاً على نفس الموجة.

هذا هو اللغز العظيم في الخليقة: أن وعي جميع المخلوقات **وعي إلهي** واحد. ولكن هذا **الوعي الإلهي** بمجرد أن يظهر نفسه ويتخذ هيئات خارجية ويصبح فعالاً فيها، فإنه يجزئ نفسه إلى أجزاء لا حصر لها لكي يتوسع، وكل من هذه الأجزاء يصبح بداية وأصلاً لكيان متفرد. أصل كل هيئة متفردة هو قانون هذه الهيئة أو حقيقتها. لو لم يكن هناك قانون أو حقيقة لكل شكل أو هيئة، لأصبح التمييز بين الأشكال غير ممكن ولأصبح هناك توسع لا حدود له، ربما تكون فيه نقاط تركيز وتجمعات، ولكن لن يكون هناك وعي متفرد. كل شكل من الأشكال إذاً يمثل عنصراً واحداً في الانتقال من الوحدانية إلى الكثرة. هذا التعدد ينتج قوانين وأنماط وعي وحقائق لا حصر لها تنتشر في الكون وتصبح في النهاية أفراداً متميزين. وهكذا يبدو أن الكائن الفرد يبتعد بالضرورة من أصله أكثر وأكثر في عملية تجزأ **الواحد الإلهي.** ولكن متى تم هذا التجزأ والتفرد، يصبح ممكناً، عن طريق التعرف والتطابق الداخلي، أن نُرجع التعدد مرة أخرى إلى الوحدة الأصلية. هذا هو **سبب وجود** الكون حسب نظرتنا إلى الأمور ونحن نرى أن الكون قد خلق لكي تتمكن هذه الظاهرة من الحدوث. أي أن **الواحد-الكل*** قد جعل نفسه ملموساً ومحسوساً [في الكون] لكي يصبح واعياً بنفسه. على أي الأحوال، هذا هو السبب الجوهري في الخلق.

أفضل ما نستطيع أن نفعل هو أن نتقبل الكون بالرضى، وأن نستفيد من حياتنا على الأرض أقصى استفادة... كل ما عدا ذلك سيأتي في أوانه.

Bases of the Integral Yoga — أسس اليوغا المتكاملة

It is purposely, mind you, that I have not mentioned the ego as one of the causes of the sense of individuality. For the ego being a falsehood and an illusion, the sense of individuality would itself be false and illusory (as Buddha and Shankara* affirm), whereas the origin of individualization being in the Supreme Himself, the ego is only a passing deformation, necessary for the moment, which will disappear when its utility is over, when the Truth-Consciousness will be established.

3 March 1951

Living on the Surface and Living within

Almost totally, everybody lives on the surface, all the time, all the time on the surface. And for them it's even the only thing which exists — the surface. And when something compels them to draw back from the surface, some people feel that they are falling into a hole. There are people who, if they are drawn back from the surface, suddenly feel that they are crumbling down into an abyss, so unconscious they are!

They are conscious only of a kind of a small thin crust which is all they know of themselves and things and the world, and it is so thin a crust! Many! I have experienced, I don't know how often... I tried to interiorize some people and immediately they felt they were falling into an abyss, and at times a black abyss. Now this is the absolute inconscience. But a fall, a fall into something which for them is like a non-existence, this happens very often. People are told "Sit down and try to be silent, to be very quiet"; this frightens them terribly.

A fairly long preparation is needed in order to feel an increase of life when one goes out of the outer consciousness. It is already a great progress. And then there is the culmination, that when one is obliged for some reason or other to return to the outer consciousness. It is there that one has the impression of falling into a black hole, at least into a kind of dull, lifeless greyness, a chaotic mixture of disorganized things, with the faintest light, and all this seems so dull, so dim, so dead that one wonders how it is possible to remain in this state — but this is of course the other end — unreal, false, confused, lifeless!

24 August, 1955

تعمدت ألا أذكر الأنا* كأحد أسباب إحساسنا بالتفرد والتميز لأن الأنا وهم زائف، وحيث أن أصل التفرد والتميز يرجع الى **الواحد-الكل***، لا أعتبر الإحساس بالتفرد والتميز زور ووهم باطل (كما يراه بوذا و شانكارا*)، بل أرى أن الأنا تحريف وقتي كان له نفعه في مرحلة ما ولكن مصيره إلى الزوال عندما ينتهي نفعه ويترسخ **وعي-الحقيقة** على الأرض.

3 مارس 1951

الحياة على السطح والحياة في الداخل

الغالبية العظمى من الناس يعيشون باستمرار على سطح كيانهم ولا يتصورون وجود أي شيء آخر غير هذا السطح. وهم يعيشون في اللاوعي لدرجة أنهم إذا سُحبوا من السطح واضطروا إلى مغادرة هذه القشرة الخارجية من كيانهم يشعرون على الفور أنهم يقعون في في هاوية!

هذه القشرة الخارجية الرفيعة هي كل ما يعلمه هؤلاء القوم عن أنفسهم وعن سائر العالم... وهؤلاء حسب خبرتي المتكررة ليسوا أقلاء، بل هناك الكثيرون منهم... كلما حاولت أن أسعدهم على سحب وعيهم إلى الداخل، يشعرون للتو أنهم يقعون في هاوية، بل أحيانا في هاوية ليس فيها بصيص من نور. هذا هو اللاوعي المطلق. وهذه الهاوية تمثل لهم اللاوجود والعدم. وهذا هو ما يرعبهم أشد الرعب عندما أنصحهم بأن يجلسوا ويحاولوا يكونوا صامتين وفي هدوء تام.

نحتاج إلى إعداد طويل إلى حد ما لكي نبدأ في إدراك أننا بالخروج من الوعي السطحي والتعمق في داخل كياننا نجد حياة أوسع وأكثر ثراء. وعندما ننجح في ذلك، يكون ذلك دليلاً على أننا أحرزنا تقدماً كبيراً [في اليوغا]. هذا التقدم يبلغ قمته عندما نعتاد الحياة في الداخل إلى درجة أن نشعر، إذا اضطررنا لسبب ما إلى الرجوع إلى الوعي السطحي، كما لو كنا قد وقعنا في ثقب أسود ونجد الحياة على السطح مملة ورتيبة وخليطاً معتماً ومشوشاً من أشياء خامدة لا نظام فيها، لدرجة أن نتعجب كيف أمكننا الحياة على مثل هذه الحال من قبل — هنا نكون بالطبع قد توصلنا إلى الطرف الآخر وتقدمنا من اللاوعي التام إلى الوعي التام.

24 أغسطس 1955

Bases of the Integral Yoga — أسس اليوغا المتكاملة

Matter and Body

> *Each Spot of the body is symbolical of an inner movement; there is there a world of subtle correspondences. But this is a long and complex subject and we cannot enter into its details just now. The particular place in the body affected by an illness is an index to the nature of the inner disharmony that has taken place. It points to the origin, it is a sign of the cause of the ailment. It reveals too the nature of the resistance that prevents the whole being from advancing at the same high speed. It indicates the treatment and the cure. If one could perfectly understand where the mistake is, find out what has been unreceptive, open that part and put the force and the light there, it would be possible to re-establish in a moment the harmony that has been disturbed and the illness would immediately go." (The Mother)*

Why is "each spot of the body symbolical of an inner movement"?

Because the whole physical world is the symbol of universal movements. So our body is the symbol of our inner movements. The whole world, the whole physical world is like a materialization, a crystallization — of the movements in other planes of the universe. It is like a finalization, it is as though a projection on something that retains the image, fixes the image. Therefore, at every point it is the same thing as in the whole material universe.

The material is a plane, isn't it?

Yes, it is a final result. There is an increasing materiality and a decreasing materiality, and the physical plane is at the center: it is like a screen on which all the intervening vibrations are projected and held, as upon a screen — it is an image, an image of all that is happening. We notice it because it is a thing done, something concrete. It is as though you viewed the whole universe as a movement of force and this movement of force were projected till it met a screen and on the screen it made an image, and this image on the screen is the physical world. And it is a mere image. The physical world which everyone takes as the only reality is simply an image. It is the image of all that happens in what we call the invisible. It becomes visible to us because there is a screen that intervenes and stops the vibrations and that produces an image. If there were no such screen, the vibrations would move on and nothing would be seen. And yet all the movements would exist. But for us they would be invisible, if there were no screen to stop the vibrations.

المـادة والبـدن

"كـل موقـع فـي البـدن يرمـز إلـى حركـة داخليـة، وهنـا نجـد عالمـاً مـن التوافقـات الدقيقـة. ولكـن ذلـك موضـوع متشـعب لا نسـتطيع أن نـدخل فـي تفاصيله الآن. الموقـع المعيـن الـذي يتـأثر بمـرض مـا يشـير إلـى طبيعـة اختلال التـوازن والانسـجام الـذي حـدث وبالتـالي إلـى أصـل المـرض وسـببه. وهـو يشـير أيضـاً إلـى طبيعـة المقاومـة التـي تمنـع أجـزاء البـدن مـن التقـدم كلهـا بنفـس السـرعة العاليـة. وهـو يشـير أخيـراً إلـى طريقـة العـلاج وإلـى الـدواء. لـو أمكننـا أن نتعـرف بدقـة علـى مكـان الخطـأ، علـى العضـو الـذي لا يتجـاوب، وأن نفتـح هـذا العضـو **للقـوة والنـور**، لأمكـن فـي لحظـة اسـترجاع التناسـق الـذي اختـل وبـذلك يـزول المـرض علـى الفـور." (الأم)

ما هو السبب في أن كل موقع في البدن يرمز إلى حركة داخلية؟

السـبب هـو أن العـالم الفيزيائـي بأجمعـه يرمـز إلـى حركـات كونيـة. وبالمثـل بـدننا هـو رمـز لحركاتنـا الداخليـة. العـالم الفيزيائـي بأجمعـه يشـبه تجسـداً أو تبلـوراً لحركـات تحـدث علـى مسـتويات كونيـة أخـرى، كأنـه إسـقاطاً لهـذه الحركـات الكونيـة علـى شـيء يحتفـظ بصـورتها ويثبتهـا. وبـذلك تمثـل كـل نقطـة مـن عالمنـا الفيزيائـي موقعـاً مـن مواقـع الكـون المـادي.

هل يمكن اعتبار عالمنا المادي مستوى قائماً بذاته؟

نعـم. إنـه نتيجـة نهائيـة. هنـاك درجـات مختلفـة مـن التجسـد المـادي، وعالمنـا الفيزيائـي يوجـد فـي مركزهـا كمـا لـو كـان شاشـة تُسـقط عليهـا ذبـذبات كـل المسـتويات الوسـيطة، وتُحفَظ عليهـا صـورة إجماليـة لكـل مـا يحـدث فـي الكـون. هـذه الصـورة هـي العـالم الفيزيائـي، وهـي مجـرد صـورة. أي أن العـالم الفيزيائـي الـذي يعتبـره الجميـع الحقيقـة الوحيـدة مـا هـو إلا صـورة لكـل مـا يحـدث فـي عوالـم غيـر المرئيـة. عالمنـا الفيزيائـي مرئـي لنـا لأن هنـاك شاشـة تعتـرض طريـق تموجـات الإسـقاط وتحتفـظ بصـورة لهـا. لـو لـم تكـن هنـاك شاشـة تعتـرض طريـق الذبـذبات الكونيـة لكـان عالمنـا أيضـاً غيـر مرئيـاً.

Bases of the Integral Yoga — أسس اليوغا المتكاملة

For the ordinary consciousness it is the image alone that is true, and what happens behind it is more or less problematical, but in the true consciousness, all that happens behind or before is the true thing and what one sees externally is only an image, that is to say, a projection on a screen, of something that exists altogether independently. So, our body represents a small fragment in this set of images that is projected and it is a fragment which expresses exactly all the vibrations of the inner state corresponding to this little point that is the body.
23 September 1953

The True Body

There is a physical Nature which is perfectly harmonious, which has an absolutely... how to put it... yes, harmonious working, without any disorder, without disequilibrium, without any rupture of harmony, which would be expressed, if it existed upon earth, by a perfect health, a growing force, a continuous progress; and then all that one would like to obtain from one's body one would obtain; and this can go as far as an almost unimaginable progress of perfection.

The physical state as we see it with all its disharmonies, its weaknesses, its uglinesses, is the same deformation as that which has changed the higher vital, the true vital, into the kind of vital we see. And this comes from the same cause; it is cut off from its Origin, with an acute sense of separation which makes one live in an absolutely obscure consciousness which has become totally ignorant, instead of living in the consciousness of One's origin. Now to ask why it is like that is to ask too much. That's all?

I did not understand very well, Sweet Mother.

You haven't understood what the true physical is, because it is not a question of understanding. One is not conscious of it because one is not inside it, one doesn't live in it. But can't you conceive a body which would be perfectly beautiful, perfectly harmonious, which would function perfectly well and would never be ill, never tired, and would be in a state of constant progress? First it would become taller and taller until it reaches its maximum height, and then it would become stronger and stronger, more and more skillful, more and more conscious, and always in a perfect harmony: never any illness and never any fatigue, never any error, making no mistakes, knowing exactly at each moment what ought to be done and why.
29 June 1955

Bases of the Integral Yoga — أسس اليوغا المتكاملة

الـوعي العـادي يأخـذ الصـورة علـى أنهـا كـل الحقيقـة، ولا يفهم جيداً مـاذا يحـدث وراء هـذه الصـورة، ولكـن الـوعي الحقيقـي يـرى أن مـا يحـدث وراء أو قبـل الصـورة هـو الشـيء الحقيقـي، وأن مـا نـراه ليس إلا صـورة ظاهريـة، أي إسقاطاً علـى شاشـة لشـيء لـه وجـود مستقل تمامـاً. وبـذلك يمثـل بـدننا هـذا الجـزء الصـغير مـن تلـك المجموعـة مـن الصـور الـذي يعبـر عـن كـل ذبـذبات الحالـة الداخليـة التـي تتوافق معه.
23 سبتمبر 1953

البدن الحقيقي

هنـاك **طبيعـة** فيزيائيـة كاملـة فـي تناسـقها، تجـري حركاتهـا فـي اتسـاق وتـوازن تـام لا ينتابـه الخلـل او الصـدع. لـو تحققـت هـذه الطبيعـة علـى الأرض، تكـون نتيجتهـا الصـحة الكاملـة والقـوة الناميـة والتقـدم المستمر؛ وكل ما نتمنى أن تقدر أبداننا على فعله... وكل ذلك في تقدم مطرد يصعب تخيله.

حالـة أبـداننا التـي نراهـا بكـل مـا فيهـا مـن خلـل وضـعف وقبح نتجت مـن نفس التحريـف الـذي حـرف المجـال الحيـوي الأعلـى، أو الكيـان الحيـوي الحقيقـي إلـى الكيـان الحيـوي الـذي نـراه اليـوم فـي الإنسـان العـادي. هذا التحريـف أوجبـه نفـس السـبب: ألا وهو الانفصـال مـن **الأصـل** [الإلهـي]، ومـا نتـج عـن ذلـك مـن إحسـاس الإنسـان بالبعـد والعزلـة والانفصـال ومـن تَـرَدِّيه فـي وعـي الجهـل بـدلاً مـن وعـي الوحـدة الأصـلية. أمـا سـبب حـدوث هـذا الانفصـال، فإنـه يتخطـى حـدود موضـوعنا الحـالي... هـل هنـاك سـؤال آخر؟

مريد: لم أفهم عنك جيداً أيتها الأم العذبة.

أنـت لـم تفهـم مـا هـو البـدن الحقيقـي لأن المسـألة ليسـت مسـألة فهـم. أنـت لا تعـي البـدن الحقيقـي لأنـك لسـت بداخلـه ولأنـك لا تعيـش فيـه. ولكـن ألا تسـتطيع أن تتصـور بـدناً كامـلاً فـي جمالـه وتناسـقه، فـي حالـة تقـدم مستمر، يـؤدي وظائفـه علـى أحسـن صـورة ولا يمـرض أبـداً؟ بـدن [يتطـور مـن بـدننا الحـالي بـأن] يبـدأ أولاً فـي النمـو فـي الطـول إلـى أن يبلـغ طولـه الأقصـى، ثـم ينمـو باضـطراد فـي القـوة والمهـارة والـوعي، ويكـون دائمـا فـي اتسـاق تـام، ولا يقـع أبـداً فريسـة للتعـب أو المـرض أو الخطـأ، ويعلـم فـي كـل لحظة ما هو مطلوب منه والغرض منه.
29 يونيو 1955

Influences from Outside

Naturally these influences are of very diverse kinds. They may be studies from a psychological point of view or from an almost mechanical standpoint, the one usually translating the other, that is, the mechanical phenomenon occurs as a sort of result of the psychological one.

In very few people, and even in the very best at very rare moments in life, does the will of the being express that deep inner, higher truth.

(After a silence the Mother continues:) The individual consciousness extends far beyond the body; we have seen that even the subtle physical which is yet material compared with the vital being and in certain conditions almost visible, extends at times considerably beyond the visible limits of the physical body. This subtle physical is constituted of active vibrations which enter into contact or mingle with the vibrations of the subtle physical of others, and this reciprocal contact gives rise to influences — naturally the most powerful vibrations get the better of the others. For example, as I have already told you several times, if you have a thought, this thought clothes itself in subtle vibrations and becomes an entity which travels and moves about in the earth atmosphere in order to realize itself as best it can, and because it is one among millions, naturally there is a multitude and involved interaction as a result of which things don't take place in such a simple and schematic fashion.

What you call yourself, the individual being enclosed within the limits of your present consciousness, is constantly penetrated by vibrations of this kind, coming from outside and very often presenting themselves in the form of suggestions, in the sense that, apart from a few exceptions, the action takes place first in the mental field, then becomes vital, then physical. I want to make it clear that it is not a question of the pure mind here, but of the physical mind*; for in the physical consciousness itself there is a mental activity, a vital activity and a purely material activity, and all that takes place in your physical consciousness, in your body consciousness and bodily activity, penetrates first in the form of vibrations of a material nature, and so in the form of suggestions. Most of the time these suggestions enter you without your being in the least conscious of them; they go in, awaken some sort of response in you, then spring up in your consciousness as though they were your own thought, your own will, your own impulse; but it is only because you are unconscious of the process of their penetration.

مؤثرات من الخارج

تؤثر على وعينا، بطبيعة الحال، مؤثرات من كل الأنواع. يمكن دراسة هذه المؤثرات من الناحية السيكولوجية ويمكن أيضاً أن ننظر إليها بنظرة آلية توازيي النظرة الأولى وتكاد تكون نتيجة لها.

إرادة الكيان البشري لا تعبر عن الحقيقة الباطنية في عمقها وسموها إلا في أفراد قليلين، بل إن ذلك لا يحدث إلا نادراً في أفضل هؤلاء الأفراد.

(الأم تستأنف بعد فترة صمت:) الوعي الفردي يمتد خارج حدود البدن بكثير؛ وقد رأينا سابقاً أن الكيان الفيزيائي الدقيق يكون في ظروف معينة مرئياً، على الرغم من أنه أكثر مادية من الكيان الحيوي، وأنه يمتد أحياناً إلى حدود أبعد كثيراً من حدود البدن. كياننا الفيزيائي الدقيق يكون من ذبذبات تدخل في وتمتزج مع ذبذبات الآخرين، وهذا التفاعل يؤثر على جميع الأطراف بحيث تتغلب الذبذبات الأقوى على الذبذبات الأضعف. أذكركم بمثال الأفكار الذي ضربته لكم مرات عديدة من قبل: الأفكار تكتسي في أذهانكم بذبذبات دقيقة وتصبح كياناً مستقلاً يتحرك ويتنقل في جو الأرض ليحقق نفسه بأحسن ما يمكنه، ويتفاعل مع ذبذبات الآخرين، ولكن نظراً لوجود أعداد هائلة من الأفكار البشرية في الجو فأن هذه التفاعلات تكون معقدة ومركبة ولا تتم بطريقة سهلة يمكن التنبؤ بنتائجها.

ما تسميه "نفسك"، أي هذا الكائن الفردي المحدود داخل وعيك الحالي، معرض على الدوام لذبذبات الآخرين التي تأتي من الخارج وتتخلله، والتي كثيراً ما تأتي في صورة إيحاءات في العقل، بمعنى أن التأثير يحدث، بصرف النظر عن أحوال نادرة، أولاً في المجال الذهني ثم في المجال الحيوي وأخيراً في المجال المادي. أرجو أن يكون واضحاً أن العقل الذي أعنيه هنا ليس العقل البحت [عقل التفكير] ولكن العقل الفيزيائي* (فالوعي الفيزيائي يشمل، إلى جانب نشاط العقل الفيزيائي، نشاط حيوي ونشاط مادي بحت، وكل ذلك يظهر في وعي البدن* ونشاطه). وبالتالي فإن هذا التأثير الذي يدخلنا من الخارج، يدخلنا أولاً كإيحاءات لها طابع مادي. وفي أغلب الأحوال، تدخلنا هذه الإيحاءات بدون أن ندركها وتؤثر فينا كما لو كانت قد نشأت من تفكيرنا الخاص أو إرادتنا الخاصة أو دفعتنا الخاصة، وما ذلك إلا لأننا لم نعي طريقة دخولها فينا.

Bases of the Integral Yoga — أسس اليوغا المتكاملة

These suggestions are very numerous, manifold, varied, with natures which are very, very different from each other, but they may be classified into three principal orders. First — and they are hardly perceptible to the ordinary consciousness; they become perceptible only to those have already reflected much, observed much, deeply studied their own being — they are what could be called collective suggestions.

When a being is born upon earth, he is inevitably born in a certain country and a certain environment. Due to his physical parents he is born in a set of social, cultural, national, sometimes religious circumstances, a set of habits of thinking, of understanding, of feeling, conceiving, all sorts of constructions which are at first mental, then become vital habits and finally material modes of being. To put things more clearly, you are born in a certain society or religion, in a particular country, and this society has a collective conception of its own, this religion has a collective "construction" of its own which is usually very fixed. You are born into it. Naturally, when you are very young, you are altogether unaware of it, but it acts on your formation — that formation, that slow formation through hours and hours, through days and days, experiences added to experiences, which gradually builds up a consciousness. You are underneath it as beneath a bell-glass. It is a kind of construction which covers and in a way protects you, but in other ways limits you considerably. All this you absorb without even being aware of it and this forms the subconscious* basis of your own construction.

This subconscious basis will act on you throughout your life, if you do not take care to free yourself from it. And to free yourself from it, you must first of all become aware of it; and the first step is the most difficult, for this formation was so subtle, it was made when you were not yet a conscious being, when you had just fallen altogether dazed from another world into this one (laughing) and it all happened without your participating in the least in it. Therefore, it does not even occur to you that there could be something to know there, and still less something you must get rid of. And it is quite remarkable that when for some reason or other you do become aware of the hold of this collective suggestion, you realize at the same time that a very assiduous and prolonged labour is necessary in order to get rid of it. But the problem does not end there.

أسس اليوغا المتكاملة — Bases of the Integral Yoga

مع أن هذه الإيحاءات تأتي بأعداد وأنواع وفيرة تختلف فيما بينها اختلافاً شديداً، يمكن إلى حد ما تصنيفها في ثلاث مجموعات. المجموعة الأولى تشمل الإيحاءات الجماعية التي يصعب على الوعي العادي أن يدركها، ولا يدركها إلا الذين أكثروا من التفكير والملاحظة ومن دراسة أنفسهم.

عندما يولد كائن بشري على الأرض، فإنه يولد بالضرورة لأبوين في بلد معين ومحيط معين، وسط مجموعة من الظروف الاجتماعية والثقافية والوطنية وأحياناً الدينية، ومعرضاً لمنظومة من عادات التفكير والفهم والشعور والتصور وجميع أنواع التركيبات التي تحدد وتقرر أسلوب حياته ذهنياً ثم حيوياً وأخيراً مادياً. أزيدكم إيضاحاً: أنتم تولدون في مجتمع معين، في ديانة معينة، في بلد معين وهذا المجتمع له مفاهيمه وتصوراته الجماعية الخاصة به، وهذه الديانة لها بناء جماعي عادة ما يكون ثابتاً وغير قابل للتغيير. في أوائل عمركم، وعندما تكونون ما زلتم صغاراً للغاية، تكونون غير واعين بالظروف المحيطة بكم، ولكنها تؤثر على تكوينكم ببطء، ساعة بعد ساعة ويوماً بعد يوم. تمرون بكل ذلك في تجارب متوالية تمتصونها بدون أي دراية منكم كما لو كنتم تعيشون تحت ناقوس زجاجي يغطيكم تماماً ويكون وقاية لكم من ناحية، ولكنه يُحدِّدكم كثيراً من الناحية الأخرى. هذا التأثير المستمر يُكوِّن تدريجياً وعيكم ويصبح أساساً لكيانكم دون الواعي.

إذا لم تعملوا بعناية على تخليص أنفسكم من هذا الأساس اللاشعوري، فإنه يؤثر عليكم طيلة حياتكم. ولكن قبل أن تتمكنوا من تخليص أنفسكم منه، يجب أن تصبحوا أولاً واعين بوجوده. هذه الخطوة الأولى هي أصعب الخطوات، لأنكم تريدون التخلص من تركيبة [نفسية] دقيقة للغاية تشكلت قبل أن تبلغوا مرحلة الإدراك، عندما كنتم ما زلتم في حالة ذهول نتج من وقوعكم من عالم آخر إلى عالمنا هذا! ولأن كل ما حدث لكم بعد ذلك حدث بدون أن أي اشتراك من ناحيتكم، لا يخطر لكم حتى على بال أن شيئاً تجهلونه يسيطر عليكم، شيئاً لا يجب أن تدركوه فحسب، بل أن تتخلصوا منه كذلك. من الملفت للنظر أنكم عندما تدركون أخيراً، لسبب أو لآخر، مدى قبضة هذا الإيحاء الجماعي عليكم، تدركون في الوقت ذاته مقدار الجهد المتواصل الذي سيكون مطلوباً منكم للتخلص منه. ولكن ليت المشكلة تقف عند هذا الحد!

Bases of the Integral Yoga — أسس اليوغا المتكاملة

You live surrounded by people. These people themselves have desires, stray wishes, impulses which are expressed through them and have all kinds of causes, but take in their consciousness an individual form. For example, to put it in very practical terms: you have a father, a mother, brothers, sisters, friends, comrades; each one has his own way of feeling, willing and all those with whom you are in relation expect something from you, even as you expect something from them. That something they do not always express to you, but it is more or less conscious in their being, and it makes formations. These formations, according to each one's capacity of thought and the strength of his vitality, are more or less powerful, but they have their own little strength which is usually much the same as yours; and so what those around you want, hope, desire or expect from you enters in this way in the form of suggestions very rarely expressed, but which you absorb without resistance and which suddenly awaken within you a similar desire, a similar will, a similar impulse... This happens from morning to night, and again from night to morning. For these things don't stop while you are sleeping, but on the contrary are very often intensified because your consciousness is no longer awake, watching and protecting you to some extent.

And this is quite common, so common that it is quite natural and so natural that you need special circumstances and most unusual occasions to become aware of it. Naturally, it goes without saying that your own responses, your own impulses, your own wishes have a similar influence on others, and that all this becomes a marvelous mixture in which might is always right!

If that were the end of the problem, one could yet come out of the mess; but there is a complication. This terrestrial world, this human world is constantly invaded by the forces of the neighboring world, that is, of the vital world, the subtler region beyond the fourfold earth atmosphere (consisting of physical, vital, mental and psychic elements); and this vital world which is not under the influence of the psychic forces or the psychic consciousness is essentially a world of ill-will, of disorder, disequilibrium, indeed of all the most anti-divine things one could imagine. This vital world is constantly penetrating the physical world, and being much more subtle than the physical, it is very often quite imperceptible except to a few rare individuals. There are entities, beings, wills, various kind of individualities in that world, who have all kinds of intentions and make use of every opportunity either to amuse themselves if they are small beings or to do harm and create disorder if they are beings if they are beings with a greater capacity. And the latter have a very considerable power of penetration and suggestion, and whenever there is the least opening, the least affinity, they rush in, for it is a game which delights them.

أنـت تعيشـون وسـط آخريـن. وهـؤلاء الآخـرون لهـم، نتيجـة لأسـباب متنوعـة، رغبـات شـاردة وشـهوات واندفاعـات تُعَبّـر عـن نفسـها مـن خلالهـم وتتخـذ فـي وعيهـم طابعـاً خاصـاً. مـن وجهـة نظـر عمليـة، كـل الـذين تـربطهم بكـم صـلات، علـى سـبيل المثـال: الأب، الأم، الأخـوة، الأخـوات، الأصدقـاء، الـزملاء يتوقعـون أشـياء منكـم، كمـا أنـك تتوقعـون أشـياء شـبيهة منهـم. ومـع أنهـم علـى وعـي إلـى حـد مـا بتوقعـاتهم، إلا أنهـم لا يُصَـرّحون لكـم بهـا، بـل يحتفظـون بهـا فـي أنفسـهم كتشـكيلات [انظـر "تشـكيل" فـي قامـوس المفـردات بـآخر الكتـاب]. قـوة هـذه التشـكيلات تتوقـف علـى الطاقـة الفكريـة والحيويـة لكـل فـرد وهـي تتشـابه إلـى حـد مـا فـي معظـم النـاس. وبـذلك تـدخل فيكـم، فـي صـورة إيحـاءات، بـدون أي مقاومـة مـن نـاحيتكم، شـهوات ورغبـات هـؤلاء القـوم وتوقـظ فيكـم رغبـات وشـهوات واندفاعـات شـبيهة تتلـون بطابعكـم الخـاص... هـذا الغـزو مـن الخـارج يسـتمر مـن الصبـاح إلـى المسـاء، ومـن المسـاء إلـى الصبـاح، ولا يتوقـف حتـى أثنـاء نومكـم، بـل أنـه يـزداد شـدة أثنـاء النـوم لأن وعيكـم أثنـاء النـوم لا يراقـب ولا يحميكـم بنفـس الدرجـة التـي يراقـب بهـا ويحميكـم فـي اليقظـة.

عمليـة الإيحـاء مـن الخـارج دائمـة الحـدوث وشـائعة لدرجـة أنهـا تمثـل الحالـة الطبيعيـة، ومـع ذلـك لا تـدركونها إلا تحـت ظـروف خاصـة وغيـر اعتياديـة. غنـي عـن الـذكر فـي هـذا المجـال أن رغبـاتكم واندفاعـاتكم تـؤثر بـدورها علـى الآخريـن تـأثيراً ممـاثلاً، وتكـون نتيجـة كـل ذلـك خليطـاً مـذهلاً يتغلـب فيـه المؤثـر القـوي علـى المؤثـر الضعيـف.

لـو كان ذلـك كل مـا فـي الأمـر، لأمكـن ربمـا الإفـلات مـن هـذه الفوضـى؛ ولكـن مـا يـزال هنـاك تعقيـد آخـر. فالبشـر علـى الأرض معرضـون باسـتمرار لهجمـات مـن العـالم المجـاور، أو بالتحديـد مـن العـالم الحيـوي* (العـالم الـدقيق وراء جـو الأرض بطبقاتـه الأربعـة: الماديـة والحيويـة والذهنيـة و السـيكية*). هـذا العـالم الحيـوي لا يخضـع لنفـوذ القـوى السـيكية أو للـوعي السـيكي، ولـذلك فهـو أسـاسـاً عـالم اضطـراب وهيجـان و سـوء نيـة وكـل الأشـياء المعاديـة للألوهيـة التـي يمكـن أن تخطـر علـى بـل. سـبب نجاحـه فـي تخلـل عالمنـا المـادي هـو أن مادتـه أكثـر دقـة مـن مـادة عالمنـا بحيـث أنـه، عندمـا يتسـلل إلينـا، لا يقـدر علـى رؤيتـه والشـعور بـه إلا أفـراد نـادرون. فـي ذلـك العـالم الحيـوي كائنـات وشخصيـات ونيـات مـن جميـع الأنـواع بحيـث نجـد أن الكائنـات الصغيـرة منهـم لا تضيـع أي فرصـة للتسـلي علـى حسـاب البشـر، أمـا الكائنـات الأقـوى فلهـا قـدرة عظيمـة علـى التخلـل والإيحـاء، وكلمـا وجـدوا ثغـرة، أو تلقـوا دعـوة مـن شـيء مشـابه لهـم فـي عالمنـا، يسـارعون بالغـزو ليشـيعوا الأذى والفوضـى لأنهـم يجـدون متعـة كبيـرة فـي ذلـك.

Bases of the Integral Yoga — أسس اليوغا المتكاملة

Besides, they are very thirsty or hungry for certain human vital vibrations which for them are a rare dish they love to feed upon; and so their game lies in exciting pernicious movements in man so that man may emanate these forces and they be able to feed on them just as they please. All movements of anger, violence, passion, desire, all these things which make you abruptly throw certain energies from yourself, project them from yourself, are exactly what these entities of the vital world like best, for, as I said, they enjoy them like a sumptuous dish. Now, their tactics are simple: they send you a little suggestion, a little impulse, a small vibration which enters deep into you and through contagion or sympathy awakens in you the vibration necessary to make you throw off the force they want to absorb.

There it is a little easier to recognize the influence, for, if you are the least bit attentive, you become aware of something that has suddenly awakened within you. For example, those are in the habit of losing their temper, if they have attempted ever so little to control their anger, they will find something coming from outside or rising from below which actually takes hold of their consciousness and arouses anger in them. I don't mean that everybody is capable of this discernment; I am speaking of those who have tried to understand their being and control it. These adverse suggestions are easier to distinguish than, for instance, your response to the will or desire of a being who is of the same nature as yourself, another human being who consequently acts on you without giving you a clear impression of something coming from outside: the vibrations are too alike, too similar in their nature, and you have to be much more attentive and have much sharper discernment to realize that these movements which seem to come out from you are not really yours but come from outside. But with the adverse forces, if you are in the least sincere and observe yourself attentively, you become aware that it is something in the being which is responding to an influence, an impulse, a suggestion, even something at times very concrete, which enters and produces similar vibrations in the being.
12 December 1956

أضف إلــى ذلـك أن كائنــات العـالم الحيـوي تتلهـف علــى امتصـاص قـوى حيويـة معينـة مـن البشـر يجـدونها طعامـاً شـهياً ونــادراً؛ ووسـيلتهم لتحقيـق غرضـهم هـي إثـارة حركـات معينـة تجعـل البشـر يطلقون هذه القوى من أنفسـهم. هذه الطاقـات التي تخرج مـن البشـر فجـأة عندما يتمكن منهم الغضب أو العنـف أو الشـهوة أو أي مشـاعر ملتهبـة أخـرى تـوفر لهـم هذا الغـذاء المفضل. ولـذلك تلجأ الكائنـات الحيويـة إلـى هـذه الخدعـة البسـيطة وهـي أن ترسـل إيحـاءات أو دفعـات أو ذبـذبات صـغيرة تـدخل في البشر وتتخللهم و تجعلهم يطلقون هذه الطاقات من أنفسهم.

هنـا يكون التعـرف علـى مصـدر المـؤثر الخـارجي أسـهل بعـض الشـيء، لأنكـم تسـتطيعون، بالقليـل مـن الانتبـاه، أن تلاحظـوا أن شـيئاً مـا قـد اسـتيقظ بـداخلكم وأثـاركم فجـأة. علـي سـبيل المثـال، يلاحظ الـذين يعـانون مـن فـورات الغضـب ويحـاولون الـتحكم فيهـا أن شـيئاً أتـي مـن الخـارج أو صـعد مـن الطبقـات السـفلى في كيـانهم واسـتحوذ علـى وعيهم وأشـعل الغضـب فيهـم. أنا لا أقول إن جميـع النـاس قـادرون علـى التمييـز بهـذا الشـكل، بـل أتكلـم فقـط عـن ذوي الخبـرة الـذين سـعوا إلـى فهـم أنفسـهم والـتحكم في ذاتهـم. التعـرف علـى الإيحـاءات المعاديـة الآتيـة مـن عـالم آخـر أسـهل مـن التعـرف علـى الإيحـاءات القادمـة مـن بشـر، لأن البشـر لهـم طبـائع متشـابهة وإيحـاءاتهم لا تلفت أنظارنـا مثلمـا تفعـل الإيحـاءات الآتيـة مـن عـالم آخـر، ولـذلك يحتـاج التعـرف علـى إيحـاءات البشـر إلـى قـدرة تمييـز أكبـر تسـمح لنـا أن نـدرك أن التـأثير الـذي نشـعر بـه لا ينبـع مـن أنفسـنا بـل مـن آخـرين. أمـا فـي حالـة القـوى الحيويـة المعاديـة، فيكفـي أن نكـون صـادقين بعـض الشـيء فـي ملاحظـة أنفسـنا لنـرى أن التـأثير الـذي حـدث فينـا يأتي من عالم من العوالم المعادية لنا.

12 ديسمبر 1956

The Complexity of our Nature

Sweet Mother, Sri Aurobindo has written: "It is part of the foundation of Yoga to become conscious of the great complexity of our nature, see the different forces that move it and get over it a control of directing knowledge." Are these forces different for each person?

Yes. The composition is completely different, otherwise everybody would be the same. There are not two beings with an identical combination; between the different parts of the being and the composition of these parts the proportion is different in each individual. There are people, primitive men, people like the yet undeveloped races or the degenerated ones whose combinations are fairly simple; they are still complicated, but comparatively simple. And there are people absolutely at the top of the human ladder, the 'elite of humanity; their combinations become so complicated that a very special discernment is needed to find the relations between all these things. There are beings who carry in themselves thousands of different personalities, and then each one has its own rhythm and alternation, and there is a kind of combination; sometimes there are inner conflicts, and there is a play of activities which are rhythmic and with alternations of certain parts which come to the front and then go back and again come to the front. But when one takes all that, it makes such complicated combinations that some people truly find it difficult to understand what is going on in themselves; and yet these are the ones most capable of a complete, coordinated, conscious, organised action; but their organisation is infinitely more complicated than that of primitive or undeveloped men who have two or three impulses and four or five ideas, and who can arrange all this very easily in themselves and seem to be very co-ordinated and logical because there is not very much to organise.

But there are people truly like a multitude, and so that gives them a plasticity, a fluidity of action and an extraordinary complexity of perception, and these people are capable of understanding a considerable number of things, as though they had at their disposal a veritable army which they move according to circumstance and need; and all this is inside them. So when these people, with the help of yoga, the discipline of yoga, succeed in centralising all these beings around the central light of the divine Presence, they become powerful entities, precisely because of their complexity.

طبيعتنا المركبة

أمـي العذبة، كتـب شـري أوروبينـدو: "مـن المهـم لكـي نرسـخ أساسـنا فـي اليوغـا، أن نصبـح واعيـن بمـدى تعقيد طبيعتنـا، وأن نـرى القـوى المختلفة التـي تحركهـا، وأن نتوصـل إلـى التحكم فيهـا عن طريق المعرفة". هل تختلف هذه القوى من شخص إلى آخر؟

نعـم. طبائـع الأفـراد تختلـف فـي بنيتهـا وتركيبهـا، ولـو لـم يكـن الأمـر كذلـك، لتسـاوى النـاس فـي كـل شـيء. لا يوجـد شخصـان بنفـس التركيبـة وتناسـب أجـزاء الكيـان المختلفـة. فـي حيـن تتصـف الشـعوب البدائيـة، التـي لـم تتمـدن أو التـي تـدهورت مـن المدنيـة إلـى البـداءة، ببنيـة داخليـة بسـيطة وخاليـة مـن التعقيـد، تبلـغ طبائـع نخبـة البشـر درجـة مـن التعقيـد تتطلـب منهـم قـدرة كبيـرة علـى مجـرد التمييـز لمجـرد فهـم العلاقـات بيـن الأجـزاء المختلفـة فـي بنيتهـم. تتكـون طبائـع تلـك النخبـة مـن آلاف الشخصيـات، كـل شخصيـة منهـا لهـا إيقاعهـا وتناوبهـا؛ وهـي تمتـزج بعضهـا مـع البعـض فـي داخلهـم، تتصـادم أحيانـاً، وتتنـاغم أحيانـاً أخـرى، وتتنـاوب بيـن احتـلال مكـان الصـدارة فـي كيـانهم وبيـن التراجـع منـه إلـى الخلفيـة. عنـدما نأخـذ كـل ذلـك فـي الاعتبـار، نـرى مـدى تعقـد بنيتهـم، ولا نتعجـب أن بعضهـم يعجـزون أحيانـاً عـن فهـم مـا ذا يـدور فـي أنفسـهم، حتـى عنـدما تكـون تحقيقـاتهم وأعمـالهم كاملـة، متناسـقة، منظمـة، وواعيـة. وهـم فـي ذلـك بعيـدون بالطبـع عـن بسـاطة الإنسـان البدائـي الـذي لا يملـك إلا دوافـع وأفـكار قليلـة يسـتطيع بسـهولة أن ينظمهـا وأن يعيـش حيـاة منسـقة ومنطقيـة بـدون حاجـة إلـى بـذل جهـد كبيـر.

يتكـون كـل مـن هـذه الأفـراد ذوي البنيـة الداخليـة المعقـدة مـن حشـد كبيـر مـن الشخصيـات المختلفـة، وهـذا هـو مـا يضـفي عليـه مرونـة ولدونـة فـي القيـام بأعمالـه وقـدرة عظيمـة علـى اسـتيعاب وفهـم الأمـور، كمـا لـو كـان هنـاك بداخلـه جيـش كامـل تحـت تصرفـه يسـتطيع أن يوجهـه حسـبما تقتضـي الظـروف. لـو هَـذَّب مثـل هـذا الشـخص نفسـه بواسـطة اليوغـا ونجـح، علـى الرغـم مـن التعقيـد الكبيـر فـي شخصيتـه، فـي تنظيـم جميـع الشخصيـات المجتمعـة فيـه حـول ضـوء **الحضـرة الإلهيـة** بداخلـه، فإنـه يكتسب قوة وقدرة عظيمتين حقاً.

Bases of the Integral Yoga — أسس اليوغا المتكاملة

So long as this is not organised they often give the impression of an incoherence, they are almost incomprehensible, one can't manage to understand why they are like that, they are so complex. But when they have organised all these beings, that is, put each one in its place around the divine centre, then truly they are terrific, for they have the capacity of understanding almost everything and doing almost everything because of the multitude of entities they contain, of which they are constituted. And the nearer one is to the top of the ladder, the more it is like that, and consequently the more difficult it is to organise one's being; because when you have about a dozen elements, you can quickly compass and organise them, but when you have thousands of them, it is difficult.
June 22, 1955

طالمــا أنـه لـم يـنظم نفسـه داخليــاً، فإنـه يبـدو للآخـرين، الـذين يعجـزون عـن فهمـه، مشوشاً ومليئـاً بالمتناقضـات وغامضـاً. أمـا لو نجح في تنظيم نفسه، فإنـه يصبح مهولاً بحق نتيجـة لقدرتـه على فعل وفهـم أي شـيء تقريبـاً. بالتناسب مـع ارتفـاع مقـام هـذا الفرد، فإنـه يجـد صعـوبة أكبـر فـي التنظيم، حيث أن العناصر التي يحتاج إلى تنسيقها تزداد بدورها.

22 يونيو، 1955

Spirit and Matter

I think one of the greatest difficulties in understanding things comes from an arbitrary simplification which puts spirit on one side and matter on the other. It is this foolishness that makes you incapable of understanding anything. There is spirit and matter – this is very convenient. So if one does not belong to spirit, one belongs to matter; if one does not belong to matter, one belongs to spirit. But what do you call spirit and what do you call matter? It is a countless crowd of things, an interminable ladder. The universe is a seemingly infinite gradation of worlds and states of consciousness, and in this increasingly subtle gradation, where does your matter come to an end? Where does your spirit begin? You speak of "spirit"— where does this spirit begin? With what you don't see? Is that it? So you include in "spirit" all the beings of the vital world*, for instance, because you don't see them in your normal state — all that belongs to "spirit"— and they may indeed be the spirit which is behind your intention — and it isn't up to much! That's it.

It is like those people who say, "When you are alive you are in matter, when you are dead, you enter the spirit. There, then! So, liberate the spirit from matter, die, and you liberate your spirit from matter." It is these stupid ties which prevent you from understanding anything at all. But all this has nothing to do with the world as it really is.

For the human consciousness as it is, there are certainly infinitely more invisible things than visible things. What you know, the things which are visible to you and which you are conscious of – it's almost like the skin of an orange compared with the orange itself — and even an orange with a very thin skin, not a thick one! And so, if you know only the skin of the orange, you know nothing about the orange.

And this is more or less what happens. All that you know about the universe is just a superficial little crust — and even this you hardly know. But that is all you know about it, and all the rest escapes you.

7 March, 1956

الروح والمادة

أعتقد أن التبسيط الاعتباطي الـذي يفصل فصلاً تـامـاً بـين الـروح والـمـادة هو أحـد أكبر العقبـات التـي تقـف فـي طريـق فهمنـا للأمـور. ربمـا يكـون مـن المـريح أن نقسـم الكـون إلـى روح ومـادة، ونعتبـر أن مـا ينتمـي إلـى الـروح لا ينتمـي إلـى المـادة ومـا ينتمـي إلـى المـادة لا ينتمـي إلـى الـروح، ولكن مثـل هـذا التبسيط هـو بالتحديـد الحمـاقـة التـي تمنعنـا مـن الفهـم. ولكـن مـا معنـى أن نقـول أن هـذا الشـيء روح وذاك الشـيء مـادة؟ الأشـياء لا حصـر لهـا بحيـث يمكـن ترتيبهـا علـى درجـات سلـم لا نهـائي، والكـون تـدرج لا نهايـة لـه مـن العـوالم وحـالات الـوعي، فـأين تريـد أن تعيـن مكانـاً محـدداً للمـادة أو مكانـاً محـدداً للـروح وسـط هـذا التـدرج الـدقيق؟ أنت تقـول "الـروح"، ولكـن أيـن يبـدأ هـذا "الـروح" وأيـن يـنتهـي؟ هـل الـروح هـو كـل مـا لا نـراه فـي حـالتنـا العـاديـة؟ ولكـن كائنـات العـالم الحيـوي*، علـى سبيـل المثـال، غيـر مرئية بالنسبة لنا، ولو اعتبرناها تابعة للروح، يصبح مفهومنا للروح غير ذي قيمة كبيرة!

بعـض النـاس يقـولـون: "عنـدما تكـون حيـاً، تنتمـي إلـى عـالم المـادة، وعنـدما تمـوت تنتمـي إلـى عـالم الـروح، ولـذا لـن تتحـرر روحـك مـن المـادة إلا بعـد موتـك!" مثـل هـاتـه الحمـاقـات هـو مـا يعتـم فهمنـا للأمـور، فهي حماقات بعيدة كل البعد عن حقيقة العالم وواقعه.

بالنسبة للـوعي البشـري السـائد حـاليـاً، عـدد الأشيـاء غيـر المرئيـة يفـوق بمراحـل عـدد الأشيـاء المرئيـة. لـو قـارنـا مـا نعلمـه ونـراه ونعيـه بمـا نجهلـه، نجـده مثـل قشـرة البرتقـالـة بالمقـارنـة بالبرتقـالـة نفسهـا، بـل إن هـذه القشـرة تكـون رفيعة للغاية. لو اقتصر علمنا على القشور، نكون جاهلين تماماً باللب نفسه.

هـذا هـو الحـال تقريبـاً مـع كـل شـيء آخـر. كـل مـا نعلمـه عـن الكـون لا يتعـدى قشـرة سطحيـة رفيعـة — وما نعلمه عن هذه القشرة لا يتعدى أقل القليل.

7 مارس، 1956

Aspiration — التطــلـع

Simply by a Sincere Aspiration

And one day, you ask yourself, "But then, why is one born? Why does one die? Why does one suffer? Why does one act?" You no longer live like a little machine, hardly half conscious. You want to feel truly, to act truly, to know truly.

Then, in ordinary life one searches for books, for people who know a little more than oneself, one begins to seek somebody who can solve these questions, lift the veil of ignorance....

We can, simply by a sincere aspiration, open a sealed door in us and find... that Something which will change the whole significance of life, reply to all our questions, solve all our problems and lead us to the perfection we aspire for without knowing it, to that Reality which alone can satisfy us and give us lasting joy, equilibrium, strength, life.

Questions and Answers, Aug 13, 1958

Bases of the Integral Yoga — أسس اليوغا المتكاملة

التطلع — Aspiration

بمجرد تطلع صادق

يأتي يوم تتساءل فيه: "ما هو السبب في أننا نولد؟ ولماذا نموت؟ وما ذا يبرر كل هذا العناء؟ وما هي الدوافع التي تحرك أفعالنا؟" فأنت لم تعد تعيش كآلةٍ صغيرة لا تعي ما تقوم به. بل إنك أصبحت الآن ترغب في أن تشعر المشاعر الصادقة وتقوم بالأعمال الحقة وتعرف المعرفة الحقيقية.

عندما يأتي هذا اليوم، تبحث في العادة عن كتب، أو عن قوم أكثر منك علماً، أو عن شخص يملك الجواب على هذه الأسئلة ويقدر على رفع نقاب الجهل عنك...

ولكننا [في هذه اليوغا لا نبحث خارجنا، بل إننا] نقدر، بمجرد تطلع صادق، أن نفتح باباً مغلقاً بداخلنا وأن نكتشف... هذا الشيء الذي سيغير تماماً معنى حياتنا، ويرد على جميع تساؤلاتنا، ويحل جميع مشاكلنا، ويقودنا بدون أن نعلم إلى الكمال الذي ننشده، إلى تلك **الحقيقة الواقعة** التي هي وحدها قادرة على أن تجيب على تطلعنا وأن تمنحنا بهجة وتوازناً وقوة وحياة لا تفنى.

أسئلة وأجوبة، أغسطس 16، 1969

46

Discrimination — القدرة على التمييز

Discovering the right thing to do

Those who wish the Light of Truth to prevail over the forces of darkness and falsehood can do so by carefully observing the initiating impulses of their movements and actions, and discriminate between those that come from the Truth and those that come from the falsehood in order to obey the first and to refuse or reject the others.

This power of discrimination is one of the first effects of the advent of the Truth's light in the earth's atmosphere.

Indeed it is very difficult to discriminate the impulses of Truth from the impulses of falsehood, unless one has received this special gift of discrimination that the Light of Truth has brought.

However to help at the beginning, one can take as a guiding rule that all that brings with it or creates peace, faith, joy, harmony, wideness, unity and ascending growth comes from the Truth; while all that carries with it restlessness, doubt, skepticism, sorrow, discord, selfish narrowness, inertia, discouragement and despair comes straight from the falsehood.

White Roses, January 1965

The Only Thing Needed

When one is assailed by the vision of...disorder and...confusion, there is only one thing to do, it is to go into the consciousness in which one knows that there is only ONE Being, ONE Consciousness, ONE Power — there is only ONE Oneness —and all those things take place within this Oneness...

That's the only thing needed, the ONLY thing; the only thing that subsists. All the rest... phantasmagoria.

It's the only thing effective in every case: when you want to do something, when you cannot do something, when you act, when the body can no longer act... In EACH and EVERY case: that alone — that alone: make conscious contact with the Supreme Consciousness, unite with it, and wait. There.

Discrimination — القدرة على التمييز

كيف نميز بين الصواب والخطأ

إذا كنـا نرغب أن يتغلب **نـور الحقيقة** علـى قوى الظـلام والـزور، نستطيع فعل ذلك بـأن نلاحظ بدقـة الـدوافع وراء حركاتنـا وأفعالنـا وأن نميـز بيـن الـدوافع التي تـأتي مـن **الحقيقـة** وتلـك التي تتبـع مـن الزور فنتبع الأولى وننبذ الثانية.

هذه القدرة على التمييز هي من أولى النتائج التي يجلبها حلول **نور الحقيقة** في جو الأرض.

وبالفعل نجد أن التمييز بيـن حوافز **الحقيقة** وحوافز الـزور صعبٌ للغايـة علـى الـذين لا يملكون هبة التمييز، هذه الهبة الخاصة الي تأتي في ركاب **نور الحقيقة**.

ومـع ذلـك، هنـاك قاعـدة نستطيع أن نقتدي بهـا في المراحـل الأولـى مـن الممارسـة: كـل مـا يجلب معـه السـلام والإيمـان والبهجـة والتناسـق والاتسـاع والوحـدة والنمـو المطـرد يـأتي مـن **الحقيقـة**؛ فـي حيـن أن كـل مـا يجلب القلـق والهيـاج والريـب والشـك والأسـى والشـقاق والضعـة الأنانيـة والخمـول والحبطـة واليأس يأتي مباشرة من الزور.

ورد أبيض، يناير 1965

الشيء الوحيد المطلوب

عندما تُطبِق علينا رؤيـة الفوضـى والتشوش [السـائدين في العـالم حولنـا]، لا يبقى أمامنـا لا مخرج واحـد، وهـو أن نـدخل في وعـي نـدرك فيـه أن الوجـود كلـه **كيـان واحـد، وعـي واحـد، قـوة واحـدة** — ليس هناك إلا **وحدانية واحدة** — وأن كل ما يحدث، يحدث في غضون هذه الوحدانية...

هذا هو الشيء الوحيد الذي نحتاجه؛ الشيء الوحيد؛ الشيء الوحيد الدائم. كل ما عدا ذلك وهم.

وهو الشيء الوحيد الفعال في جميع الحـالات: عندما نرغب في فعل شيء وعندما نعجز عن فعل شـيء؛ عندما ننشط، وعندما تعجز أبداننا عن النشاط... في **كل** حالـة وفي **جميـع الحـالات**: هـذا وحـده هـو الحـل — هـذا وحـده: أن نحقـق في قمـة وعينـا الاتصـال **بالوعي الأسمى** ونتحد بـه وننتظـر. هـذه هي خلاصة الأمر.

Then one receives the exact indication of what one has to do every minute — to do or not to do, to act or to remain still. That's all. Even to be or not to be. And it's the only solution. More and more this certitude is there: it's the only solution. All the rest is childishness.

Mother's Agenda, August 16, 1969

عندئـذ نتلقـى الإشـارة الصـحيحة التـي تُبَصِّـرنا بواجبنـا فـي كـل لحظـة: أن نفعـل أم لا نفعـل، أن ننشـط أم نظـل سـاكنين. هـذا هـو كـل مـا هـو مطلـوب. وهـذا يسـري حتـى فـي حـالات تبلـغ مـن الجديـة الخيـار بـين الحيـاة والمـوت. هـذا هـو الحـل الأوحـد. تـدريجاً سـنزداد يقينـاً بأنـه حقيقـة الحـل الوحيـد وأن كـل مـا عداه صبيانية وطفولية.

أجندة الأم، أغسطس 16، 1969

50

Bases of the Integral Yoga — أسس اليوغا المتكاملة

Effort — الـجهد

Effort leads to Joy

It is the effort which gives joy; a human being who does not know how to make an effort will never find joy. Those who are essentially lazy will never find joy — they do not have the strength to be joyful! It is effort which gives joy. Effort makes the being vibrate at a certain degree of tension which makes it possible for you to feel the joy.

It is only effort, in whatever domain it be — material effort, moral effort, intellectual effort — which creates in the being certain vibrations which enable you to get connected with universal vibrations; and it is this which gives joy. It is effort which pulls you out of inertia; it is effort which makes you receptive to the universal forces. And the one thing above all which spontaneously gives joy, even to those who do not practise yoga, who have no spiritual aspiration, who lead quite an ordinary life, is the exchange of forces with universal forces. People do not know this, they would not be able to tell you that it is due to this, but so it is.

January 13, 1951

Bases of the Integral Yoga — أسس اليوغا المتكاملة

الجهد — Effort

بذل الجهد يؤدي إلى البهجة

بـذل الجهـد يـؤدي إلـى البهجـة؛ والإنسـان الـذي لا يقـدر علـى بـذل الجهـد، لا يجـد أبـداً الطريـق إلـى الفـرح. الـذين هـم فـي جوهرهم كسـولون، لـن يتوصـلوا أبـدا إلـى أن يكونـوا فـرحين — لأن الفـرح والبهجة يتطلبان قوة ليست في حيازتهم.

الجهـد وحـده، سـواء أكـان مادياً أم أخلاقيـاً أم عقليـاً، يسـتطيع أن يخلـق فـي الكيـان ذبـذبات معينـة تمكننـا مـن الاتصـال بالذبـذبات الكونيـة؛ وذلـك هـو بالتحديـد مـا يمنحنـا البهجـة. بـذل الجهـد هـو الـذي يجتـذبنا مـن الخمـول والقصـور ويجعلنـا قـابلين لتلقـي القـوى الكونيـة. تبـادل القـوى مـع القـوى الكونيـة هـو أحـد أهـم الأشـياء التـي تهـب البهجـة تلقائيـاً، حتـى للـذين لا يمارسـون اليوغـا، والـذين ليسـت لهـم طموحـات روحيـة ويقـودون حيـاة عاديـة تمامـاً. النـاس لا يعرفـون هـذه الحقيقـة ولـذلك هـم غيـر قـادرين علـى أن يدلوك على الطريق إلى البهجة، ولكنه مع ذلك حقيقة واقعة.

13 يناير، 1951

Bases of the Integral Yoga — أسس اليوغا المتكاملة

Sincerity — الـصـدق والإخـلاص

Why our mood changes from day to day

One must have around oneself so intense an atmosphere in a total surrender to the Divine, so intensified around oneself that everything that passes through is automatically filtered. Anyhow, it is very useful in life, for there are — we spoke about this too — there are bad thoughts, bad wills, people who wish you ill, who make formations. There are all kinds of absolutely undesirable things in the atmosphere. And so, if one must always be on the watch, looking around on all sides, one would think only of one thing, how to protect oneself. First of all, it is tiresome, and then, you see, it makes you waste much time. If you are well enveloped in this way, with this light, the light of a perfectly glad, totally sincere surrender, when you are enveloped with that, it serves you as a marvellous filter. Nothing that is altogether undesirable, nothing that has ill-will can pass through. So, automatically, these things return where they came from. If there is a conscious ill-will against you, it comes, but cannot pass; the door is closed, for it is open only to divine things, it is not open to anything else. So it returns very quietly to the source from where it came.

But all these things are... One can learn how to do them through a kind of study and science. But they can be done without any study or science provided the aspiration and surrender are absolute and total. If the aspiration and surrender are total, it is done automatically. But you must see to it that they are total; and besides, as I was saying just now, you become very clearly aware of it, for the moment they are not total, you are no longer happy. You feel uneasy, very miserable, dejected, a bit unhappy: "Things are not quite pleasant today. They are the same as they were yesterday; yesterday they were marvellous, today they are not pleasing!" — Why? Because yesterday you were in a perfect state of surrender, more or less perfect — and today you aren't any more. So, what was so beautiful yesterday is no longer beautiful today. That joy you had within you, that confidence, the assurance that all will be well and the great Work will be accomplished, that certitude — all this, you see, has become veiled, has been replaced by a kind of doubt and, yes, by a discontent: "Things are not beautiful, the world is nasty, people are not pleasant." It goes sometimes to this length: "The food is not good, yesterday it was excellent." It is the same but today it is not good! This is the barometer! You may immediately tell yourself that an insincerity has crept in somewhere. It is very easy to know, you don't need to be very learned, for, as Sri Aurobindo has said in "Elements of Yoga": One knows whether one is happy or unhappy, one knows whether one is content or discontented, one doesn't need to ask oneself, put complicated questions for this, one knows it! — Well, it is very simple.

Bases of the Integral Yoga — أسس اليوغا المتكاملة

Sincerity — الصدق والإخلاص

لماذا يتغير مزاجنا من يوم إلى يوم

يجب أن نحيط أنفسنا بجوٍ من التسليم التام **للواحد الكل**، جو يبلغ من الصفاء والقوة درجة أنه ينقي ويرشح تلقائياً أي شيء يحاول المرور من خلاله. هذه حيطة تنفع كثيراً في الحياة، فنحن، كما قلنا في حديث سابق، محاطون بأفكار وإرادات سوء من قوم يرغبون في إيذائنا ويقومون بعمل تكوينات ذهنية تهدف إلى الإضرار بنا. الجو حولنا مشحون بكل ما هو كريه ومؤذٍ. ولو كان ضرورياً لكي نحمي أنفسنا أن نراقب باحتراس وحذر كل ما يأتينا من جميع الاتجاهات، لأصبحت حماية أنفسنا شغلنا الوحيد والشاغل. ولكن ذلك يكون مرهقاً وبالإضافة مضيعة كبيرة للوقت. أما إذا أحطنا أنفسنا بجو التسليم وعشنا في نوره، وكان تسليمنا صادقاً ومفعماً بالثقة والاطمئنان، فإن هذا الجو نفسه يعمل كمُرَشِّح يخلصنا من كل الشوائب ويمنع كل ما هو كريه وضار من النفاذ إلينا، إذ يجد نفسه أمام باب مغلق لا يسمح بالمرور إلا للأشياء الإلهية وحدها فيرتد إلى مصدره الذي أتى منه.

تستطيع حماية نفسك من إرادات السوء بدراسة وبمعرفة خاصة [الأم تشير هنا إلى العلوم الغيبية]. ولكنك تستطيع أيضاً حماية نفسك بدون حاجة إلى أي دراسة عندما يصبح تطلعك كاملاً وتسليمك تاماً وتصير الحماية تلقائية. ولكن يجب أن تحرص على أن يكون تطلعك وتسليمك كاملين بالفعل. فإذا لم يكونا كذلك، ستلحظ ذلك مباشرة. ستلحظ مثلاً أنك قد فقدت حبورك فجأة وأن نوعاً من التعاسة قد تملّك منك وتشعر بعدم الارتياح والشقاء والإحباط. عندئذ ربما تقول: "يا له من يوم تعس! الظروف اليوم هي نفس ظروف الأمس: ومع ذلك فقد كان الأمس يوماً رائعاً، في حين أني أشعر اليوم بالكآبة!" وتتساءل عن السبب. السبب هو أن تسليمك كان بالأمس كاملاً، أو قريباً من الكمال — ولكنك اليوم في حالة مختلفة. هذا هو السبب في أن ما كان جميلاً بالأمس فقد جماله في نظرك اليوم. تلك البهجة التي كنت تشعر بها، هذا الاطمئنان، تلك الثقة بأن كل شيء سيكون على ما يرام، وأن **المسعى** العظيم سوف يتحقق، كل ذلك قد حُجب بغطاء من الشك وبنوع من الاستياء، وإذا بك تشتكي من أن "الأشياء قد فقدت جمالها، وأن العالم قد أصبح كريهاً، وأن الناس قد أصبحوا مزعجين". بل أنك قد تذهب إلى حد أن تقول: "الأكل اليوم رديء على الرغم من أنه كان جيداً بالأمس"؛ على الرغم من أن طعام اليوم هو نفس طعام الأمس.

هذا إذاً هو البارومتر [الذي يدِلّك على تغير حالتك الداخلية]! عندما تحس فجأة بالتعاسة بدون سبب، اعلم أن الرياء وعدم الإخلاص قد تسللا إلى داخلك. اكتشاف ذلك ليس صعباً وليس ضرورياً أن تكون من العارفين لتكتشفه. وقد كتب **شري أوروبيندو** في كتابه "عناصر اليوغا": "نحن نعلم هل نحن سعداء أم لا، ونعلم هل نحن راضون أم لا، لا ضرورة للتساؤل أو لسؤال الغير أسئلة معقدة من أجل ذلك: نحن نعلم ببساطة" — وبالفعل إنه شيء بسيط للغاية.

Bases of the Integral Yoga — أسس اليوغا المتكاملة

The moment you feel unhappy, you may write beneath it: "I am not sincere". These two sentences go together: "I FEEL UNHAPPY" And "I AM NOT SINCERE."

Now, what is it that is wrong? Then one begins to take a look and to ask oneself what may be wrong, it is easy to find out...
There you are, my children.
July 7, 1954

بمجرد أن تشعر بتعاسة، تستطيع أن تقول لنفسك: "أنا لست صادقاً". هاتان جملتان تترافقان على الدوام: **"أنا أشعر بتعاسة" — "أنا لست صادقاً"**!

[هذه المعرفة تكفي لدفعك إلى] البحث عن سبب [التعاسة] بداخلك، وستجد أن اكتشافه ليس صعباً.. هذا هو ما أردت أن أقول يا أطفالي.

يوليو 7، 1954

Divine Grace — النعمة الإلهية

If one saw the Grace everywhere

...no matter how great your faith and trust in the divine Grace, no matter how great your capacity to see It at work in all circumstances, at every moment, at every point in life, you will never succeed in understanding the marvelous immensity of Its Action, and the precision, the exactitude with which this Action is accomplished; you will never be able to grasp to what extent the Grace does everything, is behind everything, organizes everything, conducts everything, so that the march forward to the divine realization may be as swift, as total and harmonious as possible, considering the circumstances of the world.

As soon as you are in contact with It, there is not a second in time, not a point in space, which does not show you dazzlingly this perpetual work of the Grace, this constant intervention of the Grace.

And once you have seen this, you feel you are never equal to it, for you should never forget it, never have any fears, any anguish, any recoils... or even suffering. If one were in union with the Grace, if one saw It everywhere, one would begin living a life of exultation, of all-power, of infinite happiness.

And that would be the best possible collaboration in the divine Work.
August 1st, 1956

النعمة الإلهية – Divine Grace

لو رأينا النعمة الإلهية في كل مكان

...مهما بلغ إيمانك وثقتك **بالنعمة الإلهية** من القوة، ومهما كانت قدرتك على أن تراها وهي تعمل في جميع الظروف وفي كل الأوقات وفي جميع مواقف الحياة، فإنك لن تنجح أبداً في فهم مدى عظمة نشاطها وفعلها ومدى الدقة والإتقان التي تؤدي بهما عملها: لن تستطيع أبداً أن تستوعب كيف أنها تقوم بجميع الأشياء وتسندها وتنظمها وتقودها بحيث تكون المسيرة نحو التحقيق الإلهي على أعلى درجة، تسمح بها ظروف العالم، من السرعة والاتساق.

بمجرد أن تحقق الصلة **بالنعمة الإلهية**، سيتجلى لك، بصورة مذهلة، عملها وتوسطها الدائمان في كل لحظة وفي كل مكان.

ومتى رأيت ذلك، ستشعر بضآلتك إزاءها وبأنك ينبغي ألا تنساها أبداً، وأن تضع جانباً كل خوف وأسى ونكوص... بل حتى كل معاناة. متى اتحدت مع **النعمة الإلهية** وأصبحت قادراً على رؤيتها والتعرف عليها في كل مكان، تصبح حياتك حياة بهجة واغتباط وقدرة شاملة وسعادة لانهائية.

وتلك تكون أفضل طريقة للمساهمة في **العمل الإلهي**.
1 أغسطس، 1956

Unfailing Help and Protection

.... the more you give yourself to the Divine the more He is with you, totally, constantly, at every minute, in all your thoughts, all your needs, and there's no aspiration which does not receive an immediate answer, and you have the sense of a complete, constant intimacy, of a total nearness. It is as though you carried… as though the Divine were all the time with you; you walk and He walks with you, you sleep and He sleeps with you, you eat and He eats with you, you think and He thinks with you, you love and He is the love you have. But for this one must give oneself entirely, totally, exclusively, reserve nothing, keep nothing for himself and not keep back anything also: the least little thing in your being which is not given to the Divine is a waste; it is the wasting of your joy, something that lessens your happiness by that much, and all that you don't give to the Divine is as though you were holding it in the way of the possibility of the Divine's giving Himself to you.

You don't feel Him close to yourself, constantly with you, because you don't belong to Him, because you belong to hundreds of other things and people; in your thought, your action, your feelings, impulses… there are millions of things which you don't give Him, and that is why you don't feel Him always with you, because all these things are so many screens and walls between Him and you. But if you give Him everything, if you keep back nothing, He will be constantly and totally with you in all that you do, in all that you think, all that you feel, always, at each moment. But for this you must give yourself absolutely, keep back nothing; each little thing that you hold back is a stone you put down to build up a wall between the Divine and yourself. And then later you complain: "Oh, I don't feel Him!"
July 20, 1955

عون وحماية لا يفتران

... كلمـا وهبـت نفسـك **للواحـد الكـل*** كلمـا زاد حضـوره فـي نفسـك قـوة إلـى أن يصبـح حضـوراً كليـاً، ثابتـاً، محسوسـاً فـي كـل لحظـة، فـي جميـع أفكـارك وكـل حاجاتـك. عندئـذ يكافـأ توقـك وتطلعـك باستجابـة فوريـة، وتشـعر بأنسـة وألفـة شـامـلتين ودائمتيـن، وتـزول المسـافة بينـك وبينـه زوالاً تامـاً. فيكـون ذلـك كمـا لـو كـان **الواحـد الكـل** معـك طـوال الوقـت؛ عنـدما تمشـي يمشـي معـك؛ وعنـدما تنـام ينـام معـك، وإذا أكلـت يأكـل معـك، وعنـدما تفكـر يفكـر معـك، وإذا أحببـت، فإنـه يكـون حبـك ذاتـه. لكـن لبلـوغ تلـك الحالـة، يجـب أن تهـب نفسـك وهبـاً تامـاً وشـاملاً **للواحـد الكـل** وحـده ولا لشـيء غيـره؛ بحيـث لا تحتفـظ لنفسـك بـأي شـيء أو تمتنـع عـن وهـب أي شـيء: فأقـل القليـل فـي كيانـك الـذي لا تهبـه يكـون مضيعـة لسـرورك وفرحـك، وينتقـص مـن سـعادتك بنفـس القـدر الـذي تبخـل بـه، وأي شـيء تبخـل بـه يكـون مثـل عقبـة تضعـف فرصتـك فـي أن يمنـح **الواحـد الكـل** نفسـه لـك.

أنـت لا تشـعر بقربـه وبأنـه معـك علـى الـدوام لأنـك لا تنتمـي إليـه فـي فكـرك ونشـاطك ومشـاعرك ودوافعـك، بـل تنتمـي إلـى مئـات مـن الأشـياء والأشـخاص الأخريـن... ولأنـك تحتفـظ لنفسـك وتبخـل بملاييـن مـن الأشـياء التـي تقيـم حواجـز وجـدران بينـك وبينـه. هـذا هـو السـبب فـي أنـك لا تشـعر بوجـوده معـك علـى الـدوام. أمـا لـو وهبتـه كـل شـيء ولـم تحتفـظ لنفسـك بـأي شـيء، فإنـه يكـون معـك دائمـاً فـي كـل لحظـة وبصـورة شـاملة فـي كـل مـا تفكـر وتشـعر. ولكـن لتنـال هـذا القـرب يجـب أن تهـب نفسـك وهبـاً قاطعـاً ولا تبخـل بـأي شـيء، فأصغـر شـيء تبخـل بـه يصبـح لبنـة فـي جـدار تقيمـه بينـك وبيـن **الواحـد الكـل**. لـو بخلـت بنفسـك، لا يحـق لـك أن تشـكو بعـد ذلـك مـن أنـك لا تشـعر بـه!
20 يوليو، 1955

60

Bases of the Integral Yoga — أسس اليوغا المتكاملة

The Intervention of the Grace

If you see some catastrophe coming, can you, Mother, by your effort change it?

That depends upon the nature of the event. There are many things.... That depends also upon the level from which one sees. There is a plane where there are all the possibilities, and on that level, as there are all the possibilities, there is the possibility also of changing these possibilities. If a catastrophe is foreseen in that plane, one can have the power of preventing it also. In other cases, even though one is forewarned, one has no action upon the event. And yet there, it depends from the level from where one sees.

A case of this kind was reported to me once when the very seeing prevented it from happening. An American gentleman had arrived at one of those big American hotels where there are lifts (you do not go down a stairway, you take a lift to go up or come down); now early in the morning just before getting up, he had a dream which he remembered well: he had seen a boy dressed as a lift-boy and making the same movement as a lift-boy makes directing you to get in. He was there. And then, at the end of the movement, instead of a lift, there was a hearse! [...] And the boy was signing to him to get into the carriage. When he came out of his room, the boy was there with the lift to take him down; exactly the same boy, the same face, the same dress, the same gesture. He remembered the hearse... he did not get into the lift. He said: "No, no!" and he walked down. And before he reached the ground floor, he heard a terrible noise and the lift had crashed down to the ground and all who were in it were killed. It was because of the dream that he had not got in, for he had understood.

Therefore in such a case when you have the vision, you can avert the catastrophe.

There are other cases, as I said, when you are simply forewarned. You are forewarned. In reality, it is to help you to prepare within for what must come, so that you take the right inner attitude to face the event. It is like a lesson telling you, "This is what it must teach you." You cannot change the thing, but you can change your attitude and your inner reaction. Instead of having a bad reaction, a wrong attitude towards the experience that occurs, you have a good reaction, a good attitude, and you derive as much benefit as possible out of what has happened.
29 July 1953

عمل النعمة الإلهية

أمي: عندما نرى كارثة ما مقبلة نحونا، هل يكون في وسعنا أن نغيرها بمجهودنا الشخصي؟

هـذا يتوقـف علـى طبيعـة الحـادث نفسـه و علـى مسـتوى الـوعي الـذي نـتكلم منـه... هنـاك نقـاط عديـدة جـديرة بالاعتبـار... مسـتوى الـوعي الأعلـى يسـمح بوجـود جميـع الاحتمـالات، وبالتـالي يكـون فيـه تغييـر بعـض هـذه الاحتمـالات ممكنـاً. علـى هـذا المسـتوى إذا رأى المـرء كارثـة [جماعيـة] علـى وشـك الحـدوث، يمكنـه أحيانـاً أن يمنـع حدوثها، فـإن لـم يقـدر علـى منعهـا، تنفعـه رؤيتـه المبكـرة كإنـذار بـأن يبتعـد [عن مكان الكارثة]. الأمر إذاً يتوقف على مستوى الوعي الذي ينظر المرء منه.

أضـرب لكـم كمثـال حادثـة بلغنـي خبرُهـا أدت الرؤيـة فيهـا إلـى منـع حادثـة مـن الوقـوع: نـزل رجـل أمريكـي فـي أحـد الفنـادق الأمريكيـة الكبيـرة التـي تملـك مصـاعد يسـتخدمها النـزلاء فـي انتقـالهم بـين الأدوار. فـي صبـاح يـوم مـن الأيـام حلـم الرجـل حلمـاً انطبـع جيـداً علـى ذاكرتـه: حَلِـم أنـه رَى غلامـاً يرتـدي زي عمـلاء المصـاعد يدعوه، كعـادة غلمـان المصـاعد إلـى الـدخول، ولكـن بـدلاً مـن المصـعد، كانـت هنـاك عربـة مـن عربـات نقـل المـوتى. استيقظ الرجـل مـن نومـه وتأهـب للخـروج وعنـدما غـادر غرفتـه توجـه إلـى المصـعد لينـزل إلـى الطابـق الأرضـي، وفوجئ بـأن غـلام المصـعد يكـاد يكـون نسـخة مـن الغـلام الـذي رآه فـي حلمـه. تذكـر الرجـل عربـة المـوتى وأنِـف مـن ركـوب المصـعد مؤثـراً استعمال السـلالم فـي النـزول. قبـل أن يبلـغ الرجـل الـدور الأرضـي سـمع ضجـة هائلـة سـببها سـقوط المصـعد واصطدامه بـالأرض اصطداماً نـتج عنـه قتـل جميـع الركـاب. وهكـذا كـان الحلـم إنـذاراً أتـاح للرجـل أن يتجنب الموت وإن كان لم يمنع الكارثة من الوقوع.

أصحاب الرؤيـة إذاً يسـتطيعون فـي بعـض الحـالات تجنـب الكـوارث، إذ تعمـل الرؤيـة كإنـذار بالنسـبة لهـم. ولكـن هنـاك حـالات أخـرى لا يمكـن فيهـا تجنـب الكارثـة وعندئـذ يقتصـر نفـع الإنـذار فيهـا علـى أن يسـاعد صـاحب الرؤيـة فـي إعـداد نفسـه للحادثـة التـي لا مفـر منهـا، وعلـى اتخـاذ الموقـف السـليم إزائهـا، كمـا لـو كـان الإنـذار يقـول لـه: "هذه الحادثـة درس يجـب أن تتعلمـه. لـن تقـدر علـى تغييـر مـا هـو آتٍ ولكنـك تسـتطيع أن تغيـر رد فعلـك البـاطني وتتخـذ الموقـف الصـحيح وتسـتفيد إلـى أقصـى درجـة ممكنـة مما سيصادفك."

29 يوليو 1953

Bases of the Integral Yoga — أسس اليوغا المتكاملة

Faith and Trust — الإيمـان والثقـة

Give yourself entirely

…. Faith — that kind of unshakable certitude in the very existence of God — faith is something that seizes the whole being. It is not only mental, psychic or vital: it is the whole being, entirely, which has faith. Faith leads straight to experience…

[It] does not put any questions, does not think of the results; it gives itself entirely — it gives itself, and then that's all. It is something that absorbs one completely… One has faith in the Divine, that it is the Divine who is all, and can do all, and does all… and who is the only real existence — and one gives oneself entirely to this faith, to the Divine, that's all…

And this is an absolute fact, that is, the moment one gives oneself entirely to the Divine, without calculating, in a total faith, without bargaining of any kind — one gives oneself, and then, come what may! "That does not concern me, I just give myself" — automatically it will always be for you, in all circumstances, at every moment, the best that will happen… not the way you conceive of it (naturally thought knows nothing), but in reality. Well, there is a part of the being which can become aware of this and have this confidence. This is something added on to the faith which gives it more strength, a strength — how shall I put it? — of total acceptance and the best utilization of what happens.
May 5, 1954

Bases of the Integral Yoga — أسس اليوغا المتكاملة

Faith and Trust — الإيمـان والثقـة

هَـب نـفسك كـلياً

... الإيمـان نـوع مـن اليقيـن الراسـخ في وجـود الله — وهـو شـيء يسـتحوذ على الكيـان كلـه. أي أنـه لا يقتصـر على تملـك الكيـان الـذهني أو السـيكي* أو الحيـوي* فحسـب، بـل يشـمل الكيـان البشـري بأكملـه. وهو يؤدي مباشرة إلى الخبرة الفعلية...

الإيمـان لا يتسـاءل ولا يفكر في النتـائج؛ بـل يهب نفسـه كلياً — ويجد في هذا الوهب رضـاء وكفايته. وهـو يسـتحوذ علـى المـؤمن تمامـاً... عندئـذ يـؤمن المـرء بـأن **الواحـد الكـل*** هـو الوجـود الوحيد الحقيقي، يشـمل كل شـيء وقـادر على كل شـيء وأنـه هو في الحقيقـة من يقوم بالأعمـال جميعـاً.. ثم يهب المرء نفسه كلياً لهذا الإيمان أو **للواحد الكل*** ولا يبتغي وراء ذلك أي شـيء آخر...

وإنهـا لحقيقـة مطلقـة، أنـك بمجـرد أن تهب نفسـك وهبـاً تامـاً **للواحـد الكـل***، في إيمـان شـامل وبدون أي حسـاب أو مسـاومة أو توقـع لنتيجـة، بمجـرد أن تهب نفسـك لمجـرد الوهـب، فـإن كل مـا يحدثُ لـك بعـد ذلـك في الحيـاة يصـبح، بصـورة تلقائيـة، أفضـل مـا يمكـن أن يحـدث لـك... إلا أن هـذا "الافضل" لا يكـون بالضـرورة حسـب تصـوراتك، فتفكيـر الإنسـان لا يسـتطيع أن يعـرف مـا هـو أفضـل، بـل يكـون "الأفضـل" حسـب رؤيـة **الواحـد الكـل**. في الكيـان البشـري جـزء قـادر علـى أن يعـي هـذه الحقيقـة ويثـق بهـا. هـذا الـوعي وهـذه الثقـة يُتِمِّـان الإيمـان ويزيـداه قـوة ويمكنـان المـؤمن مـن تقبل كل مـا يـأتي تقبلاً تامـاً وأن يسـتغل كل مـا يصـادفه أحسـن اسـتغلال [للتقدم الروحي].

5 مايو، 1954

64

Bases of the Integral Yoga — أسس اليوغا المتكاملة

Faith and Personal Effort

"… Faith is indispensable to man, for without it he could not proceed forward in his journey through the Unknown; but it ought not to be imposed, it should come as a free perception or an imperative direction from the inner spirit. A claim to unquestioned acceptance could only be warranted if the spiritual effort had already achieved man's progression to the highest Truth-Consciousness total and integral, free from all ignorant mental and vital mixture. This is the ultimate object before us, but it has not yet been accomplished, and the premature claim has obscured the true work of the religious instinct in man, which is to lead him towards the Divine Reality, to formulate all that he has yet achieved in that direction and to give to each human being a mould of spiritual discipline, a way of seeking, touching, nearing the Divine Truth, a way which is proper to the potentialities of his nature."

Sri Aurobindo, The Life Divine

Sweet Mother, can faith be increased by personal effort?

Faith is certainly a gift given to us by the Divine Grace. It is like a door suddenly opening upon an eternal truth, through which we can see it, almost touch it.

As in everything else in the ascent of humanity, there is the necessity – especially at the beginning – of personal effort. It is possible that in some exceptional circumstances, for reasons which completely elude our intelligence, faith may come almost accidentally, quite unexpectedly, almost without ever having been solicited, but most frequently it is an answer to a yearning, a need, an aspiration, something in the being that is seeking and longing, even though not in a very conscious and systematic way. But in any case, when faith has been granted, when one has had this sudden inner illumination, in order to preserve it constantly in the active consciousness individual effort is altogether indispensable. One must hold on to one's faith, will one's faith; one must seek it, cultivate it, protect it.

الإيمان والمجهود الشخصي

... "الإيمان لا غنى عنه للإنسان، وبدونه لا يقدر الإنسان على متابعة رحلته في عالم **مجهول**؛ ولكن الإيمان لا ينبغي أن يُفرَض على الناس، بل أن ينبع في حرية من رؤيتهم أو من إرشاد حاسم من الروح بداخلهم. لا يصح أن نددعي أننا تخطينا في إيماننا مرحلة الشك إلا عندما نبلغ في تطورنا أسمى مراحل وعي الحقيقة الشامل الذي لا يشوبه أي جهل ذهني أو حيوي. هذا هو الهدف النهائي الأقصى الذي نتحرك نحوه، ولكننا لم نبلغه بعد. واجب الحاسة الدينية في الإنسان هو أن تقوده إلى **الحقيقة الإلهية** وأن تصيغ كل أعماله بصيغة روحية وأن تعطي كل فرد نظاماً روحياً وطريقاً للسعي يقارب به **الحقيقة الإلهية** على مسار يوائم طاقاته الطبيعية الدفينة. ولكن ادعاء بلوغ الهدف النهائي قبل الأوان يعتم عمل هذه الحاسة الدينية".

شري أوروبيندو، الحياة الإلهية

أيتها الأم الحنون، هل يمكن أن نُقوّي إيماننا بواسطة مجهودنا الشخصي؟

لا شك في أن الإيمان هدية تهبنا إياها **النعمة الإلهية**. وهو مثل باب ينفتح فجأة على حقيقة خالدة، نستطيع من خلاله أن نرى هذه الحقيقة، ونقترب منها إلى أن نكاد نلمسها.

وكما هو الحال في كل ما يخص ارتقاء الإنسان، المجهود الشخصي ضروري، خاصة في البداية. يحتمل، في بعض الظروف الاستثنائية ولأسباب تتخطى تماماً قدرتنا على الفهم، أن يأتينا الإيمان فجأة كما لو كان مصادفة من غير قصد أو توقع وبدون أي طلب أو استجداء من ناحيتنا، ولكنه يكون في تلك الحالة على الأغلب استجابة لتشوق أو توق روحي أو حاجة فينا أو لشيء في كياننا كان يبحث عنه، حتى وإن لم يكن بحثه واعياً أو الوعي أو منهجياً ومنتظماً. وعلى أي حال، لو حصلنا على هبة الإيمان وشعرنا فجأة بنوره في داخلنا، لا مفر من أن نبذل الجهد لنحتفظ بإيماننا يقظاً على الدوام في وعينا العامل. يجب أن نتمسك بالإيمان ونرغبه ونسعى إليه ونتعهده ونصونه.

Bases of the Integral Yoga — أسس اليوغا المتكاملة

In the human mind there is a morbid and deplorable habit of doubt, argument, scepticism. This is where human effort must be put in: the refusal to admit them, the refusal to listen to them and still more the refusal to follow them. No game is more dangerous than playing mentally with doubt and scepticism. They are not only enemies, they are terrible pitfalls, and once one falls into them, it becomes tremendously difficult to pull oneself out.

Some people think it is a very great mental elegance to play with ideas, to discuss them, to contradict their faith; they think that this gives them a very superior attitude, that in this way they are above "superstitions" and "ignorance"; but if you listen to suggestions of doubt and scepticism, then you fall into the grossest ignorance and stray away from the right path. You enter into confusion, error, a maze of contradictions....You are not always sure you will be able to get out of it. You go so far away from the inner truth that you lose sight of it and sometimes lose too all possible contact with your soul.

Certainly a personal effort is needed to preserve one's faith, to let it grow within. Later — much later — one day, looking back, we may see that everything that happened, even what seemed to us the worst, was a Divine Grace to make us advance on the way; and then we become aware that the personal effort too was a grace. But before reaching that point, one has to advance much, to struggle much, sometimes even to suffer a great deal. To sit down in inert passivity and say, "If I am to have faith I shall have it, the Divine will give it to me", is an attitude of laziness, of unconsciousness and almost of bad-will. For the inner flame to burn, one must feed it; one must watch over the fire, throw into it the fuel of all the errors one wants to get rid of, all that delays the progress, all that darkens the path. If one doesn't feed the fire, it smoulders under the ashes of one's unconsciousness and inertia, and then, not years but lives, centuries will pass before one reaches the goal.

One must watch over one's faith as one watches over the birth of something infinitely precious, and protect it very carefully from everything that can impair it.

In the ignorance and darkness of the beginning, faith is the most direct expression of the Divine Power which comes to fight and conquer.
9 July 1958

Bases of the Integral Yoga — أسس اليوغا المتكاملة

يعـاني ذهـن الإنسـان مـن عـادة سـقيمة ومؤسـفة، ألا وهـي الشـك والريـب وحـب الجـدال. جهـد الإنسـان إذاً يجـب أن ينحـو نحـو رفـض هـذه الأشـياء: رفـض الاسـتماع لهـا وبالأحـرى الامتنـاع عـن تلبيـة إيحاءاتها. اللعـب ذهنيـاً بالشـك والريـب هـو أخطـر الألعـاب كافـة، فهـذه الشـكوك ليسـت أعـداءنا فحسـب، بـل هي أشـراك مهـولة، لو وقعنا في شـرك منها يكون الخـروج منه صعبـاً للغاية.

بعـض النـاس يتـأنقون بالتلاعـب بالأفكـار ومناقشـتها ومعارضـة إيمـانهم، ويظنـون أن ذلـك دليـل على تفـوقهم وارتفـاعهم فـوق "الخرافـات" و"الجهـل"، ولكنـك باسـتماعك واتباعـك لمـا تـوحي بـه الشـكوك، تقـع في أحلـك أشـكال الجهـل وتنحـرف عـن الطريـق السـوي. وبذلك تـدخل في الحيـرة والخطأ وفـي متاهـات المتناقضـات التـي قـد لا تسـتطيع الخـروج منهـا، وتـزداد الشـقة بينـك وبيـن الحقيقـة الباطنيـة بحيث تغيـب عـن بصـرك وأحيانـاً تفقـد كل إمكانيـات الاتصـال بروحـك.

بالتأكيـد، المجهـود الشخصـي ضـروري للحفـاظ علـى إيمانـنا وللسـماح لـه بـالنمو في داخلـنا. فيمـا بعـد — بعـد وقـت طويـل — ربمـا نجـد، عنـدما نتـذكر الماضـي، أن كل مـا صـادفنا، حتـى مـا بـدا لنـا في وقتـه أسـوء الأحـداث، كـان **نعمـة إلهيـة** دفعتـنا إلـى التقـدم علـى الطريـق، وعنـدئذ نـدرك أيضـاً أن المجهـود الشخصـي كـان **نعمـة** في حـد ذاتـه. ولكننـا لـن نبلـغ هـذه النقطـة ونحقـق هـذا الوعـي إلا بعـد تقـدم كبيـر وكفـاح طويـل بـل وأحيانـاً بعـد الكثيـر مـن المعانـاة. لـو أردنـا أن نجلـس في سـلبية الكسـل ونقـول، "لـو كـان مقـدراً لـي أن أؤمـن، فـإن ذلـك سـوف يحـدث لـي عنـدما يهبنـي **الواحـد-الكـل الإيمـان**." ذلـك يكـون موقـف تكاسـل ولاوعـي ويكـاد يكـون موقـف سـوء نيـة. لكـي يشـتعل اللهـب الداخلـي، لا بـد أن ننفـخ فيـه ونتعهـده ونغذيـه بوقـود جميـع الأخطـاء التـي نرغـب في التخلـص منهـا وبكـل مـا يـؤخر تقدمـنا وبكـل مـا يعتـم مسـارنا. إذا لـم نغـذي النـار، فإنهـا تخبـو تحـت رمـاد لاوعينـا وخمولنـا، وعنـدئذ نحتـاج، لا إلى سـنين فحسـب، بـل إلى حيـوات وقـرون لكـي نبلـغ **الهـدف**.

يجـب أن نتعهـد إيمانـنا بالرعايـة كأننـا نتعهـد ولادة شـيء ذي قيمـة لا نهائيـة، وأن نحميـه بعنايـة مـن كـل مـا قـد يضعفه.

في جهـل البدايـة وظلامهـا، الإيمـان هـو أوضـح تعبيـر عـن **القـدرة الإلهيـة** التـي تتنـزل لتحـارب وتنتصـر.

9 يوليو 1958

Trust in the Body

if you live normally, under quite normal conditions — without having extravagant ideas and a depressing education — well, through all your youth and usually till you are about thirty, you have an absolute trust in life. If, for example, you are not surrounded by people who, as soon as you have a cold in the head, get into a flurry and rush to the doctor and give you medicines, if you are in normal surroundings and happen to have something — an accident or a slight illness - there is this certainty in the body, this absolute trust that it will be all right: "It is nothing, it will pass off. It is sure to go. I shall be quite well tomorrow or in a few days. It will surely be cured" — whatever you may have caught. That is indeed the normal condition of the body. An absolute trust that all life lies before it and that all will be well. And this helps enormously. One gets cured nine times out of ten, one gets cured very quickly with this confidence: "It is nothing; what is it after all? Just an accident, it will pass off, it is nothing." And there are people who keep it for a very long time, a very long time, a kind of confidence — nothing can happen to them. Their life is all before them, fully, and nothing can happen to them. And what will happen to them is of no importance at all: all will be well, necessarily; they have the whole of life before them. Naturally, if you live in surroundings where there are morbid ideas and people pass their time recounting disastrous and catastrophic things, then you may think wrongly. And if you think wrongly, this reacts on your body.
October 7, 1953

الثقـة في البـدن

عنـدما تحيـون حيـاة عاديـة، تحـت ظـروف طبيعيـة تمامـاً — ومـا لـم تكونـوا متطـرفين في آرائكـم، أو تكـن تـربيتكم [السـابقة] قـد أحبطـتكم – فـإنكم تملكـون طـوال طفـولتكم وشبـابكم، حتى سـن الثلاثـين تقريبـاً، ثقـة تامـة بالحيـاة. ومـا لـم تكونـوا محـاطين، علـى سـبيل المثـال، بقـوم يرتبكـون ويتهيجـون بمجـرد إصـابتكم بنوبـة بـرد بسـيطة ويسـارعون إلـى الطبيـب ويعطـوكم أدويـة، ولـو كنتـم تعيشـون في محيـط عـادي، وتصـادف أن وقـع لكـم شـيء مـا، حادثـة أو اعتـلال طفيـف – فسـيكون هنـاك في أبدانكـم هذا اليقـين، سيكون علـى مـا يصـادفكم، أيـاً كـان مـا يصـادفكم، سيكون علـى مـا يـرام: "لا داعـي للقلـق، كـل شـيء سـيعود إلـى مـا كـان عليـه، سأصـبح بخيـر غـداً أو في ظـرف أيـام قليلـة، الأمـور ستتحسـن بالتأكيـد". هذا هـو حـال البـدن بالفعـل في الظـروف الطبيعيـة: فهـو يثـق ثقـة مطلقـة بـأن الحيـاة بأكملهـا مازالـت أمامـه وأن كـل شـيء سينتهي بسـلام. وهـذه الثقـة تسـاعده كثيـرا: بهـا يتحقـق لـه الشـفاء تسـع مـرات مـن كـل عشـرة، و بهـا ينـال الشـفاء بسـرعة كبيـرة: "إنـه لا شـيء. مـا الأمـر في آخـر المطـاف؟ مجـرد حادثـة بسـيطة تمـر بسـلام." هنـاك قـوم يحتفظـون بهـذه الثقـة وقتـاً طـويلاً، طـويلاً للغايـة – وهؤلاء لا يمكـن أن يصـيبهم شـيء، و تنبسـط الحيـاة بأكملهـا أمـامهم، ومـا مـن شـيء يقـدر أن يمسـهم. وإذا مـا وقـع لهـم شـيء، لا تكـون لـه أي أهميـة [لأنهـم يعلمـون أن] كـل شـيء سـينتهي بالتأكيـد نهايـة طيبـة. وبـالطبع، إذا كنتـم علـى العكـس تعيشـون في بيئـة تسـود فيهـا الأفكـار السـقيمة، ويتسـلى النـاس فيهـا بالتحـدث عـن المصـائب والكـوارث، فقـد ينحـرف تفكيركم. وإذ انحـرف تفكيركم، سيكون لذلك تأثيره على أبدانكـم...

7 أكتوبر، 1953

70

Bases of the Integral Yoga — أسس اليوغا المتكاملة

The Essential Delight — الهناء الجوهري

The Delight of Existing

There comes a time when one begins to be almost ready, when one can feel in everything, every object, in every movement, in every vibration, in all the things around – not only people and conscious beings, but things, objects; not only trees and plants and living things, but simply any object one uses, the things around one – this delight, this delight of being, of being just as one is, simply being. And one sees that all this vibrates like that. One touches a thing and feels this delight. But naturally, I say, one must have followed the discipline I spoke about at the beginning; otherwise, so long as one has a desire, a preference, an attachment or affinities and repulsions and all that, one cannot – one cannot.

And so long as one finds pleasures – pleasure, well, yes, vital or physical pleasure in a thing – one cannot feel this delight. For this delight is everywhere. This delight is something very subtle. One moves in the midst of things and it is as though they were all singing to you their delight. There comes a time when it becomes very familiar in the life around you. Of course, I must admit that it is a little more difficult to feel it in human beings, because there are all their mental and vital formations* which come into the field of perception and disturb it. There is too much of this kind of egoistic asperity which gets mixed with things, so it is more difficult to contact the Delight there. But even in animals one feels it; it is already a little more difficult than in plants. But in plants, in flowers, it is so wonderful! They speak all their joy, they express it. And as I said, in all familiar objects, the things around you, which you use, there is a state of consciousness in which each one is happy to be, just as it is. So at that moment one knows one has touched true Delight. And it is not conditioned. I mean it does not depend upon...it depends on nothing. It does not depend on outer circumstances, does not depend on a more or less favourable state, it does not depend on anything: it is a communion with the raison d'être of the universe.

And when this comes it fills all the cells of the body. It is not even a thing which is thought out – one does no reason, does not analyse, it is not that: it is a state in which one lives. And when the body shares in it, it is so fresh – so fresh, so spontaneous, so...it no longer turns back upon itself, there is no longer any sense of self-observation, of self-analysis or of analysing things. All that is like a canticle of joyous vibrations, but very, very quiet, without violence, without passion, nothing of all that. It is very subtle and very intense at the same time, and when it comes, it seems that the whole universe is a marvellous harmony. Even what is to the ordinary human consciousness ugly, unpleasant, appears marvellous.

The Essential Delight — الـهنـاء الجـوهـري

هنـاء الوجـود

يـأتي وقت نكون قد تقـدمنا فيه وأصبحنا علـى وشـك التحقيـق، عندئـذ نصبح قـادرين علـى الشـعور بالهنـاء الجـوهـري، هنـاء الوجـود، الهنـاء الـذي ينتج مـن مجـرد وجودنا وكينونتنا [كوننا ببسـاطة مـا نحـن عليـه]، أن نشـعر بهـذا الهنـاء في جميع الأشيـاء وجميـع الكائنـات وجميـع الحركـات وفي كـل مـا حولنـا — لا نشـعر بـه في النـاس والكائنـات الواعيـة فحسب، بـل أيضـا في جميـع الأشيـاء المنظـورة، لا في الأشـجار والنباتـات والكائنـات الحيـة فحسب، بـل أيضاً في كـل الأدوات التي نستعملهـا. عندئـذ نـرى كـل هـذه الأشيـاء وهـي تـرتعش بموجـات الهنـاء ونتلقـاه منهـا بمجـرد اللمـس. ولكن لْكـي نصـل إلـى هـذا التحقيـق، لا بـد مـن أن نكون قد مارسنا النظام الـذي ذكرتـه في حديث سـابق؛ أمـا لـو كنا مـا نـزال نطـوي في أنفسـنا شـهوات وأفضليات وارتباطـات ونتذبـذب بـين الاستحسـان والنفـور، سيتعذر علينا إدراك هذا الهناء.

طالمـا أننـا نجـد مسرتنا في الأشيـاء [الخارجيـة]، سـواء أكـانت مسـرة حيويـة أو بدنيـة، سـيتعذر علينـا الشـعور بالهنـاء [الجـوهـري]. فهـذا الهنـاء شـيء دقيق للغايـة. عنـدما نتـروض، نشـعر كمـا لْـو كـانت الأشيـاء حولنا تنشـد وتتغنـى لنا بهـذا الهنـاء. إلـى أن يـأتي وقت يصبح فيـه هـذا الهنـاء مألوفـاً في كـل صـور الحيـاة التي تنبـض مـن حولنـا. هنا يجب أن أقـر بـأن اكتشـاف الهنـاء في البشـر أنفسـهم أصعب بعـض الشـيء نتيجـة لكـل تشـكيلاتهم* الفكريـة والحيويـة التـي تـدخل مجـال إدراكنـا وتشوشـه. هاتـه التشـكيلات تضفـي غلظـة وفظاظـة تمتـزج مـع الأشيـاء وتجعـل استشـفاف الهنـاء الـدائم فيهـا صـعباً. الشعور بهذا الهنـاء سـهل في حالة الحيوانـات، وممكن وإن كـان أصعب في حالة النباتـات. النباتـات والزهـور لهـا روعـة خاصـة وهـي تُعَبِّر بفصـاحة عـن كـل بهجتها. وكمـا سـبق أن قلت، عنـدما نتقـدم في الـوعي، نستشـف في كـل مـن الأشيـاء المألوفـة التـي تحيـط بنـا وفـي تلـك التـي نستعملهـا، سـعادة دائمـة، كمـا لـو أنهـا كـانت سـعيدة لمجـرد كونهـا علـى مـا هـي عليـه. وهـي سـعادة لا تتوقف علـى أي شيء أو على ظروف خارجية أو على حالة معينة، بل تنتج من الاتصال الوثيق بعلة وجود الكون.

عندما نحقـق هـذا الـوعي الشـفاف، تمتلأ بـه خلايـا أبـداننا، بـدون أن نحتـاج إلـى أي تفكيـر أو تعقل أو تحليـل ذهني، بـل إننا نعيش هـذه الحالـة تلقائيـاً. اشـتراك البـدن يملأنـا بالنضـرة والنشـاط، ويغنينـا عـن ضـرورة التراجـع داخـل أنفسـنا للمراقبة والتحليـل أو أي شـيء آخـر مـن هـذا القبيـل. عندئـذ نعيش في ترنيمـة بهجـة، هادئـة غايـة الهـدوء، لا عنف فيهـا أو عواطف متقـدة... كلمـا أتت هـذه الحالـة التـي تجمع بـين الإرهـاف والحـدة يبدو لنـا الكون في انسجام رائـع، يشـمل كـل شـيء حتى مـا يعتبـره الـوعي الآدمي العادي قبيحاً أو كريهاً...

Unfortunately, as I said, people, circumstances, all that, with all those mental and vital formations – that disturbs it all the time. Then one is obliged to return to this ignorant, blind perception of things. But otherwise, as soon as all this stops and one can get out of it...everything changes. And it is all Delight, true Delight, real Delight.

This demands a little work. ...It comes, it will come, even if it takes much longer – when one asks nothing, expects nothing, hopes for nothing, when it is simply that, it is self-giving and aspiration, and the spontaneous need without any bargaining – the need to be divine, that's all.

23 January 1957

Bases of the Integral Yoga — أسس اليوغا المتكاملة

للأسف كما سبق أن قلت، هذه الحالة الرائعة لا تدوم بسبب الناس والظروف وما يأتون به على الدوام من تشكيلات* ذهنية وحيوية تضطرنا إلى الرجوع إلى الإدراك العادي بجهله وعماه. وبمجرد أن ننجح في الخروج من هذا الوعي الجاهل مرة أخرى، يحدث التغيير الشامل، ونعود إلى **الهناء**، ونخبر **الهناء الحقيقي.**

تحقيق هذه الشفافية يحتاج إلى بعض الإعداد والعمل... ولكنه ممكن وسوف يأتي، حتى لو احتاج إلى وقت طويل، على شرط أن نكف عن الإلحاف والتوقعات والآمال والمساومات، ونكتفي بوهب أنفسنا وبتطلعنا وتوقنا وحاجتنا التلقائية إلى نكون إلهيين. هذا هو كل ما في الأمر.

23 يناير 1957

Love — الـــحـــب

Love: Human and Divine

What is the relation of human love to Divine Love? Is the human an obstacle to Divine love? Or is not rather the capacity for human love an index to the capacity for Divine love? Have not great spiritual figures, such as Christ, Ramakrishna* and Vivekananda*, been remarkably loving and affectionate by nature?

Love is one of the great universal forces; it exists by itself and its movement is free and independent of the objects in which and through which it manifests. It manifests wherever it finds a possibility for manifestation, wherever there is receptivity, wherever there is some opening for it. What you call love and think of as a personal or individual thing is only your capacity to receive and manifest this universal force. But because it is universal, it is not therefore an unconscious force; it is a supremely conscious Power. Consciously it seeks for its manifestation and realisation upon earth; consciously it chooses its instruments, awakens to its vibrations those who are capable of an answer, endeavours to realise in them that which is its eternal aim, and when the instrument is not fit, drops it and turns to look for others.

Men think that they have suddenly fallen in love; they see their love come and grow and then it fades – or, it may be, endures a little longer in some who are more specially fitted for its more lasting movement. But their sense in this of a personal experience all their own was an illusion. It was a wave from the everlasting sea of universal love.

Love is universal and eternal; it is always manifesting itself and always identical in its essence. And it is a Divine Force; for the distortions we see in its apparent workings belong to its instruments. Love does not manifest in human beings alone; it is everywhere. Its movement is there in plants, perhaps in the very stones; in the animals it is easy to detect its presence. All the deformations of this great and divine Power come from the obscurity and ignorance and selfishness of the limited instrument. Love, the eternal force, has no clinging, no desire, no hunger for possession, no self-regarding attachment; it is, in its pure movement, the seeking for union of the self with the Divine, a seeking absolute and regardless of all other things. Love divine gives itself and asks for nothing. What human beings have made of it, we do not need to say; they have turned it into an ugly and repulsive thing.

Love — الـحـب

الحب: بـشـري وإلـهـي

مـا هـي العلاقـة بـين الحـب البشـري والحب الإلهي؟ هـل يقف الحب البشري عقبة فـي طريـق الحب الإلهي؟ أليست طاقة المـرء علـى الحـب البشـري بـالأحرى مؤشراً علـى طاقتـه علـى الحب الإلهي؟ ألـم يكـن عظمـاء الروحية مثل المسيح و رامـا كريشـنا* وفيفيك أنانـدا* بطبيعتهم مفعمين بالحب والود؟

الحب قوة مـن أعظم القوى الكونيـة؛ وهـو قـائم بذاتـه ولا يعتمد علـى الأشياء التـي يتجلى فيها أو يمـر مـن خلالهـا. كمـا أنـه يتجلـى كلما سنحت لـه الفرصة وكلما صـادف قبـولاً واستعداداً لتلقيه. مـا نسميه "حبـاً" ونظنه شيئاً فرديـاً يتعلق بنا شخصياً، مـا هـو إلا تعبيـر عـن طاقتنا علـى تلقـي وتجليـة هـذه القوة الكونيـة. ولكـن كـون الحـب قـوة كونيـة لا يعنـي أنـه قـوة لاواعيـة، فهـو قـوة واعيـة للغايـة. وهـو يسعى إلـى إظهـار وتحقيـق نفسـه علـى الأرض بـأن يختار أدواتـه [مـن البشر وغيـرهم] ويوقظ منهم من هم قـادرون علـى الاستجابـة لـه ويعمـل علـى تحقيق هدفـه الأبـدي فيهم، وعندما يجـد أداة لا تصلـح لأغراضه، يتخطاها ويبحث عن أداة أخرى بدلاً منها.

يظن النـاس أنهم يقعون فجـأة فـي الحـب؛ ويـرون حبهم يـأتي وينمو وسرعان مـا يـذبل — وأحيانـا يـدوم أطـول قلـيلاً فـي المحبـين الـذين يميلـون إلـى العواطف المستديمة. ولكـن لـو اعتقد المحـب أن تجربـة حبـه تلـك كانت تجربـة شخصية تنتمي إليـه بالـذات، يكـون ذلـك وهمـاً، فحبـه لـم يكن إلا موجـة من موجات الحب الكوني.

الحب **قـوة إلـهيـة** كونيـة وأبديـة تجلـي نفسـها دائمـاً ولا تتغيـر فـي جوهرهـا. التحريفـات والتشـويهات التـي نراهـا فـي أعمـال الحـب الظاهريـة، تنتمـي إلـى أدواتـه البشـرية. الحب لا يتجلـى فـي البشر وحدهم؛ فهو منتشر فـي كل مكان، فـي النباتات، وربمـا أيضا فـي الأحجار نفسها؛ أمـا فـي الحيوانات فهـو جلـي وواضـح. جميع تحريفـات هـذه القوة الإلهيـة الأبديـة العظيمـة تـأتي مـن الإظـلام والجهل والأنانيـة فـي الأداة البشـرية المحـدودة، أمـا الحـب نفسـه، فهـو بـرئ مـن هـذه التحريفـات ومـن شـوائب التعلق والشهوة و حب التملك والرغبة فـي الارتبـاط لأغـراض شخصية. **الحب الإلهي،** فـي عنصـره الخـالص، هـو تشوق النـفس إلـى الاتحاد مـع **الواحد-الكـل*** تشوقاً بحتـاً يتعالـى علـى كـل شـيء آخـر. وهـو يهب نفسـه ولا يطلب أي شـيء مقابل ذلـك. غني عـن الذكر هنـا أن هـذا الحـب قد تحول علـى يـد البشر إلى شيء قبيح ومنفر.

And yet even in human beings the first contact of love does bring down something of its purer substance; they become capable for a moment of forgetting themselves, for a moment its divine touch awakens and magnifies all that is fine and beautiful. But afterwards there comes to the surface the human nature, full of its impure demands, asking for something in exchange, bartering what it gives, clamouring for its own inferior satisfactions, distorting and soiling what was divine.

To manifest the Divine love you must be capable of receiving the Divine love. For only those can manifest it who are by their nature open to its native movement. The wider and clearer the opening in them, the more they manifest love divine in its original purity; the more it is mixed with the lower human feelings, the greater is the deformation. One who is not open to love in its essence and in its truth cannot approach the Divine. Even the seekers through knowledge come to a point beyond which if they want to go farther, they are bound to find themselves entering at the same time into love and to feel the two as one, knowledge the light of the divine union, love the very heart of knowledge. There is a place in the soul's progress where they meet and you cannot distinguish one from the other. The division, the distinction between the two that you make in the beginning are a creation of the mind: once you rise to a higher level, they disappear.

Among those who have come into this world seeking to reveal the Divine here and transform earthly life, there are some who have manifested the Divine love in a greater fullness. In some the purity of the manifestation is so great that they are misunderstood by the whole of humanity and are even accused of being hard and unloving, although the Divine love is there. But it is in them divine and not human in its form as in its substance. For when man speaks of love, he associates it with an emotional and sentimental weakness. But the divine intensity of self-forgetfulness, the capacity of throwing oneself out entirely, making no restriction and no reservation, as a gift, asking nothing in exchange, this is little known to human beings. And when it is there unmixed with weak and sentimental emotions, they find it hard and cold; they cannot recognise in it the very highest and intensest power of love.

ومع ذلك نجد حتى في البشر أن لمسة الحب الأولى تجلب معها ومضة من عنصره النقي تمكنهم من أن ينسوا أنفسهم ولو للحظة قصيرة توقظ وتجلي كل ما هو رقيق وجميل فيهم. ولكن الطبيعة البشرية، بكل ما فيها من تطلب وفصال ورغبة في الحصول على مقابل وإصرار على المنفعة الذاتية، تتغلب مرة أخرى وبذلك تشوه وتلوث ما كان إلهياً.

الذين يرغبون في إظهار **الحب الإلهي** وتجليته يجب أن يكونوا متفتحين لحركته الأصيلة وقادرين على تلقيها. وكلما كان انفتاحهم أوسع وأكثر شفافية، كلما كانوا أقدر على إظهاره في نقائه الأصلي؛ وبالقدر الذي يختلط فيهم **الحب الإلهي** بالعواطف البشرية الأدنى، كلما زاد تشوهه وتحريفه. أما الذين يغلقون أبوابهم في وجه الحب وحقيقته، فهؤلاء لن يقدروا على الاقتراب من **الواحد-الكل***. حتى أولئك الذين يسعون إلى **الواحد-الكل*** عن طريق المعرفة يصلون إلى نقطة معينة إذا أرادوا أن يتخطوها يجدون أنفسهم مضطرين إلى سلوك طريق الحب وأن يدركوا التطابق بين الحب والمعرفة وأن يفهموا أن المعرفة هي نور الاتحاد الإلهي، وأن الحب هو صميم المعرفة. في سياق تطور روح [الممارس]، تأتي مرحلة يتلاقى فيها الحب والمعرفة ويمتزجان بحيث يصبح التمييز بينهما مستحيلاً. من الشائع في أول الممارسة أن يُمَيِّز المرء بين الحب والمعرفة ولكن هذا التمييز ما هو إلا منتج من منتجات الذهن يزول عندما يتقدم المرء إلى مراحل أعلى.

من بين الذين أتوا إلى عالمنا بهدف إظهار الألوهية فيه وتحويل الحياة الأرضية [إلى حياة أفضل] فئة جسدت وجلت **الحب الإلهي** بصورة أتم وأشمل. وقد كان نقاء تجلية بعضهم عظيماً لدرجة أن الناس من حولهم لم يفهموهم واتهموهم بالقسوة وعدم القدرة على الحب. كان الحب في هذه النخبة في هيئته وعنصره إلهياً وفائقاً للحب البشري. فالحب يختلط في مفهوم الناس عادة بوع من الضعف والميل نحو العاطفية والوجدانية المفرطة. الناس لا يعلمون كثيراً عن صفات **الحب الإلهي** مثل النسيان التام للذات أو الوهب الكامل للنفس بدون توقع لأي مقابل. وعندما يصادف هؤلاء الناس **الحب الإلهي** خالصاً من كل عواطف الضعف والوجدانية المفرطة، يجدونه قاسياً وبارداً ولا يقدرون على أن يتعرفوا فيه على أسمى وأشد صور الحب.

Bases of the Integral Yoga — أسس اليوغا المتكاملة

The manifestation of the love of the Divine in the world was the great holocaust, the supreme self-giving. The Perfect Consciousness accepted to be merged and absorbed into the unconsciousness of matter, so that consciousness might be awakened in the depths of its obscurity and little by little a Divine Power might rise in it and make the whole of this manifested universe a highest expression of the Divine Consciousness and the Divine love. This was the supreme love, to accept the loss of the perfect condition of supreme divinity, its absolute consciousness, its infinite knowledge, to unite with unconsciousness, to dwell in the world with ignorance and darkness. And yet none perhaps would call it love; for it does not clothe itself in a superficial sentiment, it makes no demand in exchange for what it has done, no show of its sacrifice. The force of love in the world is trying to find consciousnesses that are capable of receiving this divine movement in its purity and expressing it. This race of all beings towards love, this irresistible push and seeking out in the world's heart and in all hearts, is the impulse given by a Divine love behind the human longing and seeking. It touches millions of instruments, trying always, always failing; but this constant touch prepares these instruments and suddenly one day there will awake in them the capacity of self-giving, the capacity of loving.

The movement of love is not limited to human beings and it is perhaps less distorted in other worlds than in the human. Look at the flowers and trees. When the sun sets and all becomes silent, sit down for a moment and put yourself into communion with Nature: you will feel rising from the earth, from below the roots of the trees and mounting upward and coursing through their fibres up to the highest outstretching branches, the aspiration of an intense love and longing, — a longing for something that brings light and gives happiness, for the light that is gone and they wish to have back again.

There is a yearning so pure and intense that if you can feel the movement in the trees, your own being too will go up in an ardent prayer for the peace and light and love that are unmanifested here. Once you have come in contact with this large, pure and true Divine love, if you have felt it even for a short time and in its smallest form, you will realise what an abject thing human desire has made of it. It has become in human nature something low, brutal, selfish, violent, ugly, or else it is something weak and sentimental, made up of the pettiest feeling, brittle, superficial, exacting. And this baseness and brutality or this self-regarding weakness they call love!

نـزول حـب **الواحـد-الكـل** إلـى العـالم كـان تضـحية عظمـى ووهب للـذات فـي أكمـل صـورد. ذلـك أن **الـوعي الأسـمى** أخـذ علـى عاتقـه أن يـدخل المـادة غيـر الواعيـة، وأن يتخللهـا ليـوقظ الـوعي فـي أعماقهـا المظلمـة ويبـث فيهـا **القـدرة الإلهيـة**، وأن يجعل الكون الظاهر بأكملـه تعبيـراً تامـاً عـن **الـوعي الإلهـي والحـب الإلهـي.** ذلـك كـان الحـب فـي أقصـى صـوره لأن **الواحـد-الكـل** ضحـى بمقامـه الإلهـي الأسـمى وبوعيـه الكامـل ومعرفتـه اللانهائيـة مـن أجل الاتحـاد مـع لاوعـي الحيـاة الأرضيـة بكـل جهلـه وظلامـه. هـذه التضـحية قـد لا يسـميها الكثيـرون حبـاً لأنهـا لا تتـزين وتتبـاهى بـرداء العاطفيـة السـطحية ولا تطالب بمقابـل لمـا قدمتـه. قوة الحـب التي تعمل في عالمنـا الآن تبحـث عـن أفراد يكون وعيهم قـادراً علـى تلقي هـذا **الحـب الإلهـي** الخـالص وعلـى التعبيـر عنـه. **الحـب الإلهـي** هـو القـوة الدافعـة وراء تشـوق البشر وسـعيهم التـي تـدفعهم إلـى التسـابق ليكتشـفوا الحـب فـي قلـب العـالم وفـي جميـع القلـوب. الحـب يحـاول دائمـاً ويفشل مـرات ومـرات؛ ولكـن لمسـته المتكررة تُعِّد البشـر إلـى أن تسـتيقظ فيهـا ذات يـوم القـدرة علـى الحـب ووهب الذات.

الحب لا يقتصـر علـى البشـر، وربمـا يكون أقـرب إلـى عنصـره الخـالص فـي عـوالم أخرى غيـر عالمنـا الآدمـي. انظر مـثلاً إلـى الـورود والأشـجار. عندما تغـرب الشـمس ويصـبح كـل شـيء سـاكناً، اجلس لحظـة وادخل فـي تواصـل مـع **الطبيعـة**: ستشـعر بتشـوق وتوق يتصـاعدان مـن أسـفل جذور الأشـجار ويرتفعـان فـي أليافهـا حتى يبلغـان أعلـى الجذور الممتـدة نحو السـماء، تشـوق كأنـه حب وحنين إلـى شـيء يجلب النـور والسـعادة، إلـى النـور الـذي غـاب بغـروب الشـمس والـذي تأمل هـذه النباتـات فـي رجوعه.

هـذا الحنين نقي وشـديد لدرجـة أنـك لـو أمكنـك أن تشـعر بـه يتصـاعد مـن الأشـجار، تجـد كيـانك أيضـاً يتسـامى فـي صـلاة تـدعو إلـى نـزول السـلام والنـور والحـب الـذين لـم يتحققـوا بعـد علـى أرضنـا. إذا مـا حققـت الاتصـال بهـذا **الحـب الإلهـي**، الصـادق، الطـاهر، الشاسـع وشـعرت بـه ولـو لوقـت قصـير وحتى لـو كـان فـي أوهـى صـوره، سـتدرك مـدى التشـوه الـذي يعانيـه هـذا الحـب علـى يـد شـهوات بنـي آدم التـي تـدخل فيـه إمـا التـدني والقبـح والأنانيـة والوحشـية والعنـف أو السـطحية والعاطفيـة المفرطـة والهشاشـة والضـعف والتفاهة. وبعـد كـل ذلـك يطلـق النـاس علـى هـذه الضـعة والوحشـية وهـذا الضـعف الأنـاني اسم الحب!!

Bases of the Integral Yoga — أسس اليوغا المتكاملة

Is our vital* being to take part in the Divine love? If it does, what is the right and correct form of participation it should take?

Where is the manifestation of Divine love intended to stop? Is it to be confined to some unreal or immaterial region? Divine love plunges its manifestation upon earth down into the most material matter. It does not indeed find itself in the selfish distortions of the human consciousness; but the vital in itself is as important an element in Divine love as it is in the whole of the manifested universe. There is no possibility of movement and progress without the mediation of the vital; but because this Power of Nature has been so badly distorted, some prefer to believe that it has to be pulled out altogether and thrown away. But it is only through the vital that matter can be touched by the transforming power of the Spirit. If the vital is not there to infuse its dynamism and living force, matter will remain dead; for the higher parts of the being will not come into contact with earth, will not be concretised in life, and they will depart unsatisfied and disappear.

The Divine love of which I speak is a Love that manifests here upon this physical earth, in matter, but it must be pure of its human distortions, if it is to incarnate. The vital is an indispensable agent in this as in all manifestation. But as has happened always, the adverse powers have put their hold on this most precious thing. It is the energy of the vital that enters into dull and insensitive matter and makes it responsive and alive. But the adverse forces have distorted it; they have turned it into a field of violence and selfishness and desire and every kind of ugliness and prevented it from taking part in the divine work. The one thing to be done is to change it, not to suppress its movement or destroy it. For without it no intensity is possible anywhere. The vital is in its very nature that in us which can give itself away. Just because it is that which has always the impulse and the strength to take, it is also that which is capable of giving itself to the utmost; because it knows how to possess, it knows also how to abandon itself without reserve. The true vital movement is the most beautiful and magnificent of movements; but it has been twisted and turned into the most ugly, the most distorted, the most repulsive. Wherever into a human story of love, there has entered even an atom of pure love and it has been allowed to manifest without too much distortion, we find a true and beautiful thing. And if the movement does not last, it is because it is not conscious of its own aim and seeking; it has not the knowledge that it is not the union of one being with another that it is seeking after but the union of all beings with the Divine.

هل ينبغي أن يساهم كياننا الحيوي في إظهار **الحب الإلهي**؟ لو كان الأمر كذلك، ما هي الهيئة الصحيحة واللائقة لفعل ذلك؟*

أين تريد أن نرسم حدوداً **للحب الإلهي** عندما يتخذ هيئة ويتجسد على الأرض؟ هل تريد ن نقصر حدوده داخل مجال لا مادي ووهمي فقط؟ **الحب الإلهي**، عندما يتجلى على الأرض، يتظللها إلى أقصى أعماق المادة. ومع أنه يقاسي في أجزاء الوعي البشري التي شوهتها الأنانية، إلا أنه لا يستطيع تجاهل الكيان الحيوي كلياً، فالكيان الحيوي عنصر هام من عناصر الكون الظاهر وبدون وساطته وتأثيره لا تكون هناك أي حركة أو تقدم. الكيان الحيوي طاقة من طاقات **الطبيعة** التي تشوهت كثيراً على يد البشر (تشوهت لدرجة أن البعض يعتقدون في ضرورة استئصالها والتخلص منها)، إلا أنها الطاقة الوحيدة التي يستطيع بها **الروح الإلهي** أن يحقق الصلة مع المادة ويحوّلها لأن الطاقات الأعلى في الكيان البشري [كالذهن مثلاً] تترفع عن الاتصال بالأرض والانشغال بالحياة. **الحب الإلهي** يجد نفسه مضطراً إلى التعامل مع الكيان الحيوي لأنه الجزء الوحيد فينا الذي ينفث الديناميكية وقوة الحياة في المادة ليخرجها من خمولها.

الحب الإلهي الذي أتحدث عنه هو حب يظهر ويتجسد في المادة على هذه الأرض، ولكن هذا التجسد يتشوه عندما يُحَرَّف الحب في الطبيعة البشرية. الكيان الحيوي عامل لا يمكن لاستغناء عنه في هذا الإظهار (وفي كل إظهار) فطاقته هي التي تدخل في المادة الخاملة عديمة الحساسية وتبث فيها الحياة وتجعلها متجاوبة [مع التأثير الإلهي]. ولكن القوى المعاكسة، كعادتها، تتملك من هذا **الحب الإلهي** لتمنعه من الاشتراك في العمل الإلهي، وتشوهه وتدخل فيه العنف والأنانية والشهوة وكل ما هو قبيح ومنفّر. لكي نُقَوّم ذلك يجب أن نغير الكيان الحيوي نفسه، دون أن نكبت حركته أو نقتله، لأننا لو قتلناه، نقتل أيضاً حماسنا وقدرتنا على التحقيق. الكيان الحيوي هو هذا الجزء فينا الذي يستطيع أن يهب نفسه كلياً. وبالتحديد لأنه الجزء الدافع القادر على الاخذ، فهو قادر على وهب نفسه إلى أقصى مدى؛ وبالتحديد لأنه يعرف كيف يستولي ويتملك، فهو قادر على نسيان نفسه بدون تحفظ. الحركة الحيوية الصادقة هي أجمل وأروع الحركات؛ ولكنها شوهت في البشر وحوّلَت إلى أبشع الحركات وأكثرها تنفيراً. كلما دخلت في قصة حب بشري ولو ذرة واحدة من الحب النقي وسُمح لها بأن تتجلى بدون أن تتشوه كثيراً، تكتسب هذه القصة بعض الحقيقة والجمال. وحتى عندما يزول هذه الحب سريعاً، يكون ذلك نتيجة لأن الوعي نسي هدفه والغرض من سعيه؛ ولأنه يجهل أن غايته الحقيقية ليست الاتحاد بين كائنين، وإنما اتحاد جميع الكائنات مع **الواحد-الكل.**

Bases of the Integral Yoga — أسس اليوغا المتكاملة

Love is a supreme force which the Eternal Consciousness sent down from itself into an obscure and darkened world that it might bring back that world and its beings to the Divine. The material world in its darkness and ignorance had forgotten the Divine. Love came into the darkness; it awakened all that lay there asleep; it whispered, opening the ears that were sealed, "There is something that is worth waking to, worth living for, and it is love!" And with the awakening to love there entered into the world the possibility of coming back to the Divine. The creation moves upward through love towards the Divine and in answer there leans downward to meet the creation the Divine Love and Grace. Love cannot exist in its pure beauty, love cannot put on its native power and intense joy of fullness until there is this interchange, this fusion between the earth and the Supreme, this movement of Love from the Divine to the creation and from the creation to the Divine. This world was a world of dead matter, till Divine love descended into it and awakened it to life. Ever since it has gone in search of this divine source of life, but it has taken in its search every kind of wrong turn and mistaken way, it has wandered hither and thither in the dark. The mass of this creation has moved on its road like the blind seeking for the unknown, seeking but ignorant of what it sought. The maximum it has reached is what seems to human beings love in its highest form, its purest and most disinterested kind, like the love of the mother for the child. This human movement of love is secretly seeking for something else than what it has yet found; but it does not know where to find it, it does not even know what it is. The moment man's consciousness awakens to the Divine love, pure, independent of all manifestation in human forms, he knows for what his heart has all the time been truly longing. That is the beginning of the Soul's aspiration, that brings the awakening of the consciousness and its yearning for union with the Divine. All the forms that are of the ignorance, all the deformations it has imposed must from that moment fade and disappear and give place to one single movement of the creation answering to the Divine love by its love for the Divine. Once the creation is conscious, awakened, opened to love for the Divine, the Divine love pours itself without limit back into the creation. The circle of the movement turns back upon itself and the ends meet; there is the joining of the extremes, supreme Spirit and manifesting Matter, and their divine union becomes constant and complete.

الحـب قـوة عظمـى أرسلها **الـوعي الأبـدي** مـن ذاتـه إلـى عالمنـا المـادي المظلم الجاهل ليسترجعه بكل كائناتـه إلـى **الواحـد-الكـل**. نـزل الحـب فـي هـذا الظـلام وأيقـظ كـل مـا كـان يغـط فـي نومـه، وهمـس فـي الآذان المغلقـة: "اسـتيقظوا! هنـاك شـيء جـدير بالاسـتيقاظ، وجـدير بـأن يكـون محـور الحيـاة ألا وهـو الحـب!". بعـد هـذا الاسـتيقاظ، أصبـح الرجـوع إلـى **الواحـد-الكـل** ممكنـاً. الخليقـة تتصـاعد عـن طريـق الحـب إلـى **الواحـد-الكـل**، وفـي الوقـت نفسـه يجـاوب **الحـب الإلهـي والنعمـة الربانيـة** علـى ذلـك بالنـزول إلـى الأرض. إلـى أن يـتم هـذا التبـادل وهـذه الحركـة الدائمـة بـين صـعود ونـزول وهـذا الانـدماج بـين الأرض وخالقهـا الأسـمى، لا يقـدر الحـب علـى بلـوغ أقصـى صـور جمالـه وقوتـه الأصـلية وبهجتـه الشـاملة. كـان عالمنـا مـادة ميتـة إلـى أن نـزل **الحـب الإلهـي** فيـه وأيقـظ المـادة للحيـاة. منـذ ذلـك الحـين عالمنـا عـن هـذا المنبـع الإلهـي ليسـتمد حياتـه منـه، وفـي بحثـه هـذا يضـل طريقـه فـي متاهـات عديـدة ويتخـبط كثيـراً فـي الظـلام. معظـم الخليقـة تسـعى نحـو الحـب سـعي العميـان الـذين يبحثـون عـن شـيء لا يـدرون ماهيتـه. أقصـى مـا توصـل البشـر إليـه ومـا يبـدو لهـم أسـمى صـور الحـب وأنقـاها وأقلهـا أنانيـة هـو حـب الأم لطفلهـا. الحـب البشـري مـا زال يبحـث عـن علـم عـن شـيء آخـر لـم يجـده بعـد، ولكنـه لا يعلـم أيـن يجـده، ولا يعلـم حتـى ماهيتـه. فـي اللحظـة التـي يسـتيقظ فيهـا وعـي الإنسـان **للحـب الإلهـي** فـي نقائـه، هـذا الحـب الإلهـي الـذي لا يعتمـد علـى أي إظهـار فـي هيئـة بشـرية، عندئـذ يكتشـف الإنسـان مـا كـان قلبـه يتـوق إليـه حقـاً. هـذا يكـون بدايـة تـوق **الـروح** الـذي يـؤدي إلـى تيقـظ الـوعي وإلـى الحنـين للاتحـاد مـع **الواحـد-الكـل**. بعـد ذلـك ينبغـي أن تـزول جميـع أشـكال الجهـل ومـا يتبعـه مـن تحريفـات بحيـث لا تبقـى إلا حركـة واحـدة: حركـة تُجَـاوب فيهـا الخليقـة علـى **الحـب الإلهـي** بحبهـا المقابـل **للواحـد-الكـل**. متـى أصبحـت الخليقـة واعيـة ومتيقظـة ومتفتحـة لحـب **الواحـد-الكـل**، يتنـزل عليهـا **الحـب الإلهـي** كالسـيل المنهمـر. عندئـذ تكتمـل الـدائرة ويلتقـي الطرفـان ويلتحـم النقيضـان: **الـروح الإلهـي** والإظهـار المـادي، فـي اتحـاد كامـل ودائـم.

Bases of the Integral Yoga — أسس اليوغا المتكاملة

Great beings have taken birth in this world who came to bring down here something of the sovereign purity and power of Divine love. The Divine love has thrown itself into a personal form in them that its realisation upon earth may be at once more easy and more perfect. Divine love, when manifested in a personal being, is easier to realise; it is more difficult when it is unmanifested or impersonal in its movement. A human being, awakened by this personal touch, with this personal intensity, to the consciousness of the Divine love, will find his work and change made more easy; the union for which he seeks becomes more natural and close. And the union, the realisation will become for him, too, more full, more perfect; for the wide uniformity of a universal and impersonal Love will be lit up and vivified with the colour and beauty of all possible relations with the Divine.

2 June, 1929

See what is behind Love

It is said that to be conscious of divine Love all other love has to be abandoned. What is the best way of rejecting the other love which clings so obstinately (Laughter) and does not easily leave us?

The Mother: To go through it. Ah! To go through, to see what is behind it, not to stop at the appearance, not to be satisfied with the outer form, to look for the principle which is behind this love, and not be content until one has found the origin of the feeling in oneself. Then the outer form will crumble of itself and you will be in contact with the divine Love which is behind all things.

That is the best way.

To want to get rid of the one in order to find the other is very difficult. It is almost impossible. For human nature is so limited, so full of contradictions and so exclusive in its movements that if one wants to reject love in its lower form, that is to say, human love as human beings experience it, if one makes an inner effort to reject it, one usually rejects the entire capacity of feeling love and becomes like a stone. And then sometimes one has to wait for years or centuries before there is a reawakening in oneself of the capacity to receive and manifest love.

Therefore, the best way when love comes, in whatever form it may be, is to try and pierce through its outer appearance and find the divine principle which is behind and which gives it existence. Naturally, it is full of snares and difficulties, but it is more effective. That is to say, instead of ceasing to love because one loves wrongly, one must cease to love wrongly and want to love well.

أتت إلى هذه الأرض كائنات عظيمة لتجلب لها نصيباً من نقاء وقدرة **الحب الإلهي**، كائنات اتخذ **الحب الإلهي** فيها هيئة شخصية لكي يجعل تحقيق مهمته على الأرض أيسر وأكثر كمالاً. ذلك أن التعرف على **الحب الإلهي** في هيئة شخصية أسهل [بالنسبة للبشر] من التعرف عليه لو كـن مجرداً من كل هيئة. عندما تمس الإنسان لمسة شخصية توقظ وعيه **للحب الإلهي** بكل شدته وقوته، يكون ذلك عوناً كبيراً يساعده في عمله وتطوره، وييسر له الاتحاد الإلهي الذي ينشده، وبذلك تتفتح أمامه جميع العلاقات الممكنة مع **الواحد-الكل** في كل جمالها وبهجتها - في ضوء حب إلهي كوني لا يتغير ولا يعتمد على أشخاص معينة.

2 يونيو 1929

استَثِبِف ما وراء الحب

يقال إننا لكي نصبح واعيين بالحب الإلهي، يجب أن نتخلى عن جميع أشكال الحب الأخرى. ما هي أفضل طريقة للتخلص من الحب الآخر الذي يتشبث بنا بعناد (ضحك) ولا يغادرنا إلا بصعوبة؟

الأم: أفضل طريقة هي أن تذهب في الحب حتى نهايته وترى ما يكمن وراءه، ألا تتوقف عند المظاهر، وألا تقنع بالأشكال الخارجية، وأن تبحث عن جوهر هذا الحب الذي تشعر به وتواظب على البحث حتى تكتشف منبعه في نفسك. عندئذ تتهافت الهيئة الخارجية تلقائياً وتَمَّس **الحب الإلهي** الكامن في جميع الأشياء.

هذه هي أفضل طريقة.

أما لو أردت أن تتخلص من الحب البشري لكي تحل محله **الحب الإلهي**، فذلك طريق صعب للغاية ويكاد يكون مستحيلاً. فالطبيعة البشرية محدودة جداً ومليئة بالمتناقضات وحصرية في حركاتها بحيث إننا لو أردنا أن نتخلص من الحب في صوره الدنيا، أي الحب البشري كما يخبره البشر، وبذلنا الجهد لنطرحه جانباً، تكون النتيجة أننا نتخلص كذلك من ملكة الشعور بالحب إطلاقاً ونصبح مثل الأحجار عديمة الإحساس. وربما اضطررنا عندئذ إلى الانتظار لسنين وقرون قبل أن تستيقظ فينا مرة أخرى القدرة على تلقي الحب والتعبير عنه.

ولذلك أفضل طريق نسلكه عندما يأتي الحب، مهما كانت الصورة التي يأتي عليها، هي ن نحاول أن نخترق مظهره الخارجي ونكتشف المبدأ الإلهي الذي يستند عليه هذا الحب. هذا الطريق بالطبع لا يخلو من الأشراك والمصاعب، ولكنه مع ذلك أكثر فاعلية [من طريق التخلص من الحب]. أي أننا، بعبارة أخرى، بدلاً من أن نمتنع عن الحب لأننا نحب بطريقة خاطئة، يجب أن نطرح جانباً الطريقة الخاطئة وأن نتعلم الحب بالطريقة الصحيحة.

Bases of the Integral Yoga — أسس اليوغا المتكاملة

For instance, love between human beings, in all its forms, the love of parents for children, of children for parents, of brothers and sisters, of friends and lovers, is all tainted with ignorance, selfishness and all the other defects which are man's ordinary drawbacks; so instead of completely ceasing to love — which, besides, is very difficult as Sri Aurobindo says, which would simply dry up the heart and serve no end — one must learn how to love better: to love with devotion, with self-giving, self-abnegation, and to struggle, not against love itself, but against its distorted forms: against all forms of monopolising, of attachment, possessiveness, jealousy, and all the feelings which accompany these main movements. Not to want to possess, to dominate; and not to want to impose one's will, one's whims, one's desires; not to want to take, to receive, but to give; not to insist on the other's response, but be content with one's own love; not to seek one's personal interest and joy and the fulfilment of one's personal desire, but to be satisfied with the giving of one's love and affection; and not to ask for any response. Simply to be happy to love, nothing more.

If you do that, you have taken a great stride forward and can, through this attitude, gradually advance farther in the feeling itself, and realise one day that love is not something personal, that love is a universal divine feeling which manifests through you more or less finely, but which in its essence is something divine.

The first step is to stop being selfish. For everyone it is the same thing not only for those who want to do yoga but also in ordinary life: if one wants to know how to love, one must not love oneself first and above all selfishly; one must give oneself to the object of love without exacting anything in return. This discipline is elementary in order to surmount oneself and lead a life which is not altogether gross.

As for yoga we may add something else: it is as I said in the beginning, the will to pierce through this limited and human form of love and discover the principle of divine Love which is behind it. Then one is sure to get a result. This is better than drying up one's heart. It is perhaps a little more difficult but it is better in every way, for like this, instead of egoistically making others suffer, well, one may leave them quiet in their own movement and only make an effort to transform oneself without imposing one's will on others, which even in ordinary life is a step towards something higher and a little more harmonious.

19 September 1956

Bases of the Integral Yoga — أسس اليوغا المتكاملة

على سبيل المثال، الحب بين البشر في جميع أشكاله (حب الآباء لأولادهم، حب الأولاد لآبائهم، الحب بين الأخوة والأخوات، الحب بين الأصدقاء والمحبين)، يشوبه الجهل والأنانية وكل العيوب والنقائص الأخرى التي يتصف بها البشر العاديون. ولذلك بدلاً من الامتناع كلياً عن الحب — وهو، كما أوضح شري أوروبيندو، شيء صعب للغاية ويؤدي إلى تجفيف القلب — يجب أن نتعلم كيف نحب بطريقة أفضل: أن نحب بإخلاص وأن نهب أنفسنا، وبدلاً من أن نكافح ضد الحب نفسه، أن نكافح ضد صوره المشوهة بكل أشكالها: الاحتكار والتعلق والغيرة وكل المشاعر التي تصاحب هذه الرذائل. أن نمتنع عن حب التملك والرغبة في السيادة وفرض إرادتنا الشخصية وتحقيق نزواتنا وشهواتنا، وأن نعطي بدلاً من أن نصمم على الأخذ والتلقي، وألا نصر على أن يتصرف الطرف الآخر بالطريقة التي نهواها، بل أن نقنع ونرضى بحقيقة إننا نحب، وألا نسعى إلى تحقيق مصالحنا وتتبع مسراتنا وإشباع شهواتنا، بل أن نقنع بأن نهب حبنا ومودتنا بدون توقع لأي رد فعل معين. أي ببساطة أن نكون سعداء لمجرد أننا نحب ولا شيء أكثر من ذلك.

عندما تفعل ذلك، تتقدم خطوة عظيمة إلى الأمام، ولو واظبت على موقفك هذا، يمكنك أن تنمو تدريجياً في شعور الحب نفسه إلى أن تصل ذات يوم إلى إدراك أن الحب ليس شيئاً شخصياً وإنما شعور إلهي كوني يحقق نفسه من خلالك بدرجات مختلفة من الدقة، وإنه في جوهره إلهي.

الخطوة الأولى هي أن تكف عن الأنانية. هذه قاعدة تصلح للجميع وليس فقط للذين يريدون ممارسة اليوغا، بل تصلح أيضاً في الحياة العادية: لو كنت تريد أن تعرف كيف تحب يجب ألا تحب نفسك أولاً وأخيراً وقبل كل شيء آخر، وأهم من ذلك ألا تحب نفسك بأنانية؛ بل يجب أن تهب نفسك إلى من تحب بدون أن تطلب أي شيء في مقابل ذلك. هذا تهذيب مبدئي يُمَكِّنَك من أن تتغلب على نفسك وأن تعيش حياة خالية من الفظاظة والبذاءة.

أما لو كنت من ممارسي اليوغا، أضف إلى ذلك ما سبق أن قلته في البداية: أن ترغب في تخطي هيئة الحب البشري المحدودة لتكتشف **الحب الإلهي** وراءها. عندئذ تتوصل تأكيداً إلى نتيجة طيبة. هذا أفضل من تجفيف قلبك [باستئصال الحب البشري]. قد تكون هذه الطريقة أصعب قلباً ولكنها أفضل من جميع النواحي؛ لأنها تجنبك من أن تفرض إرادتك على الآخرين ومن أن تكون بأنانيتك سبباً في شقائهم، وتتيح لك أن تتركهم في سلام ليتابعوا حركتهم الذاتية، في حين تَكَتَفي أنت بالسعي لتحويل نفسك، وذلك يكون، حتى في الحياة العادية، بمثابة خطوة إلى الأمام نحو شيء أعلى وأكثر اتساقاً.

19 سبتمبر 1956

Bases of the Integral Yoga — أسس اليوغا المتكاملة

Meditation — التأمل

The Hours of Meditation

Is not an increasing effort of meditation needed and is it not true that the more hours you meditate the greater progress you make?

The number of hours spent in meditation is no proof of spiritual progress. It is a proof of your progress when you no longer have to make an effort to meditate. Then you have rather to make an effort to stop meditating: it becomes difficult to stop meditation, difficult to stop thinking of the Divine, difficult to come down to the ordinary consciousness. Then you are sure of progress, then you have made real progress when concentration in the Divine is the necessity of your life, when you cannot do without it, when it continues naturally from morning to night whatever you may be engaged in doing. Whether you sit down to meditation or go about and do things and work, what is required of you is consciousness; that is the one need, – to be constantly conscious of the Divine.

But is not sitting down to meditation an indispensable discipline, and does it not give a more intense and concentrated union with the Divine?

That may be. But a discipline in itself is not what we are seeking. What we are seeking is to be concentrated on the Divine in all that we do, at all times, in all our acts and in every movement. There are some here who have been told to meditate; but also there are others who have not been asked to do any meditation at all. But it must not be thought that they are not progressing. They too follow a discipline, but it is of another nature. To work, to act with devotion and an inner consecration is also a spiritual discipline. The final aim is to be in constant union with the Divine, not only in meditation but in all circumstances and in all the active life.

There are some who, when they are sitting in meditation, get into a state which they think very fine and delightful. They sit self-complacent in it and forget the world; but if they are disturbed, they come out of it angry and restless, because their meditation was interrupted. This is not a sign of spiritual progress or discipline. There are some people who act and seem to feel as if their meditation were a debt they have to pay to the Divine; they are like men who go to church once a week and think they have paid what they owe to God.

If you need to make an effort to go into meditation, you are still very far from being able to live the spiritual life. When it takes an effort to come out of it, then indeed your meditation can be an indication that you are in the spiritual life.
April 21, 1929

Meditation — التأمل

ساعات التأمل

هل بذل الجهد في التأمل ضروري للتقدم الروحي وهل صحيح أننا نتقدم أسرع كلما أكثرنا من التأمل؟

زيادة ساعات التأمل لا يؤدي بالضرورة إلى التقدم الروحي. الدليل على أنك تقدمت روحياً يأتي عندما تتمكن من التأمل بدون حاجة إلى بذل أي جهد بل على العكس، تحتاج إلى جهد لتتوقف عن التأمل، و تجد صعوبة في التوقف عن التفكير في **الواحد-الكل***، وتجد صعوبة في الهبوط إلى الوعي العادي. تستطيع أن تكون متأكداً من أنك قد تقدمت حقاً عندما يصبح التركيز على **الواحد-الكل** ضرورة حياتك التي لا يمكنك الاستغناء عنها، وعندما يستمر هذا التركيز تلقائياً من الصباح إلى المساء مهما يكون نوع العمل الذي تكون منشغلاً به. على أي حال، ما هو مطلوب منك، سواء أكنت جالسا للتأمل، أو كنت تتحرك وتقوم بكل أنواع الأعمال، هو أن تكون واعياً **بالواحد-الكل** بصفة مستمرة.

*ولكن أليس الجلوس للتأمل أحد التمارين الضرورية [في اليوغا]، وأليس صحيحاً أن التأمل يؤدي إلى وحدة أوثق مع **الواحد-الكل**؟*

ربما كان الأمر كذلك. ولكننا هنا لا نرغب المناهج والتمارين من أجل ذاتها. ما نسعى إليه هو أن نكون مركزين على **الواحد-الكل** في جميع الأوقات وفي كل ما نفعل وفي كل تصرفاتنا وحركاتنا. لذلك ننصح بعض المريدين بالتأمل في حين لا ننصح آخرين بذلك. ولكن لا تفهم من ذلك أن الذين لا يتأملون لا يتقدمون روحياً، فهم أيضاً يمارسون ويتدربون ولكن بطريقة مخالفة. العمل بتكريس وإخلاص هو أيضاً تدريب روحي. هدفنا النهائي هو أن نتحد مع **الواحد-الكل**، لا أثناء التأمل فحسب، بل في كل الظروف وفي وسط الحياة العاملة في كل صورها.

هناك قوم يدخلون أثناء التأمل في حالة يجدون فيها متعة رفيعة، تجعلهم يستمرون فيها راضين عن أنفسهم وينسون العالم؛ ولكن لو أزعجهم شيء، يخرجون من تلك الحالة مهتاجين وغاضبين لأن تأملهم قد انقطع. هذا تصرف لا يدل على تقدم روحي أو تمالك للنفس. وهناك آخرون يشعرون عندما يتأملون أنهم يسدّدون دينهم نحو **الواحد-الكل** ويكونون في ذلك مثل الذين يذهبون إلى الكنيسة مرة كل اسبوع ويظنون أنهم بذلك قد أدوا دينهم للرب.

لو كنت تحتاج إلى بذل جهد لكي تتأمل، فاعلم أنك ما زلت بعيداً جداً عن الحياة الروحية. فقط عندما تحتاج بالعكس إلى بذل جهد لتكف عن التأمل، يكون ذلك دليلاً على أنك تعيش حياة روحية.
21 أبريل، 1929

Bases of the Integral Yoga — أسس اليوغا المتكاملة

Day-to-Day Life — الحياة اليومية

Make Use of Reason

Ordinary people enter life without even knowing what it is to live, and at each step they have to learn how to live. And before knowing what they want to realise, they must at least know how to walk; as we teach a tiny little child how to walk, in life one has also to learn how to live. Which people know how to live? And it is through experience, through mistakes, through all kinds of misfortunes and troubles of every sort that gradually one begins to be what is called reasonable, that is, when one has made a mistake a certain number of times and has had troublesome consequences from this mistake, one learns not to make it again. But there is a moment, when the brain is developed enough and you can use the reason, well, reason can help you to reduce the number of these mistakes, to teach you to walk the path without stumbling too often.

The immense majority of human beings are born, live and die without knowing why this has happened to them. They take it… it is like that; they are born, they live, they have what they call their joys and their sorrows, and they come to the end and go away. They came in and went out without learning anything. This indeed is the immense majority.

There is among them a small number of people called the élite, who try to know what has happened to them, why they are upon earth and why all that happens to them happens. Then among these there are some who use their reason and they find a way of walking properly on the path, much faster than the others. These are reasonable beings.

Now there is a handful — a big handful — of people who are born with the feeling that there is something else to find in life, a higher purpose to life, that there is an aim, and they strive to find it. So for these the path goes beyond reason, to regions which they have to explore either with or without help, as chance takes them, and they must then discover the higher worlds. But there are not many of this kind. I don't know how many of these there are now in the world, but I have the impression that they could still be counted. So for these it depends on when they begin.

Bases of the Integral Yoga — أسس اليوغا المتكاملة

الحياة اليومية — Day-to-Day Life

استعمل عقلك

يقضي النـاس العـاديون حيـاتهم بـدون أن يعرفـوا كيـف هـم يعيشـون، ويجـدون أنفسـهم مضـطرين فـي كـل خطـوة أن يتعلمـوا الحيـاة [كمـا لـو كـانوا لـم يعيشـوا مـن قبـل]. يجـب أن نـتعلم الحيـاة كمـا يـتعلم الطفـل الصـغير المشـي. كـم مـن النـاس يعرفـون حقـاً كيـف يعيشـون؟ وكـم يلزمنـا مـن تجـارب وأخطـاء ومصـائب ومشـاكل مـن جميـع الأنـواع لكـي نبلـغ تـدريجياً بعـض الحصـافة والرشـد ولكـي نصـل إلـى درجـة مـن الحكمـة تسـمح لنـا إذا مـا وقعنـا تكـراراً فـي خطـأ وعانينـا مـن عواقبـه بـأن نتجنـب الوقـوع فيـه مـرة أخـرى؟ ولكـن يـأتي يـوم تبلـغ أمخاخنـا، فيـه درجـة كافيـة مـن النضـوج تمكننـا مـن اسـتخدام بصـائرنا فـي تجنـب الأخطـاء وتحاشـي الوقـوع المتكـرر فيهـا.

الغالبيـة العظمـى مـن البشـر يولـدون ويعيشـون ويموتـون بـدون أن يجـدوا أي مغـزى لحيـاتهم. فهـم يأخـذون الحيـاة علـى علاتهـا: يولـدون ويعاشـون ويخبـرون المسـرات والأحـزان وعنـدما تصـل نهايـة حيـاتهم يغـادرون. أي أنهـم يـأتون ويـذهبون دون أن يتعلمـوا أي شـيء. هـذا هـو حـال الغالبيـة العظمـى منهـم.

ولكـن مـن النـاس نخبـة يحـاولون أن يفهمـوا مـاذا يحـدث لهـم وسـبب قـدومهم إلـى الأرض ومغـزى كـل هـذه الأحـداث. ومـن بـين هـؤلاء قلـة يسـتخدمون عقـولهم لتهـديهم إلـى الصـراط المسـتقيم، ويتقـدمون بسـرعة تفـوق سـرعة الآخـرين بكثيـر. هـؤلاء هـم الحصـفاء الراشـدون. ولكـن مـن النـاس نخبـة يحـاولون أن يفهمـوا مـاذا يحـدث لهـم وسـبب قـدومهم إلـى الأرض ومغـزى كـل هـذه الأحـداث. ومـن بـين هـؤلاء قلـة يسـتخدمون العقـل فـي اكتشـاف طريقـة للمشـي السـوي علـى الصـراط، بسـرعة تفـوق سـرعة الآخـرين بكثيـر. هـؤلاء هـم الحصـفاء الراشـدون.

وهنـاك أيضـاً حفنـة مـن النـاس — حفنـة كبيـرة — يـأتون إلـى الأرض علـى علـم بـأن الحيـة لهـا أبعـاد أخـرى وأن لهـا قصـد وهـدف أسـمى جـدير بـأن يجتهـدوا فـي اكتشـافه. مسـار تلـك الحفنـة يتخطـى العقـل ويـدخل فـي مجـالات تنـاديهم إلـى اكتشـافها، وهـم يسـعون إلـى اكتشـاف هـذه المجـالات الأعلـى، سـواء أمـدتهم الظـروف بـالعون أم لا. ولكـن هـؤلاء ليسـوا كثيـرين. لا أعلـم كـم مـن هـؤلاء يتواجـدون علـى هـذه الأرض فـي لحظتنـا هـذه، وأنـا أميـل إلـى الاعتقـاد بـأنهم لا معـدودون. بالنسـبة لتلـك الحفنـة، السـؤال المهـم هـو متـى يبـدؤون.

Bases of the Integral Yoga — أسس اليوغا المتكاملة

Now there are beings, I think, who are born and whose rational period of life may begin very early, when they are very young, and it may last for a very short time; and then they are almost immediately ready to set out on new and unexplored paths towards the higher realities. But in order to set out on these paths without fear and without any danger, one must have organised his being with the help of reason around the highest centre he consciously possesses, and organised it in such a way that it is inwardly in his control and he has not to say at every moment, "Ah! I have done this, I don't know why. Ah! That's happened to me, I don't know why" — and always it is "I don't know, I don't know, I don't know", and as long as it is like that, the path is somewhat dangerous. Only when one does what he wants, knows what he wants, does what he wants and is able to direct himself with certitude, without being tossed about by the hazards of life, then one can go forward on the suprarational paths fearlessly, unhesitatingly and with the least danger. But one need not be very old for this to happen. One can begin very young; even a child of five can already make use of reason to control himself; I know it. There is enough mental organisation in the being in these little tots who look so spontaneous and irresponsible: there is enough cerebral organisation for them to organise themselves, their life, their nature, their movements, actions and thoughts with reason.

There are some little ones here of this kind. They are not all like that but there are some. There are some like that here, I know them. So if these were taught how to use their reason properly while still very young, they would be ready to start on the great adventure. They would gain much time. But one must not set out on this road with a baggage of impulses and desires, for that brings along all kinds of serious disturbances....

Do the laws of Nature follow the law of human reason?

Oh, no!

Then how can we explain so many laws of Nature by human reason?

Because human reason is higher than Nature.

Nature is infra-rational. The laws of Nature are infra-rational laws. So when men come along and tell you, "But what do you want, it is the law of Nature", as for me, it makes me laugh. It is not worth being a man, it would be better for you to be a monkey or an elephant or a lion. The laws of Nature are infra-rational.

اعتقد أن بعض الناس يبلغون مرحلة التعقل في سن مبكرة للغاية، وربما تخطوا حتى مرحلة العقل بعد فترة قصيرة بعدها يكونون مستعدين لمبادرة سبل جديدة سعياً وراء الحقائق العليا. ولكن لكي يسلك المرء في هذه الطرق بدون خوف وبدون التعرض للخطر، يجب أن يكون قد نظَّم، بمعونة عقله الحصيف، كيانه حول درجات الوعي الأعلى في نفسه، وأن يكون قد بلغ درجة من التحكم الداخلي تغنيه عن التساؤل في كل خطوة عن أسباب تصرفاته وعن علل الأحداث التي يصادفها. طالما احتاج المرء للتساؤل في كل خطوة، يكون السعي على الطرق التي تتخطى العقلانية محفوفاً بالأخطار. فهذه الطرق لا تصبح آمنة إلا عندما يبلغ المرء مرحلة من النضوج يكون عندها على علم ودراية بأهدافه وقادراً على توجيه ذاته بخطوات أكيدة تحميه من تلاعب أمواج الحياة. ومع ذلك، أنا أعلم، عن تجربة، أن البدء المبكر ممكن، وأن الأطفال، حتى في سن الخامسة، قادرون على استخدام عقولهم للتحكم في أنفسهم وعلى تنظيم أنفسهم ذهنياً وعلى التحكم في طبائعهم وحركاتهم وتصرفاتهم وأفكارهم.

يوجد هنا [في الأشرام*] صغار من هذا النوع، أنا أعرفهم، ولكن كل الأطفال ليسوا كذلك. لو عَلَّمنا هاته النخبة في سنهم المبكر كيف يستخدمون عقولهم بحصافة، سيكونوا مستعدين للبدء في المغامرة العظيمة بدون أن يفقدوا الكثير من الوقت. ولكنهم لا ينبغي أن يخطوا على الطريق حاملين معهم متاع الاندفاعات والشهوات، الذي قد يعرضهم لجميع أنواع الخلل والاضطراب.

*هل تخضع **الطبيعة** لقانون العقل البشري؟*

بالطبع لا!

*إذاً كيف يمكننا أن نفسر الكثير من قوانين **الطبيعة** بواسطة العقل؟*

ذلك ممكن لأن مقام العقل البشري أعلى من مقام **الطبيعة.**

الطبيعة تقف [على سلم الارتقاء] على درجة أدنى من درجة العقل البشري وقوانينها أدنى مقاماً من قوانين العقل. ولذلك عندما يتخذ الناس **الطبيعة** حجة [لتبرير أفعالهم] ويقولون إنهم إنما يتصرفون تبعاً لقوانين **الطبيعة**، فإني ذلك يدفعني إلى الضحك. لو كان الأمر كما يقولون، لما كانت لبشريتنا أي قيمة، ولكان أجدر بنا أن نكون قردة أو فيلة أو أسوداً.

This is the only superiority that man has, his having a reason, and when he doesn't make use of it he becomes absolutely an animal.

That's the last excuse to give: "What do you want, it's the law of Nature!"
25 May, 1955

البشر يتفوقون في ناحية واحدة فقط، ألا وهي قدرتهم على استخدام العقل، وإذا لم يفعلوا ذلك لا يكونون أكثر من حيوانات.

التحجج بقوانين الطبيعة هو آخر عذر استطيع أن أقبله!
25 مايو 1955

Attraction and Repulsion

Sweet Mother, why does one feel attracted at first sight to some people and feel a repulsion for others?

Usually this is based on vital affinities, nothing else. There are vital vibrations which harmonise and vital vibrations which don't. It is usually this, nothing else. It is vital chemistry.

One would have to be in a much deeper and more clear-sighted consciousness for it to be otherwise. There is an inner perception based on a psychic consciousness, which makes you feel which people have the same aspiration, the same aim, and can be your companions on the way; and this perception also makes you clear-sighted about those who follow a very different way or carry in them forces which are hostile to you and may harm you in your development. But to attain such a perception one must oneself be exclusively occupied with one's own spiritual progress and integral realisation. Now, that is not often the case. And usually too, when one has attained this inner clear-sightedness, it is not expressed by attraction and repulsion, but by a very "objective" knowledge, it might be said, and a kind of inner certainty which makes you act calmly and reasonably, and without attractions and repulsions.

Therefore, it may be said in a general and almost absolute way that those who have very definite and impulsive likes and dislikes live in a vital consciousness. Mixed with this, there may be mental affinities; that is, some minds like to have relationships in common activities, but here too, these are people on a much higher level intellectually, and this is also expressed even more by a comparative ease in relationships and by something much more calm and detached. One takes pleasure in speaking with certain people, for others there is no attraction, one gains nothing from it. It is a little more distant and quiet; it belongs more to the field of reason.

But likes and dislikes clearly belong to the vital world. Well, there is a vital chemistry just as there is physical chemistry: there are bodies which repel each other and others which attract; there are substances which combine and others which explode, and it is like that. There are some vital vibrations which harmonise, and harmonise to such an extent that ninety-nine times out of a hundred these sympathies are taken for what men call love, and suddenly people feel, "Oh! he is the one I was waiting for", "Oh! she is the one I was seeking!" (laughing), and they rush towards each other, till they find out that it was something very superficial and that these things can't last. There.

الانجذاب والنفور

أيتها الأم العذبة، لماذا نشعر، من أول نظرة، بالانجذاب نحو بعض الناس وبالنفور من آخرين؟

ذلك يرجع إلى مجرد توافق حيوي* لا أكثر. من التموجات الحيوية ما ينسجم بعضه مع البعض ومنها ما يتنافر. هذا هو عادة السبب. إنها كيمياء حيوية.

لكي نرتفع فوق الانجذاب والنفور، يجب أن نعيش في وعي أكثر عمقاً واشراقاً. هناك إدراك باطني، يستند على وعي سيكي*، يمكنك من أن تتعرف على الناس الذين يشاركونك نفس التشوق الروحي ونفس الهدف ويصلحون لأن يكونوا رفاقك على الطريق؛ وفي ذات الوقت يحذرك هذا الوعي من الذين يتبعون طريقاً يخالف طريقك ويأوون بداخلهم قوى معادية قد تلحق الضرر بتطورك. لبلوغ هذا الإدراك يجب أن تكون منشغلاً حصرياً بتطورك الروحي وبرغبتك في تحقيقه تحقيقاً شاملاً؛ ولكن مثل هذا التركيز ليس شائعاً بين الناس. عندما نحقق هذه البصيرة الداخلية المشرقة، نكتسب معرفة "موضوعية" ونوعاً من الثقة الداخلية تمكننا من العمل في هدوء وتعقل وبدون انجذاب أو نفور.

يمكن القول بصفة عامة وجازمة، أن الذين يستسلمون كلياً لأحاسيس الانجذاب والنفور يعيشون في وعي حيوي*. أحياناً يمتزج [مع إحساس الانجذاب الحيوي] تقارب ذهني، بمعنى أن بعض الناس يجدون متعة في تكوين علاقات متبادلة والاشتراك في نشاطات ذهنية. هؤلاء يكونون عادة على مستوى فكري أعلى بكثير من المستوى الحيوي. فتراهم مثلاً يجدون في التحدث مع بعض الناس متعة لا يجدونها في التحدث مع آخرين. هذه العلاقات الذهنية تتميز [إذا قورنت بالعلاقات الحيوية] بالطمأنينة والسكينة والتحرر من التعلق المفرط.

الانجذاب والنفور ينتميان إلى العالم الحيوي*. وكما أن هناك كيمياء فيزيائية، هناك كيمياء حيوية كذلك: فمن الأبدان ما يجذب بعضه بعضه البعض ومنها ما ينفر بعضه من البعض، ومن المواد ما يمتزج إذا خُلِط مع مواد أخرى ومنها ما ينفجر، وهكذا. وأحياناً تنسجم ذبذبات الرجل الحيوية مع ذبذبات المرأة لدرجة أنهما، في تسع وتسعين حالة من مائة، يطلقان على التقارب الذي ينشأ بينهما لقب **الحب**. وإذا بالرجل يشعر فجأة أنه قد " قد وجد أخيراً المرأة التي كان ينتظرها"، في حين تشعر المرأة أنها قد "وجدت أخيراً الرجل الذي كانت تبحث عنه"! ثم يندفعان أحدهما إلى الآخر، وسرعان ما يكتشفان أن حبهما كان سطحياً للغاية وأن العلاقات السطحية لا يمكن أن تدوم.

Bases of the Integral Yoga — أسس اليوغا المتكاملة

So the first advice given to those who want to do yoga: "Rise above likes and dislikes." This is something without any deeper reality and it can at the very least lead you into difficulties which are at times quite hard to overcome. You can ruin your life with these things. And the best thing is not to take any notice of them – to draw back a little into yourself and ask yourself why – it's nothing very mysterious – you like to meet this person, don't like to meet that one.

But, as I say, there comes a moment when one is exclusively occupied with one's Sadhana*, when one can feel – but both more subtly and much more quietly – that a particular contact is favourable to sadhana* and another harmful. But that always takes a much more "detached" form, so to say, and often it even contradicts the so-called attractions and repulsions of the vital; very often it has nothing to do with them.

So, the best thing is to look at all that from a little distance and to lecture yourself a little on the futility of these things.

Obviously there are some natures which are almost fundamentally bad, beings who are born wicked and love to do harm; and logically, if one is quite natural, not perverted, natural as animals are – for from this point of view they are far superior to men; perversion begins with humanity – then one keeps out of the way, as one would stand aside from something fundamentally harmful. But happily these cases are not very frequent; what one meets in life are usually very mixed natures where there is a kind of balance, so to say, between the good and the bad, and one may expect to have both good and bad relations. There is no reason to feel any deep dislike, for, as one is quite mixed oneself (laughing), like meets like!

It is also said that some people are like vampires, and when they come near a person they spontaneously suck up his vitality and energy, and that one should beware of them as of a very serious danger. But that also...Not that it doesn't exist, but it is not very frequent, and certainly not so total that one need run away when one meets such a person.

So, essentially, if one wants to develop spiritually, the first thing to do is to overcome one's dislikes...and one's likes. Look at all that with a smile.
11 September 1957

Bases of the Integral Yoga — أسس اليوغا المتكاملة

هذا هو السبب في أن أول نصيحة تعطى للذين يرغبون في ممارسة اليوغا هي أن يرتفعوا [في وعيهم] فوق أحاسيس الانجذاب والنفور، لأنها في حقيقتها أحاسيس قليلة العمق وكفيلة، على أقل تقدير، بأن تزج بهم في مشاكل قد لا يستطيعون التخلص منها بسهولة. أفضل طريقة للتعامل مع هذه الأحاسيس هي ألا نعيرها التفاتاً وأن نتراجع منها قليلاً إلى داخل أنفسنا وعندئذ نرى أنها أحاسيس عادية [تحدث لكل الناس في جميع الأوقات].

أقول مرة أخرى، أن الممارس يبلغ في سياق تطوره مرحلة يكون فيها منهمكاً — في هدوء وبدون حاجة إلى إعلان ذلك للجميع — في ممارسته لدرجة أن يصير تلقائياً قادراً على التمييز بين العلاقات التي تنفع ممارسته وتلك التي تضر بها وقادراً على النظر إلى العلاقات كهـا بدون ارتباط [وانفعال زائد] وبدون اعتبار لعامل الانجذاب والنفور.

أفضل طريقة إذا [للتحرر من الانجذاب والنفور] هي [ألا تقع في حبالها] وأن تنظر إليها من بعد وأن تُوَعِّي نفسك بأنها عبث لا جدوى فيه.

هناك بشر يميلون أساساً إلى السوء ويحبون الشر والأذية منذ ولادتهم، ومن المنطقي أن يتجنب كل شخص "طبيعي" لا عوج فيه هذه الكائنات المؤذية. ما أعنيه بشخص "طبيعي" هو أنه يلبي سجية الطبيعة ويحذو حذو الحيوانات التي تمكنها غريزتها تجنب ما يضرها — هذا، على فكرة، مجال يتفوق فيه الحيوان على الانسان بكثير. من حسن الحظ، هذه الطبائع الشريرة نادرة نسبياً، والبشر الذين نصادفهم في الحياة عادة مزيج، في حالة توازن حرج، بين طبائع الخير والشر، بحيث يمكننا أن نتوقع في علاقاتنا معهم الطيب والسيء في نفس الوقت. ولكن لا داعي لأن نُعيَّرهم بذلك إذا كنا أنفسنا مُخَّلطين، فلا عجب في أن يلاقى الشبيه شبيهه!

يقال أيضاً أن بعض الناس يشبهون ماصي الدماء من حيث أنهم يمتصون الطاقة والحيوية من الآخرين، وأنهم يمثلون خطراً كبيراً يجب أن نتجنبه. هؤلاء الناس يوجدون بالفعل، ولكنهم، لحسن الحظ، قليلون وليسوا أقوياء لدرجة أننا ينبغي أن نهرب في هلع لو صادفناهم!

الخلاصة إذاً هي: إذا أردت أن تتقدم روحياً، عليك أولاً وقبل كل شيء أن تتغلب على مشاعر الاستحسان والكره وأن تنظر إليها جميعاً بابتسامة من علو.
11 سبتمبر 1957

No Two Things Are Identical

It is said that there are people who are very intelligent, and others who are foolish. Why?

Why? But, my child, there are all kinds of things in Nature! No two things are identical. All the possibilities exist in Nature: everything you can imagine and a hundred million times more. So you notice that there are intelligent people and again others who are not. And then there are others still who are unbalanced. And yet, your observations cover a very narrow field. But you can tell yourself that all this exists and hundreds of thousands of millions of other things also exist, and that no two things are alike in the world. And I don't think there is anything one can imagine which doesn't exist somewhere. This is exactly what amuses Nature most - she tries out everything, does everything, makes everything, undoes everything, and she makes all possible combinations and goes on changing them, re-handling them, remaking them, and it is a perpetual movement of all the possibilities following one another, clashing, intermingling, combining and falling apart. No two moments of terrestrial life are alike; and for how long has the earth existed?.. Very well-informed people will perhaps tell you approximately. And for how long will it yet live? They will perhaps tell you that also: figures with many zeros, so many zeros that you won't be able to read them. But it won't ever be the same thing twice over nor will there be two similar moments. If you find things looking alike, that is only an appearance. There are no two things alike, and no two identical moments. And all this goes so far back that you cannot keep count. And it goes so far forward that you can't keep count either. And it will never be twice the same thing. So, you can't ask me why this exists and why that exists!..

...Do you ever really have two similar moments? No. You know very well that you are not today what you were yesterday and you won't be tomorrow what you are today.. and that if you went back only.. say, ten years, you wouldn't recognise yourself at all any longer! You don't know even what you used to think about, granting that you thought about anything! So, there is no problem. All that you can do is to try and investigate the field of experience given to you which is extremely limited, to see all the possibilities. And you could begin noting them; you would see that it would make a huge volume immediately, simply in that tiny little field of experience which is yours!

And what are you?.. One second in Eternity!
12 August, 1953

لا يتساوى شيئان كل التساوي

يقال أن بعض الناس يتحلون بذكاء عظيم وأن بعضهم يتصفون بالحماقة؟ ما السبب في ذلك؟

السبب؟ ولكن، يا طفلي، **الطبيعة** تشمل أشياء من جميع الأنواع وما من شيئين فيها يتطابقان كل التطابق. كل شيء ممكن في **الطبيعة**: كل ما يمكنك أن تتصوره بالإضافة إلى ملايين الأضعاف من تصوراتك. لقد لاحظت أن بعض الناس أذكياء وأن البعض الآخر ليسوا كذلك، وآخرين مختلون ذهنياً، ولو اقتصرت على هؤلاء يكون مجال رؤيتك محدوداً للغاية. كل هذه الأشياء موجودة و أشياء أخرى لا حصر لها موجودة كذلك، ومع ذلك لا يتساوى شيئان فيهم كل التساوي. أعتقد أن كل شيء يمكنك أن تتصوره موجود بالضرورة في مكان ما [إما في عالمنا أو في عوالم أخرى]. التعدد هو بالتحديد المجال الذي تتجلى فيه براعة **الطبيعة**: فهي تجرب وتخلق وتنقض الأشياء ثم تركب منها جميعاً تركيبات ثم تغير هذه التركيبات وتحقق كل الأشكال الممكنة في حركة تتابع فيها هذه الأشكال وتمتزج وتتصادم ويلغي بعضها البعض. ومع ذلك لا تتساوى لحظتان من تاريخ الحياة على الأرض على الرغم من الآماد السحيقة التي توالت على هذه الحياة!.. ذوو العلم يستطيعون أن يعطوك رقم الأرقام، وهي أرقام تحتوي أصفاراً عديدة لدرجة أنك لن تستطيع قراءة هذه الأرقام.. ومع ذلك لا يتكرر أي من هذه اللحظات على نفس الصورة تماماً وحتى لو تشابهت لحظتان فإن ذلك التشابه يقتصر على المظاهر الخارجية فقط. هذه اللحظات المتباينة تمتد إلى الخلف إلى ماضي سحيق وإلى الأمام نحو مستقبل بعيد يتخطيان قدرتك على العد والحصر... لذلك سؤالك عن أسباب وجود الأشياء على ما هي عليه لا محل له...

... هل خبرت أبداً لحظتين متشابهتين كل التشابه؟ لا. أنت تعلم جيداً أنك لست اليوم ما كنته بالأمس وأنك لن تكون غداً ما أنت عليه اليوم... وأنك لو رجعت في الوقت عشر سنوات مثلاً، لن تتمكن أن تتعرف على نفسك من فرط التغير. لقد انمحت اليوم الأشياء التي كنت تفكرها عندئذ، هذا بافتراض أنك كنت تفكر وقتها على الإطلاق! لماذا تتعجب إذاً على اختلاف الناس في الذكاء؟! لو جَمَّعت في مجال خبرتك المحدودة كل الاحتمالات الممكنة سترى أنها تُكوّن مجلداً ضخماً على الرغم من خبرتك القليلة.

وماذا أنت؟... مجرد لحظة في زمان لا نهائي!
12 أغسطس 1953

The Need for Diversity

If you arrive at the conception of the world as the expression of the Divine in all His complexity, then the necessity for complexity and diversity has to be recognised, and it becomes impossible for you to want to make others think and feel as you do.

Each one should have his own way of thinking, feeling and reaction; why do you want others to do as you do and be like you? And even granting that your truth is greater than theirs—though this word means nothing at all, for, from a certain point of view all truths are true; they are all partial, but they are true because they are truths but the minute you want your truth to be greater than your neighbour's, you begin to wander away from the truth.

This habit of wanting to compel others to think as you do, has always seemed very strange to me; this is what I call "the propagandist spirit", and it goes very far. You can go one step further and want people to do what you do, feel as you feel, and then it becomes a frightful uniformity.

In Japan I met Tolstoy's son who was going round the world for "the good of mankind's great unity". And his solution was very simple: everybody ought to speak the same language, lead the same life, dress in the same way, eat the same things…. And I am not joking, those were his very words. I met him in Tokyo; he said: "But everybody would be happy, all would understand one another, nobody would quarrel if everyone did the same thing." There was no way of making him understand that it was not very reasonable! He had set out to travel all over the world for that, and when people asked him his name he would say "Tolstoy"— now, Tolstoy, you know… People said, "Oh! — 'some people didn't know that Tolstoy was dead — and they thought: "Oh! what luck, we are going to hear something remarkable" — and then he came out with that!

Well, this is only an exaggeration of the same attitude.

Anyway, I can assure you that there comes a time when one no longer feels any necessity at all, at all, of convincing others of the truth of what one thinks.
4 April, 1956

الحاجة إلى التعدد والتنوع

عندما تصل [في نموك الروحي] إلى المرحلة التي ترى فيها أن العالم تعبير عن **الواحد-الكل*** بكل شموله وإحاطته، تدرك ضرورة الاعتراف بالتعدد والتنوع، وتفقد كلياً الرغبة في جعل الآخرين يفكرون ويشعرون على نفس نمط تفكيرك وشعورك.

لماذا تريد أن تجعل الآخرين يحذون حذوك ويكونون مثلك؟ ينبغي أن نترك للناس حرية التفكير والشعور والتصرف. وحتى لو زعمت أن "حقيقتك" أعظم من "حقيقتهم"، فإن ذلك يكون من السخف، لأن الحقائق كلها "حقة"، وكل منها ما هو إلا تعبير جزئي عن **الحق الأعظم**. في اللحظة التي ترغب فيها أن تكون حقيقتك أعظم من حقيقة جارك، تبدأ في الانحراف عن الحق.

تَطَلُّب الناس أن يفكر الآخرون مثل ما يفكرون هي عادة بدت لي دائماً غريبة. وهي تعبير عن ما أسميه "حب الإعلان والدعاية". وهم لا يتوقفون عند حد التفكير، بل يتوسعون ويتوقعون أن يعمل الآخرون ويشعروا مثل ما يعملون ويشعرون. ولو تمكنوا من تحقيق ما يريدون، فإن ذلك يؤدي في نهاية المطاف إلى مساواة نظامية مرعبة.

قابلت في اليابان ابن [الكاتب الروسي] تولستوي الذي كان يطوف العالم آنذاك داعياً إلى ما كان يسميه "توحيد العالم لصالح البشر". كان المنهج الذي يقترحه بسيطاً للغاية: أن يتحدث البشر جميعاً نفس اللغة، ويعيشون على نفس النمط، ويرتدون نفس الزي، ويأكلون نفس الطعام. لا أقول ذلك من باب الفكاهة، بل تلك كانت كلماته بالفعل. قابلته في طوكيو وقال لي: "مثل هذا التوحيد يجلب السعادة للجميع، لأنه يجعلهم قادرين على التفاهم، وعندما يفعل الجميع نفس الشيء، تنتفي أسباب الشجار بينهم!" كان من المستحيل إقناعه بأن مقترحاته ليست معقولة! ولكنه استمر في الطواف في العالم [لِيُروّج أفكاره] وكان إذا سئل عن اسمه يجيب: "تولستوي"، مما كان له تأثير بالغ على بعض الناس الذين كانوا يظنونه تولستوي الأب وأن ما يقوله لا بد أن يكون دُرراً من الحكمة...

ما كان تولستوي الابن يريده ما هو إلا نزعة تقليص التعدد والتنوع في أقصى مداها.

على أي حال، أؤكد لكم أننا عندما نتطور روحياً نبلغ مرحلة نفقد فيها كل رغبة في إقناع الآخرين بالحقيقة التي نؤمن بها.
4 أبريل 1956

Education – الــتربية

The Art of Living – فـن الحيـاة

To live in the right way

Usually you are taught very few things — you are not taught even to sleep. People think that they have only to lie down in their bed and then they sleep. But this is not true! One must learn how to sleep as one must learn how to eat, learn to do anything at all. And if one doesn't learn, well, one does it badly! Or one takes years and years to learn how to do it, and during all those years when it is badly done, all sorts of unpleasant things occur. And it is only after suffering much, making many mistakes, committing many stupidities, that, gradually, when one is old and has white hair, one begins to know how to do something. But if, when you were quite small, your parents or those who look after you, took the trouble to teach you how to do what you do, do it properly as it should be done, in the right way, then that would help you to avoid all — all these mistakes you make through the years. And not only do you make mistakes, but nobody tells you they are mistakes! And so you are surprised that you fall ill, are tired, don't know how to do what you want to, and that you have never been taught. Some children are not taught anything, and so they need years and years to learn the simplest things, even the most elementary thing: to be clean.

It is true that most of the time parents do not teach this because they do not know themselves! For they themselves did not have anyone to teach them. So they do not know… they have groped in the dark all their life to learn how to live. And so naturally they are not in a position to teach you how to live, for they do not know it themselves. If you are left to yourself, you understand, it needs years, years of experience to learn the simplest thing, and even then you must think about it. If you don't think about it, you will never learn.

To live in the right way is a very difficult art, and unless one begins to learn it when quite young and to make an effort, one never knows it very well. Simply the art of keeping one's body in good health, one's mind quiet and goodwill in one's heart — things which are indispensable in order to live decently — I don't say in comfort, I don't say remarkably, I only say decently. Well, I don't think there are many who take care to teach this to their children.
2 June 1954

التربية – Education

The Art of Living – فـن الحيـاة

الحياة بالطريقة الصحيحة

أنتم لا تُعلَّمُـون إلا أقـل القليـل — لدرجـة أنكـم لا تُعلَّمُـون حتى الطريقة الصحيحـة للنـوم. يعتقد معظم النـاس أن كل مـا يلزمهم لكـي ينامـوا هو أن يرقدوا في السـرير. ولكن ذلك غير صحيح! ينبغي أن يتعلم المـرء كيفيـة النـوم كما يتعلم كيفية الأكـل وكما يتعلم فعل أي شيء آخـر على الإطـلاق. بديهـي أن المـرء بدون تعليم لا يتقن أفعالـه، أو أنـه ربمـا يحتاج إلى سنوات وسنوات لكـي يـتمكن مـن ذلك، و كم تسبب لـه أعمالـه غير المتقنة مـن المكروهـات في هذه السنوات. وكثيراً مـا نـرى النـاس لا يتعلمـون إلا بعد عناء كبير واقتراف الكثيـر مـن الأخطـاء والحماقـات عندما يصبحون شيوخاً يداخلهم الشيب. في حين لـو كلـَّف الآبـاء أو المُربُّـون أنفسهم مشقة تعليم الأطفـال فـي صغرهم الطريقـة الصحيحة للقيـام بالأعمـال، فـإن ذلك يجنبهم الناشئين الكثيـر مـن الأخطـاء على مـدى السنين. والأدهى مـن ذلك هـو أن النـاس لا يقعون في الأخطـاء فحسـب، بـل أنهم لا يدركون حتى أنها أخطـاء. وبعد ذلك يندهشـون عندما يمرضـون أو عنـدما يحسـون بالتعـب وعنـدما يجدون أنهـم لا يعلمـون حتى مـاذا يريـدون أن يفعلـوه. أمـا الأطفـال الـذين لا يتلقون أي تعليم على الإطـلاق، فهم يحتـاجون إلى سنوات عديدة لكي يتعلموا أبسط الأشياء البدائية مثل النظافة.

في معظـم الأحـوال يرجـع هـذا التقصيـر فـي تعليم الأطفـال إلى جهـل الآبـاء أنفسهم. فهم أنفسـهم لـم يجدوا مـن يُعلِّـمَهم واضطروا بدورهم إلى التخبط في طويـلاً في الظلام لكـي يتعلمـوا كيف ينبغي أن يعيشـوا. وطبيعـي أنهـم لا يسـتطيعون تعليم أطفـالهم مـا هـم أنفسـهم يجهلـون. وهكـذا [الأم مخاطبـة الأطفـال] فـإنكم لـو تُركتم لأنفسكم كليـاً، سـوف تحتـاجون إلى سنين عديدة مـن التجـارب لكـي تتعلمـوا أبسـط الأشيـاء، وحتـى فـي تلـك الحالـة سيكون لزامـاً عليكم أن تتـزوّروا وتفكروا فـي الأمـور، لأنكـم، بدون رؤية وتفكر لن تتعلموا أبداً.

الحيـاة بالطريقـة الصحيحـة فـن صعـب للغايـة، و مـا لـم يتعلم المـرء هـذا الفـن فـي سـن مبكـر، ويبـذل الجهـد فـي تعلمـه، فـأن المـرء لا يجيد هـذا الفن. اعتبر أبسـط الأمـور مثل الاحتفـاظ بالبـدن في صحـة طيبـة وتهدئـة الـذهن وزرع النوايا السـليمة في القلب — وكلهـا أمـور لا غنـى عنهـا لكـي يعيـش المـرء حيـاة كريمـة — لاحظ إنني لا أقول حياة مريحـة أو حيـاة بـاهرة، بـل حيـاة كريمـة لا أكثـر مـن ذلك. لا أعتقد أن الكثيرين يهتمون بتعليم أطفالهم هذه البديهيات.

2 يونيو 1954

Education – التــربية

Distinguishing between Good and Evil – التمييز بين الخير والشر

The Aspiration towards Perfection

There is another quality that must be cultivated in a child from very young age: that is the feeling of uneasiness, of a moral unbalance which it feels when it has done certain things, not because it has been told not to do them, not because it fears punishment, but spontaneously. For example, a child who hurts its comrades through mischief, if it is in the normal, natural state, will experience uneasiness, a grief deep in its being, because what it has done is contrary to its inner truth.

For in spite of all teachings, in spite of all that thought can think, there is something in the depths which has the feeling of a perfection, a greatness, a truth, and is painfully contradicted by all the movements opposing this truth. If a child has not been spoiled by its milieu, by deplorable examples around it, that is, if it is in the normal state, spontaneously, without it being told anything, it will an uneasiness when it has done something against the truth of its being. And it is exactly upon this that later its effort for progress must be founded.

For if you want to find one teaching, one doctrine upon which to base your progress, you will never find anything — or, to be more exact, you will find something else, for in accordance with the climate, the age, the civilization, the teaching given is quite conflicting. When one person says, "This is good", another will say, "No, this is bad", and with the same logic, the same persuasive force. Consequently, it is not upon this that one can build. Religion has always tried to establish a dogma, and it will tell you that if you conform to the dogma you are in the truth and if you don't you are in the falsehood. But all this has never led to anything and has only created confusion.

There is one true guide, that is the inner guide, who does not pass through the mental consciousness.

التمييز بين الخير والـشر – Distinguishing between Good and Evil

التوق إلى الكمـال

هنـاك صفـة أخـرى يجب أن ننميهـا فـي الطفل فـي سن مبكـر، ألا وهـي الشـعور بعـدم الارتيـاح وبـوخز الضـمير عنـدما يفعل أشيـاء معينـة مثـل أذيـة الغيـر، بشـرط أن يـأتي هـذا الشـعور مـن داخلـه تلقائيـاً ولـيس لمجـرد أن هـذه الأشيـاء ممنوعـة أو لأنـه يخشـى العقوبـة. الطفـل الـذي يضـر برفقـائه مـن بـاب الشيطنة وحب الأذية يشـعر فـي الحالـة الطبيعيـة المعتـادة بـالغم وعـدم الارتيـاح فـي أعمـاق كيانـه لأن هذه التصرفات تناقض حقيقته الداخلية.

فـي أعمـاق الانسـان، علـى الـرغم ممـا تقولـه بعـض التعـاليم ومـا يزعمـه بعـض المفكريـن، تـوق إلـى الكمـال والعظمـة والحقيقـة، وهـذا التـوق يجعلـه يتـألم مـن جميـع الحركـات التـي تناقـض حقيقـة كيانـه. طالمـا أن الطفـل لا يحـاط فـي الوسـط الـذي يعيـش فيـه بأمثلـة مؤسفة تفسـده، أي طالمـا أنـه يعيـش فـي ظـروف طبيعيـة، نجـد أنـه يشـعر، تلقائيـاً وبـدون أي إيعـاز مـن الآخريـن، بـالحرج وعـدم الارتيـاح عنـدما يفعل شـيئاً يناقـض حقيقـة كيانـه. هـذا الشـعور هـو بالتحديـد الأسـاس الـذي يجـب أن يبنـي عليـه الطفل فيما بعد جهوده نحو التقدم.

لـو كنـت تأمـل فـي أن تجـد نظامـاً وحيـداً مـن التعـاليم أو مـذهباً واحـداً يصلـح أن يكـون أساسـاً لتقدمك، فإنـك لـن تجـد مـا تريـده. فالتعـاليم المختلفـة تتضـارب وتختلـف كثيـراً فيمـا بينهـا تبعـاً للجـو والزمـان والحضـارة التـي نشـأت فيهـا. وكثيـراً مـا يُعتبـر نفـس الشـيء فـي بعـض التعـاليم خيـراً، فـي حيـن تجـده تعـاليم أخـرى شـراً، وكثيـراً مـا تـدافع هـذه التعـاليم عـن وجهـات نظـر متضـاربة بـنفس قـوة الإقنـاع وبـنفس المنطـق. هـذا التعـاليم لا تصـح أن تكـون أساسـاً نبنـي عليـه. حاولـت الأديـان دائمـا فـرض نظـم مـن العقـائد الجامـدة أعلنـت أن مـن يلتـزم بهـا يكـون فـي الحـق ومـن يخالفهـا يكـون فـي الباطـل. ولكـن كل ذلك لم يؤد على مدى تاريخها الطويل إلا إلى التشوش والاضطراب.

المرشد الوحيد الذي لا يضل هو المرشد الباطني الذي يتخطى الوعي الذهني.

Education – الـتـربية

Naturally, if a child gets a disastrous education, it will try ever harder to extinguish within itself this little true thing, and sometimes it succeeds so well that it loses all contact with it, and also the power of distinguishing between good and evil. That is why I insist upon this, and I say that from their infancy children must be taught that there is an inner reality — within themselves, within the earth, within the universe — and that they, the earth and the universe exist only as a function of this truth, and that if it did not exist the child would not last, even the short time that it does, and that everything would dissolve even as it comes into being. And because this is the real basis of the universe, naturally it is this that will triumph: and all that opposes this cannot endure as long as this does, because it is That, the eternal thing which is at the base of the universe.

It is not a question, of course, of giving a child philosophical explanations, but he could very well be given the feeling of this kind of inner comfort, of satisfaction, and sometimes, of an inner joy when he obeys this little very silent thing within him which will prevent him from doing what is contrary to it. It is on an experience of this kind that teaching may be based. The child must be given the impression that nothing can endure if he does not have within himself this true satisfaction which alone is permanent.

Can a child become conscious of this inner truth like an adult?

For a child this is very clear, for it is a perception without any complication of word or thought — there is that puts him at ease and that which makes him uneasy (it is not necessarily joy or sorrow which come only when the thing is very intense). And all this is much clearer in the child than in an adult, for the latter has always a mind which works and clouds his perception of the truth. To give a child theories is absolutely useless, for as soon as his mind awakes he will find a thousand reasons for contradicting your theories, and he will be right.

This little true thing in the child is the divine presence in the psychic* — it is also there in plants and animals. In plants it is not very conscious. In animals it begins to be conscious, and in children it is very conscious. I have known children who were much more conscious of their psychic being* at the age of five than at fourteen, and at fourteen than at twenty-five; and above all, from the moment they go to school where they undergo that kind of intensive mental training which draw their attention to the intellectual part of their being, they lose almost always and almost completely this contact with their psychic being.

التربية – Education

عندما تكون تربية الطفل مأساوية، نجده يحاول أكثر فأكثر أن يخمد في نفسه صوت المرشد الداخلي الخافت الحق، وأحياناً ينجح في ذلك إلى درجة أن يفقد كل صلة به، وبذلك يفقد القدرة على التمييز بين الخير والشر. هذا هو السبب في أني أصمم على ضرورة توعية الأطفال في سن مبكر بوجود هذه الحقيقة الداخلية — بداخلهم، وبداخل الأرض وداخل الكون — وبأنهم والأرض والكون لا يتواجدون إلا بفضل هذه الحقيقة وكتوابع لها، وبأنه إذا لم توجد هذه الحقيقة، لن يمكنهم أن يستمروا في الحياة حتى الفترة القصيرة التي يعيشوها، وبدونها تتلاشى جميع الأشياء وتنحل بمجرد دخولها في عالم الوجود. هذه الحقيقة هي الأساس الحقيقي الأبدي الذي ينبني عليه الكون، ومن الطبيعي أنها ستنتصر في النهاية، وكل ما يعارضها سيكون مصيره الزوال.

ذلك لا يعني بالطبع أننا يجب أن نشرح كل ذلك للطفل فلسفياً، بل يجب أن نساعده على إدراك الراحة الداخلية والرضا والبهجة التي سينالها إذا ما أطاع هذا الشيء الصغير الساكن الصامت بداخله، هذا الشيء الذي يمنعه من أن يخالف حقيقة كيانه. هذا هو نوع التجارب التي يمكن أن نؤسس تربية الطفل عليها. يجب أن يفهم الطفل تدريجياً أن الأشياء لا دوام لها ما لم يشعر بداخله بهذا الرضا الحقيقي الذي وحده له الدوام.

هل يمكن أن يكون الطفل واعياً بحقيقته الداخلية مثل الشخص البالغ؟

الطفل يستطيع بسهولة أن يعي حقيقته الداخلية بنوع من الفطنة التي لا تتوقف على كلمات أو أفكار — فالطفل يقدر على تمييز ما يسبب له الراحة وما يسبب له عدم الارتياح (إنه شعور مرهف وليس بالضرورة على نفس الدرجة من القوة مثل مشاعر البهجة أو الأسى). بل أن هذا التمييز أسهل بالنسبة للأطفال لأن أذهانهم لا تعمل بنفس النشاط الذي تعمل به في البالغين، والنشاط الذهني هو الذي يعتم الحقيقة. لا فائدة من فرض نظريات على الطفل، لأنه سيجد، بمجرد أن يستيقظ ذهنه، آلاف الأعذار والطرائق لكي يناقض هذه النظريات، ولا لوم عليه لو فعل ذلك.

هذا الإحساس الخافت بالحق بداخل الطفل هو الحضرة الإلهية في كيانه السيكي* — وهي حاضرة كذلك في النبات وفي الحيوان. الوعي بالحضرة الإلهية يبدأ في النبات، ويصبح ملحوظاً في الحيوان وملموساً تماماً في الأطفال. عرفت قوماً كان وعيهم بكيانهم السيكي في سن الخامسة يفوق وعيهم به عندما بلغوا الرابعة عشر، وكان وعيهم في الرابعة عشر يفوق وعيهم به في الخامسة والعشرين؛ ولاحظت في كثير من الأحوال أن الأطفال بمجرد أن يلتحقوا بإحدى المدارس التي تشدد على التربية الذهنية وتركز انتباههم على الجزء العقلي من كيانهم يفقدون صلتهم بكيانهم السيكي بصورة تكاد تكون تامة.

110

Education – التــربية

If only you were an experienced observer, if you could tell what goes on in a person, simply by looking into his eyes!... It is said that the eyes are the mirrors of the soul; that is a popular way of speaking but if the eyes do not express to you the psychic, it is because it is very far behind , veiled by many things. Look carefully, then, into the eyes of little children, and you will see a kind of light — some describe it as frank — but so true, so true, which looks at the world with wonder. Well, this sense of wonder, it is the wonder of the psychic which sees the truth but do not understand much about the world, for it is too far from it. Children have this but as they learn more, become more intelligent, more educated, this is effaced, and you see all sorts of things in their eyes: thoughts, desires, passions, wickedness — but this kind of little flame, so pure, is no longer there. And you may be sure it is the mind that has got in there, and the psychic has gone very far behind.

Even a child who does not have a sufficiently developed brain to understand, if you simply pass on to him a vibration of protection or affection or solicitude or consolation, you will see that he responds. But if you take a boy of fourteen, for example, who is at school, who has ordinary parents and has been ill-treated, his mind is very much in the forefront; there is something hard in him, the psychic being has gone behind. Such boys do not respond to the vibration. One would say they are made of wood or plaster.

If the inner truth, the divine presence in the psychic is so conscious in the child, it could no longer be said that a child is a little animal, could it?

Why not? In animals there is sometimes a very intense psychic truth. Naturally, I believe that the psychic being is a little more formed, a little more conscious in a child than in an animal. But I have experimented with animals, just to know; well, I assure you that in human beings I have rarely come across some of the virtues which I have seen in animals, very simple, unpretentious virtues. As in cats, for example:

التربية – Education

ليتكم كنتم ضليعين في فن الملاحظة وكنتم قادرين على أن تستشفوا ما ذا يدور بداخل الناس بمجرد النظر في أعينهم!... الحكمة الشائعة تقول إن الأعين هي مرآة الروح... ولكننا نعجز كثيراً عن استشفاف الروح في أعين بعض الناس، وما ذلك إلا لأن روحهم قد توارت إلى الخلف وحُجبت وراء العديد من الأشياء. إذا نظرت بعناية في أعين الأطفال، سترى ضوءً، يصفه البعض بأنه ضوء الصراحة والصدق، وهو بالفعل ضوء ينبع من صدق خالص ينظر إلى العالم في دهشة. دهشة الكيان السيكي* [الروح] تأتي من أنه يعلم الحقيقة ويجد أن واقع عالمنا يخالفها. أعين الأطفال الصغار تشع هذا الضوء، ولكن بنمو الأطفال في التعلم والذكاء والخبرة يفقدون الضوء تدريجياً، وعندئذ ترى في أعينهم خليطاً من جميع الأشياء: أفكار، رغبات، عواطف متقدة، بل وأحياناً بعض الخبث وحب الشر — أي أن هذا اللهب الصغير النقي لم يعد يسطع من خلال أعينهم. من المؤكد في هذه الحالة أن تَدَخُّل الذهن هو الذي دفع بالكيان السيكي إلى الخلف.

لو منحت طفلاً، حتى لو كان يفتقد النمو الذهني الكافي للفهم، بعض الحماية أو الود أو العناية الحانية أو العزاء، فإنه يتجاوب معها. ولكنك لو فعلت المثل مع صبي مراهق يتعلم في مدرسة، وينتمي إلى أبوين عاديين أساءوا معاملته، ستجد أن النشاط الذهني في الصبي قد أصبح في مقدمة كيانه وأن كيانه السيكي قد توارى إلى الخلف وستلاحظ في الصبي بعض الجمود والقسوة. أحياناً لا يبدي مثل هذا الصبي استجابة مع ما تقدمه له من عطف أو ود كما لو كان قد شق من حجر أو صنع من جبس.

لو كان الطفل قادراً على وعي حقيقته الداخلية أو الحضرة الإلهية في كيانه السيكي، هل يصح بعد ذلك أن يقال أن الطفل حيوان صغير؟*

وماذا يمنع من ذلك؟ كثيراً ما تكون الحقيقة السيكية واضحة إلى حد بعيد في الحيوانات. أنا لا أنكر أن الأطفال أكثر وعياً بكيانهم السيكي من الحيوانات وأن كيانهم السيكي أكثر تبلوراً. استناداً على تجارب قمت بها مع بعض الحيوانات لتوضيح هذه النقطة، أؤكد لك أني وجدت في الحيوانات فضائل قلما وجدتها في البشر لأنها فضائل بسيطة لا ادعاء فيها. خذ القطط، على سبيل المثال.

Education – التــربية

I have studied cats a lot; if one knows they, well, they are marvelous creatures. I have known mother-cats which have sacrificed themselves entirely for their babies — people speak of maternal love with such admiration, as though it were purely a human privilege, but I have seen this love manifested by mother-cats to a degree far surpassing ordinary humanity. I have seen a mother-cat which would never touch her food until her babies had taken all they needed. I have seen another cat which stayed eight days beside her kittens, without satisfying any of her needs because she was afraid to leave them alone; and a cat which repeated more than fifty times the same movement to teach her young to jump from a wall unto a window, and I may add, with a care, an intelligence, a skill which many uneducated women do not have. And why is it thus? — because there was no mental intervention. It was altogether spontaneous instinct. But what is instinct? — it is the presence of the Divine in the genus of the species, and that, that is the psychic* of animals; a collective, not an individual psychic.

I have seen in animals all the reactions, emotional, affective, sentimental, all the feelings of which men are proud. The only difference is that animals cannot speak of them and write about them, so we consider them inferior beings because they cannot flood us with books on what they have felt.

When I was a child if I did something bad immediately I felt uneasy and I would decide never to do that again. Then my parents also used to tell me never again to do it. Why? Because I had myself decided not to do it anymore?

A child should never be scolded. I am accused of speaking ill of parents! But I have seen them at work, you see, and I know that ninety percent of parents snub a child who comes spontaneously to confess a mistake: "You are very naughty. Go away, I am busy" — instead of listening to the child with patience and explaining to him where his fault lies, how he ought to have acted. And the child who had come with good intentions, goes away quite hurt, with the feeling: "Why am I treated thus?" Then the child sees his parents are not perfect — which is obviously true of them today — he sees that they are wrong and says to himself: "Why does he scold me, he is like me!"
8 January, 1951

التربية – Education

درست القطط دراسة مستفيضة؛ ووجدت إننا عندما نعرفها معرفة جيدة، نكتشف إنها مخلوقات رائعة. عرفت أمهات قطط ضحت بأنفسها كلياً في سبيل أطفالها الرضيعة — الناس يتحدثون عن حب الأم كما لو كان حباً يقتصر على البشر، ولكني وجدت حب الأمومة في القطط يفوق كثيراً حب الأمومة في البشر العاديين. عرفت قطة أم لم تكن تمس الطعام على الإطلاق حتى يأخذ أطفالها كل كفايتهم. ورأيت قطة أخرى بقيت بجوار أطفالها ثمانية أيام خوفاً من تركهم وحدهم بدون أن تشبع أو ترضي أياً من حاجاتها الطبيعية. كما شاهدت قطة تكرر أكثر من خمسين مرة نفس الحركة لتعلم صغارها القفز من حائط إلى نافذة مقابلة، وقد فعلت ذلك بعناية وذكاء ومهارة لا تتوفر في كثير من النساء غير المتعلمات. لو بحثنا عن السبب في هذا التفوق في الحيوان، نجد أنه يرجع إلى أن الحيوان لا يعاني من التدخل الذهني بنفس درجة الإنسان، فهو يتصرف بدافع من الغريزة التلقائية. ولكن ما هي تلك الغريزة؟ إنها الحضرة الإلهية في النوع او الفصيلة، وهذه الحضرة هي الكيان السيكي في الحيوان: وهو كيان جماعي، وليس كياناً فردياً.

لاحظت أن الحيوانات قادرة على جميع الأحاسيس العاطفية والوجدانية التي يفتخر بها البشر. الفارق الوحيد هو أن الحيوانات لا تستطيع التكلم عن هذه المشاعر أو على وصفها كتابةً، ونحن نعتبرهم كائنات أقل درجة منا لأنهم لا يمطرون علينا وابلاً من الكتب التي تصف مشاعرهم!

في طفولتي كنت إذا ما فعلت فعلاً شريراً أشعر للتو بعدم الارتياح وأعقد العزم على ألا أعود إلى مثل هذا الفعل أبداً. ولكن والداي كانا ينهياني بدورهم عن هذا الفعل. فما هو السبب في هذا النهي بعد أن قررت أنا نفسي الامتناع؟

يجب ألا ننهر الأطفال أبداً. يتهمني البعض بأني أظلم الآباء. ولكني راقبت الآباء في تعاملهم مع أطفالهم ولاحظت أنهم في تسعين في المائة من الأحوال يزجرون طفلهم إذا ما أتى ليعترف تلقائياً بخطئه ويقولون له: "إنك طفل سيء السلوك. اذهب ولا تزعجنا، فنحن مشغولون الآن" — بدلاً من أن يستمعوا له بصبر ويشرحوا ويبينوا له طبيعة خطئه و يبينوا له الفعل الصائب الذي كان ينبغي أن يفعله. وهكذا يذهب الطفل الذي أتى بنوايا سليمة وقد جُرحت مشاعره ويتعجب: "لماذا يعاملني أبواي بهذه الطريقة؟" ثم أن الطفل كثيراً ما يرى عيوب والديه — وكم من العيوب سنرى في البالغين لو نظرنا حولنا — ويتساءل: "لماذا ينهرني أبواي مع أنهما يقترفان أخطاء مثلي تماماً؟"

8 يناير، 1951

114

Education – التـربية

Learning to Know Oneself — اعـرف نـفسـك

The true Reason for Living

Essentially there is but one single true reason for living: it is to know oneself. We are here to learn — to learn what we are, why we are here, and what we have to do. And if we don't know that, out life is altogether empty — for ourselves and for others.

And so, generally, it is better to begin early, for there is much to learn. If one wants to learn about life as it is, the world as it is, and then really know the why and the how of life, one can begin when very young, from the time one is very, very tiny — before the age of five. And then, when one is hundred, he will still be able to learn. So it is interesting. And all the time one can have surprises, always learn something one didn't know, meet with an experience one did not have before, find something one was ignorant of. It is surely very interesting. And the more one knows, the more aware does one become that one has everything to learn. Truly, I could say that only fools believe they know.

3 February, 1954

Learning to Know Oneself — اعرف نفسك

السبب الحقيقي للحياة

أساساً، هناك سبب واحد حقيقي للحياة: أن نعرف أنفسنا. لقد أتينا على ظهر الأرض لنكتشف من نحن و ما السبب في وجودنا هنا وما هو العمل المطلوب منا؛ بدون تلك المعرفة تكون حياتنا فارغة وخالية من أي معنى بالنسبة لنا وبالنسبة للآخرين.

من الأفضل أن نبدأ مبكرين بالتعلم، لأن ما ينبغي أن نتعلمه كثير. لو أردنا أن نعرف حقيقة الحياة ومُسَوّغاتها وطبيعتها وأن نفهم العالم كما هو في الواقع، أي نبدأ بالتعلم قبل عامنا الخامس ولا نكف عن التعلم حتى لو بلغنا مائة عام. أن نتعلم أشياء لم نكن نعلمها من قبل ونمر بخبرات لم نمر بها سابقاً ونكتشف أشياء كنا نجهل وجودها: هذا هو ما يجعل الحياة مشوقة وزاخرة بالمفاجآت. كلما ارتفعنا في المعرفة، كلما أدركنا أن ما نجهله يفوق كثيراً ما نعلمه. أستطيع أن أقول بحق إن الذين يعتقدون إنهم على علم لا بد أن يكونوا سفهاء..

3 فبراير، 1954

Education – الـــتربية

Learning as a Choice, not a Compulsion – التعلم اختياراً لا إرغاماً

The Right to Choose

I think it was just today or perhaps yesterday, I was pleading for the right of everyone to remain in ignorance if it pleases him…. I am not speaking of ignorance from the spiritual point of view, the world of Ignorance in which we live, I am not speaking of that. I am speaking of ignorance according to the classical ideas of education. Well, I say that if there are people who don't want to learn and don't like to learn they have the right not to learn.

The only thing it is our duty to tell them is this, "Now, you are of an age when your brain is in course of preparation. It is being formed. Each new thing you study makes one more little convolution in your brain. The more you study, the more you think, the more you reflect, the more you work, the more complex and complete does your brain become in its tiny convolutions. And as you are young, it is best done at this time. That is why it is common human practice to choose youth as the period of learning, for it is infinitely easier." And it is obvious that until the child becomes at least a little conscious of itself, it must be subjected to a certain rule, for it has not yet the capacity of choosing for itself.

The age is very variable; it depends on people, depends on each individual. But still, it is understood that in the seven-year period between the age of seven and fourteen, one begins to reach the age of reason. If one is helped, one can become a reasoning being between seven and fourteen.

Before seven there are geniuses — there are always geniuses, everywhere — but as a general rule the child is not conscious of itself and doesn't know why or how to do things. That is the time to cultivate its attention, teach it to concentrate on what it does, give it a small basis sufficient for it not to be entirely like a little animal, but to belong to the human race through an elementary intellectual development.

After that there is a period of seven years during which it must be taught to choose — to choose what it wants to be. If it chooses to have a rich, complex, well-developed brain, powerful in its functioning, well, it must be taught to work; for it is by work, by reflection, study, analysis and so on that the brain is formed. At fourteen you are ready — or ought to be ready —to know what you want to be.

التعلم اختياراً لا إرغاما – Learning as a Choice, not a Compulsion

حـق الاختيـار

دافعت اليـوم، أو ربما كـان ذلك بـالأمس، عـن حـق الأفـراد فـي أن يظلـوا جهلاء إذا كانـت تلك هـي رغبتهم... أنـا لا أتكلـم هنا عمـا يسميه العـالمون بـأمور الـروح جهـلاً (أي الجهـل بأسمى لـمعارف الروحيـة)، بـل أعنـي الجهـل حسب مفهـوم التربيـة الشـائعة [فـي المـدارس والجامعـات]. أقـول أنـه لـو كان قوم لا يريدون أو لا يحبون أن يتعلموا، لا يصح أن نرغمهم على التعلم.

ومـع ذلك، فـإن مـن واجبنا أن نحـث صغـار السـن على التعلم بـأن نقول للتلميـذ: "مخك فـي هـذا السن المبكـر مـا يـزال فـي مرحلـة الإعـداد والتكـوين، وكـل شـيء جديـد تتعلمـه يخلـق تلفيفـاً مخبـأ جديـداً يضـاف إلـى تلافيـف مخك. كلما أكثـرت مـن الدراسـة أو التفكير أو الاستقصاء أو العمـل كلمـا زادت تلافيف مخك شمـولاً وكمـالاً. السـن المبكـر هـو السـن المناسب للتعلم وقد أجمع النـاس على أن التعلم فـي سـن مبكـرة أسـهل كثيـراً منـه في سـن متقدمـة". مـن الواضـح أن الطفـل طالمـا لـم يبلـغ علـى الأقـل درجـة معينـة مـن الـوعي بالنفس، فإنـه لا يقـدر علـى الاختيـار لنفسـه ويجب أن يخضع لبعض التوجيـه والإرشاد.

لـو تساءلنا عـن العمـر الـذي يبلـغ فيـه الطفـل هـذه الدرجـة مـن الـوعي والإدراك، نجـده يختلـف كثيـراً وانـه يتوقـف علـى الأفـراد أنفسـهم. لكن مـن المتعارف عليـه أن الطفـل، مـع بعض العـون وامساعدة، يبلـغ هذا الإدراك ويصبـح كيانـاً عاقلاً بين السابعة والرابعة عشر.

الطفـل، بصفـة عامـة، قبـل سـن السـابعة لا يكـون واعيـاً بنفسـه ولا يعلـم أسـباب الأمـور أو كيفيـة أدائهـا، باستثناء العبـاقرة منـهم (العبـاقرة يتواجـدون فـي كـل مكـان). السـابعة إذاً هـي السـن المناسـب لتنميـة ملكـة الانتبـاه في الطفـل ولتعليمـه التركيز على مـا يفعل، ولإعطائه الأسـاس الكـافي لكـي يرتفـع فـوق مرتبة الحيوان الصغير ولينضم، عن طريق النمو الذهني، إلى سائر الجنس البشري.

تـلي ذلك فتـرة سـبع سنوات يجب أن يتعلم فيها الطفل كيف يختار: أن يختـار مـا ذا يريد أن يصبح. لـو اختـار أن يمتلـك ذهنـاً نامـياً، متعـدد النـواحي وقويـاً فـي نشـاطه، لابـد إذاً أن ننصـحه بالعمـل والاجتهاد؛ فالذهن ينمو عـن طريق العمل وإعمال الفكر والدراسة والتحليل وما شابه ذلك فـي سن الرابعـة عشـر يصبـح الطفـل — أو يتوقـع أن يكـون الطفـل — مسـتعداً وقـادراً علـى أن يختـار مـا ذا يريد أن يكون في مستقبله.

Education – التـربية

And so I say: if at about that age some children declare categorically, "Intellectual growth does not interest me at all, I don't want to learn, want to remain ignorant in the ordinary way of ignorance", I do not see by what right one could impose studies on them nor why it should be necessary to standardize them.

There are those who are at the bottom and others who are at another level. There are people who may have very remarkable capacities and yet have no taste for intellectual growth. One may warn them that if they don't work, don't study, when they are grown up, they will perhaps feel embarrassed in front of others. But if that does not matter to them and they want to live a non-intellectual life, I believe one has no right to compel them. That is my constant quarrel with the teachers of the [Ashram] school! They come and tell me" "If they do don't work, when they are grown up they will be stupid and ignorant. I say: "But if it pleases them to be stupid and ignorant, what right have you to interfere?" One can't make knowledge and intelligence compulsory. That's all.

Now, if you believe that by abstaining from all effort and all study, you will become geniuses and supramental geniuses at that, don't have any illusions, it won't happen to you. For even if you touch a higher light, through an inner aspiration or by a divine grace, you will remain quite nebulous and won't in any way change your outer life. But if it pleases you to be like this, nobody has the right to compel you to be otherwise. You must wait till you are sufficiently conscious to be able to choose.

Of course, there are people who at fourteen are yet like children of five. But these — there's little hope for them. Especially those who have lived here.

Here's something then which already changes your outlook on education completely.

Essentially, *the only thing* you should do assiduously is to teach them to know themselves and choose their own destiny, the path they will follow; to teach them to look at themselves, understand themselves *and* to will what they want to be. That is infinitely more important than teaching them what happened on earth in former times, or even how the earth is built, or even… indeed all sorts of things which are quite a necessary grounding if you want to live the ordinary life in the world, for if you don't know them, anyone will immediately put you down intellectually: "Oh, he is an idiot, he knows nothing."

التربية – Education

ولـذلك أقـول: لـو قـرر طفـل فـي هـذا العمـر وقـال بصـورة قاطعـة: "النمـو العقلـي لا يشَـوّقني علـى الإطـلاق، وأنـا لا أرغـب فـي التعلم، ولا أمـانع فـي أن أظـل جـاهلاً بـالمواد التـي تعلمهـا المـدارس"، فـإني لا أرى مـن أيـن يكـون لنـا الحـق فـي أن نعتبـر تعليـم [المـدارس] معيـاراً لا يصـح الحيـاد عنـه، ونفرض هذا التعليم عليه ضد رغبته.

الناس يختلفون فـي مسـتوياتهم وبعضهـم قـد تكـون لهـم طاقـات ومواهـب رائعـة علـى الـرغم مـن أنهـم لا يجـدون أي تشـويق فـي النمـو العقلـي. هـؤلاء يمكننـا أن نحـذرهم ونـوعيهم بـأنهم لـو لـم يعملـوا ويدرسـوا، فربمـا يشـعرون عنـدما يكبـرون، بـالإحراج والخجـل فـي صحبـة الآخرين. فلـو لـم يكـن لهـذا العامـل أي أهميـة بالنسـبة لهـم وكـانوا يريـدون أن يعيشـوا حيـاة غيـر حيـاة الفكـر والثقافـة، أعتقـد أننـا لا نملـك الحـق فـي إرغامهـم. هـذه النقطـة محـل خـلاف مسـتمر بينـي وبيـن مدرسـي مدرسـة الأشـرام* الـذين يـأتون إلـي قـائلين: "لـو لـم يعمـل التلاميـذ، سيصبحون أغبيـاء وجهـلاء عنـدما يكبـرون". وأنـا أرد عليهـم: "إذا كـانوا يحبـون أن يكونـوا أغبيـاء وجهـلاء، مـن أيـن لكـم الحـق فـي التدخل؟" النقطـة الأساسية هنا هي أن المعرفة والذكاء لا يأتيان بالإرغام.

[في الفقرة التاليـة توجـه الأم الحـديث إلـى التلاميـذ] لـو كنتـم تعتقـدون أنكـم، بامتنـاعكم عـن بـذل الجهـد وعـن الدراسـة، سـتصبحون عباقـرة أو حتـى عباقـرة تخطـوا مرحلـة العقـل إلـى مرحلـة "مـا بعـد العقـل"، فأنصـحكم بـأن تتخلـوا عـن هـذه الأوهـام، فـذلك لـن يحـدث لكـم. لأنكـم حتـى لـو توصلتـم، عـن طريـق التـوق أو بفضـل العنايـة الإلهيـة، إلـى نـور أعلـى، سـتظلون فـي غيـام ولـن يمكنكـم أن تغيـروا حيـاتكم بـأي صـورة. لـو كـان هـذا يَسُـرُّكم، فليـس لأي شـخص الحـق فـي إرغـامكم. ولكـن يجـب أن تنتظـروا حتى تصبحوا واعيين بأنفسكم إلى درجة تمكنكم من الاختيار.

بعـض الشـباب يظلـون حتـى عـامهم الرابـع عشـر مثـل أطفـال فـي عـامهم الخامـس. بالنسـبة لهـؤلاء الأمـل ضعيف [في أن يكونوا قادرين على الوعي والاختيار]، خاصة للذين نشأوا هنا منهم.

[في الفقـرة التاليـة توجـه الأم حـديثها إلـى مدرسـي ومدرسـات مدرسـة الأشـرام] مـا قلنـاه حتـى الآن كافٍ لتغيير نظرتكم إلى التربية تغييراً كلياً.

أساسـاً، الشـيء الوحيـد الـذي يجـب أن تحرصـوا علـى تعليمـه الأطفـال هـو أن يعرفـوا أنفسـهم وكيـف يختـارون مصيـرهم والمسـار الخـاص الـذي سـيتبعونه؛ أن تعلمـوهم أن ينظـروا إلـى أنفسـهم ويفهمـوا أنفسـهم، وأن يختـاروا مـاذا يريـدون أن يصبحـوا فـي المسـتقبل. هـذا أهـم بكثيـر مـن تعليمهـم مـاذا حـدث علـى الأرض فـي الأزمـان السـابقة، وكيفيـة تركيـب الأرض... أي أهـم مـن كـل هـذه الأشـياء التـي تعتبـر أساسـاً ضـرورياً لمـن يرغبـون أن يعيشـوا حيـاة العـالم العاديـة، والتـي بـدونها يكـون المـرء عرضة لاستهزاء الآخرين الذين يعتبرونه أبلهاً جاهلاً.

120

Education – التــربية

But still, at any age, if you are studious and have the will to do it, you can also take up books and work; you don't need to go to school for that. There are enough books in the world to teach you things. There are even many more books than necessary. [...]

But what is very important is to know what you want. And for this a minimum of freedom is necessary. You must not be under a compulsion or an obligation. You must be able to do things wholeheartedly. If you are lazy, well, you will know what it means to be lazy... You know, in life idlers are obliged to work ten times more than others, for what they do they do badly, so they are obliged to do it again. But these are things one must learn by experience. They can't be instilled in you.

The mind, if not controlled, is something wavering and imprecise. If one doesn't have the habit of concentrating it upon something, it goes on wandering all the time. It goes on without a stop anywhere and wanders into a *world* of vagueness. And then, when one wants to fix one's attention, it hurts! There is a little effort there, like this: "Oh! How tiring it is, it hurts!" So one does not do it. And he lives in a kind of cloud. And your head is like a cloud; it's like that, most brains are like clouds: there is no precision, no exactitude, no clarity, it is hazy — vague and hazy. You have impressions rather than a knowledge of things. You live in an approximation, and you can keep within you all sorts of contradictory ideas made up mostly of impressions, sensations, feelings, emotions — all sorts of things like that which have very little to do with thought and ... which are just vague ramblings.

But if you want to succeed in having a precise, concrete, clear, definite thought on a certain subject, you must make an effort, gather yourself together, hold yourself firm, concentrate. And the first time you do it, it literally hurts, it is tiring! But if you don't make a habit of it, all your life will be living in a state of irresolution. And when it comes to practical things, when you are faced with — for, in spite of everything, one is always faced with — a number of problems to solve, of a very practical kind, well, instead of being able to take up the elements of the problem, to put them all face to face, look at the question from every side, and rising above and seeing the solution, instead of that you will be tossed about in the swirls of something grey and uncertain, and it will be like so many spiders running around in your head — but you won't succeed in catching the thing.

Education – التربية

على أي حال، يستطيع المرء في أي عمر، لو كان يميل إلى الدراسة ويرغبها، أن يستعين بالكتب؛ ولا حاجة له لأن يلتحق بمدرسة من أجل ذلك. هناك كتب كافية في العالم للتعليم، بل هناك فائض منها يزيد على الحاجة. [...]

ولكن ما هو في غاية الأهمية هو أن تعرف ما ذا تريد. ومن أجل ذلك يجب ألا تكون خاضعاً لإكراه ولا بد أن يتوفر لك قدر معين من الحرية يتيح لك أن تفعل الأشياء بكل قلبك وبكل حماسك. لو فضلت التكاسل، حسناً، ستكتشف مصير الكسولين... فالحياة تضطر المتثاقلين، الخاملين إلى أن يعملوا عشرة أضعاف ما يعمله الآخرون، ذلك لأنهم لا يتقنون عملهم ويضطرون إلى إعادة ما يفعلون. ولكن هذه أشياء يجب أن تتعلمها بالخبرة ولا يستطيع الغير أن يغرسها فيك.

إذا لم نخضع أذهاننا للتوجيه والتنظيم، تصبح عرضة للتذبذب وعدم الدقة. ولو لم نعودها على التركيز على الأشياء، فإنها تتجول بدون انقطاع من موضوع لآخر وينتابها الغموض. فإذا ما رغبنا في تركيز انتباهنا، نجد التركيز مؤلماً ويتطلب بذل الجهد. وهذا بدوره يصبح سبباً في أننا نصرف النظر عن التركيز كلياً فنصير كالذين يعيشون في السحاب. معظم الأمخاخ ضبابية وغامضة وتفتقد الدقة والوضوح، وبدلاً من أن تتوصل إلى المعرفة، تكتفي بمجرد انطباعات عن الأشياء. وبذلك لا تعرف هذه الأذهان الأمور إلا بصورة تقريبية وتكون زاخرة بجميع أنواع الآراء المتناقضة وبخليط من الانطباعات والأحاسيس والمشاعر والعواطف وبأشياء أخرى من هذا القبيل لا علاقة لها بالفكر ولا تتعدى أن تكون تسكعاً ذهنياً بدون غاية أو نظام.

لكن لو أردنا أن يتسم تفكيرنا في مواضيع معينة بالدقة والتماسك والوضوح والتأكيد، يجب أن نبذل الجهد، وأن نلم أشتاتنا ونطرح التسيب جانباً ونركز. عندما نفعل ذلك لأول مرة، نشعر بالألم والإجهاد. وإذا لم نعود أنفسنا على ذلك، نظل طوال حياتنا في حالة من التردد والتذبذب. فإذا ما صادفتنا مشاكل ذات طابع عملي — وهو ما يحدث دائماً في الحياة — نجدنا عاجزين عن تحليل هذه المشاكل إلى عناصرها والتوفيق بين هذه العناصر والنظر إلى المشكلة من جميع أوجهها وندخل في دوامات معتمة من الالتباس تتقاذفنا في جميع الأنحاء، كما لو كانت هناك أفواج من العناكب تتجول في رؤوسنا.

Education – التـربية

I am speaking of the simplest of problems, you know, I am not speaking of deciding the fate of the world or humanity, or even of a country — nothing of the kind. I am speaking of the problems of your daily life, of every day. They become something quite woolly.

Well, it is to avoid this that you are told, when your brain is in course of being formed, "Instead of letting it be shaped by such habits and qualities, try to give a little exactitude, precision, capacity of concentration, of choosing, deciding, putting things in order, try to use your reason."

Of course, it is well understood that reason is not the supreme capacity of man and must be surpassed, but it is quite obvious that if you don't have it, you will live an altogether incoherent life, you won't even know how to behave rationally. The least thing will upset you completely and you won't even know why, and still less how to remedy it. While someone who has established within himself a state of active, clear reasoning, can face attacks of all kinds, emotional attacks or any trials whatever; for life is entirely made up of these things — unpleasantness, vexations — which are small but proportionate to the one who feels them, and so naturally felt by him as very big because they are proportionate to him. Well, reason can stand back a little, look at all that, smile and say, "Oh! No, one must not make a fuss over such a small thing."

If you do not have any reason, you will be like a cork on a stormy sea. I don't know if the cork suffers from its condition, but it does not seem to me a very happy one.

Now, after having said all this — and it's not just once I have told you this but several times I think, and I am ready to tell it to you again as many times as you like — after having said this, I believe in leaving you entirely free to choose whether you want to be the cork on the stormy sea or whether you want to have a clear, precise perception and a sufficient knowledge of things to be able to walk to — well, simply to where you want to go. For there is a clarity that's indispensable in order to be able even to follow the path one has chosen.

I am not at all keen on your becoming scholars, far from it! For then one falls into the other extreme: one fills one's head with so many things that there is no longer any room for the higher light; but there is a minimum that is indispensable for not... well, for not being the cork.

Education – التربية

أتحدث هنا عن شئون عادية، ولست أتحدث عن تقرير مصير العالم أو الإنسانية أو حتى مصير بلد واحد — لا أعني أي شيء من هذا القبيل. ما أعنيه هو مشاكل الحياة اليومية. الذهن غير المدرب يجد أبسط المشاكل غامضة ومبهمة.

[الأم تعود إلى مخاطبة التلاميذ] لتجنب هذا الغموض نقول لكم حين تكون أمخاخكم ما زالت في مرحلة التكوين: "بدلاً من أن تتركوا أذهانكم عرضة للتشتت والالتباس، مرّنوها على شيء من الدقة ولا تحرموها من القدرة على التركيز والانتقاء واتخاذ القرارات ووضع الأمور في مكانها الصحيح. باختصار، حاولوا أن تستغلوا قدرتكم على التفكير."

من المفهوم هنا بالطبع، أن القدرة على التفكير ليست أعظم طاقات الإنسان وأنه يجب تخطيها، ولكن واضح أيضاً أن حياتكم بدونها تكون مشوشة تماماً لدرجة أنكم تصبحوا عاجزين عن التصرف بطريقة منطقية وتكونوا عرضة للانزعاج من أقل الشيء بدون أن تفهموا حتى سبب هذا الانزعاج، ناهيكم عن أن تتمكنوا من على علاج الموقف. أما الذين رَسَّخُوا في أنفسهم القدرة على التفكير والتعقل، فإنهم يستطيعون مواجهة جميع أنواع الهجمات، عاطفية أو غير ذلك فالحياة مشحونة بأسباب الغيظ والنكد والمضايقات — أمور صغيرة في حد ذاتها ولكن من يشعر بها يجدها كبيرة للغاية وأكثر من طاقته. ذو العقل يستطيع أن يتراجع قليلاً ويراقب الموقف ويبتسم قائلاً، "كلا، لا ضرورة للاضطراب على مثل هذه التوافه."

بدون القدرة على التفكير المنطقي يصبح المرء مثل فلينة طافية على بحر عاصف. لا أعلم مشاعر الفلينة في مثل هذا الوضع، ولكنه لا يبدو لي وضعاً سعيداً على أي حال!

والآن، وبعد أن أخبرتكم بكل ذلك — وتلك ليست المرة الأولى، بل أعتقد إني قلته مرات عديدة من قبل، ومستعدة لتكراره كلما رغبتم في ذلك — أعتقد إني أوضحت نيتي على منحكم الحرية الكاملة لتختاروا بين أن تكونوا الفلينة على البحر العاصف أو أن تكونوا ذوي بصائر مستنيرة ودقيقة وعلم كافٍ بالأمور يمنحكم القدرة على الخطو نحو الهدف الذي ترغبون في الوصول إليه. فالبصيرة المستنيرة شرط لا غنى عنه لكي يتمكن المرء من الخطو نحو هدفه المنشود.

لا أعلق أهمية خاصة على أن انقطاعكم للدراسة والتعمق، بل إني بعيدة كل البعد عن ذلك. لأنكم في تلك الحالة تتطرفون إلى الناحية الأخرى وتملئون رؤوسكم بأشياء كثيرة لا تدع أي مجال للنور الأعلى لأن يدخل فيها. المهم هو أن تحوزوا حداً أدنى من المعرفة يتيح لكم أن تتجنبوا مصير الفلينة التي تلعب بها الأمواج.

124

Education – التـــربية

Mother, some say that our general inadequacy in studies comes from the fact that too much stress is laid on games, physical education. Is this true?

Who said that? People who don't like physical education? Stiff old teachers who can't do exercises any longer? These? — I am not asking for names!

Well, I don't think so. You remember the first article Sri Aurobindo wrote in the Bulletin? He answers these people quite categorically.

… I don't think it is that. I am quite sure it is not that, I believe rather — and I put all the blame on myself — that you have been given a fantastic freedom, my children, Oh! I don't think there is any other place in the world where children are so free. And, indeed, it is very difficult to know how to make use of a freedom like that.

However, it was worthwhile trying the experiment. You don't appreciate it because you don't know how it is when it is not like that; it seems quite natural to you. But it is very difficult to know how to organize one's own freedom oneself. Still, if you were to succeed in doing that, in giving yourself your own discipline — and for higher reasons, not in order to pass exams, to make a career, please your teachers, win many prizes, or all the ordinary reasons children have: in order not to be scolded, not to be punished, for all that: we leave out all these reasons — if you manage to impose a discipline upon yourself — each one his own, there is no need to follow someone else's — a discipline simply because you want to progress and draw the best out of yourself, then…. Oh! You will be far superior to those who follow the ordinary school disciplines. That is what I wanted to try. Mind you, I don't say I have failed: I still have great hope that you will know how to profit by the unique opportunity. But all the same, there is something you must find out: it is the *necessity* of an inner discipline. Without discipline you won't be able to get anywhere, without discipline you can't even live the normal life of a normal man. But instead of having the conventional discipline of ordinary societies or ordinary institutions, I would have liked and I still want you to have the discipline you set yourselves, for the love of perfection, your own perfection, the perfection of your being.

التـربية – Education

أمـي، يقـول الـبعض أن قصـورنا العـام فـي الدراسـة يرجـع إلـى أن نظـام تعليمنـا يفـرط فـي الميـل نحو التربية البدنية والمباريات. هل هذا صحيح؟

مـن قـال هـذا؟ قـوم لا يحبـون التربيـة البدنيـة؟ مدرسـون قـد شـاخوا وتصلبـوا وأصبحـوا لا يقـدرون علـى القيام بالتمارين الرياضية؟ على فكرة، أنا لا أريد أن أعرف أسماءهم.

لا أعتقـد أن مـا يزعمـون صحيـح. لعلكـم تتـذكرون أول مقـال كتبـه شـري أوروبينـدو فـي النشـرة؟ لقـد رد فيه على هذه النقطة رداً قاطعاً.

... لا أعتقـد أن التمـارين الرياضيـة هـي المسـئولة. بـل إنـي أعتقـد — وفـي ذلـك آخـذ كـل اللـوم علـى نفسـي — أن السـبب فـي تقصيركـم فـي الدراسـة هـو الحريـة الفائقـة التـي تتمتعـون بهـا يـا أطْفالي! لا أعتقـد أن هنـاك أي مكـان آخـر علـى ظهـر الأرض يتمتـع فيـه التلاميـذ بمثـل هـذه الحريـة. وأنـا أوافـق تمامـاً على أن الاستفادة من مثل هذه الحرية صعب للغاية.

ومـع ذلـك، أعتقـد أن مـنحكم هـذه الحريـة كـان تجربـة جديـرة بالمحاولـة. أنتـم لا تُقَـدّرُون حـريّتكم حـق قـدرها لأنكـم لا تعلمـون كيـف تكـون الحيـاة بـدونها؛ ولـذا تبـدو لكـم الحريـة التامـة شـيئاً مسـلماً بـه وبـديهياً. تنظيـم الحريـة الشـخصية شـيء صعـب للغايـة. لـو نجحتـم فـي أن يفـرض كـل مـنكم عـى نفسـه نظامـه الخـاص — علـى شـرط أن يكـون ذلـك مـن أجـل دوافـع أسـمى، لا بغـرض النجـاح فـي الامتحانـات، أو التقـدم فـي الوظائـف أو إرضـاء المدرسـين أو الفـوز بجوائـز، أو لأي هـدف آخـر مـن الأهـداف العاديـة التـي يبتغيهـا الأطفـال مثـل تجنـب التوبيـخ والعقـاب ومـا شـابه ذلـك: دعونـا نسـتبعد كـل هـذه الأهـداف — أي لـو نجـح كـل مـنكم فـي أن يفـرض علـى نفسـه نظامـه الخـاص، لا نظـام شـخص آخـر — لا لأي سـبب سـوى أن يتقـدم وأن يسـتخلص مـن نفسـه خيـر مـا فيهـا، فـإن ذلـك يكـون تحقيقـاً أعظـم بمراحـل مـن التفـوق فـي المـدارس العاديـة. هذا هـو مـا أردت أن أحاولـه معكـم. لاحـظ إنـي لا أقـول إنـي فشـلت: فمـا زال أملـي كبيـراً فـي أنكـم سـتعرفون كيـف تسـتفيدون مـن الفرصـة الفريـدة المتاحـة لكـم. علـى أي حـال، الشـيء المهـم الـذي يجـب أن تتوصلـوا إليـه، هـو ضـرورة النظـام الـداخلي. بـدون نظـام لـن تنجحـوا فـي تحقيـق أي شـيء فـي الحيـاة، ولا حتـى فـي أن تعيشـوا الحيـاة المعتـادة التـي يعيشـها الرجـل العـادي. ولكـن بـدلاً مـن أن تتبعـوا النظـم التقليديـة السـارية فـي المجتمعـات والهيئـات العاديـة، وددت، ومـا زلـت أود، أن تتبعـوا نظمكـم التـي تفرضونهـا علـى أنفسكـم حبـاً فـي تحقيـق ذاتكـم كمالكـم الذاتـي.

Education – التــربية

... Note that if one didn't discipline the body, one would not even be able to stand on two legs, one would continue like a child on all fours. You could do nothing. You are obliged to discipline yourself; you could not live in society, you could not live at all, except all alone in the forest; and even then, I don't quite know. It is absolutely indispensable. I have told you this I don't know how often. And because I have a very marked aversion for conventional disciplines, social and others, it does not mean that you must abstain from all disciplines. I would like everyone to find his own, in the sincerity of his inner aspiration and the will to realise himself.

And so the aim of all those who know, whether they are teachers, instructors or any others, the very purpose of those who know, is to inform you, to help you. When you are in a situation which seems difficult to you, you put your problem and, from their personal experience, they can tell you, "No, it is like this or like that, and you must do this, you must try that. "So, instead of forcing you to absorb theories, principles and so-called laws, and a more or less abstract knowledge, they would be there to give you information about things, from the most material to the most spiritual, each one within his own province and according to his capacity.

It is quite obvious that if you are thrown into the world without the least technical knowledge, you may do the most dangerous things. Take a child who knows nothing, the first thing he will do if has any matches, for instance, is to burn himself. So, in that field, from the purely material point of view, it is good that there are people who know and who can inform you; for otherwise, if each one had to learn from his own experiences, he would spend several lives learning the most indispensable things. That is the usefulness, the *true* usefulness of teachers and instructors. They have learnt more or less by practice or through a special study, and they can teach you those things it is indispensable to know. That makes you save time, a lot of time. But that is their only usefulness: to be able to answer questions. And, in fact, you should have a brain which is lively enough to ask questions. I don't know, but you never have anything to ask me or it is so seldom.
13 June, 1956

التربية – Education

... لاحظوا أيضاً أنكم لو لم تنظموا أبدانكم، سوف تجدوا أنفسكم عاجزين عن فعل أي شيء، ولن تقدروا حتى على الوقوف على أرجلكم وتصبحوا مضطرين إلى الزحف على أربع مثل الأطفال. بدون تنظيم، تصبحوا غير صالحين للحياة في المجتمع وربما غير صالحين للحياة على الإطلاق، باستثناء لو أردتم أن تعيشوا بمفردكم في الغابات، ولكني لست متأكدة من صلاحيتكم حتى لهذا. لا أنكر إني شديدة النفور من النظم التقليدية، اجتماعية أكانت أو غير ذلك، ولكن ذلك لا يعني إني أتوقع منكم أن تتجنبوا جميع أنواع الأنظمة. كم وددت لو وجد كل منكم نظامه الخاص النابع من توقه المخلص الصادق ورغبته في تحقيق ذاته.

[الأم تخاطب التلاميذ مرة أخرى] هدف ذوي العلم والخبرة، سواء أكانوا مدرسين أو مدربين، وواجبهم الحقيقي يجب أن يكون توفير المعلومات لكم ومساعدتكم، بحيث أنكم عندما تواجهون صعوبة وتعددون أسئلتكم، تحصلون منهم على إرشادات تساعدكم على التغلب على هذه الصعوبة. وبدلاً من أن يرغمكم المدرسون على تقبل نظريات ومبادئ وألوان من المعرفة التجريدية وما يسمونه قوانين الطبيعة، فإنهم يوفرون لكم ما تحتاجونه من معلومات في مجالات تمتد من أقصى الماديات حتى أقصى الروحيات، كل مدرس في مجال تخصصه وحسب قدراته.

واضح أنكم، لو انطلقتم في العالم بدون أي معرفة تقنية، قد تقومون بأعمال على قدر كبير من الخطر. أول شيء يفعله طفل لا يعلم أي شيء إذا وقعت في يده علبة كبريت، هو أن يحرق نفسه. ولذا، فإنه من الخير والضروري، من وجهة النظر المادية البحتة، أن يكون هناك من يستطيعون تزويدكم بالمعلومات؛ لأنه لو كان على كل فرد أن يتعلم من تجاربه الخاصة فقط، لاحتاج إلى حيوات عدة لكي يتعلم أبسط الضروريات. هذا إذا هو النفع، النفع الحقيقي للمدرسين والمدربين. فهم قد تعلموا، إما بالتجربة أو بالدراسة المتخصصة، ويستطيعون أن يعلموكم الأشياء المبدئية التي لا يمكن الاستغناء عنها. بذلك توفرون وقتاً كثيراً. ولكن فائدتهم تنتهي عند هذا الحد: أن يكونوا قادرين على إجابة أسئلتكم. كذلك يجب أن تكون أمخاخكم نشطة بدرجة تمكنكم من أن تسألوا الأسئلة. لا أدري لماذا لا تقدمون لي أسئلة أو لماذا لا تفعلون ذلك إلا في القليل النادر.
13 يونيو، 1956

Education — التــربية

A Child's Dreams — أحــلام الطـفـل

Do not discourage the dreams of a child

When one is very young and as I say "well-born", that is born with a conscious psychic being within, there is always, in the dreams of the child, a kind of aspiration, which for its child consciousness is a sort of ambition, for something which would be beauty without ugliness, justice without injustice, goodness without limits, and a conscious, constant success, a perpetual miracle. One dreams of miracles when one is young, one wants all wickedness to disappear, everything to be always luminous, beautiful, happy, one likes stories which end happily. This is what one should rely on. When the body feels its miseries, its limitations, one must establish this dream in it — of a strength which would have no limit, a beauty which would have no ugliness, and of marvelous capacities; one dreams of being able to rise into the air, of being wherever it is necessary to be, of setting things right when they go wrong, of healing the sick; indeed one has all sorts of dreams when one is young… Usually parents or teachers pass their time throwing cold water on it, telling you, "Oh, it is a dream, it is not a reality." They should do the very opposite! Children should be taught, "Yes, this is what you must try to realise and not only is it possible but it is certain if you come in contact with the part in you which is capable of doing this thing. This is what should guide your life, organize it, make you develop in the direction of the true reality which the ordinary world calls illusion."

This is what it should be, instead of making children ordinary, with that dull, vulgar common sense which becomes an inveterate habit and, when something is going well, immediately brings up in the being the idea: "Oh, that won't last!", when somebody is kind, the impression, "Oh, he will change!", when one is capable of doing something, "Oh, tomorrow I won't be able to do it so well." This is like an acid, a destructive acid in the being, which takes away hope, certitude, confidence in the future possibilities.

When a child is full of enthusiasm, never throw cold water on it, never tell him, "You know, life is not like that!" You should always encourage him, tell him, "Yes, at present things are not always like that, they seem ugly, but behind this there is a beauty that is trying to realise itself. This is what you should love and draw towards you. This is what you should make the object of your dreams, of your ambitions."

أحلام الطفل – A Child's Dreams

لا تُثَبِّط أحلام الطفل

عندما يكون الطفل في سن مبكر ويكون، على حسب تعبيري، "قد أُحسِنَت ولادته"، أي يكون قد وُلِد وكيانه السيكي* حي بداخله، فإن أحلام هذا الطفل تنطوي دائماً على نوع من التوق والتشوق، وحتى إن بدا هذا التشوق في وعيه الطفولي كضرب من الطموح، إلا أنه في الحقيقة حنين إلى جمال لا يشوبه القبح، وعدالة لا يعكرها ظلم، وطيبة لا حدود لها، ونجاح واع مستمر، ومعجزات تتجدد بدون انقطاع. نحن نحلم في طفولتنا بالمعجزات ونتمنى أن يزول الخبثُ والمكر من عالمنا وأن تكون الأشياء نورانية وجميلة وسعيدة، ونستحسن القصص التي تنتهي نهاية سعيدة. هذا هو نوع الأحلام التي ينبغي أن نعتمد ونبني عليها. عندما يشعر البدن ببؤسه وآلامه وِالحدود المفروضة عليه، يجب أن نغرس فيه هذا الحلم: أن يحلم بقوة لا حدود لها وبجمال لا يداخله القبح وبأننا نمتلك طاقات باهرة مثل الارتفاع في الهواء حيثما تقتضي الضرورة وإصلاح الأمور متى فسدت وشفاء المرضى: هذه هي الأحلام التي يحلمها الأطفال ولكن، للأسف، كثيراً ما يُلقي الآباء والمعلمون دشاً بارداً عليها عندما يقولون للطفل: "هذه مجرد أحلام لا نصيب لها من الحقيقة"، في حين أن ما ينبغي أن يفعلوه هو العكس من ذلك تماماً، أي أن يعلموا الطفل أن يرى في حمه مثلاً أعلى يحاول تحقيقه، ويغرزوا فيه الثقة أن التحقيق ممكن، وإنه بالتأكيد سيكتشف يوماً ما هذا الجزء فيه الذي هو قادر على التحقيق، وأن هذا النوع من الأحلام هو الشيء الذي ينبغي أن يرشد حياته وينظمها وهو الذي سيساعده على النمو نحو الحقيقة الحقة حتى لو اعتبرها الناس العاديون وهماً.

هذه الأحلام هي نموذج لما ينبغي أن تكون الأمور عليه بدلاً من المفهوم الاعتيادي المتشائم الرتيب الذي ينشأ عليه الأطفال والذي يتمكن منهم ويصبح عادة يصعب التخلص منها، هذا التشاؤم الذي يجعلك ترى أن الأمور، عندما يكون كل شيء على ما يرام، سرعان ما تتعكر بالضرورة، أو عندما تصادف لطفاً من شخص آخر أن هذا اللطف لا يمكن أن يدوم، أو إذا كنت قادراً عَلى فعل شيء، لا بد ستفقد هذه القدرة يوماً ما. هذا تشاؤم يهدم الكيان ويذيب الأمل والثقة والإيمان في إمكانيات المستقبل مثلما يذيب الحامض المعادن.

عندما ترى الطفل مليئاً بالحماس، لا تلقي أبداً بماء بارد عليه بحجة أن حماسه لا مبرر له وأن الحقيقة تخالف ما يتصوره. بل شجع الطفل دائماً بأن تقول له، "نعم، قد تخالف الأمور تصورك في الوقت الحالي وقد تبدو قبيحة، ولكن هناك وراء هذا القبح جمال يحاول أن يحقق ذته. هذا الجمال هو ما ينبغي أن تحب وأن تجتذب نحوك، وهو ما ينبغي أن تهدف إليه في أحلامك وفي طموحك."

Education – التــربية

And if you do this when you are very small, you have much less difficulty than if later on you have to undo, undo all the bad effects of a bad education, undo that kind of dull and vulgar common sense which means that you expect nothing good from life, which makes it insipid, boring, and contradicts all the hopes, all the so-called illusions of beauty. On the contrary, you must tell a child — or yourself if you are no longer just a baby — "Everything in me that seems unreal, impossible, illusory, that is what is true, that is what I must cultivate." When you have these aspirations: "Oh, not to be limited all the time by some incapacity, held back all the time by some bad will!", you must cultivate in yourself the certitude that that is what is essentially true and that is what must be realised.

Then faith awakens in the cells of the body. And you will see that you find a response in your body itself. The body itself will feel that if its inner will helps, fortifies, directs, leads, well, all its limitations will gradually disappear.

And so, when the first experience comes, which sometimes begins when one is very young, the first contact with the inner joy, the inner beauty, the inner light, the first contact with *that*, which suddenly makes you feel, "Oh! That is what I want," you must cultivate it, never forget it, hold it constantly before you, tell yourself, "I have felt it once, so I can feel it again. This has been real to me, even for the space of a second, and that is what I am going to receive in myself"... And encourage the body to seek it — to seek it, *with the confidence* that it carries the possibility within itself and that if it calls for it, it will come back, it will be realised again.

That is what should be done when one is young. This is what should be done every time one has the opportunity to recollect oneself, commune with oneself, seek oneself.

When you are normal, that is to say, not spoiled by bad teaching and bad examples, when you are born and live in a healthy and relatively balanced and normal environment, the body, spontaneously, without any need to intervene mentally or even vitally, has the certitude that even if something goes wrong it will be cured. The body carries within itself the certitude of cure, the certitude that the illness or disorder is sure to disappear.

التربية – Education

تشجيع الطفل في أول طفولته على هذا النحو يجنبه الكثير من المصاعب في مستقبل حياته ويغنيه في مستقبل حياته عن مشقة محو آثار تربية رديئة توطد الطفل على ألا يتوقع أي خير من الحياة وتجعل الحياة عديمة الطعم ومملة وتقف عقبة في طريق كل أمل وتَدمغ أي توق إلى الجمال بأنه وهم. يجب أن نقول للطفل — أو لأنفسنا إذا كنا قد تخطينا سن الرضاعة! — أن ما يبدو فينا مخالفاً للواقع ومستحيلاً ووهمياً، ذاك هو بالتحديد الحقيقة التي يجب أن نتعهدها بالرعاية. ويجب أن نساعد الطفل على فهم اننا عندما نتوق إلى التغلب على كل عجز فينا وكل إرادة سوء تجذبنا إلى الوراء، فإن ذلك التوق جوهره صادق وحقيقي وهو الشيء الذي يجب أن نحققه.

عندئذ يستيقظ الإيمان في خلايا البدن. وسترى كيف يتجاوب بدنك ويقتنع بأن كل حدوده وقيوده ستختفي بالتدريج لو أن إرادته الداخلية أخذت زمام القيادة والتوجيه وساندته وشدت من عزمه.

عندما تأتي التجربة الأولى، وهي قد تأتي أحياناً في سن مبكرة جداً، ويتم أول اتصال بالبهجة الداخلية، بالنور الباطني، أول اتصال بذاك الذي يجعلك تشعر فجأة، "هذا هو تماماً ما أريد"، يجب أن تتعهد هذا الشعور بالرعاية، وألا تنساه أبدا وأن تضعه على الدوام نصب عينيك وأن تقول لنفسك، "ما دمت قد خبرت هذا الشعور مرة، وحتى ولو كان ذلك لفترة وجيزة، فأنا قادر على أن أخبره مرة أخرى. لقد كان شعوراً حقيقياً بالنسبة لي، وسوف أكون قادراً على الشعور به في ذاتي مستقبلاً"... ثم تشجع بدنك على أن يبحث عنه، واثقاً من قدرته على ندائه واسترجاعه وتحقيقه مرة أخرى.

هذا هو ما يجب أن نفعله في طفولتنا وهذا هو ما يجب أن نفعله في كل مرة تتاح لنا فيها الفرصة لأن نجمع أشتاتنا ونتواصل مع أنفسنا ونبحث عن ذاتنا.

عندما تكون طبيعياً وعادياً، بمعنى أن لم يُفسِدُك تعليم رديء أو قدوة سيئة، ولو كنت قد وُلدت وكنت تعيش في محيط متوازن وطبيعي إلى حد ما، يكون جسمك تلقائياً وبدون أية حاجة لتدخل من الذهن أو من الكائن الحيوي* واثقاً من الشفاء إذا ما اختل شيء فيه. فالبدن يحمل بداخله اليقين بالشفاء وبأن المرض أو العلة سيزولان بالتأكيد.

Education – الـتـربية

Only through false education from the environment is the body gradually taught that there are incurable diseases, irreparable accidents, and that one grows old, and all these stupidities which undermine its faith and confidence. But normally, the body of a normal child — the body, I am not speaking of the mind — the body itself feels when something goes wrong that it will certainly be all right again. And if it is not like that, it means that it has already been perverted. It seems *normal* for it to be in good health, it seems quite abnormal to it if something goes wrong and it falls ill; and in its instinct, its spontaneous instinct, it is sure that everything will be all right. It is only the perversion of thought which destroys this; as one grows up, the thought becomes more and more distorted, there are all the collective suggestions, and so, little by little, the body loses its trust in itself, and naturally, losing its self-confidence, it also loses the spontaneous capacity of restoring its equilibrium when it has been disturbed.

But if when very young, from your earliest childhood, you have been taught all sorts of discouraging, depressing things — things that cause decomposition, so to speak, or disintegration — then this poor body does its best, but it has been perverted, corrupted, and no longer has the sense of its inner strength, its inner force, its power to react.

If you take care not to corrupt it, the body carries within itself the certitude of victory. Only the wrong use we make of thought and its influence on the body robs it of this certitude of victory. So the first thing to do is to cultivate this certitude instead of destroying it. And when it is there, no effort is needed to aspire, but simply a flowering, an unfolding of that inner certitude of victory.

The body carries within itself the sense of its divinity. This is what you must try to recover in yourself if you have lost it.

When a child tells you a beautiful dream in which he had many powers and all things were very beautiful, be very careful never to tell him, "Oh! Life is not like that", for you would be doing something wrong. You must on the contrary tell him, "Life *ought to be* like that, and *it will be* like that!"
31 July 1957

Education – التربية

التربية الخاطئة وحدها هي التي تعلِّم البدن تدريجياً أن مصيرنا إلى العجز وأن هناك أمراض مستعصية وحوادث ذات عواقب لا رجعة فيها... وكل الحماقات الشبيهة التي تُقَوِّض إيمانه وثقته. ولكن بدن الطفل السوي – أنا لا أتحدث عن العقل بل عن البدن نفسه – البدن نفسه يشعر، في الوضع الطبيعي، عندما يختل شيء فيه، أنه سيشفى بالتأكيد. وإذا لم يشعر بذلك، فذلك معناه أنه قد أُفسِد وحُرِّف بالفعل. البدن يجد الصحة الطيبة شيئاً طبيعياً، ويجد المرض والخلل شيئاً غير طبيعي؛ وهو يثق غريزياً وتلقائياً بأن كل شيء سيصبح على ما يرام. تلك الثقة لا يُقَوِّضُها إلا تحريف الفكر؛ إذ أننا عندما نكبر، يأخذ تفكيرنا في الانحراف شيئا فشيئا بسبب كافة الإيحاءات الجماعية، وهكذا يفقد البدن بالتدريج ثقته في نفسه. وبطبيعة الحال، فقدان الثقة بالنفس يؤدي إلى فقدان القدرة التلقائية على استعادة التوازن المختل.

لو أدخل الآخرون في رأسك منذ نعومة أظافرك، منذ طفولتك المبكرة، جميع أنواع الأشياء المُثَبِّطة للعزيمة والمُحبِطة – الأشياء التي تؤدي، إذا جاز التعبير، إلى التفكك والتحلل، وحتى لو بذل جسمك المسكين قصارى جهده، فإنه بعد تحريفه وإفساده، يكون قد فقد إحساسه بقوته الداخلية وبعزيمته وقدرته على الأداء الصحيح.

البدن يحمل بداخله اليقين بالنصر على شرط أن نحرص بعناية على ألا نفسده. ولا يَحرم البدن من هذه الثقة إلا الاستخدام الخاطئ للفكر وتأثير هذا الفكر عليه. فأول ما يجب علينا أن نفعله إذاً هو تنمية هذا اليقين بدلا من تقويضه. وعندما يتوافر هذا اليقين، فإن التطلع* يصبح ممكناً بدون جهد، ويكون ازدهاراً وتفتحاً لهذا اليقين الداخلي بالنصر.

البدن يحمل بداخله الحس بكماله المطلق. هذا هو الحس الذي يجب أن نعيد اكتشافه في أنفسنا، إذا كنا قد فقدناه.

عندما يَقُصُّ عليك طفل حلماً كانت له فيه قدرات مذهلة وكانت جميع الأشياء جميلة، فاحرص على ألا تقول له أبداً، "نعم، نعم، ولكن الحياة غير ذلك"، لأنك تظلمه لو فعلت ذلك. ما يجب أن تقوله للطفل هو أن الحياة هي التي ينبغي أن تكون مثل حلمه وإنها ستكون كذلك يوماً ما.
31 يوليو، 1957

Education – الـتــربية

Diplomas and Certificates – الديبلومات والشهادات

Sweet Mother, Why are no diplomas and certificates given to the students of the Centre of Education [of the Sri Aurobindo Ashram]?*

For the last hundred years or so mankind has been suffering from a disease which seems to be spreading more and more and which has reached a climax in our times; it is what we may call "utilitarianism". People and things, circumstances and activities seem to be viewed and appreciated exclusively from this angle. Nothing has any value unless it is useful. Certainly something that is useful is better than something that is not. But first we must agree on what we describe as useful — useful to whom, to what, for what?

For, more and more, the races who consider themselves civilized describe as useful whatever can attract, procure or produce money. Everything is judged or evaluated from a monetary angle. That is what I call utilitarianism. And this disease is highly contagious, for even children are not immune to it.

At an age when they should be dreaming of beauty, greatness and perfection, dreams that may be too sublime for ordinary common sense, but which are nevertheless far superior to this dull good sense, children now dream of money and worry about how to earn it. So when they think of their studies, they think above all about what can be useful for them, so that later on when they grow up can earn a lot of money.And the thing that becomes most important for them is to prepare themselves to pass examinations with success, for with diplomas, certificates and titles they will be able to find good positions and earn a lot of money. For them study has no other purpose, no other interest.

To learn for the sake of knowledge, to study in order to know the secrets of Nature and life, to educate oneself in order to grow in consciousness, to discipline oneself in order to become master of oneself, to overcome one's weaknesses, incapacities and ignorance, to prepare oneself to advance in life towards a goal that is nobler and vaster, more generous and more true — they hardly give it a thought and consider it all very utopian. The only thing that matters is to be practical, to prepare themselves and learn how to earn money.

Education – التربية

الديبلومات والشهادات — Diplomas and Certificates

أمـي العذبـة، مـا هـو السـبب فـي عـدم إعطـاء ديبلومـات وشـهادات لطلبـة مركـز التربيـة [فـي أشرام شري أوروبيندو]؟*

منـذ حـوالي مائـة عـام تعـاني الإنسانية مـن مـرض استشـرى استشـراءً مضـطرداً بلـغ قمتـه فـي يومنـا هـذا؛ هـذا المـرض يمكـن أن نسـميه "النفعيـة" وأعراضـه هـي النظـر إلـى النـاس والأشياء ولْظروف والأنشـطة المختلفـة وتقيّـمُها تبعـاً لنفعهـا المباشـر، واعتبار كـل مـا ليـس لـه نفـع مباشـر عديـم القيمـة. واضـح أن النـافع أفضـل مـن غيـر النـافع؛ ولكنـا يجـب أن نتفـق أولاً علـى تعريـف كلمـة "نـافع": نـافع لمن؟ وما هو بالتحديد هذا النفع؟

يقتصـر مفهـوم "نـافع"، فـي نظـر الـذين يصـفون أنفسـهم بـأنهم متمدنون، علـى كـل مـا يجتـذب المـال أو يولـده أو يـوفره، وهـم يُقَيّـمُون جميـع الأمـور والأشـياء مـن وجهـة ماليـة بحتـة. هـذا هـو مـا أسـميه "النفعيـة". وهو مرض معدٍ للغاية ولا يسلم منه أحد، حتى الأطفال.

فالأطفـال أصبحـوا اليـوم يحلمـون بالمـال ويُقلِقـون أنفسـهم بالتفكيـر فـي كيفيـة اكتسـابه فـي سـن مبكرة كـان ينبغـي لأحلامهـم فيهـا أن تـدور حـول الجمـال والعظمـة والكمـال. أي حـول مثاليـات تتعـالى علـى هـذا الحـس العـادي وعلـى ذاك المنطـق النفعـي الممـل الكليـل. تجـد الأطفـال عندمـا يفكـرون فـي دراسـتهم، يفكـرون أولاً وقبـل كـل شـيء فـي مـا يمكنهـم مـن اكتسـاب المـال الكثيـر عندمـا يكبـرون. وبالتـالي يصـبح أهـم شـيء بالنسـبة لهـم هـو إعـداد أنفسـهم للتفـوق فـي الامتحانـات، لأن الشـهادات والـديبلومات والألقـاب تفتـح أبـواب الوظائـف المربحـة. وبـذلك لا تكـون لهـم فـي الدراسـة أي متعـة أو هدف وراء ذلك.

قلمـا يخطـر علـى بـال تلاميـذ اليـوم أن يتعلمـوا ابتغـاءً للمعرفـة أو أن يدرسـوا لكـي يكتشـفوا أسـرار **الطبيعـة** والحيـاة أو لكـي يهـذبوا أنفسـهم ويَنَـَّمُوا وعيهـم، أو ليخضـعوا أنفسـهم لنظـام يـؤدي بهـم إلـى اكتسـاب السـيادة علـى أنفسـهم، أو ليعـدوا أنفسـهم مبكـراً لبلـوغ هـدف أكثـر نبـلاً وسـعة وجـوداً وصـدقاً — بـل يعتبـر هـؤلاء التلاميـذ كـل ذلـك خيـالاً وأحلامـاً. كـل مـا يهتمـون بـه هـو أن يكونـوا عمليين وأن يتعلموا الطرق السهلة لاكتساب المال .

Education — التـربية

Children who are infected with this disease are out of place at the Centre of Education of the Ashram. And it is to make this quite clear to them that we do not prepare them for official examinations or competitions or give them diplomas or titles which they can use in the outside world. We want here only those who aspire for a higher and better life, who thirst for knowledge and perfection, who look forward eagerly to a future that will be more totally true.

There is plenty of room in the world for all others.
17 July 1960

السـبب فــي أننـا لا نُعِّـد التلاميـذ لامتحانـات أو مباريـات رسـمية وأننـا لا نعطـيهم ديبلومـات وألقـاب تـنفعهم فـي العـالـم الخـارجي هـو بالتحديـد أننـا نريـد هنـا تلاميـذ يبتغـون المعرفـة لوجـه المعرفـة، أمـا الأطفـال المصـابون بمـرض المنفعيـة، فهنـاك أمكنـة كافيـة لهـم فـي مـدارس العـالم الخـارجي. نريـد هنـا فقـط التلاميـذ الـذين يطمحـون إلـى حيـاة أسـمى وأرفـع، ويتحرقـون للمعرفـة والكمـال ويـأملون فـي مستقبل أكثر صدقاً وأقرب إلى الحقيقة الشاملة.

هناك أمكنة كافية لجميع الآخرين في مدارس العالم الخارجي.
11 يوليو 1960

Education — الـتـربية

Girls and Physical Education — الفتيات والتربية البدنية

The following questions were addressed to the Mother by a disciple teaching in the "Sri Aurobindo International Centre of Education" and published, together with the answers of the Mother, under the title "To Women about their Body":

Sweet Mother,
While handling children in the Group for Physical Education we meet certain problems with girl students. Most of these are suggestions put upon them by their friends, older girls, parents and the doctor. Please throw light on the following questions so that we may be better equipped in our knowledge to execute our responsibilities more efficiently.

1. *What attitude should a girl take towards her monthly periods?*
2. *Should a girl participate in her normal program of Physical education during her periods?*
3. *Why are some girls completely run down during their periods and suffer from pains in the lower back and abdomen while others may have a slight or no inconvenience at all?*
4. *How can a girl overcome her suffering and pains during periods?*
5. *Do you think there should be different types of exercises for boys and girls? Will a girl bring harm to her genital organs by practicing the so-called manly sports?*
6. *Will a girl's appearance change and become muscular like a man's and make her look ugly if she practices vigorous exercises?*
7. *Will the practice of vigorous types of exercises bring difficulties in child-birth if the girls want to marry and have children afterwards?*
8. *What should be the ideal of Physical Education for a girl from the point of view of her sex?*
9. *What roles should man and woman play in our new way of life? What shall be the relation between them?*
10. *What should be the ideal of a woman's physical beauty?*

Before answering your questions I wish to tell you something which you know no doubt, but which you must never forget if you wish to learn how to lead a wise life.

Education — التـربية

Girls and Physical Education — الفتيات والتربية البدنية

الأسئلة التالية وجهتها إلى الأم مـُعلمة في "مركـز شـري أوروبينـدو الـدولي للتربية" وقـد نُشِرَت، مع إجابات الأم، في مقال بعنوان "إلى النساء بخصوص بدنهم":

أمي العذبة،

نواجـه كمعلمـين صعـوبات معينة في مجمـوعة التربيـة البدنيـة أثنـاء تعاملنـا مـع البنـات بخصـوص أبدانهم. هـذه الصعـوبات تنبـع مـن إيحـاءات تـأتيهم مـن صديقاتهم الأكبر سنًا ومـن الوالـدين ومـن الطبيب. رجاء الإجابـة علـى الأسئلة التاليـة لعلنـا نـتمكن مـن القيـام بمسؤولياتنا بفعالية أكبر.

1. ما هو الموقف الذي ينبغي أن تتخذه الفتاة إزاء الدورة الشهرية؟
2. هل ينبغي أن تشترك الفتاة في برنامج التربية البدنية المعتاد أثناء الدورة الشهرية؟
3. . لمـاذا تشـعر بعـض الفتيات بالإرهـاق الشـديد وتعـانين مـن آلام أسـفل الظهـر والـبطن فـي حـين لا تشـعر أخريـات بـأي شـيء علـى الإطـلاق أو يقتصـر الأمـر علـى مجـرد تعب بسيط؟
4. ماذا ينبغي أن تفعل الفتاة لكي تتغلب على معاناتها وآلامها أثناء الدورة الشهرية؟
5. هـل تعتقـدين بضـرورة وجـود تمـارين خاصـة للفتيـات تختلـف عـن تمـارين الصبيان؟ هـل يمكن أن تسـبب الفتـاة ضـرراً لأعضـائها التناسلية لـو مارسـت تمرينـات "رجولية"؟
6. هـل يتغيـر مظهـر الفتـاة وتصبح مفتولة العضـلات كالرجـال وقبيحـة لـو مارسـت تمرينات تنمية العضلات ورفع الأثقال؟
7. بالنسبـة إلـى الفتيـات التـي يـرغبن فـي الـزواج وإنجاب الأطفال، هـل تسـبب هـذه التمرينات العنيفة صعوبات في الولادة فيما بعد؟
8. ما هو المثل الأعلى للتربية الرياضية بالنسبة للفتاة من حيث أنها أنثى؟
9. مـا هـو الـدور الـذي يلعبـه الرجل والمرأة فـي نظـام حياتنـا الجديـد؟ ومـا ذا يـبغي أن تكون العلاقة بينهما؟
10. ما هو المثل الأعلى لجمال المرأة من الناحية البدنية؟

قبـل أن أرد علـى أسئلتك أود أخبـرك شـيئاً لا بـد أنك تعلمينه، ولكن يجب ألا تنسيه أبداً لـو رغبـت أن تعرفي الطريق إلى حياة تسودها الحكمة والحصافة.

Education – الـتـربية

It is true that we are, in our inner being, a spirit, a living soul that holds within it the Divine and aspires to become it, to manifest it perfectly; it is equally true, for the moment at least, that in our most materia external being, in our body, we are still an animal, a mammalian, of a higher order no doubt, but made like animals and subject to the laws of animal Nature.

You have been taught surely that one peculiarity of the mammal is that the female conceives the child, carries it and builds it up within herself until the moment when the young one, fully formed comes out of the body of its mother and lives independently. In view of this function Nature has provided the mother with an additional quantity of blood which has to be for the child in the making, the surplus blood has to be thrown out to avoid excess and congestion. This is the cause of the monthly periods. It is a simple natural phenomenon, result of the way in which woman has been made and there is no need to attach to it more importance than to the other functions of the body. It is not a disease and cannot be the cause of any weakness or real discomfort. Therefore, a normal woman, one who is not ridiculously sensitive, should merely take the necessary precautions of cleanliness, never think of it anymore and lead her daily life as usual without any charge in her program. This is the best way to be in good health.

Besides, even while recognizing that in our body we still belong dreadfully to animality, we must not therefore conclude that this animal part, as it is the most concrete and the most real for us, is one to which we are obliged to be subjected and which we must allow to rule over us. Unfortunately this is what happens most often in life and men are much more slaves than masters of their physical being. Yet it is the contrary that should be, for the truth of the individual life is quite another thing.

We have in us an intelligent will more or less enlightened which is the first instrument of our psychic* being. It is this intelligent will that we must use in order to learn to live not like an animal man but as a human being, candidate for Divinity.

And the first step towards this realization is to become master of this body instead of remaining an impotent slave.

صحيح أننـا، فـي كياننـا الداخلي، روح مـن **الواحـد-الكـل*** ونتـوق إلـى أن نتطابـق معـه وأن نحققـه كليـاً، ولكـن صحيـح أيضـاً أننـا مـا زلنـا، فـي كياننـا الخـارجي المـادي، أي فـي بـدننا، حيوانـات وثدييات، حيوانـات مـن مرتبـة أعلـى بـدون شـك، ولكننـا مـع ذلـك لا نختلـف كثيـراً فـي خلقتنـا عـن الحيـوان ونخضع مثله لقوانين **الطبيعة** الحيوانية.

لا بـد أنـك تعلمـين أن الثدييـات تتميـز بـأن الأنثـى تحبل بـالجنين وتُكَوِّنـه بـداخلها وتحمله حتى تحيـن الـولادة وعندئـذ يخـرج المولـود تـام التكويـن مـن بـدن الأم ليعيـش مسـتقلاً. لكـي تصبـح هـذه العمليـة ممكنـة، تـزود **الطبيعـة** الأم بكميـة إضافيـة مـن الـدم لاسـتخدامها فـي تكويـن الجنـين، وعنـدما ينتهـي الحمـل بـالولادة، تحتـاج الأم إلـى التخلـص مـن هـذا الدم حتـى لا يتراكم فـي بـدنها. هـذا هو سـبب الـدورة الشـهرية. هـي إذا ظاهـرة بسـيطة ونتيجـة طبيعيـة لتركيـب الأنثـى وليـس هنـاك أي ضـرورة لأن نعطيهـا مـن الأهميـة أكثـر ممـا نعطـي أيـاً مـن وظائـف البـدن الأخـرى. فالدورة الشـهرية ليسـت مرضاً ولا يمكـن أن تكـون السـبب فـي أي ضعـف أو إزعـاج حقيقـي. ولـذلك فـإن المـرأة الطبيعيـة، إذ لـم تكـن مفرطـة الحساسـية إلـى درجـة السـخف، تسـتطيع، بعـد مراعـاة مقتضيـات النظافـة، أن تعيـش حياتهـا كالعـادة وبـدون أي تغييـر فـي برنامجهـا اليـومي وبـدون أن تفكـر فـي الـدورة الشـهرية أبعـد مـن ذلـك. هذه أفضل طريقة للبقاء بصحة جيدة.

وبالإضافـة: حتـى لـو وافقنـا علـى أننـا مـا زلنـا نخضـع في بـدننا لقوانين الحيـوان، لا ينبغـي أن نسـتنتج مـن ذلـك أننـا ملزمـون بالخضـوع لهـذه الناحيـة الحيوانيـة فينا لمجـرد أننـا نراهـا ملموسـة وأكثـر واقعيـة مـن ناحياتنـا الأخـرى. للأسـف، ذلـك الخطـأ كثيـراً مـا نجـد في الحيـاة أن الغالبيـة العظمـى مـن البشـر عبيـد بدنهم بدلا مـن أن يكونـوا سـادته. العكس تمامـاً هـو مـا ينبغـي أن يحـدث، فحقيقة حياة الفرد شـيء آخـر تمامـاً [عـن واقـع بدنه].

كـل منـا لـه إرادة ذكيـة ومتنـورة إلـى حـد مـا وهـي الأداة الأولـى لكياننـا السـيكي*. هـذه الإرادة الفطنـة هـي بالتحديـد الأداة التـي يجـب أن نسـتعين بهـا إذا أردنـا أن نتعلـم كيـف نعيـش ككائنـات آدميـة علـى الطريـق نحو الربانية بدلاً مـن أن نعيش مثـل الحيوانات.

الخطـوة الأولـى نحـو هـذا التحقيـق هـي أن نكتسـب السـيادة علـى بـدننا بـدلاً مـن أن نظـل عبيـداً لـه لا حول لهم ولا قوة.

Education – التــربية

One most effective help towards this goal is physical culture. For about a century there has been a renewal of a knowledge greatly favored in ancient times, partially forgotten since then. Now it is reawakening, and with the progress of modern science, it is acquiring quite a new amplitude and importance. This knowledge deals with the physical body and the extraordinary mastery that can be obtained over it with the help of this enlightened and systematized physical education.

This renewal has been the result of the action of a new power and light that have spread upon the earth in order to prepare it for the great transformation that must take place in the near future.

We must not hesitate to give primary importance to this physical education whose very purpose is to make our body capable of receiving and expressing the new force which seeks to manifest upon earth.

This said, I now answer the questions you put to me:

1. *What attitude should a girl take towards her monthly period?*

The attitude you take towards something quite natural and unavoidable. Give it as little importance as possible and go on with your usual life, without changing anything because of it.

2. *Should a girl participate in her program of Physical Education during her period?*

Certainly if she is accustomed to physical exercise, she must not stop because of that. If one keeps the habit of leading one's normal life always, very soon one does not even notice the presence of the menses.

3. *Why are some girls completely run down during their periods and suffer from pain in the lower back and abdomen while others may have slight or no inconvenience at all?*

Education – التربية

التربيـة البدنيـة وسيلة عظيمـة الفاعليـة تساعدنا علـى بلـوغ هـذا الهـدف. وقـد أعطيـت فـي الأزمـان القديمـة أهميـة كبيـرة، ولكـن هـذه المعرفـة آلـت إلـى النسيـان إلـى حـد مـا بمـرور الوقـت إلـى أن شهدت صحـوة كبيـرة فـي القـرن الأخيـر نتيجـة للتقدم العلمـي وأصبحت التربيـة البدنيـة تحتـل مـرة أخـرى مكانـاً مرموقـاً. علـم التربيـة البدنيـة يختـص بالبـدن وبالسيطـرة المذهلـة التـي يمكـن أن نفرضهـا عليـه بواسـطة برامج تربوية بدنية متنورة.

رجـوع التربيـة البدنيـة إلـى مكانتهـا السـابقة كـان نتيجـة لانتشـار قـوة ونـور جديـدين علـى الأرض يُعِّدَانها للتحول العظيم الذي يجب أن يحدث في المستقبل القريب.

ولـذلك يجـب ألا نتـردد فـي إعطـاء مكانـة كبـرى للتربيـة البدنيـة التـي تهـدف بالتحديد إلـى جعـل أبداننا قادرة على تلقي هذه القوة الجديدة التي تسعى إلى تحقيق نفسها على الأرض.

بعد هذا التقديم، أرد الآن على الأسئلة التي وجهتيها إلي:

1. ما هو الموقف الذي ينبغي أن تتخذه الفتاة إزاء الدورة الشهرية؟

نفـس الموقـف الـذي تتخذينـه إزاء أي شـيء طبيعـي ولا مفـر منـه. لا تهتمـي كثيـراً بالـدورة الشهرية وتابعي حياتك العادية دون أي تغيير في برنامجك بسببها.

2. هـل ينبغـي أن تستمر الفتـاة فـي المشاركة فـي برنامج التربية البدنية المعتـاد أثنـاء دورتهـا الشهرية؟

نعـم بالتأكيـد. لـو كانـت الفتـاة معتـادة علـى ممارسـة التماريـن الرياضيـة، لا ينبغـي أن توقفهـا بسبب الـدورة الشهريـة. لـو اتخـذت الفتـاة هـذا الموقـف وثابـرت عليـه، سـرعان مـا تفقـد الـدورة الشهريـة أهميتها وأخيراً لا تلحظ الفتاة أي تغير أثناء الدورة الشهرية.

3. لمـاذا تشعر بعض الفتيات بالإرهـاق الشديد وتعانين مـن آلام أسفل الظهـر والبطن فـي حيـن لا تشعر أخريات بأي شيء أو بمجرد تعب بسيط؟

144

Education – التــربية

It is a question of temperament and mostly of education. If from her childhood a girl has been accustomed to pay much attention to the slightest uneasiness and to make a fuss about the smallest inconvenience, then she loses all capacity of endurance and anything becomes the occasion for being pulled down. Especially if the parents themselves get too easily anxious about the reactions of their children. It is wiser to teach a child to be a bit sturdy and enduring than to show much care for these small inconveniences and accidents that cannot always be avoided in life. An attitude of quiet forbearance is the best one can adopt for oneself and teach to the children.

It is a well-known fact that if you expect some pain you are bound to have it and, once it has come, if you concentrate upon it, then it increases more and more it becomes what is usually termed as "unbearable", although with some will and courage there is hardly any pain that one cannot bear.

4. How can a girl overcome her suffering and pain during periods?

There are some exercises that make the abdomen strong and improve the circulation. These exercises must be done regularly and continued even after the pains have disappeared. For the grown-up girls, this kind of pain comes almost exclusively from sexual desires. If we get rid of the desires, we get rid of the pain. There are two ways of getting rid of desires; the first one, the usual one, is through satisfaction (or rather what is called satisfaction, because there is no such thing as satisfaction in the domain of desire); this means leading the ordinary human-animal life, marriage, children and the rest of it.

There is, of course, another way, a better way, — control, mastery, transformation*; this is more dignified and also more effective.

5. Do you think there should be different types of exercises for boys and girls? Will a girl bring harm to her genital organs by practicing the so-called manly sports?

In all cases, as well as for boys as for girls, the exercises must be graded according to the strength and the capacity of each one. If a weak student tries at once to do hard and heavy exercises, he may suffer for his foolishness. But with a wise and progressive training, girl as well boys can participate in all kinds sports, and thus increase their strength and health.

ذلك يتوقف على مزاج الفتاة وإلى حد بعيد على تربيتها. لو كانت الفتاة قد اعتادت منذ طفولتها على الانزعاج والشكوى من أقل مضايقة، فإنها تصير بمرور الوقت مفرطة الحساسية و تفقد قدرتها على التحمل. هذا يحدث على الأخص لو كان الأب والأم أنفسهما ينزعجان بصورة مفرطة لأقل شيء يمس أطفالهما. إنه أقرب إلى الحكمة أن يُعَوِّد الأهل الطفل على التجلد والتماسك بدلاً من الإفراط في إظهار العطف عند وقوع أبسط المضايقات والحوادث، فالحوادث البسيطة لا يمكن تلافيها كلياً في الحياة. أفضل موقف يمكن أن يتخذه البالغون وأن يعلموه للأطفال هو موقف التحمل في صبر وهدوء.

إنها حقيقة معروفة، إنك عندما تتوقع الألم تجده حاضراً، ومتى أتى الألم، إنك لو ركزت عليه، إنه يتزايد إلى أن يصبح غير محتمل. كل ألم يصبح محتملاً عندما تواجهه ببعض الشجاعة وقوة الإرادة.

4. ماذا ينبغي أن تفعل الفتاة لكي تتغلب على معاناتها وآلامها أثناء الدورة الشهرية؟

هناك تمرينات لتقوية البطن وتنشيط الدورة الدموية، وهي تمارين يجب ممارستها بانتظام والاستمرار فيها حتى بعد زوال الآلام. في حالة البنات البالغات، تنشأ هذه الآلام عادة من الرغبات الجنسية وتزول بالتخلص من هذه الرغبات. هناك طريقتان للتخلص من الرغبات: الأولى، وهي الطريقة المعتادة، عن طريق الإشباع (أو ما يُسَمَّى الإشباع)، ففي الحقيقة الإشباع مستَحيل في مجال الرغبات والشهوات)؛ وهي تؤدي إلى الحياة العادية التي يكون فيها المرء مزيجاً من الإنسان والحيوان، أي حياة الزواج والإنجاب ... إلى آخره.

وهناك بالطبع طريقة أخرى أفضل: بواسطة التحكم والسيطرة على النفس وتحويل* الكيـان، وهي تؤدي إلى حياة أكثر وقاراً وأكثر فاعلية.

5. هل تعتقدين بضرورة وجود تمارين خاصة للفتيات تختلف عن تمارين الصبيان؟ هل يمكن أن تسبب الفتاة ضرراً لأعضائها التناسلية لو مارست التمرينات التي توصف بأنها "رجولية"؟

في جميع الحالات، سواء كان الطالب فتى أو فتاة، يجب اختيار التمرينات تبعاً لمقدرة اطالب أو الطالبة وطاقتهما. لو حاول طالب ضعيف البنية أن يمارس فوراً تمرينات شديدة وصعبة، ربما يكون لهذا التهور نتائج غير مرغوبة. ولكن بواسطة تمارين حصيفة ومتدرجة، يستطيع الجميع، فتياناً وفتيات، الاشتراك في كل أنواع الرياضة وبذلك ينمون عضلاتهم ويحسنون صحتهم.

Education – التــربية

To become strong and healthy can never bring harm to a body, even if it is a woman's body!

6. *Will a girl's appearance change and become muscular like a muscular man's and make her look ugly if she practices vigorous exercises?*

Weakness and fragility may look attractive in the view of a perverted mind, but it is not the truth of Nature, nor the truth of the Spirit.

If you have ever looked at the photos of the women gymnasts you will know what perfectly beautiful bodies they have; and nobody can deny that they are muscular!

7. *Will the practice of vigorous types of exercises bring difficulties in child-birth if the girls want to marry and have children afterwards?*

I never came across such a case. On the contrary, women who are trained to do strong exercises and have a muscular body go through the ordeal of child-formation and child-birth much more easily and painlessly.

I heard the authentic story of one of these African women who are accustomed to walk for miles carrying heavy loads. She was pregnant and the time of delivery came during one of the day's marches. She sat on the side of the track, under a tree, gave birth to the child, waited for half an hour, then she rose and the new-born babe went on her way quietly, as if nothing had happened. This is a splendid example of what a woman can do when she is in full possession of her health and strength.

Doctors will say that such a thing cannot occur in a civilized world with all the so-called progress that humanity has achieved; but we cannot deny that, from the physical point of view, this is a more happy condition than all the sensitiveness, the sufferings and the complications created by the modern civilizations.

Moreover, usually doctors are more interested in the abnormal cases, and they judge mostly from that point of view. But for us, it is different; it is from the normal that we can rise to the supernormal, not from the abnormal which is always a sign of perversion and inferiority.

كل ما يؤدي إلى القوة والصحة لا يمكن أن يضر البدن، حتى لو كان بدن امرأة!

6. هل يتغير مظهر الفتاة وتصبح قبيحة ومفتولة العضلات كالرجال لو مارست تمرينات تنمية العضلات ورفع الأثقال؟

قد تكون للضعف والهشاشة جاذبية خاصة لذوي العقول المنحرفة، ولكن الضعف والهشاشة لا يتمشيان مع حقيقة **الطبيعة** أو حقيقة **الروح.**

لو نظرتِ إلى صور (فوتوغرافية) للاعبات الجمباز، سترين مدى جمال أبدانهم؛ هذا على الرغم من أنهن بالطبع مفتولات العضلات!

7. بالنسبة إلى الفتيات التي يرغبن في الزواج وإنجاب الأطفال، هل تسبب هذه التمرينات العنيفة صعوبات في الولادة فيما بعد؟

لم أصادف حتى الآن أي حالة تبرر هذه المخاوف. بل على العكس، نجد أن الحمل والولادة يكونان أيسر كثيراً بالنسبة للنساء اللاتي تمارس تمارين القوة واللاتي يمتلكن أبداناً قوية.

سمعت قصة موثوق فيها عن امرأة إفريقية من النساء اللاتي يحملن الأثقال الكبيرة ويتنقلن بها مسافات طويلة سيراً على الأقدام. كانت المرأة حبلى، وفي ذات مرة أثناء مسيرتها اليومية المعتادة، آن أوان وضعها. جلست المرأة ببساطة بجوار الطريق ووضعت طفلها، ثم انتظرت نصف ساعة وقامت وتابعت سيرها، كما تفعل كل يوم، حاملة رضيعها، بالإضافة إلى أحمالها الأخرى. هذا مثال رائع لما تقدر المرأة على أدائه عندما تكون في كامل صحتها وقوتها.

ربما يقول الأطباء أن مثل هذا الأداء لا يمكن أن يتكرر في العالم المتمدن بكل تحقيقته التي يعتبرها الناس تقدماً، ولكننا لا نستطيع أن ننكر أن التصرف البدائي الوارد في هذه الحادثة أفضل كثيراً، من الناحية البدنية، من كل أشكال الحساسية والمعاناة والتعقيدات التي أنجبتها الحضارات الحديثة.

أضف إلى ذلك أن الأطباء يركزون دائماً على الحالات الشاذة ويُصدرون أحكامهم عادة من وجهة نظر هذه الحالات. الأمر يختلف بالنسبة لنا: فنحن نريد أن نسمو من "الطبيعي" إلى "ما يتخطى الطبيعي"، ولا نريد أن نأخذ منطلقنا من "الشاذ" لأن الشاذ كثيراً ما يقترن بالانحراف والدونية.

Education – التـربية

8. *What should be the ideal of physical education for a girl from the point of view of her sex?*

I do not see why there should be any special ideal of physical education for girls other than boys.

Physical education has for its aim to develop all the possibilities of a human body, possibilities of harmony, strength, plasticity, cleverness, agility, endurance, and to increase the control over the functioning of the limbs and the organs, to make of the body a perfect instrument at the disposal of a conscious will. This program is excellent for all human beings equally, and there is no point in wanting to adopt another one for girls.

9. *What roles should man and woman play in our new way of life? What shall the relation between them?*

Why make at all a distinction between them? They are all equally human beings, trying to become fit instruments for the Divine Work, above sex, caste, creed and nationality, all children of the same Infinite Mother and aspirants to the one Eternal Godhead.

10. *What should be the ideal of a woman's physical beauty?*

A perfect harmony in the proportions, suppleness and strength, grace and force, plasticity and endurance, and above all, an excellent health, unvarying and unchanging, which is a result of a pure soul, a happy trust in life and an unshakable faith in the Divine Grace.

One word to finish:
I have told you these things, because you needed to hear them, but not to make of them absolute dogmas, for that would take away their truth.
23 July 1960

8. ما هو المثل الأعلى للتربية الرياضية بالنسبة للفتاة من حيث أنها أنثى؟

لا أرى ضرورة لأن يختلف المثل الأعلى للتربية البدنية في حالة الفتيان عنه في حالة الفتيات.

التربية البدنية تهدف إلى تنمية جميع إمكانيات وطاقات البدن التي تشمل التناسق والقوة والليونة والحذق والمرونة والتحمل، وإلى تحسين التحكم في وظائف الجوارح والأعضاء، وإلى جعل البدن أداة كاملة في خدمة الإرادة الواعية. برنامجنا الحالي ممتاز ويصلح للجميع. لا ضرورة على الإطلاق لبرنامج مختلف للفتيات.

9. ما هو الدور الذي يلعبه الرجل والمرأة في نظام حياتنا الجديد؟ وما ذا ينبغي أن تكون العلاقة بينهما؟

هل هناك أي داعي إلى التمييز بين الرجل والمرأة؟ الرجال والنساء جميعاً كائنات بشرية، يحاولون جميعاً أن يكونوا أدوات صالحة **للعمل الإلهي** وتخطي الجنس والطبقية والعقائد والجنسيات، وهم جميعاً أطفال **الأم اللانهائية** ويطمحون إلى **خلود الألوهية.**

10. ما هو المثل الأعلى لجمال المرأة من الناحية البدنية؟

تناسق كامل في أبعاد البدن، المرونة والطاقة والقوة، الرشاقة والتحمل، اللدونة والقوة، وأهم من كل ذلك الصحة الممتازة التي لا تتغير ولا تتبدل، والتي تنتج من روح نقية ومن الثقة المبتهجة في الحياة والإيمان الثابت **بالنعمة الإلهية.**

كلمة صغيرة في النهاية:
لقد أخبرتك بهذه الأشياء لأنك كنت تحتاجين إلى سماعها، ولم أخبرك بها لكي تجعلي منها عقائد ومبادئ مطلقة، لأن ذلك يبطل حقيقتها.
23 يوليو 1960

A different Outlook – نـظـرة جـديـدة

About Illness and Healing – عـن المـرض والشـفـاء

The Protective Envelope

Illnesses enter through the subtle body*, don't they? How can they be stopped?

... If one is very sensitive, very sensitive – one must be very sensitive – the moment they touch the subtle body and try to pass through, one feels it. It is not like something touching the body, it is a sort of feeling. If you are able to perceive it at that moment, you have still the power to say "no", and it goes away. But for this one must be extremely sensitive. However, that develops. All these things can be developed methodically by the will. You can become quite conscious of this envelope, and if you develop it sufficiently, you don't even need to look and see, you feel that something has touched you. I can give you an instance of this, there are many similar ones.

Someone was seeking to establish a constant and conscious contact – absolutely constant and conscious – with the inner Godhead, not only with the psychic being but the divine Presence in the psychic being, and she had decided that she would be like this, that she would busy herself with nothing else, that is to say, whatever she might be doing, her concentration was upon this, and even when she went out walking in the street, her concentration was upon this. She lived in a big city where there was much traffic: buses, tramways, etc..., many things, and to cross the street one had to be considerably careful, wide-awake and attentive, otherwise one could get run over, but this person had resolved that she would not come out of her concentration. One day when she was crossing one of the big avenues with all its cars and its tramways, still deep in her concentration, in her inner seeking, she suddenly felt at about an arm's length a little shock, like this; she jumped back and a car passed just by her side. If she had not jumped back she would have been run over... This is an extreme point, but without going so far one can very easily feel a kind of little discomfort (it is not something which is imposed with a great force), a little uneasiness coming near you from anywhere at all: front, behind, above, below.

A different Outlook – نـظـرة جديـدة

About Illness and Healing — عن المرض والشـفـاء

الـغـلاف الـواقي

الأمراض تغزونا عن طريق البدن الدقيق*، أليس كذلك؟ كيف يمكن إيقافها قبل أن تستفحل؟

... عنـدما تكـون حساسـاً للغايـة — الحساسيـة المرهفـة شـرط أساسـي — تشـعر بـالأمـر ض فـي اللحظـة التـي تمـس فيهـا بـدنـك الـدقيـق وتحـاول المـرور الـى داخلـك. لمستها ليست بالقوة التـي يصطدم بها جسم مـادي بك، ولكنـه إحسـاس شبيه. لـو كنت متنبهـاً في لحظة اللمس وأدركت مـا حـدث، تكـون مـا زلت قـادراً علـى رفض المرض وطرحـه بعيداً عنك. ولكن يجب أن تكـون فـي غايـة الحساسية لتقـدر علـى فعل ذلـك. علـى أي حـال، مـن الممكـن تنميـة الحساسيـة. كـل هـذه الأشيـاء قابلـة للتنميـة منهجيـاً بواسطـة الإرادة. فـي مقدورك إلـى حـد بعيد أن تصبـح واعيـاً ببـدنـك الـدقيق الـذي يحيـط بـك ويُغلِّـفك، ولـو كـان وعيـك بـه كافيـاً، لا تحتـاج [لحمايـة نفسـك مـن غـزو الأمـراض] إلـى فحـص هـذا الغـلاف باستمرار أو التركيـز عليـه، بـل إنـك تشعـر كلمـا مسـه شـيء. للتوضيـح، أضـرب نـك مثـلاً واحداً من أمثلة كثيرة شبيهة.

أرادت امرأة [الأم تقص هنا تجربتها الذاتيـة باستخدام ضميـر الغائـب] أن تعقـد صلـة دائمـة وواعيـة تمامـاً بالألوهيـة الكامنـة بـداخلها، لا بالكيـان السـيكي* فحسـب، بـل **بالحضـرة الإلهيـة** فـي الكيـان السـيكي. كانـت قد عقدت العزم علـى ذلك وقـررت ألا تشغل نفسها بـأي شـيء آخـر، إلـى درجـة أنها حتـى أثنـاء مشيها في الشوارع كانت تركـز علـى تحقيق رغبتها هـذه. كانـت المـرأة تعيـش فـي مدينـة كبيـرة شـوارعها تعـج بعربـات التـرام والأتوبيس وأشيـاء كثيـرة أخرى بحيـث كـان مجـرد عبـور بعـض الشـوارع يستلزم التنبـه التـام لتجنـب الحـوادث. ولكـن هـذه السيدة كانـت مصممـة علـى عـدم الخـروج مـن تركيزهـا. ذات يـوم، أرادت أن تعبـر واحـداً مـن الطـرق الأساسيـة كثيـرة الازدحـام، وكانـت مستغرقـة فـي تركيزهـا العميـق علـى سـعيها الـداخلي عندما شعرت بهـزة صغيـرة علـى بعـد ذراع أمامها جعلتها تقفز متراجعـة إلـى الـوراء في نفس اللحظـة التـي مرت فيها عربة مسرعة بحيـث أنها لـو لـم تتراجـع فـي اللحظـة المناسبة، كانـت العربـة ستمر فوقها. هـذا مثـال لحالـة متطرفـة... ولكن هنـاك أمثلة أقـرب إلى موضوعنا، إذ إننا نستطيع أن نشـعر [عندما يقترب منا مرض مثلاً] بنـوع من عـدم الارتياح (ليس بالضـرورة بصـدمة عنيفـة كمـا لـو كـان جسـم مـا قـد صدمنا)، كأنمـا أُقبـل علينـا شيء غير مرغوب من ناحية ما: من الأمام، الخلف، من أعلى، أو من أسفل.

152

A different Outlook – نـظـرة جـديـدة

If at that moment you are sufficiently alert, you say "no", as though you were cutting off the contact with great strength, and it is finished. If you are not conscious at that moment, the next minute or a few minutes later you get a queer sick feeling inside, a cold in the back, a little uneasiness, the beginning of some disharmony; you feel a maladjustment somewhere, as though the general harmony had been disturbed. Then you must concentrate all the more and with a great strength of will keep the faith that nothing can do you harm, nothing can touch you. This suffices, you can throw off the illness at that moment. But you must do this immediately, you understand, you must not wait five minutes, it must be done at once. If you wait too long and begin to feel really an uneasiness somewhere, and something begins to get quite disturbed, then it is good to sit down, concentrate and call the Force, concentrate it on the place which is getting disturbed, that is to say, which is beginning to become ill.

But if you don't do anything at all, an illness indeed gets lodged somewhere; and all this, because you were not sufficiently alert. And sometimes one is obliged to follow the entire curve to find the favourable moment again and get rid of the business. I have said somewhere that in the physical domain all is a question of method – a method is necessary for realising everything. And if the illness has succeeded in touching the physical-physical, well, you must follow the procedure needed to get rid of it. This is what medical science calls "the course of the illness". One can hasten the course with the help of spiritual forces, but all the same the procedure must be followed.

There are some four different stages. The very first is instantaneous. The second can be done in some minutes, the third may take several hours and the fourth several days. And then, once the thing is lodged there, all will depend not only on the receptivity of the body but still more on the willingness of the part which is the cause of the disorder. You know, when the thing comes from outside it is in affinity with something inside. If it manages to pass through, to enter without one's being aware of it, it means there is some affinity somewhere, and the part of the being which has responded must be convinced

لـو كنـا في تلك اللحظـة متيقظين بدرجـة كافية ورفضنا هذا التدخل كما لـو كنا نقفل بابـاً بحـزم، فـإن الأمـر ينتهي ويفشل المرض في هجمته. أمـا لـو كنا في تلك اللحظـة غافلين، فإننا نشعر فـي الدقيقـة التاليـة أو بعد بضعة دقائق بإحسـاس مرضـي غريب، وربما ببـرد في ظهورنا، كمـا لـو كـان كياننا يوشـك على الـدخول في فوضـى عامة واختلال تـوازن. عندئـذ يجب أن نركـز بقوة أكبـر وأن نتمسك بإيماننـا بأننـا فـي الحمايـة وأن لا شـيء يستطيع أن يضر بنا. ولكننا يجب أن نفعل ذلك على الفـور، وألا نؤجل خمس دقائق مثلاً، لأننا لو تأخرنا وبدأنا نشعر باختلال فعلي في موضع مـا، يكـون من المستحسن أن نجلس ونركز ونـدعو **القوة الإلهيـة** ونسددها على الموضـع الـذي بـدأ فـي الاستسلام للمرض والاختلال.

أمـا لـو لـم نقـاوم على الإطـلاق، فـإن المرض يتمكن منـا، وكـل ذلك لأننا لـم نكن يقظين بالدرجـة الكافيـة. عندئـذ نضطر إلى تتبـع مسـار المرض إلى أن تسنح لنـا فرصـة أخرى للتخلص منـه. لقد أخبرتكم ذات مرة أننـا نحتـاج دائمـاً فـي المجـال الفيزيـائي البدني إلى مـنهج لـو أردنـا أن نحقق أي شـيء. لـو نجح المـرض في أن يمس البـدن الفيزيـائي، سنكون ملـزمين باتبـاع المـنهج المطلـوب للتخلص منـه. هذا هو مـا يسمى في علم الطب "أن نـدع المرض يجري مجراه". يمكننـا أن نسرع عمليـة الشفـاء بالاستعانة بـالقوى الروحية، ولكننا سنحتاج على الـرغم ذلك إلى اتبـاع المـنهج الخـاص الذي يناسب ذلك المرض المعين.

مـنهج الشفـاء يتكون إذاً مـن أربـع مراحـل: الأولـى فوريـة والثانيـة يمكن القيـام بهـا فـي ظـرف دقائق والثالثـة تحتـاج إلى بضع ساعات والرابعـة إلى بضعة أيـام. ولكـن الشفـاء سيتوقف علـى تفنح الجزء المصـاب [للقـوى الإلهيـة]، وعلـى رغبـة هذا الجزء في الشفـاء. ذلك أنـه عندما يغزونا شـيء مـن الخـارج، يكون هنـاك دائمـا شـيء في داخلنا في حالـة توافق مـع المرض. نجـاح أي مـرض فـي التسلـل إلى داخلنا دليـل علـى أن جـزء مـن أجزائنا تضامن مـع هذا المـرض. فـي هذه الحالـة، لا مفر مـن اقناع الجزء المريض بأن [يكف عن تمسكه بالمرض] وأن يرغب في الشفـاء.

A different Outlook – نــظـرة جـديــدة

I have known some truly extraordinary instances... Wait, take an example which is quite concrete: sunstroke. This upsets you considerably, it is one of the things which makes you most ill – a sunstroke upsets everything, it disturbs the inner functions, it generally causes a congestion in the head and very high fever. So, if this has happened, if it has succeeded in getting through the protection and entering you, well, if you can just go into a quiet place, stretch yourself out flat, go out of your body (naturally, you must learn this; there are people who do this spontaneously, for others a long discipline is necessary), go out of your body, remain above in a way to be able to see the body (you know the phenomenon, seeing one's body when one is outside ? This can be done at will, going out of one's body and remaining just above it), the body is stretched out on a bed, a bench, on the ground, anywhere; you are stretched just above it and from there, consciously, you pull the Force from above, and if you are used to doing it, if your aspiration is strong enough, you get the answer; and then, from there, taking care not to re-enter your body, you begin to push these forces into the body, like that, regularly, until you see the body receiving them (for, the first few moments they don't enter, because the body is quite upset by the illness, it is not receptive, it is curled up), you push them gently, gently, quietly, without nervousness, very peacefully, into the body. But you must not be disturbed by anyone. If someone comes along, sees you stretched out and shakes you, it is extremely dangerous. You must do this in quiet conditions, ask people not to disturb you or better shut yourself up where they can't disturb you. But you can concentrate slowly (this takes more or less time – ten minutes, half an hour, one hour, two hours – depends upon the seriousness of the disorder which has set in), slowly, from above, you concentrate the Force until you see that the body is receiving, that the Force is entering, the disorder is being set right and there is a relaxation in the body itself. Once that is done you can get back and you are cured.

This has been done for a sunstroke, which is a fairly violent thing, and also for typhoid fever, and many other illnesses, as, for instance, for a liver which was suddenly upset somehow (not due to indigestion, but a liver which doesn't function properly for the moment); it may also be cured in the same way. There was a case of cholera which was healed like that. The cholera had just been caught, had entered, but was not yet lodged; it was completely cured. Consequently, when I say that if one masters the spiritual force and knows how to use it, there is no malady which cannot be cured. I don't say it just like that in the air; it is said from experience with the thing. Of course, you will say you don't know how to go out of the body, draw the Force, concentrate it, have all this mastery... It is not very frequent, but it is not impossible. And one can be sure that if one is helped... In fact, there is a much easier method, it is to call for help.

A different Outlook – نظرة جديدة

لقد خبرت حالات ملفتات للنظر بحق... خذ ضربة الشمس كمثال ملموس تماماً: ضربة الشمس هي أحد الأشياء التي تجعلك مريضاً للغاية وتربك كل شيء وتزعج الوظائف الداخلية وتسبب عادة احتقاناً في الرأس وارتفاعاً شديداً في درجة الحرارة. فإذا أصابتك ونجحت في اختراق الغلاف الواقي واستقرت، حسناً، لو أمكنك أن تذهب إلى مكان هادئ وتتمدد أفقياً وتخرج من بدنك (بالطبع يجب أن تتعلم فعل ذلك، بعض الناس يفعلونه تلقائياً، في حين يحتاج آخرون إلى تدريب طويل)، أن تخرج من بدنك وتظل محلقاً فوقه بحيث يمكنك أن تراه (هل تعرف هذه الظاهرة: أن ترى نفسك من الخارج؟ هذا شيء يمكن عمله إرادياً): بدنك إذاً ممدد على الفراش أو على مقعد طويل أو على الأرض في مكان ما، وأنت تحلق فوقه مباشرة، ومن هناك تجذب واعياً **القوة** من أعلى. لو كنت معتاداً على فعل ذلك، وكان تطلعك شديداً بدرجة كافية، ستحصل على القوى التي تنشدها، ثم تشرع في دفع هذه القوى برفق إلى داخل بدنك، مع مراعاة ألا ترجع أنت نفسك إلى بدنك مرة أخرى، وتستمر في ذلك حتى ترى أن بدنك بدأ يتقبل القوى (قد لا ينجح ذلك في الدقائق الأولى عندما يكون البدن ما زال منزعجاً بشدة المرض وغير متقبل ومقفلاً ومتقوقعاً على نفسه). ولكن استمر بلطف بالغ وبهدوء وبدون أي توتر وفي سلام تام. احرص على ألا يزعجك حد أثناء وجودك خارج بدنك، إذ أنه لو مر أحدهم ورآك ممدداً وهزّك، يكون ذلك في غاية الخطورة. لذلك يجب أن تفعل ذلك في محيط هادئ وأن تطلب من الناس ألا يزعجوك، والأفضل من ذلك هو أن تكون في مكان لا يقدر الآخرون على ازعاجك فيه. استمر في تركيز **القوة الإلهية** (الوقت قد يطول أو يقصر: عشر دقائق، نصف ساعة، ساعة أو ساعتين — تبعاً لشدة الاضطراب الذي نشأ في البدن نتيجة لضربة الشمس) إلى أن ترى أن البدن بدأ في تقبل **القوة** و الاسترخاء وأن الخلل بدأ يزول. متى تم ذلك تستطيع أن ترجع إلى بدنك وتكون بذلك قد شفيت.

لقد نجح هذا المنهج في حالة ضربة شمس، وهي شيء عنيف نوعاً ما، وأيضاً في حالة حمى التيفويد وأمراض أخرى كثيرة غيرها... استناداً إلى ذلك، عندما أقول إننا لو أحسنا استعمال القوة الروحية وعرفنا كيف نستخدمها، لا يستعصي علينا اشفاء أي داء، أتحدث عن تجربة وخبرة بهذه الأمور. بالطبع ستقول إنك لا تعلم كيف تخرج من بدنك أو كيف تجتذب **القوة** أو كيف تركز وتحقق كل هذا التحكم في البدن... صحيح أن كل ذلك يحتاج إلى معرفة خاصة، ولكن الخروج من البدن ليس مستحيلاً. كن واثقاً أنه لو كان العون الإلهي معك [لم تكمل الأم جملتها]... في الواقع هناك طريقة أسهل بكثير، وهي أن تستنجد وتسأل العون.

A different Outlook – نــظـرة جديـدة

But the condition in every case – in every case – whether one does it oneself and depending only on oneself or whether one does it by asking someone to do it for one, the first condition: not to fear and to be calm. If you begin to boil and get fidgety in your body, it is finished, you can do nothing.

For everything – to live the spiritual life, heal sickness – for everything, one must be calm.
March 31, 1951

Stopping Illness before it is too late

Sweet Mother, when one sees an illness coming, how can one stop it?

Ah! First of all, you must not want it and nothing in the body must want it. You must have a very strong will not to be ill. This is the first condition.

The second condition is to call the light, a light of equilibrium, a light of peace, quietude and balance, and to push it into all the cells of the body, enjoining them not to be afraid, because that again is another condition.

First, not to want to be ill, and then not to be afraid of illness. You must neither attract it nor tremble. You must not want illness at all. But you must not because of fear not want it; you must not be afraid; you must have a calm certitude and a complete trust in the power of the Grace to shelter you from everything, and then think of something else, not be concerned about this any longer. When you have done these two things, refusing the illness with all your will and infusing a confidence which completely eliminates the fear in the cells of the body, and then busying yourself with something else, not thinking any longer about the illness, forgetting that it exists... there, if you know how to do that, you may even be in contact with people who have contagious diseases, and yet you do not catch them. But you must know how to do this.

Many people say, "Oh, yes, here I am not afraid." They don't have any fear in the mind, their mind is not afraid, it is strong, it is not afraid; but the body trembles, and one doesn't know it, because it is in the cells of the body that the trembling goes on. It trembles with a terrible anxiety and this is what attracts the illness.

ولكن الشـرط في كل حالـة — في جميع الحـالات — سـواء أكنـت تعمـل بمفردك معتمداً على نفسك فقـط أو تسـتعين بـآخرين، الشـرط الأول هـو ألا تخـاف وأن تظـل هادئـاً. لـو بـدأ بـدنك فـي الغليـان والتململ، فقد انتهى الأمر ولن تتمكن من فعل أي شيء.

الشـرط الضرـوري فـي جميـع الأحـوال — لكـي تعيش حيـاة روحيـة أو لتشـفي مـرض — هـو أن تبقـى هادئاً.
31 مارس، 1951

إيقاف المرض قبل أن يستفحل

أيتها الأم العذبة، كيف يمكن إيقاف مرض نراه مقبلاً علينا؟

آه! قبل كـل شـيء يجب ألا تكون راغبـاً فـي المـرض، ويجب ألا يرغبـه أي شـيء فـي بـدنك. يجب أن تكون مصمماً تماماً على رفض المرض. هذا هو الشرط الأول.

الشـرط الثـاني هـو أن تـدعو النـور: نـور اتـزان وسـلام وهـدوء وتعـادل، وأن تدفعـه فـي كـل خلايـا البدن، وأن تحث الخلايا على عدم الخوف. ذلك هو الشرط الثاني.

أولاً، عدم الرغبـة فـي المـرض، وثانيـاً عـدم الخـوف منـه. يجـب مـن ناحيـة ألا تجتـذب المـرض، و مـن الناحيـة الأخـرى يجـب ألا تـرتعش خوفـاً منـه. يجـب ألا تتـوق إلـى المـرض بـأي صـورة. ولكـن لا ينبغـي أن يكـون الخـوف هـو مـا يدفعـك إلـى تجنب المـرض؛ لأنـك يجب أن تتجنـب الخـوف كـذلك. يجـب أن تتحلى بـاليقين الهـادئ وبالثقـة التامـة فـي قـدرة **الفضـل الإلهـي** علـى حمايتـك مـن كـل شـيء، وأن تصـرف ذهنـك إلـى شـيء آخـر ولا تعيـر الأمـر اهتمامـاً بعـد ذلك. عندما تفعـل هـذين الشـيئين: تـرفض المـرض بكـل إرادتـك وتغـرس فـي خلايـا بـدنك ثقـة تسـتأصل الخـوف منهـا، ثـم تشـغل نفسـك بشـيء آخـر متحاشيـاً التفكيـر في المـرض وناسـياً وجـوده... لـو اسـتطعت فعـل ذلك، تكـون قـادراً علـى الاتصـال مـع مرضـى ذوي أمـراض معديـة دون أن تلتقـط المـرض منـهم. ولكـن يجـب أن تعـرف كيفيـة فعل ذلك.

كثيـرون سـيحاجون قـائلين: "ولكنـي لا أخـاف المـرض!" ربمـا كانـت أذهـانهم قويـة فعـلاً لا يعتريهـا الخـوف؛ ولكـن أبـدانهم تـرتعش خوفـاً وهـم لا يـدركون أن الارتعـاش يحـدث فـي خلايـاهم. إنهـا تـرتعش في حالة من القلق الفظيع، وهذا هو ما يجتذب المرض.

A different Outlook – نـظـرة جديـدة

It is there that you must put the force and the quietude of a perfect peace and an absolute trust in the Grace. And then, sometimes you are obliged to drive away with a similar force in your thought all suggestions that after all, the physical world is full of illnesses, and these are contagious, and because one was in contact with somebody who is ill, one is sure to catch it, and then, that the inner methods are not powerful enough to act on the physical, and all kinds of stupidities of which the air is full. These are collective suggestions which are passed on from one person to another by everybody….

When Sri Aurobindo says that illness comes from outside, what exactly is it that comes?

It is a kind of vibration made up of a mental suggestion, a vital force of disorder and certain physical elements which are the materialisation of the mental suggestion and the vital vibration. And these physical elements can be what we have agreed to call germs, microbes, this and that and many other things. It may be accompanied by a sensation, may be accompanied by a taste, also by a smell, if one has very developed subtle senses. There are these formations of illness which give a special taste to the air, a special smell or a slight special sensation. People have many senses which are asleep. They are terribly [lazy and indolent]. If all the senses they possess were awake, there are many things they would perceive, which can just pass by without anyone suspecting anything. For example, many people have a certain kind of influenza at the moment. It is very wide-spread. Well, when it comes close, it has a special taste, a special smell, and it brings you a certain contact (naturally not like a blow), something a little more subtle, a certain contact, exactly as when you pass your hand over something, backwards over some material… You have never done that? The material has a grain, you know; when you pass your hand in the right direction or when you pass it like this (gesture), well, it makes you… it is something that passes over your skin, like this, backwards…

الخلايـا هـي الموقـع الـذي يلـزم أن تسـددوا عليـه **القـوة الإلهيـة** والهـدوء النـابع مـن السكينة التامـة والثقـة الكاملـة فـي **الفضـل الإلهـي**. وأحيانـا يجب أن تطـردوا بحـزم مـن فكركم جميـع الإيحـاءات السـلبية التـي تنـادي بـأن العـالم المـادي، فـي آخـر المطـاف، ملـيء بـالأمراض، وأن هـذه الأمـراض معديـة، وأنكـم بالتأكيـد ستمرضـون لأنكـم كنـتم علـى اتصـال بشـخص مـريض، وأن منـاهج العـلاج الداخليـة لا تملـك القـوة الكافيـة للتـأثير علـى البـدن، وكـل الحماقـات الشـبيهة التـي يعـج بها الجـو. هـذه إيحـاءات جماعيـة يمررها الناس أحدهم إلى الآخر.

عندما يقول شري أوروبيندو أن المرض يأتي من الخارج، ما هو ذاك بالتحديد الذي يأتي؟

المـرض ذبذبـة تتكـون مـن إيحـاءات ذهنيـة وقـوة حيويـة فوضـوية وبعـض العناصـر الفيزيائيـة التـي تجسـد هـذه الإيحـاءات الذهنيـة والذبـذبات الحيويـة. هـذه العناصـر الفيزيائيـة ربمـا تكـون مـا اصطلح علـى تسـميته جـراثيم وميكروبـات، إلـى آخـره. وربمـا صـاحب المـرض إحسـاس أو مـذاق أو رائحـة، يسـتطيع ذوو الحـواس الدقيقـة المرهفـة تمييزهـا.. فـي النـاس حـواس عديـدة نائمـة نتيجـة لخمـولهم وكسـلهم، ولـو تيقظـت هـذه الحـواس كلهـا، لأصـبحوا قـادرين علـى إدراك أمـور كثيـرة لا تخطـر علـى بـالهم فـي العـادة. علـى سبيل المثـال، خـذ حالـة الإنفلونـزا الشـائعة حاليـاً. عندما يقتـرب هذا الوبـاء يكـون لـه مـذاق ورائحـة خاصـة ولمسـة خفيفـة (ليست بقـوة الضـربة بـالطبع) كمـا لـو كنـت تمـرر يـدك علـى مادة معينة في اتجاه مضاد لتكوين سطحها ويشعر جلدك بقشعريرة نتيجة لخشونة ملمسها.

160

A different Outlook – نـظرة جـديـدة

Besides, there is always a way of isolating oneself by an atmosphere of protection, if one knows how to have an extremely quiet vibration, so quiet that it makes almost a kind of wall around you. – But all the time, all the time one is vibrating in response to vibrations which come from outside… You are never in an absolutely quiet atmosphere which emanates from you, that is, which comes from inside outward (not something which comes from outside within), something which is like an envelope around you, very quiet… it is only when you have this conscious extremely calm atmosphere, and as I say, when it comes from within (it is not something that comes from outside), it is only when it's like this that you can go with impunity into life, that is, among others and in all the circumstances of every minute… Otherwise if there is something bad to be caught, for example, anger, fear, an illness, some uneasiness, you are sure to catch it….

What is to be wondered at is the unconsciousness with which men go through life; they don't know how to live, there's not one in a million who knows how to live, and they live like that somehow or other, limping along, managing, not managing; and all that for them, bah! What is it? Things that happen.

They don't know how to live. All the same one should learn how to live. That's the first thing one ought to teach children: to learn how to live.
May 11, 1955

A different Outlook – نـظـرة جديـدة

في مقـدورنا دائمـاً أن نعـزل أنفسـنا بـداخل جـو واق يحمينـا، لـو عرفنـا كيـف نغلـف أنفسـنا بذبـذبات هـدوء تكـون مثـل الحـائط مـن حولنـا. ولكننـا نتجـاوب دائمـا مـع الذبـذبات التـي تأتينـا مـن الخـارج، ولا نكـون أبـداً في جـو مـن الهـدوء التـام، هـدوء يشـع مـن داخلنـا إلـى الخـارج ويُكَـوِّن حولنـا غلافـاً واقيـاً. لـو نجحنـا في إحاطـة أنفسـنا بمثـل هـذا الغـلاف يمكننـا أن نـذهب إلـى أي مكـان ونكـون في وقايـة مـن ذبذباتـه، ونسـتطيع أن نختلـط بالنـاس تحـت جميـع الظـروف وفـي جميـع الأوقـات. بـدون هـذا الغـلاف، نكـون معرضـين لالتقـاط أي موجـة تقـدم علينـا، سـواء أكانـت موجـة غضـب أو خـوف أو مـرض أو بلبلة...

مـا يـدعو إلـى التعجب هـو مـدى اللاوعـي الـذي يعيـش فيـه النـاس. إنهـم لا يعلمـون الطريقـة الصحيحة للحيـاة، وليـس هنـاك فـرد واحـد في مليـون يعلـم ذلـك. بـل هـم يعيشـون كيفمـا اتفـق ويتخبطـون كـالعرج في حيـاتهم، ويقـدرون أحيانـاً علـى توجيـه أنفسـهم وأحيانـا يفشلـون، ولا يتعجبـون علـى حـالهم بـل يقبلونه بحجة أن هذه "أشياء عادية تحدث للجميع"..

النـاس لا يعرفـون كيف يعيشـون، ولكـن ذلـك شـيء ينبغـي أن يتعلمـوه. تربيـة الأطفـال يجـب أن تبـدأ بتعليمهم كيف ينبغي أن يعيشوا حياتهم.

11 مايو، 1955

A different Outlook – نـظـرة جديــدة

About Death – عن الـمـوت

Changing our Outlook on Death

[...] If one must for some reason or other leave one's body and take a new one, is it not better to make one's death something magnificent, joyful, enthusiastic, than to make it a disgusting defeat? Those who cling on, who try by every possible means to delay the end even by a minute or two, who give you an example of frightful anguish, show they are not conscious of their soul... After all, it is perhaps a means, isn't it? One can change this accident into a means; if one is conscious one can make a beautiful thing out of it, a very beautiful thing, as of everything. And note , those who do not fear it, who are not anxious, who can die without any sordidness are those who never think about it, who are not haunted all the time by this "horror" facing them which they must escape and which they try to push as far away from them as they can. These, when the occasion comes, can lift their head, smile and say, "Here I am."

It is they who have the will to make the best possible use of their life, it is those who say, "I shall remain here as long as it is necessary, to the last second, and I shall not lose one moment to realise my goal"; these, when the necessity comes, put up the best show. Why? — it is very simple, because they live in their ideal, the truth of their ideal; because that is the real thing for them, the very reason of their being, and in all things they can see this ideal, this reason of existence, and never do they come down into the sordidness of material life.

So, the conclusion:
One must never wish for death.
One must never will to die.
One must never be afraid to die.
And in all circumstances one must will to exceed oneself.
23 April 1951

Overcoming the Fear of Death

There are two remedies [to overcome the fear of death]. There are many, but two at least are there. In any case, the use of a deeper consciousness is essential. One remedy consists in saying that it is something that happens to everyone (let us take it at that level), yes, it is a thing that happens to everybody, and therefore, sooner or later, it will come and there is no reason why one should be afraid, it is quite a normal thing. You may add one more idea to this, that according to experience (not yours but just the collective human experience), circumstances being the same, absolutely identical, in one case people die, in another they do not — why?

عن الـمـوت — About Death

تغيير نظرتنا إلى الموت

[....] حيث أنـه مكتـوب علـى كـل منـا أن يتـرك بدنـه يومـاً مـا ويتخـذ بـدناً آخـر، ألا يكون مـن الأفضل أن نوطد أنفسنا علـى أن نعتبر المـوت شيئـاً رائعـاً بهيجـاً نتحمـس لـه بـدلاً مـن أن نعتبـره هزيمـة مقيتـة؟ أولئـك الـذيـن يتشـبثون بالحيـاة ويحـاولون بكـل طريقـة أن يَمِـدُّوا فـي عمـرهم دقيقـة أو دقيقتـين ويضـربون بأنفسـهم أمثـالاً للمفجوعـين المرعوبيـن، يُدلّـون بمـوقفهم هـذا علـى أنهـم غيـر واعيـن بـأرواحهم.... [لأنهـم لـو كـانوا واعيـن، لأدركـوا] أن المـوت ربمـا كـان وسيلة [تـؤدي إلـى شـيء أفضـل]. عنـدما نكـون واعيـن، يمكننـا أن نبـدل نظرتنـا إلـى المـوت (تمـاماً كمـا نُبَـدّل نظرتنـا إلـى أي شـيء آخـر) فنـراه شيئـاً جميـلاً لا كارثـة مرعبـة. لاحـظ أن الـذيـن لا يخشـون المـوت ولا يعيشـون فـي قلـق مسـتمر بسـببه، الـذيـن يتجاهلونـه تمامـاً ولا يستسـلمون لوسـاوس الرعـب والرغبـة فـي تأجيـل الحيـاة إلـى أبعـد مـدى، هـؤلاء يموتـون فـي كرامـة وعنـدما تـأتي ساعتهم يرفعـون رؤوسـهم مبتسـمين كمـا لـو كانوا يقولون للموت: "مرحباً، ها نحن ذا."

هـؤلاء بالتحديـد هـم أيضـاً الـذيـن يحرصـون علـى أن ينتفعـوا أعظـم النفـع مـن حيـاتهم ويكـون مـوقفهم، "سـأظل علـى قيـد الحيـاة طالمـا كـان ذلـك ضروريـاً، حتـى آخـر لحظـة، ولـن أفقـد دقيقـة واحـدة فـي تحقيـق هـدفي"؛ وهـم الـذيـن، عنـدما تحيـن سـاعتهم، يبـدون فـي أحسـن صـورهم. لمـاذا؟ — الجـواب بسـيط للغايـة: لأنهـم لا يتـدنون إلـى خسـة الحيـاة الماديـة، ويعيشـون حقيقـة مثلهـم الأعلـى، تلـك الحقيقـة التـي هي واقعهم والأسـاس المسبب لكيانهم، والحقيقة التي يرونها في كل شيء ينظرون إليه.

الاستنتاج الذي نصل إليه إذاً هو:
يجب ألا نتمنى الموت أبداً.
يجب ألا نسعى إلى الموت بأي حال.
يجب ألا نخاف الموت في أي وقت من الأوقات.
يجب أن نرغب في التفوق على أنفسنا في جميع الأحوال.
23 أبريل 1951

التغلب على خشية الموت

هنـاك وسـائل عـدة للتغلـب علـى الخـوف مـن المـوت، علـى الأقـل وسـيلتان، ولكـن الشـرط الضـروري لنجـاح هـذه الوسـائل جميعـاً هـو أن نمارسـها مـن وعـي أعمـق [مـن الـوعي العـادي]. الوسـيلة الأولـى هـي أن نقـول ببسـاطة إن المـوت يحـدث لجميـع الكائنـات الحيـة، ولـذلك لا بـد مـن أن يأتينـا عاجـلاً أو آجـلاً، وحيـث أنـه حادثـة طبيعيـة وعاديـة لا داعـي لأن نخافـه. نسـتطيع أن نضيـف إلـى مـا سـبق الملاحظـة التاليـة التـي تنبـع مـن الخبـرة البشـرية الجماعيـة وهـي أن ظـروف معينـة تـؤدي إلـى مـوت بعـض الأفـراد، في حين أن أفراد آخرين لا يموتون في ظروف مماثلة تمامـاً — فما هو السبب؟

A different Outlook – نـظـرة جـديـدة

And if you push the thing a little further still, you say to yourself that after all it must depend on something which is altogether outside your consciousness — and in the end one dies when one has to die. That is all. When one has to die, one dies, and when one has not to die, one does not die. Even when you are in mortal danger, and it is not your hour to die, you will not die, and even if you are out of all danger, just a scratch on your foot will be enough to make you die, for there are people who have died of a pin-scratch on the foot — because their time had come. Therefore, fear has no sense. What you can do is to rise to a state of consciousness where you can say, "It is like that, we accept the fact because it seems to be recognized as an inevitable fact. But I do not need to worry, for it will come only when it must come. So I don't need to feel afraid: when it is not to come, it will not come to me, but when it must come, it will come. And as it will come to me inevitably, it is better I do not fear the thing; on the contrary one must accept what is perfectly natural." This is a well-known remedy, that it to say, very much in use.

There is another, a little more difficult, but better, I believe. It lies in telling oneself: "This body is not I", and in trying to find in oneself the part which is truly one's self, until one has found one's psychic* being — And when one has found one's psychic being — immediately, you understand — one has the sense of immortality. And one knows that what goes out or what comes in is just a matter of convenience: "I am not going to weep over a pair of shoes I put aside when it is full of holes! When my pair of shoes is worn out I cast it aside, and I do not weep." Well, the psychic being has taken this body because it needed to use it for its work, but when the time comes to leave the body, that is to say, when one must leave it because it is no longer of any use for some reason or other, one leaves the body and has no fear. It is quite a natural gesture — and it is done without the least regret, that's all.

And the moment you are in your psychic being, you have that feeling spontaneously, effortlessly. You soar above the physical life and have the sense of immortality. As for me, I consider this the best remedy. The other is an intellectual common-sense, rational remedy. This is a deep experience and you can always get it back as soon as you recover the contact with your psychic being. This is a truly interesting phenomenon, for it is automatic. The moment you are in contact with your psychic being, you have the feeling of immortality, of having always been and being always, eternally. And then what comes and goes — these are life's accidents, they have no importance. Yes this is the best remedy. The other is like the prisoner finding good reasons to accept the prison. This one is like a man for whom there is no longer any prison [...].

A different Outlook – نـظرة جديدة

لـو استرسـلنا علـى هـذا الخـط مـن التفكيـر نـرى أن المـوت يتوقف حتمـاً علـى عوامـل خارجـة كليـاً عـن وعينـا — ونـدرك أننـا، فـي نهايـة المطـاف، لا نمـوت إلا عنـدما تحـين سـاعتنا. هـذا كـل مـا فـي الأمـر. إذا حانـت سـاعتنا نمـوت، وإذا كانـت لـم تحـن بعـد لا نمـوت. وحتـى لـو كنـا فـي خطـر يهـدد حياتنـا وكانـت سـاعتنا لـم تحـن بعـد، فإننـا لا نمـوت، فـي حيـن إننـا لـو كنـا فـي مـأمن مـن جميـع الأخطـار، قـد يكفـي أن تُخـدَش قدمنـا خدشـاً بسـيطاً لكـي نمـوت، وقـد مـات بعـض النـاس بالفعـل مـن وخـزة مسـمار فـي قدمهـم — لأن أوانهـم كـان قـد أتـى. الخـوف إذاً لا معنـى لـه. مـا نسـتطيع أن نفعلـه هـو أن نرتفـع فـي وعينـا إلـى مسـتوى الـوعي الـذي يسـمح لنـا بـأن نقـول، "كُتِـب المـوت علينـا، ونحـن نقبلـه لأنـه واقـع لا مفـر منـه يعتـرف بـه جميـع البشـر. ولـذلك، لا داعـي للخـوف والقلـق، فالمـوت لـن يصيبنـا قبـل أوانـه، ولـن نسـتطيع الهـروب منـه إذا حـان الأوان. وحيـث أننـا لـن نسـتطيع الفـرار منـه، مـن الأفضـل أن نضـع الخـوف جانبـاً ونتقبلـه كشـيء طبيعـي تمامـاً." هـذا عـلاج معـروف يسـتخدمه الكثيـرون لـلتخلص مـن خشية الموت.

أمـا الوسـيلة الثانيـة فهـي أصعـب قليـلاً، ولكنهـا، فـي اعتقـادي، أفضـل. خلاصتهـا أن نتراجـع مـن تطابقنـا الكلـي مـع البـدن بـأن نقـول: "أنـا لسـت هـذا البـدن" ونحـاول أن نجـد هـذا الجـزء منـا الـذي يمثلنـا بحـق، ألا وهـو الكيـان السـيكي*. بمجـرد أن نكتشـف كياننـا السـيكي، نشـعر بالأبديـة، ونـدرك أن كـل مـا يخـرج منـا ويدخـل فينـا زائـل، وأن المـوت مجـرد اصطـلاح تعـارف النـاس عليـه. وننظـر إلـى بـدننا كمـا ننظـر إلـى حـذاء بـالي آن الأوان لـلتخلص منـه وأصبـح لا يسـتحق أن نـذرف عليـه الـدمع. كياننـا السـيكي* اتخـذ بـدننا الحـالي لأنـه احتـاج لاسـتخدامه لفتـرة مـا كـأداة يعمـل بهـا، وعنـدما يتـم عملـه ويحـين الاوان لكـي يغـادر هـذا البـدن الـذي أصبـح لا ينفعـه، فإنـه يغـادره بصـورة طبيعيـة، وبـدون أن يكـون فـي كـل هـذا مكان لخوف أو لندم.

متـى بـدأت تعيـش فـي كيانـك السـيكي، تحلـق عاليـاً فـوق الحيـاة الفيزيائيـة وتكتسـب حـس الأبديـة علـى الفـور وبـدون جهـد. أنـا اعتبـر هـذه الوسـيلة أفضـل عـلاج للتغلـب علـى خشـية المـوت. الوسـيلة الأولـى تنبنـي علـى الفطـرة السـليمة والتعقـل الحصـيف. أمـا الوسـيلة الثانيـة فهـي تجربـة عميقـة يمكـن اسـترجاعها فـي كـل مـرة نحقـق فيهـا الاتصـال بكياننـا السـيكي. وهـي تجربـة مشـوقة حقـاً مـن حيـث أنهـا تلقائيـة. بمجـرد أن نحقـق الاتصـال بكياننـا السـيكي نشـعر بالأبديـة وبأننـا عشـنا منـذ الأزل وأننـا سـوف نعيـش إلـى الأبـد. أمـا مـا يأتـي ويذهـب، فإنـه حـوادث عارضـة فـي الحيـاة لا أهميـة لهـا. هـذا هـو العـلاج الأفضـل بالفعـل. العـلاج الأول يشـبه حالـة سـجين يحـاول أن يجـد مزايـا فـي سـجنه تسـهل عليـه تقبـل هـذا السـجن، أمـا العـلاج الثـاني فيشـبه حالـة الرجـل الحـر الـذي أفلـت مـن سـجنه [...].

A different Outlook – نــظرة جديــدة

Now there is a small remedy which is very, very easy. For it is based on a simple personal question of one's common sense... You must observe yourself a little and say that when you are afraid it is as though the fear was attracting the thing you are afraid of. If you are afraid of illness, it is as though you are attracting the illness. If you are afraid of an accident, it is as though you were attracting the accident. And if you look into yourself and around yourself a little, you will find it out, it is a persistent fact. So if you have just a little common sense, you say: "It is stupid to be afraid of anything, for it is precisely as though I were making a sign to that thing to come to me. If I had an enemy who wanted to kill me, I would not go and tell him: "You know, it's me you want to kill!" It is something like that. So since fear is bad, we won't have it. And if you say that you are unable to prevent it by your reason, well, that shows you have no control over yourselves and must make a little effort to control yourselves. That is all.
14 October, 1953

A different Outlook – نـظـرة جديـدة

هنـاك أيضـا عـلاج آخـر فـي غايـة السـهولة. و هـو أيضـاً ينبنـي علـى اسـتخدام شخصـي بسـيط للفطـرة السـليمة والحصـافة... لـو لاحظنـا أنفسنـا قلـيلاً، نجـد أننـا عندما نخـاف مـن أي شـيء، يكـون ذلـك كمـا لـو كنـا نجـذب هذا الشـيء إلـى أنفسنـا. لـو خشـينا المـرض، يكـون ذلـك كمـا لـو كنـا نجتـذب المـرض، ولـو خفنـا مـن الحـوادث، يكـون ذلـك كمـا لـو كنـا نجتـذب إلينـا الحـوادث. ولـو دققنـا فـي أنفسـنا وفيمـا حولنـا نكتشـف أن هـذه الملاحظـة تصـدق دائمـا. عندئـذ نـرى أن الخـوف حماقـة، لأنـه بمثابـة أن نعطـي إشـارة إلـى الشـيء الـذي نخافـه لكـي يقدم علينـا، تمامـاً كمـا يكـون مـن الحماقـة لـو كـان لنـا عـدو ينـوي قتلنـا أن نـذهب إليـه ونعرفـه بأنفسـنا! دعنـا نـرفض الخـوف إذاً حيـث أنـه ضـار ولا نفـع فيـه. أمـا لـو قلنـا إننـا عـاجزون عـن استخدام هـذه الوسـيلة لأننـا لا نسـتطيع الـتحكم فـي أفكارنـا، يكـون ذلـك دلـيلاً علـى أننـا عـاجزون إطلاقـاً عـن الـتحكم فـي أنفسـنا، وعندئـذ يكـون لزامـاً علينـا أن نجتهـد فـي تعلـم الـتحكم فـي النفس. هذا كل ما في الأمر.

14 أكتوبر، 1953

A different Outlook – نـظـرة جـديـدة

About Pain and Suffering — عـن الألـم والـمـعـانـاة

The four Stages of Pain

"There are four stages in the pain God gives to us; when it is only pain; when it is pain that causes pleasure, when it is pain that is pleasure,; and when it is purely a fiercer form of delight."
Aphorism 421, Sri Aurobindo

The Mother commented as follows on the aphorism above:
If Sri Aurobindo refers to moral pain, whatever it may be, I can say from experience that the four stages he speaks of correspond to four states of consciousness that stem from the inner development and the degree of union with the divine consciousness obtained by the individual consciousness. When the union is perfect, there only remains the 'fiercer form of delight.'

That experience I had in 1912 (1912 or 1913, I don't remember)... I was in Paris. Once I had an anxiety about someone who was to travel to Paris and arrive at a certain time; time was passing and passing, and the person didn't arrive. Then, at one point, I had a sort of anguish suddenly... You see, I was already conscious of my psychic* being (I had been for a long time), and that anguish suddenly became extraordinarily intense, and it made (bursting gesture) like fireworks — a marvel! So I understand what he means by a "fierce form of delight." But it was purely psychological, it wasn't physical...

I don't know whether he was actually referring to physical pain? If he refers to physical pain endured by the body, the experience does not follow so clearly defined an order, all the more so as union with the Divine* most often causes the pain to disappear... physically, the body's whole experience now is that it only has to give itself unreservedly, to abandon itself totally to the divine Presence, and the pain, any pain at all, disappears...

It is not that it turns into something else: it disappears. And on a physical level, it's more important because, along with the pain, the CAUSE disappears too. Which means that the disorder that had occurred is dissolved. It no longer exists. That's why I don't think Sri Aurobindo is referring to physical things, because in the physical, experiences are different.

عـن الألـم والـمـعـاناة – About Pain and Suffering

مراحل الألم الأربعة

"الألـم الـذي يفرضـه الله علينـا لـه أربعـة مراحـل: فـي الأولـى يكون مجرد ألـم، وفـي الثانيـة يمتـزج مـع الألـم بعـض المتعـة، وفـي الثالثـة يتحـول الألـم كليـاً إلـى متعـة، أمـا فـي الرابعـة والأخيرة فإنه يكون نوعاً من الهناء العاتي."

أقوال مأثورة رقم 421، شري أوروبيندو

تعليق الأم:

لـو كـان شـري أوروبينـدو يريـد هنـا الألـم النفسـي، أيـاً كـان نوعـه، أسـتطيع أن أقـول عـن تجربـة أن المراحـل الأربعـة التـي يـذكرها تقابـل أربعـة حـالات مـن الـوعي تنشـأ مـن النمـو الـداخلي وتتوقـف علـى مـدى اتحـاد الـوعي الفـردي مـع الـوعي الإلهـي. فـي المرحلـة الأخيـرة، عندمـا يكـون الاتحـاد تامـاً، لا يبقى إلا ذلك "الهناء العاتي."

لقـد مـررت بهـذه التجربـة عـام 1912 (1912 أو 1913، لا أتـذكر الآن)عندما كنـت فـي بـاريس. ذات مرة داخلنـي قلـق بخصوص شـخص كنـت أتوقعـه وكـان قـد تـأخر كثيـراً فـي الوصـول. ومـع أن كيانـي السـيكي* كـان قـد اسـتيقظ لسـنوات خلـت، تنـامى قلقـي إلـى درجـة أنـه انفجـر فجـأة كمفرقعـات الألعـاب الناريـة وكـان ذلـك شـعوراً رائعـاً! وذلـك يجعلنـي أفهـم مـا يعنيـه شـري أوروبينـدو "بنـوع مـن الهنـاء العاتي." ولكن الألم في تجربتي تلك كان نفسياً بحتاً، ولم يكن بدنياً...

لا أعلم لـو كـان شـري أوروبينـدو يشـير فـي قولـه إلـى الألـم البدنـي؟ لـو كـان الأمـر كذلـك، فإن لمراحـل، تبعـاً لخبرتـي، لا تتـوالى بهـذا الترتيـب بالضـرورة. أضـف إلـى ذلـك أن الاتحـاد مـع **الواحـد-الكـل** ينهـي الألـم كليـاً. تجربتـي الحاليـة هـي أنـه بمجرد أن يهـب البـدن نفسـه بـدون أي شـرط ويستسـلم تمامـاً **للحضـرة الإلهيـة**، فـإن الألـم، أي نـوع مـن الألـم، يـزول ويتلاشـى... هـذا معنـاه أن الألـم بـدلاً مـن أن يتحـول إلـى شـيء آخـر يـزول كليـاً. وذلـك لـه أهميـة عظيمـة علـى المسـتوى البدنـي، لأنـه مـع زوال الألـم، يـزول أيضـاً **سـبب** الألـم، وهـذا معنـاه أن الخلـل [الصـحي] الـذي سـبب الألـم أساسـاً يتلاشـى بـدوره. التجربـة فـي حالـة الألـم البدنـي تختلـف عنهـا فـي حالـة الألـم النفسـي وهـذا هـو السـبب فـي اعتقادي أن شري أوروبيندو لا يشمل الألم البدني في هذا القول.

A different Outlook – نــظـرة جـديـدة

Psychological or inner things, even sensations (sensations about events, not about the body), have a fluidity, they are quite different in character. Things of the body have a sort of... (what shall I call it?) maybe a concrete stability or fixity, I don't know. For example, if you have a pain somewhere in the heart of lungs or...some pain), it corresponds to something within, something that happened, a disorder, and the pain (when you are in a tranquil state) corresponds to what we might call the "situation" of the cells, so when the pain disappears it means the cells are back in place — it doesn't mean that the disorder is continuing but you no longer feel it, that's no it. So it is not the sensation you have that changes, it's the material FACT that has changed. And that I find much more marvelous: the contact with the true Force puts things back to order.
Mother's Agenda, 28 March, 1970

The Transformation of Suffering

Why is there suffering? How to cure suffering?

.... because that is the only kind of vibration which can pull Matter out of its inertia.

The supreme Peace, the supreme Calm are deformed and disfigured into inertia, ... , and precisely because this was the deformation of true Peace and Calm, there was no reason why it should change! A certain vibration of awakening — of reawakening – was necessary to come out of this inertia, that could not pass directly from inertia to Peace; something was needed to shake the inertia, and that is translated externally by suffering.

I am speaking here of physical suffering, because all the other sufferings – vital, mental, emotional sufferings – are due to a wrong working of the mind, and these... may simply be classed together as Falsehood, that's all. But physical suffering gives me the impression of a child being beaten, because here, in Matter, Falsehood has become ignorance; that is to say, there is no bad will – no bad will is there in Matter, all is inertia and ignorance: complete ignorance of the Truth, ignorance of the Origin, ignorance of the Possibility and ignorance even of what is to be done in order not to suffer physically.

الأمـور النفسية والباطنية مثل الأحاسيس لها طـابـع مختلـف أكثر مرونـة وليونـة مـن الأمـور البدنيـة التـي تميـل إلـى الثبـوت والصـلابـة... لا أدري. علـى سبيـل المثـال: لـو كنـت فـي حالـة هـدوء [نفسي] وكنـت تعـانـي مـن ألـم فـي القلـب أو فـي الـرئتيـن، أو مـن أي ألـم بـدنـي آخـر، تكون خلايا بـدنك هي مصـدر ألمـك، وعنـدما يختفـي الألـم، يكـون ذلـك دليـلاً علـى أن خلايـاك عـادت إلـى حالتهـا لطبيعيـة. اختفـاء الألـم دليـل علـى أن الخلـل نفسـه قـد زال وأن الواقـع المـادي قـد تغيـر. وذلـك، فـي نظـري، شـيء أروع بكثيـر، لأنـه دليـل علـى أن اتصـالك **بالقوة الحقة** [القوة الإلهية] قـد شفاك.
أجندة الأم، 28 مارس 1970

تحويل المعاناة

ما سبب وجود المعاناة؟ كيف يمكن علاجها؟

... المعانة هي النوع الوحيد من الذبذبات الذي يستطيع أن يجذب المادة من خمولها.

السـلام والسـكون [اللـذان كانـا القصـد الإلهـي]، شُـوّها ومُسِخـا وتحـولا [فـي الخليقـة] إلـى خمـول وقصـور. وفـي ذلـك الجمـود والخمـول، لـم تشـعر [الخليقـة] بـأي داع لأن تتغيـر. ومـن ثـم أصبـح ضـروريـاً أن تتـدخل رعشـة إيقـاظ لتخليـص [الخليقـة] التـي أصبحـت عـاجـزة عـن العـودة إلى **السلام الإلهي الحقيقي**، من جمودها وخمولها. رعشة الإيقاظ هذه هي ما نشعر به كألم ومعاناة.

أنـا أتحـدث هنا عـن المعانـاة البدنيـة، لأن جميـع أنـواع المعانـاة الأخـرى – حيويـة، عقليـة وعاطفيـة – سـببها أداء خـاطـئ فـي الـذهن، ويمكـن تصنيفهـا ببسـاطة تحـت مجموعـة **الباطـل**. المعانـاة البدنيـة تـذكرني بمعانـاة الطفـل الـذي يُضـرَب [بـدون سـوء نيـة]، ذلـك لأن المـادة لا تـوجـد فيهـا إرادة شـريرة، والباطـل فيهـا مـا هـو إلا خمـول وجهـل: جهـل **بالحقيقة**، جهـل **بالأصـل وبالإمكانيـات**، وجهـل حتى بمـايلزم فعلـه لتجنب المعانـاة نفسهـا. هـذا الجهـل متفشـي فـي كـل مكـان فـي الخلايـا – والتجربـة التـي تتـرجم فـي الـوعـي البـدني البـدائي بالمعانـاة – هـي التجربـة الوحيدة التي تستطيع أن تـوقظ [البشـر] وأن تستحـث فيهم الطموح والتطلع إلى المعرفة والشفاء وتزكية الذات.

172

A different Outlook – نـظرة جديـدة

This ignorance is everywhere in the cells, and it is only the experience, the experience of what is translated in this rudimentary consciousness as suffering, which can awaken, bring forth the need to know and to cure, and the aspiration to transform oneself... whenever something goes wrong in the working (that is to say, instead of being supple, spontaneous, natural, the working becomes a painful effort, a struggle against something which takes the appearance of a bad will, but is only a reticence that does not understand), at that moment, the intensity of the aspiration, of the call, is tenfold, becomes constant. The difficulty is to remain at that state of intensity. Generally everything falls back, I cannot say into a somnolence, but a kind of relaxation: you take things easy; and it is only when the inner disorder becomes painful that the intensity grows and remains permanent. For hours – hours together – without slackening, the call, the aspiration, the will to be united with the Divine, to become the Divine, is maintained at its maximum. Why? Because there was externally what is called a physical disorder, a suffering. Otherwise, when there is no suffering, from time to time one soars up, then one falls back into a slackening; again another time one soars up once more... there is no end to it. That lasts eternally. If we want things to go fast (relatively fast according to the rhythm of our life), this smack of the whip is necessary. I am convinced of it, because as soon as you are within your inner being you look upon that with contempt (as regards oneself).

But then, all of a sudden, when there comes this true Compassion of the Divine Love, and when one sees all these things that appear so horrible, so abnormal, so absurd, this great pain which is upon all beings and even upon all things... then there takes birth in this physical being the aspiration to soothe, to cure, to remove that. There is in Love, at its Origin, something which is translated constantly as the intervention of Grace: a force, a sweetness, something like a vibration of solace spread everywhere, but which an illumined consciousness can direct, concentrate on some points. And it is there, there itself that I saw the true use one can make of thought: thought serves as a kind of channel to carry this vibration from place to place, wherever it is necessary. This force, this vibration of sweetness is there in a static way upon the world, pressing in order to be received, but it is an impersonal action. And thought – illumined thought, surrendered thought, thought which is no longer anything but an instrument, which tries no longer to initiate things, which is satisfied with being moved by the higher Consciousness – thought serves as an intermediary to establish a contact, a relation, and to enable this impersonal Force to act wherever it is necessary, upon definite points.

... عنـدما يخـتـل شـيء مـا فـي أداء البـدن، ويكـف الأداء عـن أن يكـون مرنـاً وتلقائيـاً وطبيعيـا، ويتحـول إلـى مجهـود مـؤلم وصـراع (وهـو مـا قـد يبـدو كسـوء نيـة، ولكنـه لـيس إلا تـردد نـاتج عـن جهـل)، عندئـذ تتضـاعف شدة التطلـع والـدعاء عشـر مـرات وتصبـح ثابتـة. الصعوبة تكمـن فـي الحفـاظ علـى هـذه الشدة. مـا يحـدث عـادة هـو أن كـل شـيء يتهافـت، لا إلـى نعـاس ولكـن إلـى نـوع مـن الاسـترخاء: أي ننـا نأخـذ الأمـور بسـهولة، وفقـط عنـدما يصبـح الخلـل الـداخلي مؤلمـاً، يعـود [التطلـع] إلـى شـدته ويصبـح مسـتديماً. علـى مـدى سـاعات – سـاعات بأكملهـا – وبـدون تهـاون، يسـتمر الـدعاء والتطلـع بأقصـى قـوةٍ وبرغبـة فـي الاتحـاد مـع **الواحـد-الكـل*** وفـي التطـابق معـه. لمـاذا؟ بسـبب مـا تعـارف النـاس علـى تسـميته خلـلاً بـدنياً يسـبب الألـم. وفـي الحالـة الأخـرى، عنـدما لا تكـون هنـاك معانـاة، فـإن المـرء يحلـق صـاعداً مـن آن إلـى آخـر، ثـم يتهافـت عائـداً إلـى إرخـاء الشـدة، ومـرة أخـرى يعـود المـرء إلـى التحليـق...وهكـذ دوالـيك! تلـك الـدورة قـد تتكـرر إلـى مـا لا نهايـة إذا لـم يكـن هنـاك سـوط الألـم الـذي هـو وحـده قـادرة علـى تسـيير الأمـور بسـرعة تتناسـب مـع إيقـاع حياتنـا. أنـا مقتنعـة مـن ذلـك. ولكـن بمجـرد أن نـدخل كياننـا الـداخلي، نشـعر بمـرارة الإهانـة فـي حقيقـة أن السـوط ضـروري لتحريكنـا إلـى الأمـام.

ولكـن فجـأة، عنـدما تتنـزل **الشـفقة الإلهيـة** الحقيقيـة، وعنـدما ينظـر المـرء إلـى كـل هـذه الأشـياء التـي تبـدو غايـة فـي الفظاعـة والشـذوذ والسـخف، هـذا الألـم العظيـم المُسَلَّط علـى جميـع الكائنـات وحتـى علـى جميـع الأشـياء... عندئـذ يولـد فـي هـذا الكـائن المـادي التطلـع إلـى تلطيـف وشـفاء وإزالـة كـل ذلـك. هنـاك فـي جوهـر **الحـب الإلهـي** شـيء يُتَرجـم باسـتمرار إلـى تخلـل **الرحمـة الإلهيـة**: شـيء قـوي وعـذب يشـبه ذبذبـة السـلوان المنتشـرة فـي كـل مكـان بحيـث يمكـن لـوعي مسـتنير أن يوجههـا و يركزهـا علـى لمواضـع [التـي تعـاني مـن الألـم]. وهنـا أجـد بالتحديـد النقطـة التـي نسـتطيع فيهـا أن نسـتخدم الفكـر ستخدامـاً صحيحـاً: أن نجعـل مـن الفكـر قنـاة لنقـل هـذه الذبذبـة مـن مكـان لآخـر كلمـا دعـت الضـرورة. هـذه القـوة، ذبذبـة العذوبـة هـذه، منتشـرة وسـاكنة فـوق العـالم وتقـوم بالضغـط علـى انتظـار القـادرين علـى تلقيهـا، ولكـن ذلـك يحـدث بصـورة غيـر شـخصية. أمـا التفكيـر، التفكيـر المسـتنير، التفكيـر الـذي سَلَّم نفسـه، الفكـر الـذي لـم يعـد أكثـر مـن أداة، الـذي لـم يعـد يريـد أن يسـتهل الأمـور، والـذي رضـي بـأن يكـون طـوع **الـوعي الأعلـى** – هـذا الفكـر يـؤدي وظيفـة الوسـيط أو حلقـة الوصـل التـي تمكـن هـذه القـوة غيـر الشـخصية مـن أن تعمـل علـى بعـض النقـاط المحـددة، أينمـا حتَّمـت الضـرورة.

A different Outlook – نـظـرة جـديـدة

It may be said in an absolute way that an evil always carries its own remedy. One might say that the cure of any suffering coexists with the suffering. So, instead of seeing an evil "useless" and "stupid" as it is generally thought to be, you see that the progress, the evolution which has made the suffering necessary — which is the cause of the suffering and the very reason for its existence — attains the intended result; and at the same time the suffering is cured, for those who are able to open themselves and receive. The three things — suffering as a means of progress, progress, and the cure of suffering — are coexistent, simultaneous; that is to say, they do not follow each other, they are there at the same time.

If, at the moment when the transforming action creates a suffering, there is in that which suffers the necessary aspiration and opening, the remedy also is taken in at the same time, and the effect is total, complete: transformation, with the action necessary to obtain it, and, at the same time, cure of the false sensation produced by the resistance. And the suffering is replaced by... something which is not known upon this earth, but which is akin to joy, well-being, trust and security. It is a supersensation, in a perfect peace, and which is obviously the only thing that can be eternal.

This analysis expresses very imperfectly what one would call the "content" of the Essential and Eternal Bliss.

I believe it is something that has been felt, experienced, partially and in a very fleeting manner, through all the ages, but which has just begun to concentrate and almost concretise itself upon earth.
28 September 1966

نـظـرة جديـدة – A different Outlook

مـن الممكـن القـول بصـورة جازمـة أن كـل أذى يحمـل معـه دواءه وأن المعانـاة وشفـاؤها يتعايشـان سـوياً على الـدوام. ولـذلك بـدلا مـن أن تـرى مـا يصيبك مـن أذى على أنـه شيء "عديم الفائـدة" ولا طائـل مـن ورائـه، تـرى كيـف أن التقـدم أو التطـور اللـذان جعـلا المعانـاة ضـرورية – اللـذان همـا سـببها ومبرر وجودهـا – يحققـان [فـي آخـر المطـاف] النتيجـة المقصـودة؛ وكيـف أن المعانـاة تصبـح فـي الوقـت نفسـه الشفاء عنـدما نكـون قـادرين على التفتـح والتلقـي. هـذه الأشيـاء الثلاثـة تتواجـد فـي ذات الوقـت: المعانـاة كوسيلة للتقـدم، والتقـدم نفسه، والشفاء مـن المعانـاة، أي أنها لا تتابـع، بل تتزامـن سـوياً.

لـو وجـد فـي الشـخص الـذي يعـاني، فـي لحظـة المعانـاة، التَـوق* والانفتـاح الضـروريان، فـإن الشـفاء يتم تحصيلـه فـي نفـس الوقـت، والنتيجـة تكـون شـاملة وكاملـة: التحـول والعمـل المطلـوب لتحقيقـه، وفـي نفـس الوقـت الشفاء مـن الشعـور [المرضـي] الكـاذب النـاتج مـن المقاومـة. عندئـذ يحـل محـل العنـاء... شـيء غيـر معـروف علـى الأرض، ولكنـه مـزيج مـن البهجـة والصـحة والثقـة والأمـان. إنـه شـعور فـائق يصاحبه سلام تام، ومن الواضح أنه الشيء الوحيد الذي يمكن أن يدوم إلى الأبد.

هذا التحليل يعبر بصورة ناقصة للغاية عما يمكن أن نسميه "مضمون" الهناء الجوهري المستديم.

أعتقـد أن النـاس قـد شـعروا بـه وخبروه علـى مـدى العصـور بصـورة جزئيـة وعـابرة للغايـة، ولـكنـه الآن في طريقه إلى التركز والتجسد على الأرض.

28 سبتمبر، 1966

176

A different Outlook – نـظرة جديـدة

About Happiness — عن السعادة

Create your own Atmosphere

Every time you think of something, it is as though you had a magnet in your hand and were attracting that thing towards yourself – you understand. Now, there are people who have a very, very bad habit of always thinking about all possible catastrophes, and are in a sort of constant apprehension about some calamity befalling them the next moment. I know many like that, there are some here. And so, those people have as though a magnet in their hands to attract calamities, not only upon themselves but upon others also. That lays a big responsibility upon them. And if one can't stop all the time from thinking about something some have a head that runs on and they haven't found a way of stopping it – well, why not make it run on the right lines instead of letting it run on the others! Once your head begins to run, let it run on all the good things that can happen. If it is obliged to turn round and round, well, turn then to the good side! That is, if somebody is ill, instead of saying: "What is going to happen, perhaps this is going to be very serious, and if it is that disease.. and a calamity comes so quickly", instead of all that, if one thinks: "Oh! that is nothing, illnesses are outer illusions translating some deeper vibrations which are not seen, that is why one doesn't speak about them, but that's how it is. And these deeper vibrations may come and set in order what has been disturbed. And this imbalance, this illness or bad thing that has come, well, it will be absorbed by the Grace and will disappear, no trace of it will remain, except that of things agreeable and pleasant." One may continue to think in this way uninterruptedly. People always need to make their mind run, run, run, but then make it run on the right lines, you will see that it has an effect. For instance, let it go like this: that I shall learn better and better, shall know better and better, become healthier and healthier, and all difficulties will vanish, and wicked people will become sweet and good, and ill people will be cured, and houses which should be built will be built, and those things which should disappear will disappear, but giving place to better things, and the world will move in a constant progress, and at the end of that progress there will be a total harmony, and so on, and continue thus. You can go on endlessly. But then you will have around you and around your head all kinds of pretty things.
December 9, 1953

A different Outlook – نـظرة جديـدة

About Happiness — عن السعادة

اخلق جوك الخاص

في كـل مـرة تفكـر فيهـا فـي شـيء مـا، يكـون ذلك كمـا لـو كنت تجتذب بمغناطيس في يدك هـذا الشـيء نحـوك. تتفشى فـي النـاس أحيانـاً عـادة سيئة للغايـة، ألا وهـي أنهـم يفكـرون باستمرار فـي كـل الكـوارث التـي يحتمـل أن تصـيبهم، ويعيشـون فـي حالـة توقـع مسـتمر لمصـيبة أو أخـرى تـنقض عـليهم فـي اللحظـة التاليـة. أعـرف كثيرين علـى هـذا الحـال، بعضـهم موجـودون هنـا. هـؤلاء القوم يجتـذبون المصـائب ويجلبونهـا لا علـى رؤوسـهم فحسب، بـل علـى رؤوس الآخـرين أيضـاً. وهـذا يُحَمـِّلهم مسئولية كبيرة. ولكـن حتـى لـو سلمنا بـأنهم عـاجزون عـن منـع أنفسـهم مـن التفكير وعـن إيقـاف أمخـاخهم عـن النشـاط المسـتمر، لمـاذا لا يحولـون الرذيلـة إلـى فضيلـة بـأن يفكـروا أفكـار تفاؤل بـدلاً مـن أفكـار تشـاؤم؟ متـى شـرع دماغـك فـي اللـف والـدوران، اجعلـه يـدور حـول كـل الأشـياء 'الإيجابيـة الممكنة. عندما تفكـر مـثلاً فـي مـرض، بـدلاً مـن أن تبـدأ بـالقلق وتتصـور كـل الأمـراض الخطيرة المحتملـة، تفكـر فـي أن المـرض مـا هـو إلا وهـم خـارجي وترجمـة لذبـذبات باطنيـة فـي الأعمـاق لا يـتكلم عنهـا النـاس لأنهـم لا يسـتطيعون رؤيتها، وأن ذبـذبات باطنيـة أخـرى تسـتطيع أن تتـدخل وتُـقِّوم الخلـل، وأن **النعمـة الإلهيـة** كفيلـة بإزالـة المـرض بكـل أعراضـه السـيئة بحيـث لا يتبقـى مـن آثـاره إلا مـا هـو مقبـول وسـار. وليتـك تسـتمر فـي التفكيـر الإيجابـي علـى هـذا المنـوال بـدون انقطـاع. بـدلاً مـن أن تسـمح لـذهنك بـأن يتجـول هنـا وهنـاك بـدون توقـف، أجعلـه يعمـل علـى الخطـوط السـليمة — سـترى أن ذلـك سـتكون لـه نتـائج طيبـة. هـاك بعـض الأفكـار الإيجابيـة علـى سـبيل المثـال: "سـوف أتعلـم أحسـن وأحسـن، وسـوف أتقـدم فـي المعرفـة أكثـر وأكثـر، وسـوف تتحسـن صـحتي باستمـرار، وسـوف تـزول جميـع المصـاعب، وسـوف يصـبح الأشـرار طيبـين، وسـوف يشـفى المرضـى، وسـوف يجـد المتشـردون منـازل تـأويهم، وسـوف تختفـي الأشـياء التـي ينبغـي أن تـزول وتحـل محلـها أشـياء أفضـل منهـا، وسـوف يسـتمر العـالم فـي تقدمـه، وسـوف يـؤدي هـذا التقـدم فـي النهايـة إلـى انسـجام شـامل...". عنـدما تفكـر باستمرار علـى هـذا المنـوال، تحيـط نفسـك بكـل أنـواع الأشـياء الجميلـة اللطيفـة.

9 ديسمبر، 1953

178

A different Outlook – نـظـرة جديـدة

Be always kind

Be always kind, come out of all bitter criticism, see no more evil in everything, obstinately force yourself to see nothing but the kind Presence of the divine Grace and you will see not only within you but around you, an atmosphere of quiet joy, peaceful trust, luminous hope spreading more and more and not only you will feel happy and quiet yourself but the major part of your bodily disorders will disappear.

It is quite remarkable that the digestive functions are extremely sensitive to a critical, unkind, sour attitude, a harsh judgment. Nothing more than that and the functioning of digestion is disturbed. And it is a vicious circle : the more the digestive function is disturbed, the more you become unkind, critical, disgusted with life and things and persons. So you do not come out of it. There is only one cure, namely, to deliberately come out of this attitude, to refuse absolutely to have it and to force on yourself, through constant control, a willed attitude of thorough kindliness. Try and you will see that you are much better in health.
November 1956- November 1962

The Human Problem

It is obvious that what especially characterises man is this mental capacity of watching himself live. The animal lives spontaneously, automatically, and if it watches itself live, it must be to a very minute and insignificant degree, and that is why it is peaceful and does not worry. Even if an animal is suffering because of an accident or an illness, this suffering is reduced to a minimum by the fact that it does not observe it, does not project it in its consciousness and into the future, does not imagine things about its illness or its accident.

With man there has begun this perpetual worrying about what is going to happen, and this worry is the principal, if not the sole cause of his torment. With this objectivising consciousness there has begun anxiety, painful imaginations, worry, torment, anticipation of future catastrophes, with the result that most men – and not the least conscious, the most conscious – live in perpetual torment. Man is too conscious to be indifferent, he is not conscious enough to know what will happen. Truly it could be said without fear of making a mistake that of all earth's creatures he is the most miserable. The human being is used to being like that because it is an atavistic state which he has inherited from his ancestors, but it is truly a miserable condition.

كن حنوناً على الدوام

كن شفوقاً وحنوناً، دع جانباً عـادة الانتقـاد المـر، كُـف عـن توقـع الشـر فـي كـل شـيء، واستعمـل إرادتك لـكي تكون واعيـاً **بالنعمـة الإلهيـة** الرحيمـة ولا شـيء غيرهـا، عندئـذ ستشـعر، أكثـر وأكثـر، فـي داخلـك، وأيضـاً فـي كـل مـا حولـك، بجـو مـن البهجـة والهـدوء والثقـة والسـلام والأمـل والنـور. عنـدما تشعر بهذا الهدوء وهذه السعادة، يزول الجزء الأعظم من متاعبك البدنية.

مـن الملفـت للنظـر أن وظائـف الهضـم تتـأثر بشـكل حسـاس عنـدما نتخـذ موقـف النقـد الـلاذع وإصـدار الأحكـام القاسيـة علـى الأمـور. هـذا الموقـف وحـده كفيـل بـأن يخـل بعمـل الجهـاز الهضمـي ويدخلنـا فـي دورة شـر لا نقـدر علـى الإفـلات منهـا: كلمـا اختـل هضمنـا، كلمـا زدنـا قسـوة ومـرارة وقرفـاً مـن الحيـاة والنـاس والأشـياء، وكلمـا ازددنـا قسـوة ومـرارة، كلمـا زاد اختـلال هضمنـا. العـلاج الوحيـد هـو أن نصمـم علـى التخلـص مـن هـذا الموقـف وأن نرفضـه كليـاً، وأن نستعيـن بقدرتنـا علـى التحكـم فـي أنفسـنا لكي نتبنى موقف الرأفة والشفقة. حاول ذلك وسوف تخبر تحسناً ملحوظاً في صحتك.

نوفمبر 1956 – نوفمبر 1962

مشكلة الإنسان

مـن الواضـح أن الخاصـة التـي تميـز الإنسـان [عـن سـائر الخليقـة] هـي قدرتـه علـى أن يراقـب نفسـه وحياتـه. الحيـوان يعيـش تلقائيـاً، وإذا مـا راقـب نفسـه يكـون ذلـك بقـدر صغيـر للغايـة لا يسـتحق الذكـر، وهـذا هـو السـبب فـي أنـه يعيـش فـي سـلام ولا يعـرف القلـق. وحتـى عنـدما يعانـي الحيـوان نتيجـة لحادثـة أو مـرض، تكـون معاناتـه ضئيلـة إلـى أقصـى حـد لأنـه لا يلاحظهـا، ولا يركـز عليهـا فـي وعيـه ولا يحمل الهموم التي تأتي من تصور العواقب المحتملة لهذا المرض أو الحادثة في المستقبل.

القلـق المسـتمر بخصـوص مـا قـد يحـدث فـي المسـتقبل بـدأ مـع الإنسـان، وهـو السـبب الرئيسـي، وربمـا كـان السـبب الأوحـد فـي عـذاب البشـر. بنمـو الـوعي الـذي لا يعتـرف إلا بالأشـياء الملموسـة، ظهـر القلـق والعـذاب والتخيـلات المؤلمـة وتوقـع الكـوارث المسـتقبلية، ونتـج مـن ذلـك أن معظـم البشـر، حتـى أكثـرهم وعيـاً، أصبحـوا يعيشـون فـي عـذاب دائـم. وعـي الإنسـان يكفـي لكـي يجعلـه يكتـرث ويبالـي، ولكنـه لا يكفـي ليطلعـه علـى مـا سـوف يحـدث بالفعـل. حقيقـة نسـتطيع أن نقـول بثقـة تامـة أن الإنسـان هـو أكثـر المخلوقـات الأرضيـة بؤسـاً. هـذا وضـع ورثـه الإنسـان مـن أسـلافه وتعـود عليـه، وهـو وضـع يستدعي الرثاء حقاً.

A different Outlook – نـظرة جـديـدة

Of course, it is impossible for man to fall back to the level of the animal and lose the consciousness he has acquired; therefore, for him there is only one means, one way to get out of this condition he is in, which I call a miserable one, and to emerge into a higher state where worry is replaced by a trusting surrender and the certitude of a luminous culmination – this way is to change the consciousness

How can a problem be solved when one doesn't have the necessary knowledge? And the unfortunate thing is that man believes that he has to resolve all the problems of his life, and he does not have the knowledge needed to do it. That is the source, the origin of all his troubles – that perpetual question, "What should I do?." which is followed by another one still more acute, "What is going to happen?" and at the same time, more or less, the inability to answer. That is why all spiritual disciplines begin with the necessity of surrendering all responsibility and relying on a higher principle. Otherwise peace is impossible.

And yet, consciousness has been given to man so that he can progress, can discover what he doesn't know, develop into what he has not yet become; and so it may be said that there is a higher state than that of an immobile and static peace: it is a trust total enough for one to keep the will to progress, to preserve the effort for progress while ridding it of all anxiety, all care for results and consequences. This is one step ahead of the methods which may be called "quietist", which are founded on the rejection of all activity and a plunging into an immobility and inner silence, which forsake all life because it has been suddenly felt that without peace one can't have any inner realisation and, quite naturally, one thought that one couldn't have peace so long as one was living in outer conditions, in the state of anxiety in which problems are set and cannot be solved, for one does not have the knowledge to do so.

The next step is to face the problem, but with the calm and certitude of an absolute trust in the supreme Power which knows, and can make you act. And then, instead of abandoning action, one can act in a higher peace that is strong and dynamic.

This is what could be called a new aspect of the divine intervention in life, a new form of intervention of the divine forces in existence, a new aspect of spiritual realisation.
March 26, 1958

A different Outlook – نـظـرة جـديـدة

واضح أن هبـوط الإنسـان مرة أخرى إلـى مستوى الحيـوان وتخليـه عن الـوعي الـذي اكتسبه ليس حـلاً مقبـولاً؛ ولـذلك لـيس أمامـه إلا طريـق واحـد وهـو أن يخرج مـن حالتـه الراهنـة، التـي أصـفها بأنهـا بائسـة، ويرتقـي إلـى حالـة أسـمى يَحِـل فيهـا التسليم والثقـة والتأكد مـن بلـوغ القمـة محـل اقلـق؛ أي باختصار أن يغير الإنسان وعيه.

كيف يمكن للمرء أن يحـل مشـاكل لا يملـك المعرفـة الضرورية لحلها؟ لسوء حظـه يعتقد الإنسـان أنـه مطالب بـأن يحـل مشـاكل حياتـه بنفسه. تساؤل الإنسـان المستمر عـن مـا ينبغـي أن يفعله والسـؤال الآخـر الأكثـر إزعاجـاً الـذي يتبعـه: "مـاذا سيحدث؟"، همـا مصـدر وسبب كـل متاعبـه، فهي أسئلة الجـواب عليهـا لـيس في وسعه. لـذلك تنـادي جميـع المناهج الروحيـة قبـل كـل شـيء بضرورة تسليم المسئولية والاعتماد على مبدأ أكثر علواً وارتفاعاً. بدون هذا التسليم، يكون الخلاص مستحيلاً.

ومـع ذلك، مُنِـح الإنسـان وعيـاً يمكنـه مـن التقـدم واكتشـاف مـا هـو يجهله وتحقيـق مـا هـو لم يحققه بعد؛ ولـذلك نستطيع أن نقـول أن هنـاك حـال أفضـل مـن مجـرد السـلام السلبي السـاكن ألا وهو الثقـة الشـاملة التـي تتيح للإنسـان أن يحـافظ علـى إرادة التقـدم وأن يكـون فـي الوقت ذاتـه قـدراً علـى الاجتهـاد فـي السـعي نحـو التقـدم ولكـن بـدون أي قلـق بخصـوص النتـائج والعواقب. هـذه تكـون خطـوة إلـى الأمـام بالمقارنـة بالمناهـج التـي تنـادي بالسكينة التامة والصـمت الـداخلي ورفض النشـاط، والتي تهمـل الحيـاة لأنهـا تعتبـر السـلبية والسكينة التامـة شـرطاً ضروريـاً للتحقيـق الـداخلي. هـذد المناهج تعتبـر الجمـع بـين الحيـاة والتحقيـق الروحـي مستحيلاً، لأن الحيـاة لا تـوفر السـلام والسكينة اللازمـين للتحقيق.

الخطـوة التاليـة هـي أن يواجـه المـرء المشـكلة بالهـدوء والثبـات الـذين يأتيـان مـن الثقـة المطلقـة فـي **القـدرة الإلهيـة** التـي تعلـم كـل شـيء وتمكننـا مـن الفعـل والنشـاط. وبـدلاً مـن تجنـب النشـاط، يصبـح المرء قادراً على العمل في سلام أعلى لا يتعارض مع القوة والديناميكية.

هـذا هـو مـا يمكن أن نعتبره وجهـاً جديـداً مـن أوجـه التـدخل الإلهـي فـي الحيـاة، وهيئـة جديـدة لتـدخل القوى الإلهية في الوجود، ووجهـاً جديداً من أوجه التحقيق الروحي.
26 مارس، 1958

A different Outlook – نـظـرة جـديـدة

About Time – عـن الـوقـت

For each thing its own Time

For each activity, each realisation, each movement, there is a definite period of time, which differs. There are countless periods of time which are entangled; but each thing is regulated by a kind of rhythm which is this thing's own rhythm.

You see, for the facility of their outer existence, men have divided time more or less arbitrarily into years, months, weeks, days, hours, minutes, seconds, etc.; it is a rhythm that's more or less arbitrary, because it has been created by man, but it has in itself a certain reality, for it corresponds to universal movements... as far as possible. And that is why, by the way, we celebrate the birthday, for example: because there is a certain rhythm in each one's existence which is established by this regular return of circumstances analogous to those in which he was born.

And all movements – when you observe them, you become aware that they have a certain rhythm – the movements of inner consciousness, for example, not only from the point of view of understanding but that of personal reactions, of the ups and downs in progress; of a fairly regular periodic return, at once of advancing and recoiling, of difficulties and of helps. But if each person is attentive he realises that his own rhythm is absolutely particular to him, it is not the same rhythm as his neighbour's. But even as the seasons follow a certain rhythm, regular enough on the whole, so the individual life has its seasons. And when one studies oneself attentively, one finds out that there are even certain repetitions of analogous circumstances at regular intervals. Even, very sensitive people become aware that there are certain days of the week or certain hours of the day when they can do things more easily. Some of them have particular difficulties on particular days and at particular hours; some on the contrary have better inspirations at particular moments – but everyone has to find this out in himself by observation. Naturally it is far from being absolute, it is not strict, and if it is troublesome, it can be eliminated very easily simply by a little effort of resolute will. But if it helps, one can make use of it.

And all this, each thing having its own rhythm, well, it makes an extremely complicated crisscrossing of rhythms, which results in what we see: something which seems to have none – because it is too complicated, it is too complex.

عـن الوقـت — About Time

لكل شيء أوان

هنـاك أوان محـدد لكـل نشـاط ولكـل تحقيـق ولكـل حركـة. كـل شـيء يتبـع إيقاعـه الخـاص. هنـاك مواقيـت لا حصر لها، وهي متداخلة بعضها مع البعض.

اصـطلح النـاس، لتسـيير حيـاتهم الظاهريـة، علـى تقسـيم الوقـت إلـى سـنين وأشـهر وأسـابيع وأيـام وسـاعات ودقـائق وثـواني وهكـذا. ومـع أن هـذا التقسـيم اعتبـاطي إلـى حـد مـا لأنـه مـن صنـع الإنسـان، إلا أنـه يسـتند علـى حقيقـة أن الأمـور والأحـداث تحـاول بقـدر المستطاع مواءمـة حركـات كونيـة. وهـذا، علـى فكـرة، هـو السـبب في إننـا نحتفـل بأعيـاد ميلادنـا، فحيـاة كـل منـا لهـا إيقـاع خـاص بهـا يَتمثل في العـودة المتكـررة للظـروف [الفلكيـة] التي كانت سـائدة وقـت ولادتنـا

لـو دققنـا النظـر، نجـد أن حركـات وعينـا البـاطني لهـا أيضـاً إيقاعهـا الخـاص، وذلـك لا يقتصـر علـى حركـات الفكـر وردود الفعـل فحسـب، بـل يشـمل أيضـاً تنـاوب العلـو والهبـوط والتقـدم والتـأخر والأوقـات الحرجـة وأوقـات اليسـر في تقدمنـا [الروحي]. كـل فـرد يسـتطيع لـو دقـق النظـر أن إيقاعـه يخصـه شخصيـاً وأنـه يختلـف عـن إيقـاع جـاره. وكمـا أن فصـول العـام لهـا إيقـاع منتظـم إلـى حـد كبيـر، فالحيـاة الفرديـة كـذلك لهـا مواسـمها، بمعنـى أن ظـروف معينـة تتكـرر بصـورة منتظمـة. ذوو الحساسـية المرهفـة يلاحظـون أحيانـاً أن بعـض أيـام الأسـبوع وبعـض سـاعات النهـار تسـمح لهـم بـأداء شئونهم بسـهولة تفـوق تلـك التي يخبرونهـا في الأيـام والسـاعات الأخـرى. في حيـن يعـاني البعـض مـن تفـاقم المشـاكل في أيـام وسـاعات معينـة، يتلقـى البعـض الآخـر أفضـل إلهـامهم في لحظـات معينـة — ولكـن هـذه أمـور شخصيـة ينبغـي أن يكتشـفها كـل فـرد بملاحظـة مـا يـدور بداخلـه. هـذه تجـارب شخصيـة وليسـت قـوانين مطلقـة ولـو كانـت معرفتهـا مفيـدة، لا مـانع مـن اسـتخدامها، وإذا لـم تكـن، يمكن الاستغناء عنها بسهولة بواسطة الإرادة.

كـل شـيء لـه إيقـاع خـاص بـه، وذلـك يـؤدي [علـى المسـتوى الجمـاعي] إلـى شـبكة معقـدة مـن الإيقاعـات المتقاطعة تكـاد تبـدو لنـا تشوشـاً لا نظـام فيـه.

A different Outlook – نـظـرة جديـدة

How can we make use of it, Sweet Mother?

Well, if... let us say, you know... we are speaking of yoga... if you observe in yourself a certain repetition of conditions, for example, that at a particular hour, a certain time of day, in certain circumstances, it is easier for you to concentrate or meditate, well, you make use of that by doing it at that time. Naturally, you must not become its slave; one can use it but it must not become a necessity so that if the hour has gone by one can't meditate then. But if it is a good help, one uses the help; it's all a matter of observation.

If you study yourself you can become aware that in the year certain periods come due not only to personal conditions but more general ones – conditions of Nature in general. There are times when you meet more difficulties in the sadhana*; there are times, on the contrary, when you feel in yourself a greater push for the growth of knowledge and consciousness. This helps you in the sense that, if at a given time you find yourself in the midst of special difficulties or something that seems like a stoppage, instead of lamenting you tell yourself, "Why, it's the usual time; it's because we are at this particular time of the year." And you wait with patience for the time to pass; or do what you can, but without being discouraged and saying, "Ah, look, I am not getting on, I am not making any progress." It helps you to be reasonable.

And naturally one can take one more step and take precautions in such a way... inner precautions to be independent of these external influences. But this comes much later, when one begins to be the conscious master of one's sadhana*. That comes afterwards.

October 19, 1955

A different Outlook – نـظـرة جـديـدة

أيتها الأم العذبة: كيف يمكن الانتفاع من هذه المعرفة؟

حسناً، دعنـا نعتبر مجـال اليوغـا... لـو لاحظت أن التركيـز والتأمـل أيسـر بالنسبة لـك فـي وقت معين وتحـت ظـروف معينـة، تستطيع أن تمارسـهما فـي هـذا الوقت وفـي هـذه الظـروف علـى شـرط ألا تستعبدك عاداتك لدرجـة أن تصبح عـاجزاً عن الممارسـة تحت ظروف أخرى. تلك مسـألة ملاحظـة [دقيقة ومستمرة] لا أكثر.

لـو راقبت نفسك بعنـاية تكتشف، فـي سياق ممارستك، أن المصاعب تتكاثـر فـي أوقـات معينـة مـن العـام، فـي حين تشـعر فـي أوقـات أخـرى بـدوافع أقـوى للاستزادة مـن المعرفـة والـوعي، كمـا أنـك تلاحـظ أن هـذا التـأرجح لا يتوقـف فقـط علـى ظروفـك الشخصية، بـل علـى ظـروف عامـة تتعلق **بالطبيعـة**. هـذه معرفـة نافعـة لأنها تجنبك لـوم النـفس عندما تصادف مصـاعب مكثفـة تمنعك مـن الممارسـة وتتيح لـك عندئـذ أن تلقـي اللـوم علـى الظروف الموسـمية، وأن تنتظر صـابراً إلـى أن ينقضـي الموسـم، مكتفيـاً بـأن تفعل مـا فـي طاقتـك، دون أن تقع فريسـة للإحبـاط. إنها معرفة تجعلك أكثر تعقلاً.

وبـالطبع تستطيع أن تـذهب خطـوة أبعد مـن ذلك بـأن تتخـذ الاحتياطـات الداخليـة التـي تحـررك كليـاً مـن هـذه المؤثرات الخارجيـة [التي تسبب التـأرجح]. ولكن بلـوغ ذلك يتطلب وقتـاً طـويلاً ولا يـأتي إلا عندما تتقدم في الوعي وتصبح ممارساً ضليعاً في اليوغا.
أكتوبر 19، 1959

A different Outlook – نـظـرة جـديـدة

About Money – عـن الـمـال

Money as a Universal Force

> *"Money is the visible sign of a universal force, and this force in its manifestation on earth works on the vital and physical planes and is indispensable to the fullness of the outer life. In its origin and its true action it belongs to the Divine. But like other powers of the Divine it is delegated here and in the ignorance of the lower Nature can be usurped for the uses of the ego or held by Asuric [hostile] influences and perverted to their purpose. This is indeed one of the three forces – power, wealth, sex – that have the strongest attraction for the human ego and the Asura [Hostiles] and are most generally misheld and misused by those who retain them...For this reason most spiritual disciplines ...proclaim poverty and bareness of life as the only spiritual condition. But this is an error; it leaves the power in the hands of the hostile forces. To reconquer it for the Divine to whom it belongs and use it divinely for the divine life is the supramental way for the sadhaka."*
> Sri Aurobindo

How can one know if one's way of using money is in accordance with the divine Will?

One must first know what the divine Will is. But there is a surer way – to surrender money for the divine work, if one is not sure oneself. "Divinely" means at the service of the Divine – it means not to use money for one's own satisfaction but to place it at the Divine's service.

Sri Aurobindo speaks of "a weak bondage to the habits that the possession of riches creates".

When you are rich and have a lot of money to spend, generally you spend it on things you find pleasant, and you become habituated to these things, attached to these things, and if one day the money is gone, you miss it, you are unhappy, you are miserable and feel all lost because you no longer have what you were in the habit of having. It is bondage, a weak attachment. He who is quite detached, when he lives in the midst of these things, it is well with him; when these things are gone, it is well also; he is totally indifferent to both.

About Money – عن المـال

المال قوة كونية

"المـال تعبير جلي عـن قـوة كونيـة تعمـل عـلى المستويين الحيوي* والمـادي، وهـي قـوة لا يمكن الاستغناء عنهـا لكمـال الحيـاة على الأرض. قوة المـال تنتمـي فـي أساسها وعملهـا الحقيقـي إلى **الواحـد-الكـل*** [وإن كانت فـي عملهـا عـلى الأرض لا تصـدر منـه مباشـرة، بـل تعمـل بتوكيـل منـه]، لـذلك تـتمكن قـوى الأنانيـة والقـوى المعاديـة مـن الاستيلاء عليهـا واستغلالها فـي أغراضـها الخاصـة. المـال هـو أحـد القـوى الثلاثـة (السلطان والثـروة والجـنس) التي ينجـذب إليهـا "الأنـا" البشـري والقـوى المعاديـة أشـد الانجـذاب، وهـي أيضـا القـوى الثلاثـة التـي تخضـع لسيطرة هـذه القـوى المعاديـة كـل الخضـوع. هـذه هـو السبب فـي أن معظـم الأنظمـة الروحيـة تنـادي بـأن الفقـر والتقشـف شـرط أساسـي لكـل مـن يرغبـون الحيـاة الروحيـة. ولكـن هـذا ادعـاء خـاطئ؛ لأن تحقيـق هـذا الشـرط يتـرك المـال وقدرتـه فـي أيـادي القـوى المعاديـة. طريـق السـوبرامنتال* يـدعو الممـارس بـالأحرى إلى استرجاع المـال مـن القـوى المعاديـة وإعادتـه إلـى مالكـه الأصلـي **الواحـد-الكـل** واستغلالـه في خدمتـه".

شري أوروبيندو

في تعاملنا بالمـال، مـا هـو السبيل لأن نكـون علـى ثقـة بأننا نفعل ذلـك علـى نمـط يـوائم **الإرادة الإلهيـة؟**

يجب أولاً أن نعـرف مـا هـي **الإرادة الإلهيـة**. إذا لـم نكـن واثقـين مـن علمنـا، هنـاك طريـق مضمون: أن نكرس المال للعمل الإلهي بمعنى ألا ننفقه في إشباع رغباتنا وإنما في خدمة **الواحد-الكل.**

شري أوروبيندو يلمح إلى ضعف البشر وتعلقهم بالثروات التي يملكونها.

عندما تكون ثريـاً وقادراً علـى الإنفـاق بسـعة وبـذخ، فإنـك تنفق المـال عـادة على الأشياء التـي تَسُرُك ومـن ثـم تتعـود علـى هـذه الأشياء وتتعلـق بهـا. وإذا فقـدت ثروتـك لأي سبب مـن الأسبـاب، تشعر بـالبؤس لأنـك لـم تعـد تملـك الأشياء التـي تعـودت عليهـا. هـذا هـو الضعف والتعلق الـذي يشـير إليـه شـري أوروبينـدو [أعـلاه]. مـن يحـرر نفسـه كليـاً مـن التعلـق والارتبـاط، يعيش هانئـاً وراضيـاً في الرخاء وفي الشظف ولا يبالي أو يكترث كثيراً في أي من الحالين.

A different Outlook – نـظـرة جديـدة

That is the right attitude: when it is there he uses it, when it is not he does without it. And for his inner consciousness this makes no difference. That surprises you, but it is like that.

> *If one has the power to acquire a lot of money, does this mean that one has a certain control over terrestrial forces?*

This depends upon how one acquires it. If you get it by foul ways, that does not mean that you have a control. But if someone, scrupulously doing his duty, sees that money comes to him, it is evidently because he exercises a control over these forces. There are people who have the power of attracting money and they haven't the least need to practise dishonesty to get it. Others, even to get a few pennies, must make all sorts of contrivances, more or less clear. So one cannot say... We see a rich man and think he must be exercising a control over the forces of money – no, not necessarily. But if a man remains perfectly honest and does what he thinks is his duty without caring to acquire money, and yet money comes to him, evidently he has a certain affinity with those forces.

> *It is said, "One cannot make a heap without making a hole", one cannot enrich oneself without impoverishing someone else. Is this true?*

This is not quite correct. If one produces something, instead of an impoverishment it is an enrichment; simply one puts into circulation in the world something else having a value equivalent to that of money. But to say that one cannot make a heap without making a hole is all right for those who speculate, who do business on the Stock Exchange or in finance – there it is true. It is impossible to have a financial success in affairs of pure speculation without its being detrimental to another. But it is limited to this. Otherwise a producer does not make a hole if he heaps up money in exchange for what he produces. Surely there is the question of the value of the production, but if the production is truly an acquisition for the general human wealth, it does not make a hole, it increases this wealth. And in another way, not only in the material field, the same thing holds for art, for literature or science, for any production at all.

> *When I was doing business (Export-import), I always had the feeling of robbing my neighbour.*

A different Outlook – نـظـرة جـديـدة

الموقف السليم تجاه المال هو أن تستخدمه لو توفر، وإذا لم يتوفر أن تتصرف بدونه، بدون أن يتغير وعيك الداخلي في كلتا الحالتين. قد يدهشك أن مثل هذا التحرر التام من المال ممكن، ولكنه حقيقة واقعة [يتوصل إليها البعض].

هل يمكن اعتبار قدرة الحصول على المال دليلاً على قدرة التحكم في القوى الأرضية؟

هذا يتوقف على كيفية الحصول على المال. لو حصل شخص على المال بطرق ملتوية، يكون جواب سؤالك النفي. ولكن لو كان هذا الشخص يؤدي عمله بأمانة تامة في حين يسعى المال إليه، يكون ذلك دليلاً جلياً على تحكمه في القوى الأرضية. بعض الناس قادرون على اجتذاب المال بدون أي حاجة إلى اللجوء إلى الغش. وآخرون لا يقدرون على كسب أقل القليل من المال بدون اللجوء إلى حيل من جميع الأنواع. ولذلك لا يوجد جواب قاطع على سؤالك... أحيانا ننظر إلى رجل ثري ونظن أنه يتحكم في قوى المال — ولكن هذا استنتاج لا يصدق في جميع الأحوال. أما الرجل الذي يظل أميناً ويؤدي واجبه بدون اكتراث بالمال ويجد المال رغم ذلك مقبلاً عليه، يكون بالطبع في حالة تآلف مع القوى الأرضية.

يقول البعض أننا "لا نستطيع أن نكدس كوماً بدون أن نحفر حفرة"، بمعنى إننا لا نستطيع أن نجمع المال إلا على حساب قوم آخرين. هل هذا صحيح؟

هذا يتوقف على كيفية كسب المال. لأننا عندما نكسب المال من الإنتاج، نثري الآخرين ولا نُفقِرهم بأن نضيف إلى العالم شيئاً جديداً له قيمة مالية. القول الذي ذكرته [الكوم والحفرة] يصدق في حالة الاشتغال بالمضاربات في البورصات والأعمال التجارية. اكتساب المال من المضاربات يكون عادة على حساب الآخرين. ولكن ذلك لا يسري في حالة الانتاج. فالمُنتج الذي يغتني من منتجاته لا يُفقِر الآخرين إذا كانت مُنتَجاته نافعة وتضيف إلى مجموع الثروة البشرية. وذلك لا يقف عند حد الانتاج المادي فحسب، بل يسري أيضاً على الانتاج الفني والأدبي والعلمي وفي جميع مجالات الإنتاج الأخرى.

عندما كنت اشتغل بالاستيراد والتوريد، كنت أشعر دائماً بأننا أسرق من جاري.

A different Outlook – نـظـرة جـديـدة

This is living at the expense of others, because one multiplies the middlemen. Naturally, it is perhaps convenient, practical, but from the general point of view, and above all in the way it is practised, it is living at the expense of the producer and the consumers. One becomes an agent, not at all with the idea of rendering service (because there is not one in a million who has this idea), but because it is an easy way of earning money without making any effort. But of course, among the ways of making money without any effort, there are others much worse than that! They are countless.

> *Friends from outside have often asked me this question: "When one is compelled to earn his living, should one just conform to the common code of honesty or should one be still more strict?"*

This depends upon the attitude your friend has taken in life. If he wants to be a sadhak, it is indispensable that rules of ordinary morality do not have any value for him. Now, if he is an ordinary man living the ordinary life, it is a purely practical question, isn't it? He must conform to the laws of the country in which he lives to avoid all trouble! But all these things which in ordinary life have a very relative value and can be looked upon with a certain indulgence, change totally the minute one decides to do yoga and enter the divine life. Then, all values change completely; what is honest in ordinary life, is no longer at all honest for you. Besides, there is such a reversal of values that one can no longer use the same ordinary language. If one wants to consecrate oneself to the divine life, one must do it truly, that is, give oneself entirely, no longer do anything for one's own interest, depend exclusively upon the divine Power to which one abandons oneself. Everything changes completely, doesn't it? – everything, everything, it is a reversal. What I have just read from this book applies solely to those who want to do yoga; for others it has no meaning, it is a language which makes no sense, but for those who want to do yoga it is imperative. It is always the same thing in all that we have recently read: one must be careful not to have one foot on one side and the other foot on the other, not to bestride two different boats each following its own course. This is what Sri Aurobindo said: one must not lead a "double life". One must give up one thing or the other – one can't follow both.

This does not mean, however, that one is obliged to get out of the conditions of one's life: it is the inner attitude which must be totally changed. One may do what one is in the habit of doing, but do it with quite a different attitude. I don't say it is necessary to give up everything in life and go away into solitude, to an ashram necessarily, to do yoga.

نـظرة جديـدة – A different Outlook

مجـال الاسـتيراد والتوريـد يعتمـد عـادة على سماسـرة ووسـطاء، وربمـا كـان ذلك ضـروريا لتسـهيل الأعمـال، ولكـن لـو اعتبرنـا كيفيـة إدارة هـذه الأعمـال، نجـد أن الوسـطاء كثيـرا مـا يحققـون الـربح على حسـاب المنتجيـن والمسـتهلكين، فهـم يسـعون بـالطبع إلـى كسـب المـال بسـهولة وبأقـل جهـد ولا يسـعون إلـى أداء الخدمـات والمنفعـة العامـة (لـن تجـد واحـدا فـي المليـون مـنهم يفكر فـي ذلك). وهنـاك بـالطبع طـرق أخـرى أسـوأ كثيـرا مـن ذلك لكسـب المـال فوسـائل وسـبل كسـب المـال تفـوق الحصـر.

كثيـرًا مـا يسـألني صـديق لـي [مـن خـارج الأشـرام]: "عنـدما نكـون مضـطرين إلـى اكتسـاب معيشـتنا، هـل يكفـي أن نلتـزم بعـرف الأمانـة الشـائع، أم ينبغـي أن نتخطـى العـرف الشـائع إلـى عـرف أكثـر صـرامة وتشـددا؟"

هذا يتوقف على الموقف الـذي يقفـه صـديقك فـي الحيـاة. لـو كـان يريـد ممارسـة اليوغـا، لا مفر مـن أن يتخطـى عـرف الأخـلاق العـادي [إلـى أخلاقيـة أكثـر صـرامة]. أمـا لـو كـان رجـلا عاديا يعـيش حيـاة عاديـة، فإن السـؤال يـؤول إلـى اعتبـارات عمليـة بحتـة مثـل الالتـزام بقوانيـن البلـد الـذي يعـيش فيـه تجنبـا للمتاعـب. كـل الأمـور التـي لهـا أهميـة نسـبية فـي الحيـاة العاديـة والتـي يسـتطيع المـرء أن يأخـذها بتسـاهل، تتغيـر كليـا بمجـرد أن يشـرع المـرء فـي ممارسـة اليوغـا والسـعي نحـو الحيـاة الإلهيـة. مـا يعتبـر أمانـة فـي الحيـاة العاديـة قـد يكـون بعيـدا عـن الأمانـة فـي حيـاة اليوغـا التـي تنقلـب فيهـا كـل القيـم رأسـا على عقـب وتفقـد لغـة الحيـاة العاديـة صلاحيتها للاستخدام. لـو أراد المـرء أن يكـرس نفسـه للحيـاة الإلهيـة، يجـب أن يكـون تكريسـه صـادقا وشـاملا، وأن يكـف تمامـا عـن تقصـي مصـالحه الشـخصية وأن يعتمـد كليـا على **القـدرة الإلهيـة** ويهـب نفسـه لهـا. عندئـذ يتغيـر كـل شـيء تمامـا، أليـس كـذلك؟ كـل شـيء، كـل شـيء، إنـه انقـلاب فعلـي. مـا قرأتـه عليكـم مـن هـذا الكتـاب يصـلح فقـط للـذين يريـدون ممارسـة اليوغـا وهـو إلزامـي بالنسـبة لهـم، ولكنـه لا يصـلح ويفقـد معنـاه بالنسـبة لمـن سـواهم. كـل مـا قرأنـاه حديثـا يحـذرنا مـن خلـط الأمـور بعضـها مـع البعـض ومـن محاولـة ركـوب قـاربين يسـريان فـي اتجـاهين مختلفيـن بـأن نضـع قدمـا فـي أحـد القـاربين والقـدم الأخـرى فـي القـارب الآخـر. هـذا مـا عنـاه شـري أوروبينـدو عنـدما حـذرنا مـن أن نعـيش "حيـاة مزدوجـة" ونصـحنا بـأن نختـار بيـن الحيـاة العاديـة وبيـن حيـاة اليوغـا — إذ يسـتحيل أن نعـيش الحياتيـن فـي آن واحـد.

ولكـن هـذا لا يعنـي بالضـرورة أننـا ملزمـون بتغييـر ظـروف حياتنـا [الخارجيـة]: مـا يجـب أن نغيـره كليـا هـو موقفنـا الـداخلي. ليـس هنـاك مـا يمنـع [إذا أردنـا ممارسـة اليوغـا] مـن الاسـتمرار فـي أعمالنـا التـي اعتدنـا عليهـا، المهـم هـو أن نقـوم بهـذه الأعمـال مـن منطلـق مفهـوم جديـد.

192

A different Outlook – نـظـرة جديــدة

Now, it is true that if one does yoga in the world and in worldly circumstances, it is more difficult, but it is also more complete. Because, every minute one must face problems which do not present themselves to someone who has left everything and gone into solitude; for such a one these problems are reduced to a minimum while in life one meets all sorts of difficulties, beginning with the incomprehension of those around you with whom you have to deal; one must be ready for that, be armed with patience, and a great indifference. But in yoga one should no longer care for what people think or say; it is an absolutely indispensable starting-point. You must be absolutely immune to what the world may say or think of you and to the way it treats you. People's understanding must be something quite immaterial to you and should not even slightly touch you. That is why it is generally much more difficult to remain in one's usual surroundings and do yoga than to leave everything and go into solitude; it is much more difficult, but we are not here to do easy things – easy things we leave to those who do not think of transformation.

How can money be reconquered for the Mother?

Ah!...There is a hint here. Three things are interdependent (Sri Aurobindo says here): power, money and sex. I believe the three are interdependent and that all three have to be conquered to be sure of having any one – when you want to conquer one you must have the other two. Unless one has mastered these three things, desire for power, desire for money and desire for sex, one cannot truly possess any of them firmly and surely. What gives so great an importance to money in the world as it is today is not so much money itself, for apart from a few fools who heap up money and are happy because they can heap it up and count it, generally money is desired and acquired for the satisfactions it brings. And this is almost reciprocal: each of these three things not only has its own value in the world of desires, but leans upon the other two. I have related to you that vision, that big black serpent which kept watch over the riches of the world, terrestrial wealth – he demanded the mastery of the sex-impulse. Because, according to certain theories, the very need of power has its end in this satisfaction, and if one mastered that, if one abolished that from human consciousness, much of the need for power and desire for money would disappear automatically. Evidently, these are the three great obstacles in the terrestrial human life and, unless they are conquered, there is scarcely a chance for humanity to change.

Does an individual mastery over desire suffice or is a general, collective mastery necessary?

A different Outlook – نظرة جديدة

نحن لسنا مطالبين، عندما نرغب في ممارسة اليوغا، بأن نهجر كل شيء أو أن نلتحق بـ "أشرام*" أو أن ندخل في العزلة والخلوة. صحيح أن ممارسة اليوغا في العالم وفي ظروف الحياة العادية أصعب [منها في العزلة]، ولكن التحقيق في العالم أكثر شمولاً. ذلك أننا في العالم نضطر إلى مواجهة مشاكل لا يصادفها الذين يهجرون كل شيء وينعزلون. العزلة تقلل المشاكل إلى حد أدنى، في حين أن الحياة العادية تواجهنا بجميع ألوان المصاعب وأولها عدم فهم الناس المحيطين بنا والذين نحن مضطرون للتعامل معهم. لو أردنا ممارسة اليوغا في الحياة العادية، يجب أن نكون مستعدين لمواجهة هذه المشاكل ومزودين بالصبر وبالكثير من عدم الاكتراث. نقطة البداية الحاسمة في اليوغا هي أن نكف عن الاكتراث بما يظنه الناس وبما يقولوه. ينبغي أن نكون محصنين تماماً ضد آراء الناس وطريقة معاملتهم لنا. يجب أن تفقد مفاهيم الناس أهميتها في نظرنا ويجب ألا تؤثر علينا بأي صورة من الصور. هذا هو السبب في أن الممارسة تكون عادة أصعب بكثير إذا تابعنا حياتنا المألوفة عنها لو هجرنا كل شيء وانعزلنا. ومع ذلك: نحن لم نأت إلى الأرض للقيام بالأمور السهلة — دعنا نترك الأمور السهلة للذين لا يسعون إلى تغيير أنفسهم.

كيف يمكن استرجاع المال [من القوى المعادية] واستخدامه في أغراض إلهية؟

دعني أعطيك إشارة... شري أوروبيندو يذكر [في الاقتباس المذكور أعلاه] ثلاث قوى مترابطة تتوقف بعضها على البعض: السلطان والمال والجنس. اعتقد أنها مترابطة بحيث أنك لو أردت أن تتحكم في إحداها لا بد أن تتحكم في القوتين الأخريين في ذات الوقت. ما لم تتغلب على الثلاثة جميعاً (شهوة السلطان وشهوة المال وشهوة الجنس)، لن تتمكن من أن تسيطر على أي منها بصورة حاسمة وأكيدة. ما يعطي المال أهميته العظمى في العالم اليوم ليس المال في حد ذاته، فبصرف النظر عن بعض الحمقى الذين يحبون تكويم المال من أجل المال في حد ذاته، يحب الناس المال لأنه يوفر لهم مطالبهم ويتيح لهم حياة راحة ورغد. هذه الشهوات الثلاثة تؤثر بعضها على بعض بصورة متبادلة وتعزز وتغذي بعضها البعض. لقد قصصت عليكم رؤيتي التي رأيت فيها ثعباناً أسوداً كبيراً يحرس كنوز العالم وثرواته. هذا الثعبان يتطلب [من الذين يرغبون أن ينالوا من الثروات التي يحرسها] السيطرة على دوافع الجنس. تبعاً لبعض النظريات، شهوة التسلط لها جذور دفينة في الرغبة الجنسية، ولذلك لو نجح المرء في التغلب على الشهوة الجنسية وفي استئصالها من وعيه، فإن جزءاً كبيراً من حاجته وشهوته للسلطة والمال يزول تلقائياً. من الواضح أن هذه القوى الثلاث هي العقبات الكبرى في حياة البشر على الأرض، ومالم يتمكن البشر من التغلب عليها، يكون الأمل في تغير البشرية ضعيفاً للغاية.

هل يكفي لو سيطر بعض الأفراد على شهواتهم، أم أنه ضروري أن يسيطر البشر كلهم كجماعة على شهواتهم؟

A different Outlook – نـظـرة جـديـدة

Ah! There we are... Is it possible to attain a total personal transformation without there being at least a correspondence in the collectivity?... This does not seem possible to me. There is such an interdependence between the individual and the collectivity that, unless one does what the ascetics have preached, that is, escapes from the world, goes out of it completely, leaves it where it is and runs away selfishly leaving all the work to others, unless one does that... And even so I have my doubts. Is it possible to accomplish a total transformation of one's being so long as the collectivity has not reached at least a certain degree of transformation? I don't think so. Human nature remains what it is — one can attain a great change of consciousness, that yes, one can purify one's consciousness, but the total conquest, the material transformation depends definitely to a large extent, on a certain degree of progress in the collectivity. Buddha said with reason that as long as you have in you a vibration of desire, this vibration will spread in the world and all those who are ready to receive it will receive it. In the same way, if you have in you the least receptivity to a vibration of desire, you will be open to all the vibrations of desire which circulate constantly in the world. And that is why he concluded: Get out of this illusion, withdraw entirely and you will be free. I find this relatively very selfish, but after all, that was the only way he had foreseen. There is another: to identify oneself so well with the divine Power as to be able to act constantly and consciously upon all vibrations circulating through the world. Then the undesirable vibrations no longer have any effect upon you, but you have an effect upon them, that is, instead of an undesirable vibration entering into you without being perceived and doing its work there, it is perceived and immediately on its arrival you act upon it to transform it, and it goes back into the world transformed, to do its beneficent work and prepare others for the same realisation. This is exactly what Sri Aurobindo proposes to do and, more clearly, what he asks you to do, what he intends us to do: Instead of running away, to bring into oneself the power which can conquer.

Note that things are arranged in such a way that if the tiniest atom of ambition remained and one wanted this Power for one's personal satisfaction, one could never have it, that Power would never come. Its deformed limitations, of the kind seen in the vital and physical world, those yes, one may have them, and there are many people who have them, but the true Power, the Power Sri Aurobindo calls "supramental", unless one is absolutely free from all egoism under all its forms, one will never be able to manifest. So there is no danger of its being misused. It will not manifest except through a being who has attained the perfection of a complete inner detachment. I have told you, this is what Sri Aurobindo expects us to do — you may tell me it is difficult, but I repeat that we are not here to do easy things, we are here to do difficult ones. May 3, 1951

نـظرة جديـدة – A different Outlook

آه ! كنـت أتوقـع هـذا السـؤال... هـل تظـن أن الفـرد يسـتطيع أن يتغيـر كليـاً بـدون أن يكـون هنـاك علـى الأقـل بعـض التجـاوب مـن الجماعـة البشـرية؟... هـذا يبـدو لـي مسـتحيلاً... الفـرد والجماعـة يتوقفـان أحدهمـا علـى الآخـر بحيـث أن الفـرد لا ينجـح فـي تغييـر نفسـه كليـاً مـا لـم تكـن هنـاك درجـة معينـة مـن التغيـر فـي الجماعـة. وحتـى لـو سـلك الفـرد مسـلك الزاهديـن والمتقشـفين وهجـر العـالم بأكملـه بصـورة أنانيـة ليركـز علـى نفسـه فقـط، فإنـي أشـك فـي أنـه سـينجح فـي تغييـر ذاتـه: ربمـا نجـح فـي تغييـر وعيـه وجعلـه أكثـر نقـاء وصفـاء، ولكـن طبيعتـه وبدنـه سـيظلان علـى مـا همـا عليـه لأنهمـا يتوقفـان إلـى حـد بعيـد علـى تقـدم الجماعـة. قـال بـوذا أنـه طالمـا بقيـت فـي فـرد واحـد ذبذبـة شـهوة، فإنهـا تنتشـر فـي العـالم وتـؤثر علـى جميـع مـن هـم مسـتعدون لتلقيهـا. وبالمثـل، لـو كـان فيـك أقـل انفتـاح لذبـذبات الشـهوة، تكـون معرضـاً لكـل ذبـذبات الشـهوة الـي تطـوف العـالم. اسـتنتج بـوذا مـن ذلـك أن الخـلاص يكمـن فـي أن نعتبـر العـالم وهمـاً لا حقيقـة فيـه وأن نهجـره كليـاً. أنـا اعتبـر هـذا الحـل أنانيـاً إلـى حـد بعيـد، ولكنـه، علـى أي حـال، الحـل الـذي نصـح بـه بـوذا فـي ذلـك الوقـت. ولكـن هنـاك حـل آخـر: أن نتحـد مـع **القـدرة الإلهيـة** ونتطـابق معهـا إلـى درجـة تمكنـا مـن أن نـؤثر تـأثيراً واعيـاً مسـتمراً علـى جميـع الذبـذبات التـي تطـوف العـالم. عندئـذ تكـف الذبـذبات الضـارة مـن التـأثير علينـا، فـي حيـن نـؤثر نحـن عليهـا. وبـدلاً مـن أن تتسـلل هـذه الذبـذبات خلسـة إلـى داخلنـا وتمـارس نشـاطها الضـار فينـا، نكتشـفها فـور دخولهـا ونُحَوِّلها بحيـث تعـود إلـى العـالم وقـد تغيـرت إلـى ذبـذبات نافعـة تسـاعد الآخـرين علـى الوصـول إلـى نفـس التحقيـق. هـذا هـو بالتحديـد مـا يقترحـه شـري أوروبينـدو ومـا يطلبـه منـا: بـدلاً مـن أن نهـرب مـن العـالم، أن نسـتنزل فـي أنفسـنا القـدرة الظـافرة.

لاحـظ أن شـئون العـالم قـد دُبِّـرَت بحيـث أنـه لـو كـان [فـي باحـث روحـي] أقـل طمـوح ورغبـة فـي اسـتخدام **القـدرة الإلهيـة** لمصـالح شخصـية، فإنـه لا ينالهـا أبـداً. ربمـا يحصـل علـى قـدرات مُحَرَّفَـة ومحـدودة مـن قبيـل القـدرات التـي يملكهـا الكثيـرون فـي العـالمين الحيـوي والمـادي. ولكـن القـدرة الحقيقيـة التـي يسـميها شـري أوروبينـدو قـدرة السـوبرامنتال لا تتـاح إلا للـذين بلغـوا الكمـال داخليـاً وتخلصـوا مـن جميـع صـور الأنانيـة وتحـرروا كليـاً مـن التعلـق والارتبـاط، وهـي لـذلك قـدرة محصنـة ضـد سـوء الاسـتغلال. لقـد سـبق أن أخبرتكـم أن هـذا هـو مـا يتوقعـه شـري أوروبينـدو منكـم — ربمـا اعتـذرتم قائليـن إن ذلـك مطلـب صـعب، ولكنـي أكـرر لكـم إننـا لسـنا هنـا للقيـام بالأمـور السـهلة، بـل للقيـام بالأمـور الصعبـة.
3 مايو 1951

A different Outlook – نـظرة جديـدة

Money as a Curse
The more money we have, the more we need...

The more money one has the more one is in a state of calamity, my child. Yes, it is a calamity. It is a catastrophe to have money. It makes you stupid, it makes you miserly, it makes you wicked. It is one of the greatest calamities in the world. Money is something one ought not to have until one no longer has desires. When one no longer has any desires, any attachments, when one has a consciousness vast as the earth, then one may have as much money as there is on the earth; it would be very good for everyone. But if one is not like that, all the money one has is like a curse upon him. This I could tell anyone at all to his face, even to the man who thinks that it is a merit to have become rich. It is a calamity and perhaps it is a disgrace, that is, it is an expression of a divine displeasure.

It is infinitely more difficult to be good, to be wise, to be intelligent and generous, to be more generous, you follow me, when one is rich than when one is poor. I have known many people in many countries, and the most generous people I have ever met in all the countries, were the poorest. And as soon as the pockets are full, one is caught by a kind of illness, which is a sordid attachment to money. I assure you it is a curse.

So the first thing to do when one has money is to give it. But as it is said that it should not be given without discernment, don't go and give it like those who practise philanthropy, because that fills them with a sense of their own goodness, their generosity and their own importance... each one must find in his highest consciousness what the best possible use of the money he has can be. And truly money has no value unless it circulates. For each and every one, money is valuable only when one has spent it. If one doesn't spend it... I tell you, men take care to choose things which do not deteriorate, that is, gold – which does not decompose. Otherwise, from the moral point of view it rots. And now that gold has been replaced by paper, if you keep paper for a long time without taking care of it, you will see when you open your drawer that there are small silver-fish which have regaled themselves on your paper-rupees. So they will have left a lace-work which the bank will refuse.

نـظرة جديـدة – A different Outlook

لـعنـة المـال

كلما كثر ما نملكه من المال، كلما احتجنا إلى مزيد...

كلما كثر المال في حوزتنا، كلما كان ذلك مثل مصيبة تحيق بنا. نعم، إن المال مصيبة، بل هو كارثة. ذلك أن امتلاك المال يؤدي إلى الغباء والحماقة والشح والشر. إنه من أعظم المصائب التي نصادفها في هذا العالم. المال من الأشياء التي لا ينبغي أن نملكها قبل أن نتحرر كلياً من الشهوات والارتباطات لأننا عندئذ فقط نكون في وعي شامل، بحيث أننا حتى لو ملكنا ثروات الأرض كلها، نستغل هذا المال في مصلحة الجميع ونفعهم. ولكن قبل بلوغ هذه المرحلة، كل ما نملكه من المال يكون نكبة تلحق بنا. أنا لا أتردد في مواجهة أي شخص بذلك، حتى هؤلاء الذين يظنون أن الثراء دليل على الجدارة والاستحقاق. المال مصيبة وربما كان خزياً وتعبيراً عن استياء إلهي.

إنه لأسهل كثيراً على رجل فقير أن يكون طيباً وذكياً وحكيماً وكريماً من أن يتحلى رجل غني بهذه الصفات. لقد عرفت كثيراً من الناس في بلاد مختلفة، ومن بين هؤلاء وجدت أن أكثر الناس سخاء هم أشدهم فقراً. متى امتلأت جيوب شخص بالمال، فكأنما تملّك منه داء يجعله يتعلق تعلقاً خسيساً بماله. أؤكد لكم إن المال لعنة.

أفضل شيء ينبغي على صاحب المال أن يفعله هو أن يهبه. ولكن، تبعاً للنصيحة المعروفة، ينبغي ألا نهب المال بدون تمييز، وألا نفعل مثل المتصدقين الذين يتصدقون لأن التصدق يعزز فيهم الشعور بفضلهم وكرمهم وأهميتهم. كل فرد يجب أن يقرر تبعاً لأعلى درجات وعيه ما هي أفضل طريقة لاستخدام ما يملكه من مال. لو ظل المال راكداً لا تكون له قيمة حقيقية. وبالنسبة لكل فرد: المال لا قيمة إلا عندما ينفق. بعض الناس يحرصون على جمع المال على هيئة ذهب، لأن الذهب لا يتلف. ولكن، من وجهة النظر الأخلاقية، أي مال راكد يصيبه العفن. في عصرنا هذا، حلت أوراق النقد محل الذهب، وإذاً ما خزنت هذه الأوراق في أدراج مقفولة لوقت طويل بدون رعاية، فإنها تعفن بالفعل إذ تتراكم عليها حشرات السمك الفضي وتتلفها وتجعلها غير صالحة للتداول.

A different Outlook – نـظـرة جديـدة

There are countries and religions which always say that God makes those whom He loves poor. I don't know if that is true; but there is one thing which is true, that surely when someone is born rich or has become very rich, in any case when he possesses much from the point of view of material riches, it is certainly not a sign that the Divine has chosen him for His divine Grace, and he must make honourable amends if he wants to walk on the path, the true path, to the Divine.

Wealth is a force – I have already told you this once – a force of Nature; and it should be a means of circulation, a power in movement, as flowing water is a power in movement. It is something which can serve to produce, to organise. It is a convenient means, because in fact it is only a means of making things circulate fully and freely.

This force should be in the hands of those who know how to make the best possible use of it, that is, as I said at the beginning, people who have abolished in themselves or in some way or other got rid of every personal desire and every attachment. To this should be added a vision vast enough to understand the needs of the earth, a knowledge complete enough to know how to organise all these needs and use this force by these means. If, besides this, these beings have a higher spiritual knowledge, then they can utilise this force to construct gradually upon the earth what will be capable of manifesting the divine Power, Force and Grace. And then this power of money, wealth, this financial force, of which I just said that it was like a curse, would become a supreme blessing for the good of all.

... Each thing in the world has its place, its work, a real use; and if used for something else it creates a disorder, confusion, chaos. And that's because in the world as it is, very few things are utilised for their true work, very few things are really in their place, and it is because the world is in a frightful chaos that there is all this misery and suffering. If each thing was in its place, in a harmonious balance, the whole world could progress without needing to be in the state of misery and suffering in which it is. There! So there is nothing that's bad in itself, but there are many things – almost all – which are not in their place.

Perhaps in the body also it is like that. There is nothing that's bad in itself; but many things are not in their place, and that is why one becomes ill. There is created an inner disharmony. So the result is that one is ill. And people always think that it is not their fault that they are ill, and it is always their fault, and they are very angry when they are told this. "You have no pity." And yet it is true.
16 February 1955

نظرة جديدة – A different Outlook

بعض المذاهب وبعض الأديان تنادي بأن **الواحد-الكل*** يحكم على أحبائه بالفقر. لا أعلم لو كان هذا صحيحاً، ولكن ما أعتقد في صحته هو أن امتلاك شخص ما لثروات مادية طائلة، إما عن طريق الوراثة أو الاكتساب، بالتأكيد ليس دليلاً على أن **الواحد-الكل*** قد اصطفى هذا الشخص **بنعمته الإلهية**، كما أعتقد أن هذا الشخص يجب أن يبذل الكثير، من قبيل التعويض، إذا أراد أن يسير على الصراط المستقيم الذي يؤدي إلى **الواحد-الكل.**

كما سبق أن قلت، الثروة قوة من قوى **الطبيعة** ويجب أن تكون في سيولة ودوران دائم، تماماً مثل الماء في حركته ودورته. المال ينفع في أغراض الانتاج والتنظيم، ونفعه يأتي بالتحديد من حيث أنه يسهل حركة الأمور ودورانها.

كما قلت في البداية، قوة المال ينبغي أن تكون في أيادي من يستطيعون استغلالها لتحقيق أعظم النفع، أي في أيادي الذين ارتفعوا، بطريقة أو بأخرى، فوق الأنانية والشهوات والتعلق والذين اتسعت رؤيتهم لدرجة تمكنهم من فهم الاحتياجات العالمية وكيفية إشباعها باستخدام قوة المال ووسائله. عندما تكون لهؤلاء، فوق كل ذلك، معرفة روحية عالية تمكنهم من استغلال قوة المال لتحقيق **القدرة والقوة والنعمة الإلهية** على الأرض، يَكُفَّ المال عن أن يكون لعنة، ويصبح بركة قصوى لصالح الجميع.

... كل شيء في العالم له مكانه ووظيفته ونفعه، بحيث أنه لو استخدم في غير غرضه يؤدي إلى اختلال عام وارتباك وتشوش. في الوقت الحاضر، تسود عالمنا حالة فوضى شاملة يندر فيها أن تجد شيئاً في مكانه الصحيح، وهذا هو سبب ما نراه من شقاء ومعاناة. في حين أنه لو كانت جميع الأمور في مكانها في حالة توازن وانسجام، لأمكن أن يتقدم العالم بأكمله متجنباً البؤس والمعاناة السائدين حالياً. لا توجد أشياء سيئة وشريرة في حد ذاتها، ولكن معظم الأشياء، جميعها تقريباً، لا يوجد في مكانه الصحيح.

ربما يسري ذلك على البدن أيضاً. بمعنى أن كثير من الأمور البدنية ليست في مكانها الصحيح، وهذا هو ما يؤدي إلى المرض. اختلال الانسجام والتناغم الداخلي هو سبب المرض. الناس يظنون أنهم يمرضون دون أي تقصير من جانبهم، ولكنهم دائماً مسؤولون عن مرضهم، وإذا أخبرتهم بذلك يستشيطون غضباً ويتهموني بعدم الشفقة. ولكنه مع ذلك صحيح.

16 فبراير 1955

About Sleep and Dreams — عـن الـنوم والأحـلام

Conscious Sleep

How can one remain conscious in the midst of unconsciousness?
One must be vigilant.
And when asleep?
One can remain conscious in sleep, we have already explained that! One must work.
Then one doesn't sleep!

Not at all, one sleeps much better, one has a quiet sleep instead of a restless one. Most people do so many things in their sleep that they wake up more tired than before. We have already spoken about this once. Naturally, if you keep yourself from sleeping, you won't sleep. I always tell those who complain of not being able to sleep, "Meditate then and you will end up by sleeping." It is better to fall asleep while concentrating than "like that", scattered and strewn without knowing even where one is.

To sleep well one must learn how to sleep.

If one is physically very tired, it is better not to go to sleep immediately, otherwise one falls into the inconscient. If one is very tired, one must stretch out on the bed, relax, loosen all the nerves one after another until one becomes like a rumpled cloth in one's bed, as though one had neither bones nor muscles. When one has done that, the same thing must be done in the mind. Relax, do not concentrate on any idea or try to solve a problem or ruminate on impressions, sensations or emotions you had during the day. All that must be allowed to drop off quietly: one gives oneself up, one is indeed like a rag. When you have succeeded in doing this, there is always a little flame, there — that flame never goes out and you become conscious of it when you have managed this relaxation. And all of a sudden this little flame rises slowly into an aspiration for the divine life, the truth, the consciousness of the Divine, the union with the inner being, it goes higher and higher, it rises, rises, like that, very gently. Then everything gathers there, and if at that moment you fall asleep, you have the best sleep you could possibly have. I guarantee that if you do this carefully, you are sure to sleep, and also sure that instead of falling into a dark hole you will sleep in light, and when you get up in the morning you will be fresh, fit, content, happy and full of energy for the day.

A different Outlook – نـظـرة جديـدة

About Sleep and Dreams – عـن النوم والأحـلام

النوم الـواعـي

كيف يمكن للمرء أن يظل واعياً في وسط اللاوعي؟

بأن يكون يقظاً على الدوام.

حتى أثناء النوم؟

مـن الممكن أن يظـل المـرء واعيـاً أثنـاء النـوم، وقد سبق أن شـرحت ذلك! هـذه اليقظة تتطلب بعض العمل.

ولكن العمل يحول دون النوم!

كـلا على الإطـلاق، بـل أن النـوم يتحسـن كثيـراً ويصبح هادئـاً وخاليـاً مـن الاضطراب و'لهيجـان. معظـم النـاس يفعلـون أشيـاء كثيرة في نـومهم تجعلهم أشد إرهاقـاً عندما يستيقظون عما كـانوا عليـه قبل أن يدخلوا في النوم. لقد تكلمنـا عن ذلك من قبل. بـالطبع عندما تفعل مـا يستوجب اليقظة، فإنك لا تنـام. أنصح دائمـاً الـذين يشـتكون مـن الأرق أن يمارسـوا التأمـل عندما يحين وقت النـوم. والتأمـل سـيؤدي بهـم في النهايـة إلى النـوم. عنـدما يغلبهم النعـاس وهم في حالـة تركيـز، ينـامون نومـاً أفضل من لو ناموا بوعي مشتت ومبعثر.

لكي ننام جيداً، يجب أن نتعلم الوسيلة الصحيحة للنوم.

عنـدما نكـون في غايـة التعـب، يستحسـن ألا ننـام على الفـور لكي نتجنـب الوقـوع في اللاوعي. مـا ينبغي أن نفعلـه في تلك الحالـة هو أن نستلقى على الفراش ونرخـي جميـع أعصابنا الواحد بعد الآخر حتى نصبح مثـل خرقـة متشعثة ملقاة على السـرير، كمـا لـو كنا بدون عظـام أو عضـلات. ومتى مـا فعلنـا ذلك، يجب أن نرخـي أذهاننا ونمتنـع عن التركيز على الأفكـار والمشـاكل واجترار الانطباعات والأحاسيس والمشاعر التي خبرناها في يومنا. ينبغي أن ندع كل هذه الأشياء تتساقط منا في هدوء ثـم نهب أنفسنا كليـاً. إذا نجحنا في الارتخـاء على هـذا النحو، نلاحظ اللهب الصغير المشتعل بـداخلنا على الـدوام وهو يرتفع تـدريجياً متطلعـاً إلى الحقيقة والحياة و**الوعي الإلهي** ويزداد اشتعالاً إلى أن يصبح محورًا تتمحور حوله جميـع أجزاء وعينا. لـو دخلنـا في النوم على هـذ الحـال ننام أفضل نـوم ممكن. أؤكد لكم لـو اتبعتم هذه النصيحة بعناية، أنكم ستنامون في نـور داخلي متجنبين السقوط في ثقوب سوداء، وأنكـم ستكونون عند الاسـتيقاظ نضـرين ونشطـاء وراضـين وسعـداء ومـزودين بالطاقـة التي تحتاجونها ليومكم.

A different Outlook – نـظـرة جـديـدة

When one is conscious in sleep, does the brain sleep or not?

When does the brain ever sleep? When does it sleep? This is of all things the most difficult. If you succeed in making your brain sleep, it would be wonderful. How it runs on! That is vagabondage. It is this I meant when I spoke of relaxation in the brain. If you do it really well, your brain enters a silent restfulness and that is wonderful; when you attain that, five minutes of that and you are quite fresh afterwards, you can solve a heap of problems.

If the brain is always working, why don't we remember what has happened during the night ?

Because you have not caught the consciousness at its work. And perhaps because if you remembered what was going on in your brain, you would be horrified! It is really like a madhouse, all these ideas which clash, all dancing a saraband in the head! It is as if one were throwing balls in all directions at once. So, if you saw that, you would be a bit troubled.
23 April 1951

Interpreting Dreams

Sometimes, on waking up, one forgets everything, one forgets where one is. Why?

It is because you have gone into the inconscient* and lost all contact with the consciousness, and this takes a little time to be reestablished. Of course, it may happen that instead of going into the inconscient, one goes into the superconscient*, but this is not frequent. And the feeling is not the same because, instead of having this negative impression of not knowing who one is or where one is or what is what, one has a positive sensation of having risen into something other than one's ordinary life, of no longer being the same person. But when one has altogether lost contact with one's ordinary consciousness, generally it is that one has slept and been for a long time in the inconscient. Then the being is scattered, it is absorbed by this inconscient and all the pieces have to be put together again. Naturally, this is done much more quickly than at the beginning of existence, but the conscious elements have to be gathered up again and a cohesion re-formed to begin to know once more who one is.

A different Outlook – نـظـرة جديـدة

عندما نكون واعين أثناء النوم، هل ينام المخ أيضاً؟

هـل ينـام المـخ على الإطـلاق؟ متى ينـام المـخ؟ نـوم المـخ هـو أصعـب الأمـور قاطبة. لـو نجحـت في تنـويم ذهنك، يكون ذلك تحقيقاً رائعـاً. المخ يعمل بـدون انقطـاع ويتجول مـن مكـان إلى آخر هـذا هو السبـب في إنـي أنصـح بإرخـاء المـخ. لـو نجحت في ارخـاء مخك، فإنه يدخل في الراحـة والصمـت، وذلـك يكـون رائعـاً. عندئـذ تكفـي خمـس دقـائق مـن هـذا الاسترخـاء لتجديد طاقتك، وذلك يمكنك مـن التغلب على العديد من المشاكل.

إذا كان المخ يعمل على الدوام، لماذا ننسى الأحداث التي تحدث أثناء نومنا؟

لأنك لـم تحقـق الصلـة بـين وعـي اليقظـة ووعـي النـوم. وربمـا أيضـاً لأنك لـو تذكـرت مـا دار في ذهنـك أثنـاء نومـك ستـرتعب وتنـزعج. ذلـك أن المـخ أثنـاء النـوم، بكـل مـا فيـه مـن آراء تتصـادم وتتراقص وتنطلق مثل القذائف في جميع الاتجاهات، يشبه مستشفى الأمراض العقلية!
23 أبريل 1951

تـفسيـر الأحـلام

لماذا نجد أنفسنا أحياناً عند الاستيقاظ وقد نسينا كل شيء لدرجة أن نجهل حتى مكان وجودنا؟

السبـب هو أنك سقطـت في اللاوعي وفقدت كل صلـة بـالوعي، واسترجاع الصلـة يحتاج إلى بعض الوقـت. صحيح أننا نـدخل أحيانا أثنـاء النوم في الـوعي الفـائق*، ولكـن ذلـك نـادر الحـدوث، وإذا حـدث، يعطينـا شعوراً مختلفـاً عنه في حالة اللاوعي. في حالـة اللاوعـي يكـون الشعـور سلبيـاً بحيث نجهل مـن نحن وأين نحن وتختلط علينا الأمـور، أمـا في حالة الـوعي الفـائق، فإننا نحس بأنفسنا وقد ارتفعنـا فـوق وعـي الحيـاة العاديـة وتخطينا ذاتنـا. عنـدما نفقـد الصلـة مـع وعينـا العـادي، يكون ذلك دلـيلاً على أننا نمنـا طـويلاً واستغرقنا في لاوعي بعثـر وشتت كيانـنا أشتاتاً يجب، عند اليقظـة، أن نعيد جمعها في وحدة متماسكة قبل أن نسترجع ادراكنا بأنفسنا. ولكـن، بـالطبع، الوقت الـلازم للعـودة الى الوعي يتناقص كلما تقدمنا في الممارسة.

204

A different Outlook – نـظـرة جديـدة

Sometimes in dreams one goes into houses, streets, places one has never seen. What does this mean ?

There may be many reasons for this. Perhaps it is an exteriorisation: one has come out of the body and gone for a stroll. They may be memories of former lives. Perhaps one has become identified with someone else's consciousness and has the memories of this other person. Perhaps it is a premonition (this is the rarest case, but it may happen): one sees ahead what one will see later.

The other day I spoke to you about those landscapes of Japan; well, almost all – the most beautiful, the most striking ones – I had seen in vision in France; and yet I had not seen any pictures or photographs of Japan, I knew nothing of Japan. And I had seen these landscapes without human beings, nothing but the landscape, quite pure, like that, and it had seemed to me they were visions of a world other than the physical; they seemed to me too beautiful for the physical world, too perfectly beautiful. Particularly I used to see very often those stairs rising straight up into the sky; in my vision there was the impression of climbing straight up, straight up, and as though one could go on climbing, climbing, climbing... It had struck me, and the first time I saw this in Nature down there, I understood that I had already seen it in France before having known anything about Japan.

There are always many explanations possible and it is very difficult to explain for someone else. For oneself, if one has studied very carefully one's dreams and activities of the night, one can distinguish fine nuances. I was saying I thought I had a vision of another world – I knew it was something which existed, but I could not imagine there was a country where it existed; this seemed to me impossible, so very beautiful it was. It was the active mind which interfered. But I knew that what I was seeing truly existed, and it was only when I saw these landscapes physically that I realised in fact that I had seen something which existed, but I had seen it with inner eyes (it was the subtle-physical*) before seeing it physically.

Everyone has certain very small indications, but for that one must be very, very methodical, very scrupulous, very careful in one's observation and not neglect the least signs, and above all not give favourable mental explanations to the experiences one has. For if one wants to explain to oneself (I don't even speak of explaining to others), if one wants to explain the experience to oneself advantageously, to draw satisfaction, one does not understand anything anymore. That is, one may mix up the signs without even noticing that they are mixed up.

نـظرة جديدة – A different Outlook

أحيانا نحلم أننا نتجول في منازل وشوارع وأمكنة لم نرها من قبل. ما تفسير ذلك؟

قد تكون لذلك أسباب كثيرة. ربما نكون قد خرجنا من أبداننا وذهبنا في جولة. وقد تكون الأشياء التي رأيناها في الحلم ذكريات من حياة سابقة. وربما يكون وعينا قد تطابق مع وعي شخص آخر لدرجة أننا اتخذنا بعض ذكرياته. وربما (وهذا نادر) يكون الحلم هاجساً يرينا مسبقاً أشياء ستحدث في المستقبل.

أخبرتكم حديثاً كيف أتتني رؤية أجمل وأروع مناظر الطبيعة اليابانية وأنا ما زلت في فرنسا في وقت لم يسبق فيه أن رأيت أي صور فوتوغرافية لليابان. في رؤيتي كانت هذه المناظر الطبيعية خالية من البشر، مجرد الطبيعة نفسها، وخيل لي أني أرى عالماً من العوالم غير المادية، إذ أن جمال المناظر كان يفوق كل ما كنت أتصوره ممكناً على ظهر الأرض. كنت على وجه خاص كثيراً ما أحلم بأدراج ترتفع في السماء كما لو كانت تحثنا على التسلق أعلى وأعلى. انطبعت هذه المناظر في نفسي وبقيت معي حتى زرت اليابان ورأيت هذه الأشياء بالفعل وتذكرت رؤيتي السابقة.

عندما نشرع في تفسير أحلامنا، نجد أنفسنا أمام تفسيرات محتملة كثيرة. فقط من تَعَوَّد على دراسة الأحلام بعناية فائقة، يستطيع أن يميز الفروق الدقيقة في أحلامه. مثال ذلك ما قصصته عليكم للتو: أعني بذلك رؤيتي التي رأيت فيها بعيني الباطنتين مناظر ظننتها تنتمي إلى عالم آخر [لأني لم أتصور أن مثل هذا الجمال يمكن أن يوجد في عالمنا هذا] وكيف أني ظللت على هذا الحال حتى سافرت إلى اليابان ورأيت المناظر بالفعل.

أما تفسير أحلام الغير، فهو أصعب من ذلك كثيراً؛ لذلك دعنا نقتصر على تفسير أحلامنا الذاتية. كل فرد يتلقى إشارات صغيرة تساعده على تفسير أحلامه، ولكنه يجب [لكي يفسرها تفسيراً صحيحاً] أن يكون منهجياً ومدققاً، وقبل كل شيء ألا ينتقي من التفسيرات تلك التي تعجبه وتسره، لأنه لو فعل ذلك، فإن الأمور ستلتبس عليه كلياً وربما خلط الإشارات بدون حتى أن يلاحظ أنه يخلطها.

A different Outlook – نـظـرة جديـدة

For instance, when one sees somebody in a dream (I am not speaking of dreams in which you see somebody unknown, but of those where you see somebody you know, who comes to see you) there are all sorts of explanations possible. If it is someone living far away from you, in another country, perhaps that person has written a letter to you and the letter is on the way, so you see this person because he has put a formation* of himself in his letter, a concentration; you see the person and the next morning you get the letter. This is a very frequent occurrence. If it is a person with a very strong thought-power, he may think of you from very far, from his own country and concentrate his thought, and this concentration takes the form of that person in your consciousness. Perhaps it is that this person is calling you intentionally; deliberately he comes to tell you something or give you a sign, if he is in danger, if he is sick. Suppose he has something important to tell you, he begins to concentrate (he knows how to do it, as everyone does not) and he enters your atmosphere, comes to tell you something special. Now if you are passive and attentive, you receive the message. And then, two more instances still: someone has exteriorized himself more or less materially in his sleep and has come to see you. And you become conscious of this person because (almost by miracle) you are in a corresponding state of consciousness. And finally, a last instance, this person may be dead and may come to see you after his death (one part of him or almost the whole of his being according to the relation you have with him). Consequently, for someone who is not very, very careful it is very difficult to distinguish these nuances, very difficult. On the other hand, quite often imaginative people will tell you, "Oh! I saw this person – he is dead." I have heard that I don't know how many times. These are people whose imagination runs freely. It is possible that the person is dead, but not because he has appeared to you!...

... to interpret another's experiences is very difficult, unless he gives you in great detail all that surrounds the dream, the vision: the ideas he had before, the ideas he had later, the state of his health, the feelings he experienced when going to sleep, the activities of the preceding day, indeed, all sorts of things. People who tell you, "Oh! I had this vision, explain it to me !", that is childishness – unless it is someone whom you have followed very carefully, whom you yourself have taught how to recognise the planes, and whose habits, whose reactions you know; otherwise it is impossible to explain, for there are innumerable explanations for one single thing. 14 April 1951

A different Outlook – نـظـرة جـديـدة

دعنـا نعتبر مثـالاً آخر: عنـدما نـرى فـي حلم شخصـاً نعرفـه مقبـلاً علينـا، يكون لـذلك تفسـيرات شتـى محتملة. إذا كـان هذا الشخص يعيش فـي بلد أخـرى بعيـداً عنـا، يكون محتمـلاً أنـه قـد كتب لنا رسالة، وأن هـذه الرسـالة فـي طريقها إلينـا. فـي هـذه الحالـة يكـون الشخص قد أودع تشكيلاً* فكريـاً أو تركيزاً قويـاً مـن ذاتـه فـي الخطـاب يجعلنا نحلـم بـه قبـل أن يصل الخطاب بالفعل [كثيراً مـا يصل الخطاب بالبريد اليـوم التـالي!]. هذا شـيء يحـدث كثيراً. أو ربمـا تكون للشخص الـذي حلمنا به قـدرة عظيمة على التفكير ويكون قد ركز تفكيـره عليك فـي بلـده البعيد، وهـذا هو السبب فـي أنك رأيتـه فـي الحلم. أو ربمـا كـان هذا الشخص ينـاديك عامداً ليخبرك بشـيء مهـم أو ليعطيك علامـة علـى أنـه فـي خطـر أو أنـه مريض. فـإذا كان يريد أن يخبرك بشـيء هـام وكان يعـرف كيف يركز (تلك قدرة لا يملكها كل النـاس)، وكنت أنـت فـي حالـة تلقـي سلبي وتَيَـقُّـظ، فإنك تتلقـى رسالته أثنـاء نومـك. وهنـاك أيضـاً احتمـالان آخـران: لـو كـان هذا الشخص قادراً علـى مغـادرة بدنـه فـي هيئة ماديـة إلـى حد مـا، تستطيع أن تراه لـو كنت فـي وعـي ينـاسب وعيه (هـذه حالـة نـادرة يكـاد حدوثها أن يكـون معجـزة). والاحتمـال الأخير هـو أن هذا الشخص قـد مات وأتـاك بعد موتـه لرؤيتـك بجزء مـن كيانـه يتـراوح صغـراً أو كبـراً حسب علاقتك بـه. نستطيع أن نـرى مـن كـل هـذه الاحتمـالات، أنـه مـا لـم يكن مُفَسِّـر الحُلم عظيـم التـدقيق والعنـاية، فإنـه سيجد صعـوبة جمـة فـي التمييـز بين احتمـالات عديـدة لا تختلف إلا فـي فروق دقيقة. من النـاحية الأخرى، نجد كثيـراً مـن ذوي الخيـال الخصـب، عنـدما يـرون شخصـاً آخر فـي حلم، يندفعون مباشـرة إلـى استنتاج أن هـذا الشخص لا بـد قد مـات. لقـد خبرت ذلك مـرات لا حصـر لـها مـع قـوم يطلقون خيـالهم بـدون أي رابـط. [مـا أقولـه لهم هـو أن] مـن المحتمـل بالفعل أن يكون الشخص قد مات، ولكننا لا نستطيع أن نستدل على موته من مجرد ظهوره لنا في حلم!...

... تفسـير تجـارب شخص آخر وأحلامـه صعب للغايـة مـالم يعطنـا هذا الشـخص كـل لتفاصيـل المتعلقـة بـالحلم: مـاذا كانـت رؤيتـه وآراؤه قبـل الحلم وبعده، مـا هـي حالتـه الصحية، مـ ذا كانت مشاعره قبـل أن ينـام، ونشـاطاته فـي اليوم السـابق للحلم، إلـى آخـره. إذا سـألك شخص لـه رؤيـة رآهـا فـي حلم، يكـون تفسـيرك مـن بـاب العبث مـا لم تكن تعـرف هذا الشخص جيـداً وتعرف عاداتـه وردود فعلـه، وتكـون قـد عَلَّـمته أنـت نفسـك كيف يتعـرف علـى طبقـات الكيـان البشري المختلفة... بدون كل ذلك، يستحيل التفسير، إذ أن أبسط الأحلام له تفسيرات لا حصر لها.
11 أبريل 1951

The reason we forget dreams

Why do we forget our dreams?

Because you do not dream always at the same place. It is not always the same part of your being that dreams and it is not at the same place that you dream. If you were in conscious, direct, continuous communication with all the parts of your being, you would remember all your dreams. But very few parts of the being are in communication.

For example, you have a dream in the subtle physical, that is to say, quite close to the physical. Generally, these dreams occur in the early hours of the morning, that is between four and five o'clock, at the end of the sleep. If you do not make a sudden movement when you wake up, if you remain very quiet, very still and a little attentive – quietly attentive – and concentrated, you will remember them, for the communication between the subtle physical and the physical is established – very rarely is there no communication.

Now, dreams are mostly forgotten because you have a dream while in a certain state and then pass into another. For instance, when you sleep, your body is asleep, your vital is asleep, but your mind is still active. So your mind begins to have dreams, that is, its activity is more or less coordinated, the imagination is very active and you see all kinds of things, take part in extraordinary happenings After some time, all that calms down and the mind also begins to doze. The vital that was resting wakes up; it comes out of the body, walks about, goes here and there, does all kinds of things, reacts, sometimes fights or eats. It does all kinds of things. The vital is very adventurous. It watches. When it is heroic it rushes to save people who are in prison or to destroy enemies or it makes wonderful discoveries. But this pushes back the whole mental dream very far behind. It is rubbed off, forgotten: naturally you cannot remember it because the vital dream takes its place. But if you wake up suddenly at that moment, you remember it. There are people who have made the experiment, who have got up at certain fixed hours of the night and when they wake up suddenly, they do remember. You must not move brusquely, but awake in the natural course, then you remember.

لماذا ننسى الأحلام

لماذا ننسى أحلامنا؟

لأنك لا تكون دائما في نفس الجزء مـن كيانك عندما تحلم. يجب أن تكون على اتصال واع ومباشر ومسـتمر مـع جميـع أجـزاء كيانـك لكـي لا تنسـى أحلامـك. ولكـن قليـل فقط مـن أجـزاء كيانـًا يكـون متصلاً بعضه مع البعض [أثناء النوم].

افترض مـثلاً أنـك تحلم في عـالم المـادة الدقيقـة* وهـو عـالم قريـب مـن عـالم المـادة الفيزيـائيـة. أحـلام المـادة الدقيقـة تحـدث عـادة في الصبـاح المبكـر بـين الرابعـة والخامسـة، أي في آخر مراحـل النـوم. لو حرصت عند الاستيقاظ على تجنب القيام بـأي حركـة مفاجئـة وعلى البقاء في هدوء وسكـون وتنبـه وتركيز، ستتذكر حلمك، لأن الاتصال بين عالم المادة الدقيقة والعالم المادي قوي ونادراً ما ينقطع.

نحن ننسى الأحلام في العادة لأننا نحلم في وعـي معين ثم ننتقل إلى وعـي آخر. على سبب المثال، عندما نـنـام، ينـام بـدننا وكيانـنا الحيـوي، ولكـن ذهننا يظل متيقظـاً. عندئـذ يشـرع الـذهن فـي الحلم بصـورة متنـاسقة إلـى حـد مـا، ويطلـق السـراح لخيالـه ويرى أشيـاء شتـى ويسـاهم في أحـداث عجيبة. ولكنـه يهـدأ بعـد فترة ويـدخل في نعـاس. هنـا يستيقظ الكيـان الحيـوي مـن نومـه ويخرج مـن البـدن ويتجـول هنـا وهنـاك ويتفاعـل ويترقـب ويقـوم بجميـع أنـواع النشـاطات وقـد يتشـاجر أحيانـًا أو يأكـل، فالكيـان الحيـوي يحـب المغـامرات، وأحيانـاً يكـون فـي مـزاج بطـولي يجعلـه ينـدفع لإنقـاذ مسجونين أو لإبادة أعداء أو لإنجـاز اكتشـافات بـاهرة! كل ذلك يـدفع بـالحلم الـذهني إلـى خلفيـة بعيـدة ويمسـحه مـن ذاكرتنا بحيث لا نتـذكره عند اليقظـة. ولكننا لو استيقظنا فجأة قبل أن ينشط الكيـان الحيـوي، نستطيع أن نمسـك بطرف الحلم الـذهني فـي ذهننا قبـل أن يفلت مـن ذاكرتـا. هنـاك قـوم جَرَّبوا عامدين هـذا الاستيقاظ المفاجئ في أوقـات معينـة مـن الليـل، ووجدوا أنهـم يتـذكرون الأحـلام التي تسبق مباشرة لحظة استيقاظهم (لو حرصوا على عدم القيام بحركات مفاجئة أو عنيفة عند الاستيقاظ).

210

A different Outlook – نـظـرة جديـدة

After a time, the vital having taken a good stroll, needs to rest also, and so it goes into repose and quietness, quite tired at the end of all kinds of adventures. Then something else wakes up. Let us suppose that it is the subtle physical that goes for a walk. It starts moving and begins wandering, seeing the rooms and.. why, this thing that was there, but it has come here and that other thing which was in that room is now in this one, and so on. If you wake up without stirring, you remember. But this has pushed away far to the back of the consciousness all the stories of the vital. They are forgotten and so you cannot recollect your dreams. But if at the time of waking up you are not in a hurry, you are not obliged to leave your bed, on the contrary you can remain there as long as you wish, you need not even open your eyes; you keep your head exactly where it was and you make yourself like a tranquil mirror within and concentrate there. You catch just a tiny end of the tail of your dream. You catch it and start pulling gently, without stirring in the least. You begin pulling quite gently, and then first one part comes, a little later another. You go backward; the last comes up first. Everything goes backward, slowly, and suddenly the whole dream reappears: "Ah, there! it was like that."

... Even without doing this exercise which is very long and difficult, in order to recollect a dream, whether it be the last one or the one in the middle that has made a violent impression on your being, you must do what I have said when you wake up: take particular care not even to move your head on the pillow, remain absolutely still and let the dream return.

Some people do not have a passage between one state and another, there is a little gap and so they leap from one to the other; there is no highway passing through all the states of being with no break of the consciousness. A small dark hole, and you do not remember. It is like a precipice across which one has to extend the consciousness. To build a bridge takes a very long time; it takes much longer than building a physical bridge. Very few people want to and know how to do it. They may have had magnificent activities, they do not remember them or sometimes only the last, the nearest, the most physical activity, with an uncoordinated movement – dreams having no sense

نـظرة جـديـدة – A different Outlook

بعد فترة، يشبع الكيـان الحيوي مـن التجول ويشـعر بالتعب مـن كـل هـذه المغـامرات ويلجـأ بـدوره إلى السكون والراحـة. عندئـذ يستيقظ جـزء آخـر، لنفتـرض أنـه كيـان المـادة الدقيقـة، الـذي يشـرع بـدوره في الحركـة والتجـوال، ويتيقظ فضوله وينظر متعجباً إلى مـا قد يكون حدث حوله من تغيـرات. هنـا أيضـاً، لـو استيقظت وبقيت سـاكناً بـدون حركـة، سوف تتذكر حلمك. ولكن حلم المـادة الدقيقـة يدفع بحلم الكيـان الحيوي بكل مغامراتـه إلى أقصـى خلفيـة الـوعي، وبـذلك يندثر مـن ذاكرتك. ولكنك لـو لـم تكن في عجلـة عند استيقاظك وكـان فـي مقدورك البقـاء فـي السـرير حسب مشيئتك بـدون حاجـة لأن تفتح عينيك أو تحرك رأسك وأمكنك أن تركز وتجعل مـن نفسك مـرآة سـاكنة، ستتمكن من الإمسـاك بطرف مـن ذيل حلمك ومن جذبه بلطف وبـذلك تسترجعه في دفعـات صغيرة جزءاً بعد جزء في ترتيب معكوس، بحيث يأتيك آخر الحلم أولاً، ثـم تثـابر علـى ذلك إلى أن يظهر لك الحلم بعد فترة كـاملاً بكـل أجزائـه فتتعـرف عليـه. راجـع الحلم لنفسك عدة مـرات حتى يصير واضحاً فـي كـل تفاصيلـه. متـى تـم ذلك، واظب علـى السكون وحاول أن تستمر في التعمـق إلى أن تمسك بطرف شـيء آخـر، أكثر بعداً وأشد غموضاً... واظب علـى الجذب. فجأة يتغير كـل شـيء وتجد نفسك في عـالم آخر وتدخل في مغامرة جديـدة — وإذا بـك قد امسكت بحلم آخـر، وهكـذا... يجب أن تتيح لنفسك الوقت الكـافي وأن تتحلى بالصبر وأن تكـون هادئـاً للغايـة في ذهنك وفي بـدنك لكي تـتمكن من استرجاع كل أحلام ليلتك من نهايتها إلى بدايتها.

... ولكن حتـى بصرف النظـر عـن هـذه العمليـة الطويلـة الصعبة، لكي تتذكر أي مـن الأحـلام التي تركت انطباعـاً قويـاً في كيانك، سواء أكان حلمك الأخير أو الوسيط ، يجب أن تفعل مـا ذكرتـه للتو عند استيقاظك: احرص علـى عدم تحريـك رأسـك علـى الوسـادة، وواظب علـى السكون لتـام ودع الحلم يعود [إلى ذاكرتك].

قد تكون هنـاك، في بعض النـاس، فجـوات في الوصلة التـي تصـل حـالات الـوعي بعضها مـع بعض تمـنعهم مـن الانتقـال بسـهولة مـن حالـة إلى حالـة كمـا لـو كانـت تضطرهم إلى القفز فـوق جـرف ومنحـدرات. أصغر هـذه الفجـوات يكفي لجعلهم ينسون أحلامهم. بنـاء جسر للعبـور مـن حـلة وعـي إلى أخرى يحتـاج إلى وقت طويل، أطـول كثيراً من الوقت اللازم لبنـاء جسر علـى نهر مثلاً، وذلك يصد معظـم النـاس عـن الرغبة في تعلم طريقـة بنـاء جسـور الـوعي، وهكذا ينسون أحلامهـم بكل مـا فيهـا مـن نشـاطات رائعـة، وإذا تذكروا علـى الإطـلاق، لا يتـذكرون إلا آخر أحلامهـم، لأنـه الأقـرب والأكثر مادية، وإذا تذكروا على الإطلاق، يكون ما يتذكرونه غير منسق وبدون معنى.

A different Outlook – نـظرة جديـدة

.But there are as many different kinds of nights and sleep as there are different days and activities. There are not many days that are alike, each day is different. The days are not the same, the nights are not the same. You and your friends are doing apparently the same thing, but for each one it is very different. And each one must have his own procedure.

6 May 1953

The Impact of Dreams on our Lives

Sweet Mother, you have said that one can exercise one's conscious will and change the course of one's dreams.

Ah, yes, I have already told you that once. If you are in the middle of a dream and something happens which you don't like (for instance, somebody shouts that he wants to kill you), you say: "That won't do at all, I don't want my dream to be like that", and you can change the action or the ending. You can organise your dream as you want. One can arrange one's dreams. But for this you must be conscious that you are dreaming, you must know you are dreaming.

But these dreams are not of much importance, are they?

Yes, they are, and one must be conscious of what can happen. Suppose that you have gone for a stroll in the vital world; there you meet beings who attack you (that's what happens usually), if you know that it is a dream, you can very easily gather your vital forces and conquer. That's a true fact; you can with a certain attitude, a certain word, a certain way of being do things you would not do if you were just dreaming.

If in the dream someone kills, you it doesn't matter, for it is just a dream!

الليالي والنـوم يختلفـون تمامـاً مـن ليلـة إلى ليلـة كمـا تختلـف الأيـام ونشاطاتها مـن يـوم إلـى يـوم.. وكمـا أننـا قلـيلاً مـا نصـادف أيامـاً متشـابهة ولا نصـادف أبـداً يـومين متطابقين تمامـاً، فإننـا لا نصـادف ليلتين متطابقتين فـي كـل شـيء. وعلـى نفـس المنـوال، نجـد أنـه حتـى عنـدما يـؤدي النـاس ظاهريـاً نفس الأفعـال، فـأن دلالـة هـذه الأفعـال تختلـف كليـاً بالنسبة لكـل فـرد مـنهم، ولـذلك يجب أن يكـون 'كـل فـرد منهجه الخاص به.

6 مايو 1953

تأثير الأحلام على حياتنا

أمـي العذبـة، أتـذكرين إنـك قلتـي لنـا إننـا نسـتطيع بواسـطة إرادتنـا أن نغير مجـرى الأحداث فـي أحلامنا؟

نعـم، سبق أن قلت لكـم ذلك. إذا صـادفتم وأنتم تحلمـون شيئاً لا يعجبكم (على سبيل المثـال، شخصـاً يهـددكم بالقتـل)، تسـتطيعون أن تـرفضوا ذلـك وتغيـروا مسـار الحلم وتعطـوه وجهـة أخـرى تـرغبونها. الـتحكم فـي الأحـلام علـى هـذا المنـوال ممكـن. ولكـن فعل ذلـك يتطلـب أن تكونـوا واعيـن بـأنكم تحلمون.

ولكن هذه الأحلام ليست لها أهمية كبيرة، أليس كذلك؟

بلـى، وينبغي أن نكـون على وعـي بمـا قـد ينتج عنهـا. افترض إنـك ذهبت تتجـول فـي العالـم الحيوي* وتعرضت لهجمـة مـن كائنـات هـذا العالـم (ذلـك هـو مـا يحـدث عادة)، لـو كنت تعلـم إنـك تحلم، تستطيع أن تجمـع قـواك الحيويـة وتتغلـب. إنهـا لحقيقـة واقعـة أنك تسـتطيع فـي الحلم، عـن طريـق كلمـة معينـة تقولهـا أو موقـف معين تتخذه، أن تقـوم بـأمور لـن تكـون في مقـدورك لـو كنت تحلم دون علم بأنك تحلم.

ولكن حتـى لو قُتِلنَا في حلم، لا يكون لذلك أهمية، فهو مجـرد حلم!

A different Outlook – نـظـرة جديـدة

I beg your pardon! Usually, the next day you are ill, or may be a little later. That's a warning. I know someone whose eye was thus hurt in a dream, and who really lost his eye a few days later. As for me, once I happened to dream getting blows on my face. Well, when I woke up the next morning, I had a red mark in the same place, on the forehead and the cheek. Inevitably, a wound received in the vital being is translated in the physical body.

But how does it happen? There must be some intermediary?

It was in the vital that I was beaten. It is from within that this comes Nothing, nobody touched anything from outside. If you receive a blow in the vital, the body suffers the consequence. More than half of our illnesses are the result of blows of this kind, and this happens much more often than one believes. Only, men are not conscious of their vital, and as they are not conscious they don't know that fifty per cent of their illnesses are the result of what happens in the vital: shocks, accidents, fighting, ill-will. Externally this is translated by an illness. If one knows how it reacts on the physical, one goes to its source and can cure oneself in a few hours.

How is it that the symbolism of dreams varies according to traditions, races, religions?

Because the form given to the dream is mental. If you have learnt that such and such a form represents such and such a mythological person, you see that form and say: "It is that." In your mind there is an association between certain ideas and certain forms, and this is continued in the dream. When you translate your dream you give it an explanation corresponding to what you have learnt, what you have been taught, and it is with the mental image you have in your head that you know. Moreover, I have explained this to you ... in the vision of Joan of Arc (The Mother takes her book and reads):

"The beings who were always appearing and speaking to Jeanne d'Arc [Joan of Arc] would, if seen by an Indian, have quite a different appearance; for when one sees, one projects the forms of one's mind. You have the vision of one in India whom you call the Divine Mother; the Catholics say it is the Virgin Mary, and the Japanese call it Kwannon, the Goddess of Mercy; and others would give other names. It is the same force, the same power, but the images made of it are different in different faiths." Questions and Answers, 21 April, 1929

نـظـرة جديـدة – A different Outlook

أرجـو المعـذرة! لـو قتلـت فـي حلـم، سـتكون علـى الأغلـب مريضـاً فـي اليـوم التـالي أو بعـد ذلـك بقليـل. أعـرف شخصـاً تلقـى ضـربة علـى عينـه أدت، فـي ظـرف أيـام قليلـة، إلـى تلـف كامـل لعينـه. أنـا نفسـي تلقيـت فـي حلـم ضـربات علـى وجهـي ، وعندمـا اسـتيقظت فـي اليـوم التـالي وجـدت علامـات حمـراء علـى جبينـي وخـدي فـي نفـس المواضـع التـي تلقيـت فيهـا الضـربات. كل جرح يتلقاه الكيان الحيوي له بالضرورة أثره في البدن الفيزيائي.

ولكـن كيـف يحـدث ذلـك؟ لا بـد إذاً مـن وجـود وسـيط [ينقـل هـذه الضـربة مـن عـالم إلـى آخر]؟

عندما تلقيت ضربة في كيـاني الحيـوي، حـدث كل ذلك في البـاطن، فأنـا لـم أُمَّس إطلاقـاً مـن الخـارج. عندمـا تتلقـى ضـربة فـي كيانـك الحيـوي، يعـاني كيانـك البـدني تلقائيـاً نتائجهـا. مـا يزيد علـى نصـف أمراضـنا يحـدث نتيجـة لضـربات مـن هـذا النـوع؛ ذلـك شـيء يحـدث أكثـر كثيـراً ممـا نعتقـد. النـاس غيـر واعيـن بكيانهـم الحيـوي، وهـم لـذلك لا يعلمـون أن نصـف أمراضـهم هـي نتيجـة لكـل مـا يـدور فـي هـذا الكيـان مـن صـدمات وحـوادث وشـجارات وسـوء نيـة. عندمـا نكـون علـى علـم بكيفيـة تـأثير كيانـنا الحيـوي علـى كيانـنا البـدني، نسـتطيع أن نضـع يـدنا علـى أصـل المرض وأن نُـشفي أنفسنا في ساعات قليلة.

لماذا تختلف رمزية الأحلام تبعاً للتقاليد والأجناس والأديان؟

لأن الهيئـة التـي يبـدو فيهـا الحلـم تنشـأ فـي الـذهن. إذا كنـا قـد تعلمنـا وتعودنـا علـى أن شخصية معينـة مـن شخصـيات الميثولوجيـا تظهـر دائمـاً فـي هيئـة محـددة، فمـن الطبيعـي عندمـا نـرى هـذه الهيئـة فـي حلـم أن نربطهـا بتلـك الشخصـية. [أثنـاء تربيتـنا] تتكـون فـي أذهاننـا علاقـات بـين أفكـار معينـة وهيئـات معينـة، وهـذه العلاقـات تسـري علـى الأحـلام أيضـاً. عندمـا نفسـر أحلامـنا، نفعـل ذلـك تبعـاً لمـا سـبق أن تعلمنـاه ونسـتخدم الصـور الذهنيـة المُخَزَّنَـة فـي رؤوسـنا. وبالمناسبة، لقد سبق أن شرحت لكم ذلك في رؤية جان دارك (الأم تأخذ كتاباً وتقرأ:)

"نفـس الكائنـات التـي كانـت تظهـر لجـان دارك وتخاطبهـا، لـو كانـت ظهـرت لشـخص مـن ثقافـة أخـرى، شـخص هنـدي مثـلاً، كانـت سـتبدو لـه فـي هيئـة مخالفـة تمامـاً، لأن المـرء عندمـا يحلـم، يُسـقِط الأشـكال التـي فـي ذهنـه علـى الشـيء الـذي يحلمـه. ربمـا يـرى هنـدي كائنـة يطلـق عليهـا اسـم **'الأم الإلهـية'**، ولـو رأى كـاثوليكي نفـس الكائنـة ربمـا أطلـق عليهـا اسـم **'مـريم العـذراء'**، فـي حيـن أن يابـاني سيسـميها **'كوانـون'** ، إلهـة الرحمـة [فـي شـرق آسـيا]، وآخـرون سيسـتخدمون أسـماء أخـرى. أي أن نفـس القـوة ونفس القـدرة التي تمثلهـا هذه الكائنة، سوف تبدو في هيئـات مختلفة لأتبـاع أديان مختلفة."
أسئلة وأجوبة، 21 أبريل، 1929

About Free Will and Determinism — عن التخيير والتسيير

Freedom and Fatality

Can it be said in justification of one's past that whatever has happened in one's life had to happen?

Obviously what has happened had to happen; it would not have been, if it had not been intended. Even the mistakes that we have committed and the adversities that fell upon us had to be, because there was some necessity in them, some utility for our lives. But in truth these things cannot be explained mentally and should not be. For all that happened was necessary, not for any mental reason, but to lead us to something beyond what the mind imagines. But is there any need to explain after all? The whole universe explains everything at every moment and a particular thing happens because the whole universe is what it is. But this does not mean that we are bound over to a blind acquiescence in Nature's inexorable law. You can accept the past as a settled fact and perceive the necessity in it, and still you can use the experience it gave you to build up the power consciously to guide and shape your present and your future.

Is the time also of an occurrence arranged in the Divine Plan of things?

All depends on the plane from which one sees and speaks. There is a plane of divine consciousness in which all is known absolutely, and the whole plan of things foreseen and predetermined. The way of seeing lives in the highest reaches of the Supramental; it is the Supreme's own vision. But when we do not possess that consciousness, it is useless to speak in terms that hold good only in that region and are not our present effective way of seeing things. For at a lower level of consciousness nothing is realized or fixed beforehand; all is in the process of making. Here there are no settled facts, there is only the play of possibilities; out of the clash of possibilities is realized the thing that has to happen. On this plane we can choose and select, we can refuse one possibility and accept another; we can follow one path, turn away from another. And that we can do, even though what is actually happening may have been foreseen and predetermined in a higher plane.

A different Outlook – نـظرة جديـدة

About Free Will and Determinism — عن التخيير والتسيير

الحرية والجبرية

هـل يصــح أن يتحجج المـرء، تبريـراً لأخطائـه السـابقة، بـأن كل مـا حـدث فـي حياتـه الماضيـة كـان لا بد من أن يحدث؟

واضـح أن مـا حـدث فـي الماضي كـان لا بـد أن يحـدث، وهو مـا كـان سيحدث لـو لـم يكن هنـاك قصد وسـبب لحدوثـه. كـذلك الأخطـاء التـي وقعنـا فيها والمكروهـات التـي بلينـا بهـا كـان لا بـد مـن حدوثها: إمـا لضـرورة فيهـا أو لنفـع معيـن تجلبـه إلـى حياتنـا. ولكـن هـذه الأمـور لا يصـح ولا ينبغي أن تُفَسَّـر بالعقـل. مـا يحـدث لا يحـدث لإرضـاء عقولنـا، بـل يحـدث ليقودنـا إلـى مـا يتخطى تصـورات عقولنـا. ولكـن هـل هنـاك فعـلاً ضـرورة إلـى الشـرح والتفسـير؟ الكـون بأجمعـه يشـرح كل شـيء فـي كـل لحظـة، وكـل شـيء يحـدث لأن الكون موجـود علـى الحـال التـي هـو عليهـا. ولكـن ذلك ليس معنـاه أننـا مجبرون علـى قبـول قـوانين الطبيعـة المتصلبـة قبـولاً أعمـى. إذ أننـا نسـتطيع أن نقبـل الماضـي كواقـع لا نقـاش فيـه، وأن نسـتفيد فـي الوقت نفسـه مـن التجـارب التـي تعلمناهـا منـه فـي تنميـة قدرتنـا الواعـية علـى صياغـة حاضرنـا ومستقبلنا.

*إذا كانـت جميـع الحـوادث مُقَـدَّرة فـي **الخطـة الإلهيـة**، فهـل وقـت حـدوث هـذه الحـوادث مُقَـدَّر أيضاً؟*

ذلـك يتوقـف علـى مسـتوى الـوعي الـذي نشـاهد منـه. هنـاك مسـتوى مـن الـوعي الإلهـي تكـون جميـع الأمـور فيـه معروفـة بصـورة قطعيـة، وتكـون الخطـة الشـاملة مرسـومة ومحـددة. هـذا هو وعـي أعلـى مجـالات السـوبرامنتال*؛ ورؤيتـه هـي رؤيـة **الواحـد-الكـل***. ولكـن طالمـا لـم نبلـغ هـذا المسـتوى، لا فائـدة مـن التشـدق بلغـة ومفاهيـم لا تسـري إلا فيـه ولا تمثل طريقتنـا الحاليـة فـي فهم الأشـياء. أمـا علـى مسـتويات الـوعي الأدنـى، فـإن الأمـور لا تُقَـرَّر بصـورة قطعيـة مسـبقاً وإنمـا تتواجـد فـي عمليـة تطور مسـتمر تكـون فيهـا الحقـائق قابلـة للتعديل وخاضـعة لـتفاعل الاحتمـالات والإمكانيـات؛ ومـن تصـادم هـذه الاحتمـالات بعضهـا مـع بعـض يتقـرر الشـيء الـذي يجب حدوثـه. علـى هـذه المسـتويات يكـون لنـا الحـق فـي الاختيـار والانتقـاء، فنـرفض إمكانيـة معينـة ونقبـل إمكانيـة أخـرى أو نتبـع مسـاراً معينـاً ونتحاشـى مسـاراً آخـر، وكـل هذا القبـول والرفض يتم علـى الرغم مـن أن الأمـر الـذي يحـدث بالفعل قـد سبق إقراره على مستوى أعلى.

A different Outlook – نــظـرة جــديــدة

The Supreme Consciousness knows everything beforehand, because everything is realized there in her eternity. But for the sake of her play and in order to carry out actually on the physical plane what is foreordained in her own supreme self, she moves here upon earth as if she did not know the whole story; she works as if it was a new and untried thread she was weaving. In this apparent forgetfulness of her own foreknowledge in the higher consciousness that gives to the individual in the active life of the world this sense of freedom and independence and initiative. These things in him are her pragmatic tools or devices, and it is through this machinery that the movements and issues planned and foreseen elsewhere are realized here.

It may you help you understand if you take the example of an actor. An actor knows the whole part he has to play; he has in his mind the exact sequence of what is to happen on the stage. But when he is on the stage, he has to appear as if he did not know anything; he has to feel and act as if he were experiencing all these things for the first time, as if it was an entirely new world with all its chance events and surprises that was unrolling before his eyes.

Is there then no real freedom? Is everything absolutely determined, even your freedom, and is fatalism the highest secret?

Freedom and fatality, liberty and determinism are truths that obtain on different levels of consciousness. It is ignorance that makes the mind put the two on the same level and pit one against the other. Consciousness is not a single uniform reality, it is complex; it is not something like a flat plain, it is multidimensional. On the highest height is the Supreme and in the lowest depth is matter; and there is an infinite gradation of levels of consciousness between this lowest depth and the highest height.

In the plane of matter and on the level of the ordinary consciousness you are bound hand and foot. A slave to the mechanism of Nature, you are tied to the chain of Karma, and there, in that chain, whatever happens is rigorously the consequence of what has been done before. There is an illusion of independent movement, but in fact you repeat what all others do, you revolve helplessly on the crushing wheel of her cosmic machine.

A different Outlook – نـظرة جديـدة

الـوعي الأسـمى يعلـم جميـع الأمـور مسبقاً، لأن الأمـور محققـة فيـه منـذ الأزل، ولكن مـن أجـل تحقيق أغراضـه في الكـون وتنفيـذ مـا سبق أن قـرره علـى أعلـى المسـتويات، فـإن هـذا الـوعي يعمـل علـى الأرض كمـا لـو كـان يجهـل الخطـة الشـاملة وكمـا لـو كـان يعمـل علـى خطـوط جديـدة لـم يجربهـا من قبـل. هـذا "التناسـي" الظاهـري يفتـح البـاب للإمكانيـات و يعطـي الإنسـان علـى الأرض إحساسـاً بحريـة الاختيـار والاسـتقلال والقدرة علـى تـدبير شئـون حياتـه. وبـذلك يكـون هـذا الإحسـاس أداة أو جـزءاً مـن نظام يتحقق بـه علـى الأرض مـا سبق أن تقرر في عالم آخر.

لكي نـزداد فهمـاً، دعنـا نضـرب كمثـال حالـة الممثـل الـذي يعلـم، قبـل أن يخطـو علـى خشـبة لمسـرح، الـدور الـذي سيلعبـه كـاملاً ويحتفظ في ذهنـه بتسلسل فصـول المسـرحية. ومـع ذلك فهو مطالـب، أثنـاء تمثيـل منظـر معيـن، بـأن يبـدو كمـا لـو كـان لا يعلـم المنـاظر التاليـة وكأنـه يعيش الحـوادث لأول مـرة ويخبرها كمصادفات ومفاجآت.

هـل يعنـي ذلك أن الحريـة الحقيقيـة لا وجـود لهـا؟ وهـل صـحيح أن جميـع الأشيـاء قـد جُزمـت من قبل بصـورة قطعية حتـى الحريـة الشخصية وأن القدرية هـي الكلمـة النهائية في الأمـر؟

الحريـة والجبريـة، والتخييـر والتسـيير، حقائـق تنطبـق علـى مسـتويات مختلفـة مـن الـوعي، وإنـه لمـن الجهـل أن نظنهـا علـى نفـس المسـتوى ونضـاد إحـداها بـالأخرى. فالـوعي ليـس حقيقـة واحـدة متجانسـة في جميـع الأحـوال، بـل هو معقـد التركيـب؛ ولا يصـح أن نـراه كمسطح أفقـي فقط، فهو متعـدد الأبعـاد. **الكـائن الأسـمى** يسـود علـى أعلـى قمـم الـوعي في حين تسـود المـادة في أدنـى الأعمـاق؛ وهنـّك تـدرج لا نهائي من المستويات بين هذين الطرفين.

عندما نعيـش في مجـال المـادة أي علـى مسـتوى الـوعي العـادي نكـون مقيديـن مـن جميـع أطرافنـا، عبيـداً لآليـة **الطبيعـة**، وخاضعيـن لقـانون **الكـارمـا*** الـذي ينـادي بـأن كـل مـا يصـادفنا هو نتيجـة حتميـة لأفعالنـا السـابقة. الحركـة المسـتقلة تكـون هنـا مجـرد وهـم، لأننـا نكـرر في الحقيقـة مـا يفعلـه الآخرون وتـدور بـلا حـول أو قوة مقيديـن إلى عجلة الآلة الكونية التي تطحن كل شيء.

A different Outlook – نــظـرة جـديـــدة

But it need not be so. You can shift your place if you will; instead of being below, crushed in the machinery or moved like a puppet, you can rise and look from above and by changing your consciousness you can even get hold of some handle to move apparently inevitable circumstances and change fixed conditions. Once you draw yourself up out of the whirlpool and stand high above, you see you are free. Free from all compulsions, not only you are no longer a passive instrument, but you become an active agent. You are not only not bound by the consequences of your action, but you can even change the consequences. Once you see the play of forces, once you raise yourself to a plane of consciousness where lie the origins of forces and identify yourself with these dynamic sources, you belong no longer to what is moved but to that which moves.

This precisely is the aim of Yoga, — to get out of the cycle of Karma into a divine movement. By Yoga you leave the mechanical round of Nature in which are an ignorant slave, a helpless and miserable tool, and rise into another plane where you become a conscious participant and a dynamic agent in the working of Higher Destiny. This movement of the consciousness follows a double line. First of all there is an ascension; you raise yourself out of the level of material consciousness into superior ranges. But this ascension of the lower into the higher calls a descent of the higher into the lower. When you rise above the earth, you bring down too upon earth something of the above, —some light, some power that transforms or tends to transform its old nature. And then these things that were distinct, disconnected and disparate from each other — the higher in you and the lower, the inner and outer strata of your being and consciousness — meet and are slowly joined together and gradually they fuse into one truth, one harmony.

It is in this way that what are called miracles happen. The world is made up of innumerable planes of consciousness and each has its own distinct laws; the laws of one plane do not hold good for another. A miracle is nothing but a sudden descent, a bursting forth of another consciousness and its powers — most often it is the powers of the vital — into this plane of matter. There is a precipitation, upon the material mechanism, of the mechanism of a higher plane. It is as though a lightening flash tore through the cloud of our ordinary consciousness and poured into it other forces, other movements and sequences.

A different Outlook – نـظـرة جديـدة

ولكـن لا داعـي لأن تكـون الأمـور على مـا وصفناه في الفقـرة السـابقة. فنحن نستطيع، لـو شِئنا، أن نغيـر موقفنـا مـن موقـف إلـى موقـف آخر؛ وبدلا مـن أن نكون في الأسـفل طحينـاً لآلـة تسحقنا أو دُميـة تُحَـرَّك كمـا تُحَـرَّك الـدُميات في مسـرح العرائـس، يمكننـا أن نرتفـع وننظـر مـن أعلـى، بـل إننـا نسـتطيع، لـو غيرنـا وعينـا، أن نعـدِّل ونُغيّـر ظروفنـا، حتـى عندمـا تبـدو هـذه الظـروف حتميـة ولا مفر منهـا. عندئـذ يمكننـا أن نفلـت مـن قيودنـا ونرفـع رؤوسـنا ونعيـش أحـراراً. عندما نحـرر أنفسـنا مـن كـل قهـر وإرغـام، نكتشـف أننـا قـادرون علـى أن نصبـح أدوات فعالـة بعـد أن كنـا مجـرد آلات سـلبية. بل أننـا لا نتحـرر مـن الارتبـاط بنتائـج أفعالـنا فحسـب، بـل نصبـح قـادرين علـى تغييـر هـذه النتائـج نفسـها. وبمجـرد أن نفهم كيفيـة تفاعـل القـوى [الكونيـة] ونرتفـع إلـى مسـتوى الـوعي الـذي تتبـع منـه هـذه القـوى ونتعـرف علـى مصـادرها في أنفسـنا، نصبـح أنفسـنا من محركي الأمـور.

هـذا هـو بالتحديـد مـا تهـدف إليـه **اليوغـا** — أن نتحـرر مـن دورة **الكارمـا*** ونتحـرك بحريـة إلهيـة. بمسـاعدة **اليوغـا** نكـف عـن الـدوران آليـاً في دائـرة **الطبيعـة** حيـث نكـون عبيـداً جهـلاء وأدوات عـاجزة ونرتفـع إلـى مسـتوى أعلـى نشـارك فيـه ونصبـح عمـلاء قـادرين علـى خلـق **مصيـر أفضـل** لأنفسـنا. الـوعي يتحـرك في هـذه الحالـة علـى خـط مزدوج. يبـدأ أولاً بحركـة صعـود يرتفـع فيهـا مـن المسـتوى المـادي إلـى مسـتويات أسـمى. وهـذا الصعـود يسـتهل حركـة نـزول مـن أعلـى إلـى المسـتويات الأدنـى. عندمـا نرتفـع عـن الأرض، نسـتنزل في نفس الوقـت مـن أعلـى قبسـاً مـن النـور أو القـدرة الـتي تغيـر طبيعـة الأرض أو تمهـد لهـذا التغييـر. وبـذلك يتلاقـى مـا كـان منفصـلاً ومتباينـاً في كيانـنا ووعينـا — الطبقـات العليـا والسـفلى والمجـالات الباطنيـة والظاهريـة — ويمتـزج كـل ذلـك بعضـه مـع البعـض وينصهر تدريجيـاً في حقيقة واحدة واتساق واحد.

هـي الطريقـة الـتي تحـدث بهـا المعجزات. العالـم يتكون مـن مسـتويات وعـي تفـوق انحصـر كـل منهـا لـه قوانين خاصـة تميزه؛ بحيـث أن القوانين التي تسـري علـى مسـتوى معيـن لا تسـري علـى مسـتوى آخر. المعجزة مـا هـي إلا نـزول أو تدفق مفاجئ مـن وعـي وقوى مسـتوى أعلـى إلـى مسـتوى المـادة — في أغلـب الأحـوال يكـون هـذا النـزول مـن المسـتوى الحيـوي. وبذلك تنطبـع آليـة المسـتوى الأعلـى علـى آليـة المسـتوى المـادي. ويكـون ذلـك كمـا لـو أومـض بـرق واختـرق سـحاب وعينـا العـادي وصب سـيلاً من قوى وحركات وتسـلسلات من وعـي من أعلـى.

222

A different Outlook – نـظـرة جديـدة

 The result we call a miracle, because we see a sudden alteration, an abrupt interference with the natural laws of our own ordinary range, but the reason and order of it we do not know or see, because the source of the miracle lies in another plane. Such incursions of the worlds beyond into our world of matter are not very uncommon, they are even a constant phenomenon, and if we had eyes and know how to observe we can see miracles in abundance. Especially must they be constant among those who are endeavoring to bring down the higher reaches into the earth-consciousness below.
28 April 1929

A different Outlook – نـظرة جديـدة

نحـن نسـمي أي حـادث معجـزة لأننـا نـرى تغيـراً مفاجئـاً وتـدخلاً مباغتـاً فـي القـوانين الطبيعيـة التـي تسري في مجالنـا الخـاص بـدون أن نعرف سبب أو طريقـة الحدوث — حيـث أن مـا نـزل قد أتـى قد أتـى من مسـتوى آخـر. هذه الغـزوات مـن عـوالم تتخطـى عالمنـا المـادي ليسـت نـادرة الحدوث بـل هـي ظـاهرة تحـدث باستمرار، ولـو كنـا قـادرين علـى الرؤيـة ودققنـا النظـر حولنا لأمكننـا أن نتعـرف علـى الكثير مـن المعجـزات. ملكـة الرؤيـة ضـرورية بالنسـبة للـذين يسـعون إلـى اسـتنزال وعـي المسـتويات الأعلـى إلى وعي الأرض.

28 أبريل 1929

A different Outlook – نـظـرة جديـدة

About Virtue — عـن الفضيـلـة

Do not *try* to be virtuous

Examine thyself without pity, then thou wilt be more charitable and pitiful to others.
Sri Aurobindo, Aphorism Nr. 70

Following is the Mother's comment on the aphorism above:
Very good! It is very good, very good for everybody, particularly for people who think themselves very superior.

But this really corresponds to something very profound. In fact, this is an experience which I have been having for some time. It is almost like a reversal of attitude.

Indeed, men have always considered themselves victims harassed by adverse forces; those who are courageous fight, the others complain. But I have an increasingly concrete vision of the role that the adverse forces play in the creation, of the almost absolute necessity for them, so that there can be progress and for the creation to become its Origin once again – and such a clear vision that instead of asking for the conversion or abolition of the adverse forces one must realise one's own transformation, pray for it and carry it out. This is from the terrestrial point of view; I am not taking the individual standpoint. We know the individual standpoint; this is from the terrestrial point of view.

It was the sudden vision of all the error, all the misunderstanding, all the ignorance and obscurity, and even worse, all the bad will in the terrestrial consciousness which felt responsible for the perpetuation of these adverse beings and forces and which offered them in a great aspiration – more than an aspiration, a kind of holocaust – so that the adverse forces might disappear and have no further reason to exist, so that they might no longer be there to point out everything that has to be changed.

Their presence was made unavoidable by all these things that were negations of the divine life. And this movement of offering of the earth consciousness to the Supreme, in an extraordinary intensity, was like a redemption so that the adverse forces might disappear. It was a very intense experience which expressed itself like this: "Take all the faults I have committed, take them all, accept them, efface them so that these forces may disappear."

عـن الفضيلـة — About Virtue

لا تحاول أن تكون فاضلاً

امتحن نفسك بدون شفقة، عندئذ تزداد شفقة وإحساناً تجاه الآخرين.
شري أوروبيندو، قول مأثور, رقم 70

فيما يلي تعليق الأم:
رائع! إنه قول نافع للغاية، خاصة لأولئك الذين يظنون أنفسهم أفضل كثيراً من غيرهم!

في الحقيقـة، هذا القول يتفق تمامـاً مـع تجربـة أمر بها منذ فترة، تجربـة تكـاد تمثل انعكاسـاً فـي موقفي [بالنسبة للموقف الذي كنت اتخذه في الماضي].

اعتـاد البشر علـى اعتبـار أنفسهم ضحايـا تتجنـى عليهم قوى معاكسة؛ وهـم فـي العـادة إمـا يحـاربون هـذه القـوى إذا كـانوا شجعاناً، أو يكتفـون بالشكوى منهـا لـو لـم يملكـوا الشجـاعة الكافيـة. ولكـن، فـي تجربتـي أدركـت بوضوح متزايد الـدور الـذي تلعبـه القـوى المعاكسة فـي الخليقـة وضرورتها القصـوى للتقدم ولتمكين الخليقـة مـن الرجوع إلـى **الأصـل الإلهـي** — الآن أرى بوضوح أننا، بـدلاً مـن أن نأمل فـي تحويـل أو إزالة القـوى المعاكسة، يجب أولاً أن نسـعى إلـى تحويـل أنفسنا وأن نسـأل فـي صلواتنا النجـاح فـي تحقيـق ذلـك. أنـا أتكلـم مـن وجهـة نظر الأرض ككـل، لا مـن وجهـة النظـر الفرديـة (التـي نعلمها جيداً).

أدركـت فجـأة كل مـا فـي الـوعي الأرضـي مـن الخطـأ وسـوء التفاهم والجهل والإظلام، والأسـوأ مـن ذلـك، كـل النوايـا الشـريرة، وأدركـت أن كـل ذلـك هـو المسـئول عـن تكـاثر هـذه الكائنـات والقـوى المعاكسـة، ورأيـت كيـف أن الأرض تُقـدِّم كـل ذلـك فـي تطلـع عظيـم كقربـان وأضـحية، لعـل هـذه القوى المعاكسة تزول وتفقد مبرر وجودها كمؤشر يشير إلى كل ما يجب أن يتغير على الأرض.

كل مـا ينفي الحيـاة الإلهيـة علـى الأرض هـو الـذي يجعل وجـود هـذه القـوى المعاكسـة ضـرورة لا مفر منهـا. وهـذه الحركـة التـي يهب بهـا وعـي الأرض نفسـه وهبـاً تـامـاً إلـى **الكيـان الأسـمى** هـي فديـة تقدمها الأرض لعـل القـوى المعاكسة تختفـي. كانت تجربـة عميقـة وحـادة عبـرت عـن نفسـها فـي الـدعاء التالي: "تَـقَـبَّـل كل ما اقترفته من أخطـاء واعفو عنها لكي تزول هذه القوى المعاكسة."

A different Outlook – نـظرة جديـدة

This Aphorism is the same thing from the other end; it is the same thing in essence. As long as it is possible for a human consciousness to feel, act, think or be contrary to the great divine Becoming, it is impossible to blame anyone else for it; it is impossible to blame the adverse forces which are maintained in creation as the means of making you see and feel all the progress that has yet to be made.

The state I found myself in was like a memory – a memory that is eternally present – of that Consciousness of supreme Love which the Lord emanated upon earth, in the earth – in the earth to – bring it back to Him. For that was truly a descent into the most total negation of the Divine, the negation of the very essence of the divine Nature, and therefore a renunciation of the divine state in order to accept earth's obscurity and bring earth back to the divine state. And unless this supreme Love becomes all-powerfully conscious here on earth, the return can never be final.

… and I asked myself, "Since this world is progressive, since it is becoming more and more the Divine, will there not always be this intensely painful feeling of the thing which is un-divine, of the state which is un-divine compared to the one which is to come? Will there not always be what we call 'adverse forces', that is, something which is not following the movement harmoniously?" Then the answer came, the vision came: no, indeed the time for this possibility is near, the time for the manifestation of that essence of perfect Love which can transform this unconsciousness, this ignorance and the bad will which results from it into a progression that is luminous, joyful, eager for perfection and all-inclusive.

It was very concrete.

And this corresponds to a state in which one is so *perfectly* identified with all that is, that one becomes all that is anti-divine in a concrete way, and that one can offer it – one can offer it and truly transform it by offering it.

Basically, this kind of will for purity, for good, in men – which expresses itself in the ordinary mentality as the need to be virtuous – is the *great obstacle* to true self-giving. This is the origin of Falsehood and even more the very source of hypocrisy – the refusal to accept to take upon oneself one's own share of the burden of difficulties. And in this Aphorism Sri Aurobindo has gone straight to this point in a very simple way.

A different Outlook – نـظـرة جـديـدة

شـري أوروبينـدو في هذا القول المـأثور ينظر إلى الأمـر مـن الطرف الآخـر ولكنـه يقول أسـاسـاً نفس الشـيء. طالمـا كـان في مقـدور وعـي آدمـي أن يفكر ويشـعر ويتصـرف بصـورة مضـادة **للتطـور الإلهـي العظـيم**، لا يصـح أن نلقي اللـوم علـى الغيـر أو نشـتكي مـن القـوى المعاكسـة التـي هـي بالتحديد موجودة لكي تتنبهنا إلى قصورنا وإلى التقدم الذي ما يزال مطلوباً منا.

هـذه التجربـة أثارت فـي نفسي ذكـرى — ذكـرى حاضـرة إلى الأبـد —؛ تـذكرت كيف بعث **المـولى** وعـي **الحـب الأسـمى** إلـى الأرض وأطلقه فيهـا لكـي يسـترجعها إليـه [بعد ضـلالها]، وكيـف نـزل هـذا **الحب** إلـى كـل مـا ينفي **الألوهية** وينفي حتى جوهـر **طبيعتها** [هذا النفي الـذي هو بمثابة تنـازل عن المقام الإلهي وقبـول لظلام للأرض] لكـي يسـترجعه إلـى المقـام الإلهـي. ولكـن طالمـا لـم يشـمل هـذا **الحب الأسمى** وعي الأرض بأكملها، فإن الرجوع إلى المقام الإلهي لا يمكن أن يكون نهائياً.

... عندئـذ تسـاءلت: "حيـث أن العـالم يتقـدم، وحيـث أنـه يقتـرب أكثـر وأكثـر مـن الحالـة الإلهيـة، أسـيكون هنـاك دائمـا، عندما نقـارن الحالـة غير الإلهيـة الحاضـرة بالحالـة الإلهيـة المسـتقبلة هذا الإدراك المـؤلم بوجـود القوى التـي نسـميها 'القوى المعاكسـة' والتـي تمثل كـل مـا لا يتمشى مـع حركـة التطـور؟ عندئـذ أتـت الرؤيـة وأتـى الـرد: "كـلا! فقد اقتـرب الوقت حقـاً لتمكين جوهـر **الحب** الكامـل الـذي يقـدر علـى تحويـل اللاوعـي وإزالـة الجهـل ومـا يتبعـه مـن سـوء نيـة إلـى سـلسلة مـن التطـور الشامل كلها نور وبهجة وتوق إلى الكمال."

لقد كانت تجربة ملموسة تماماً.

هـذه التجربـة تمثل حالـة يكون المـرء فيهـا متطابقـاً تمامـاً مـع كـل مـا هو غير إلهي لدرجة ن يصير بصـورة ملموسـة كـل مـا هـو غيـر إلهي ولكـي يُقَـدِّم كـل ذلك [كقربـان إلى الألوهيـة]، وعـن طريق تقديمه يحقق تحويله [إلى شيء أفضل].

أساسـاً، رغبـة كـل فـرد فـي أن يكون نقيا وخيراً، التـي تعبر عن نفسها، فـي المفهـوم العـادي، بحاجتـه إلـى أن يكون فاضلاً — هـذه هـي **العقبـة الكبيـرة** التي تقـف فـي طريق وهـب النـفس وهبـاً صادقـاً. وهـي منبـع الخطـأ، بل منبـع النفـاق كـذلك — النفـاق الـذي ينشأ مـن رفض الفرد قبـول نصيبه مـن الأعبـاء والمصـاعب. فـي القـول المـأثور أعـلاه يمـس شـري أوروبينـدو هـذه النقطة بطريقة بسـيطة للغاية.

A different Outlook – نــظــرة جـديـدة

Do not *try* to be virtuous. See how much you are united, one with everything that is anti-divine. Take your share of the burden, accept yourselves to be impure and false and in that way you will be able to take up the Shadow and offer it. And in so far as you are capable of taking it and offering it, then things will change.

Do not try to be among the pure. Accept to be with those who are in darkness and give it all with total love.
21 January 1962

A different Outlook – نـظـرة جديـدة

لا تحـاول أن تكـون فاضـلاً. انظـر إلـى مـدى أنـت متداخل ومتشـابك مـع كـل مـا هـو غيـر إلـهـي. خـذ نصيبك مـن الأعبـاء، واقبـل أن تكـون فـي الخطـأ والـدنس، وبهـذه الطريقـة ستصبـح قـادراً علـى أن ترفـع **الظل** وتقدمه [إلى الألوهية]. بقدر نجاحك في حمل العبء على نفسك وتقديمه، ستتغير الأمور.

<u>لا تحـاول</u> أن تكـون مـن المتطهـرين. اقبـل أن تكـون مـع مـن هـم فـي الظـلام وقَـدِّم كـل ذلـك فـي حـب شامل.

21 يناير 1962

About Helping Others — عن مـسـاعدة الآخرين

Wish others well

You can do a lot of good to people just by sitting quietly in your room, perhaps even more good than by undergoing a lot of trouble externally. If you know how to think correctly, with force and intelligence and kindness, if you love someone and wish him well very sincerely, deeply, with all your heart, that does him much good, much more certainly than you think.

July 1, 1953

Total Kindness and Goodwill

Since we have decided to reserve love in all its splendour for our personal relationship with the Divine, we shall replace it in our relations with others by a total, unvarying, constant and egoless kindness and goodwill that will not expect any reward or gratitude or even any recognition. However others may treat you, you will never allow yourself to be carried away by any resentment; and in your unmixed love for the Divine, you will leave him sole judge as to how he is to protect you and defend you against the misunderstanding and bad will of others.

August, 1953

About Helping Others — عن مسـاعدة الآخرين

تَمَنَّى الخير للآخرين

تستطيع أن تساعد الآخرين كثيراً بمجرد جلوسك هادئاً في حجرتك، وربما استطعت بذلك أن تساعدهم أكثر مما تفعل لو أزعجت نفسك كثيراً في سبيلهم. لو كنت تعرف كيف تفكر تفكيراً صحيحاً وبقوة وذكاء وحنان، وكنت تحب شخصاً وتتمنى له الخير من صميم قلب، وتحبه بصدق وعمق وقوة، فإن ذلك يجلب له خيراً كثيراً، بالتأكيد أكثر كثيراً مما تظن.

1 يوليو، 1953

شفقة وحسن نية شاملان

ما دمنا قد نوينا على أن نحتفظ بالحب في كامل روعته لعلاقتنا الشخصية مع **الواحد-الكل***، فعلينا أن نحل محله في علاقاتنا الأخرى شفقة وحسن نية شاملين ومستديمين وخاليين من الأنانية، بدون أن نتوقع أي مكافأة أو شكر أو حتى مجرد اعتراف بالجميل في مقابل فعلنا. مهما كان تصرف الآخرين نحوك، يجب ألا تسمح للكراهية بأن تجرفك، وفي حبك **للواحد-الكل** يجب أن تجعله الحَكَم الأوحد الذي يحميك ويدافع عنك ضد سوء فهم الآخرين وسوء نواياهم.

أغسطس 1953

About Ego and Egoism – عـن الأنـا والأنانـيـة

The Ego

There are individual egos and collective egos. For example, the national ego is a collective ego. A group may have a collective ego. The human race has a collective ego. It is bigger or smaller. The individual ego is the ego of a particular person; it is the smallest kind of ego. Oh, there is of course a vital ego, a mental ego and a physical ego but these are minor individual egos. But this means the ego of a particular person.

One has many egos inside oneself. One becomes aware of them when one begins to destroy them: when one has destroyed an ego, that which was most troublesome, usually it creates a kind of inner cyclone. When one comes out of the storm, one feels, "Ah, now it is over, everything is done, I have destroyed the enemy inside me, all is finished." But after a while, one notices that there is another, and another still, and yet again another, and that in fact one is made of a heap of little egos which are absolutely a nuisance and which must be overcome one after another.

Ego means what?

I think it is the ego that makes each one a separate being, in all possible ways. It is the ego which gives the sense of being a person separate from others. It is certainly the ego which gives you the sense of the "I", "I am", "I want", "I do", "I exist", even the very famous "I think therefore I am" which is... I am sorry but I think it is a stupidity – but still it is a celebrated stupidity – well, this too is the ego. What gives you the impression that you are [such and such a person] is the ego, and that you are altogether different from this one and that one; and what prevents your body from melting away like that, dissolving in a common mass of physical vibrations, is the ego; what gives you a definite form, a definite character, a separate consciousness, the sense that you exist in yourself, independently of all others, indeed, something like that; if one does not reflect, spontaneously one has the sense that even if the world disappeared, one would be there, one would remain what one is. This of course is the super-ego.

About Ego and Egoism — عـن الأنـا والأنـانيـة

الأنـا

"الأنـا" قـد يكـون فرديـاً وقـد يكـون جماعيـاً. علـى سبيـل المثـال، كـل دولـة لهـا "أنـا" وطنـي يمثـل مجمـوع مواطنيهـا. كـل جماعـة قـد يكـون لهـا "أنـا جمـاعي". الجنـس البشـري فـي مجموعـه لـه "أنـا" جمـاعي. "الأنـا الفـردي" يمثـل ذات شخـص معيـن وهـو وحـدة صـغيرة مـن بيـن أنـواع "الأنـا". ومـع ذلـك أجـزاء هـذا الشخـص لهـا "أنـا" أيضـاً: أنـا حيـوي وأنـا ذهنـي وأنـا بدنـي تُكَـوّن كلهـا معـاً "الأنـا الفردي" لهذا الشخص.

بداخـل كـل منـا أشكـال ثانويـة مـن "الأنـا" لا نتنبـه إلـى وجودهـا إلا عندمـا نشـرع فـي التخلـص منهـا: فـي كـل مـرة نتخلـص فيهـا مـن واحـد منهـا بـادئين بأكثـرهـا إزعاجـاً، تثـور عاصفـة هوجـاء بـداخلنـا. وإذا مـا هـدأت العاصفـة، نظـن أننـا حققنـا الفـوز وانتصـرنـا علـى العـدو بـداخلنـا وأننـا نستطيـع أخيـرً أن ننعـم بالراحـة. ولكـن بعـد فتـرة نلاحـظ أن "الأنـا" مـا زال موجـوداً ولكـن فـي صـورة أخـرى، بـل فـي صـور عديـدة أخـرى، ونـدرك أننـا فـي الواقـع مكونـون مـن أشكـال عديـدة مصغـرة مـن "الأنـا" ، كلهـا غـي غايـة الإزعـاج، وكلهـا يجـب أن نتغلـب عليهـا الواحـدة بعـد الأخـرى.

مـا معنـى "الأنـا"؟

"الأنـا" هـو مـا يجعـل كـل منـا كيانـا مستقلاً بذاتـه فـي كـل ناحيـة مـن النـواحي. وهـو مـا يعطـي كـل منـا الإحسـاس بأنـه شخـص يتميـز عـن الآخـرين. وهـو بالتأكيـد مـا يجعلنـا نقـول: "أنـا"، "أنـا أريـد"، "أنـا أفعـل"، "أنـا موجـود"، وهـو وراء القـول الشهيـر "أنـا أفكـر، لـذا أنـا موجـود"، وهـو قـول اعتبـرء للأسـف حماقـة، علـى الرغـم مـن إنهـا حماقـة يحتفـي بهـا الجميـع. الأنـا هـو الـذي يعطيـك الانطبـاع أنـك "فـلان" وأنـك تختلـف تمامـاً عـن "عـلان"، وهـو الـذي يمنـع بدنـك مـن أن يـذوب ويختـلط مـع أبـدان الآخـرين فـي مزيـج مـن الذبـذبات البدنيـة، وهـو الـذي يعطيـك هيئـة محـددة، ومزاجـاً معينـاً ووعيـاً مستقلاً ويعطيـك الإحسـاس أنـك تعيـش منفصـلاً ومستقلاً عـن الآخـرين، ويجعلـك تحـس، تلقائيـاً، أنـك ستظـل موجـوداً حتـى لـو تلاشـى العالـم بأكمـله، وستبقـى نفـس الشخـص الـذي هـو أنـت الآن. هـذا بالطبـع يكـون "الأنـا" فـي أقصـى صـوره.

A different Outlook – نــظرة جـديـدة

Certainly, if one were to lose one's ego too soon, from the vital and mental point of view one would again become an amorphous mass. The ego is surely the instrument for individualisation, that is, until one is an individualised being, constituted in himself, the ego is an absolutely necessary factor. If one had the power of abolishing the ego ahead of time, one would lose one's individuality. But once the individuality has been formed, the ego becomes not only useless but harmful. And only then comes the time when it must be abolished. But naturally, as it has taken so much trouble to build you, it does not give up its work so easily, and it asks for the reward of its efforts, that is, to enjoy the individuality.
January 12, 1955

Egoism
Egoism is a relatively easy thing to correct, because everyone knows what it is. It is easy to discover, easy to correct, if one truly wants to do it and is bent on it.

But the ego is much more difficult to seize, because, in fact, to realise what the ego is one must already be out of it, otherwise one cannot find it out You are wholly moulded from it, from head to foot, from the outermost to the innermost, from the physical to the spiritual, you are steeped in ego. It is mixed with everything and you are not aware of what it is. You must have already conquered it, come out of it, freed yourself from it, at least partially, at least in some little corner of your being somewhere, in order to realise what the ego is.

The ego is what helps us to individualise ourselves and what prevents us from becoming divine. It is like that. Put that together and you will find the ego. Without the ego, as the world is organised, there would be no individual, and with the ego the world cannot become divine.

It would be logical to conclude, "Well, let us first of all become conscious individuals and then we shall send away the ego and become divine." Only, when we have become conscious individuals, we have grown so accustomed to living with our ego that we are no longer able to discern it and much labour is needed to become aware of its presence.

تأكيداً لـو فقد أي فـرد "الأنـا" قبل الأوان، فإنـه يتحول، مـن وجهـة النظـر الحيوية والذهنيـة، إلى كتلـة لا شكل لها. الأنـا هو أداة التفرد، وهذا يعني أنـه أداة ضرورية للغايـة لكـي يصبح المرء قـدراً على الاستقلال بذاتـه. لـو كانـت لأي فـرد القـدرة على إلغـاء "الأنـا" قبـل الأوان، فإنـه يفقد فرديتـه. ولكـن بمجرد أن يـتم التفرد، يفقد "الأنـا" نفعـه، و يصبح ضـاراً. وعندئذ يكـون الوقت قد حـان للتخلص منـه. ولكـن بالطبع الـتخلص من شـيء لـم يتكون إلا بعد بذل جهـود عظيمـة لـن يكـون سهـلاً، لأن هـذا الشـيء يتوقع مكافأة على ما بذلـه من جهد ويريد أن يتمتع بالفردية التي حققها.

12 يناير، 1955

الأنـــانيـة

اكتشـاف الأنانيـة سـهل وتقويمهـا فـي مقـدور كـل مـن يرغـب فعـل ذلك بصـدق وتصـميم، كمـا أن التخلص منها سهل نسبياً، لأن الجميع يعلمون مـا هي.

أمـا "الأنـا"، فـالتخلص منـه أصعب كثيراً، لأننا لكي نـدرك حقـاً ماهيـة الأنا يجب أن نكون قد خرجنـا منـه بالفعل وأصبحنا قـادرين على إدراك وجوده. ذلك أننا قد شُكِّلنا كلياً مـن الأنـا، كمـا لـو إننا كنـا منقوعين فيه مـن رؤوسنا إلى أقدامنا، مـن أكثر طبقاتنـا سطحية إلـى أكثرهـا عمقـاً، مـن كياننـا البدني إلـى كياننـا الروحي. الأنا يتخلـل ويمتزج بكل شيء فينا على غير علم منـا. هذا هو السبب في أننا لا نلاحـظ وجـوده إلا بعد أن نكـون قـد تغلبنا عليـه جزئياً وحررنـا أنفسنا منـه وخرجنا منـه على الأقل فـي ركن صغير من كياننا.

الأنا هو الـذي يساعدنا على تكوين شخصيتنا المتفردة، ولكنـه في نفس الوقت هو الـذي يمنعنـا مـن أن نصبح إلهيين. هذه هي حقيقـة الأمـر. لـو اعتبرنا الطريقة التي تُنظِّم بها عالمنـا، نرى أنـه بـدون الأنـا لا يكون هناك أفراد مميزون، وبه لا يستطيع عالمنا أن يصبح إلهياً.

الاستنتاج المنطقـي مـن ذلك هو أننا لو نجحنـا كـأفراد في أن نصبح واعيين، سنقدر على الـتخلص مـن الأنـا وبـذلك نصبح إلهيين. ولكـن مـا يحدث فعـلاً هو أننـا، حتى بفـرض كوننا أفراداً واعيين، نتعود على الحياة مع الأنا لدرجة أننا لا نلاحظ وجوده ونحتاج إلى بذل جهد كبير لمجرد اكتشافه.

A different Outlook – نـظـرة جديـدة

On the other hand, everyone knows what egoism is. When you want to pull everything towards you and other people do not interest you, that is called egoism; when you put yourself at the centre of the universe and all things exist only in relation to you, that is egoism. But it is very obvious, one must be blind not to see that one is egoistic. Everybody is a little egoistic, more or less, and at least a certain proportion of egoism is normally acceptable; but even in ordinary life, when one is a little too egoistic, well, one receives knocks on the nose, because, since everyone is egoistic, no one much likes egoism in others.

It is taken for granted, it is part of public morality. Yes, one must be a little bit egoistic, not too much, so it is not conspicuous! On the other hand, nobody speaks of the ego, because nobody knows it. It is such an intimate companion that one does not even recognise its existence; and yet so long as it is there one will never have the divine consciousness.

The ego is what makes one conscious of being separate from others. If there were no ego, you would not perceive that you are a person separate from others. You would have the impression that you are a small part of a whole, a very small part of a very great whole. On the other hand, every one of you is most certainly quite conscious of being a separate person. Well, it is the ego that gives you this impression. As long as you are conscious in this way, it means that you have an ego.

When you begin to be aware that everything is yourself, and that this is only a very small point in the midst of thousands and thousands of other points of the same person that you are everywhere, when you feel that you are yourself in everything and that there is no separation, then you know that you are on the way towards having no more ego.

There even comes a time when it is impossible to conceive oneself and say, "It is not I", for even to express it in this way, to say that the All is you, that you are the All or that you are the Divine or that the Divine is you, proves that something still remains.

There is a moment – this happens in a flash and can hardly stay when it is the All that thinks, it is the All that knows, it is the All that feels, it is the All that lives. There is not even... not even the impression that... you have reached that point. Then it is all right. But until then, there is still a little remnant of ego somewhere; usually it is the part which looks on, the witness that looks on.

A different Outlook – نـظـرة جـديـدة

التعـرف علـى الأنانيـة فـي مقـدور الجميـع. عنـدما ترغـب فـي جـذب الأشيـاء نحـوك وعنـدما تعيـش أساسـاً وقبـل كـل شـيء لنفسـك ولا تعطـي أي أهميـة للآخريـن، هـذه هـي الأنانيـة. عنـدما تعتبـر نفسـك محـور الكـون ولا تـرى الأشيـاء والأمـور إلا مـن حيـث علاقتهـا بـك، هـذه هـي الأنانيـة. الأنانيـة جليـة للعيـان، ولا بـد أن يكـون المـرء أعمـى كليـاً لكـي لا يدركهـا. كـل إنسـان فيـه إلـى حـد مـا قليـل مـن الأنانيـة، وقـدر معيـن مـن الأنانيـة يكـون عـادة مقبـولاً، ولكـن لـو تخطـى المـرء هـذه القـدر، حتـى فـي الحيـاة العاديـة، يتعـرض لنقمـة النـاس لأنهـم جميعـاً أنانيـون، ومـن الطبيعـي أن الأنـاني لا يحـب أنانيـة الآخريـن.

العـرف السـائد يقبـل الأنانيـة كـأمر مفـروغ منـه، ويـرى أن المـرء يجـب أن يكـون أنانيـاً بعـض الشـيء، بشـرط ألا يفـرط المـرء فيهـا لدرجـة أن تصبـح ملحوظـة! ومـن الناحيـة الأخـرى لا يتحـدث النـاس عـن الأنـا، لأنهـم يجهلـون ماهيتـه. الأنانيـة مثـل رفيـق حميـم تعـوَّدنا عليـه لدرجـة أننـا أصبحنـا لا نلحـظ وجـوده. ومـع ذلـك، طالمـا وجـد الأنـا، لا يسـتطيع المـرء أن ينـال الوعـي الإلهـي.

الأنـا هـو مـا يجعلـك تحـس أنـك كيـان مسـتقل عـن الآخريـن. بـدون الأنـا، تشـعر أنـك جـزء صغيـر جـداً مـن كـل كبيـر للغايـة. الواقـع الأكيـد هـو أن كـل فـرد منكـم يشـعر بأنـه شـخص مسـتقل. مـا يجعلـك تشـعر كذلـك هـو بالتحديـد الأنـا. طالمـا أنـك تشـعر كذلـك، تكـون فـي قبضـة الأنـا.

عنـدما تبـدأ فـي إدراك أن كـل شـيء ليـس إلا أنـت ذاتـك، وأنـك لسـت إلا نقطـة متناهيـة فـي الصغـر فـي وسـط آلاف مؤلفـة مـن النقـاط الأخـرى وأنهـا جميعـاً تمثـل **الشـخص الواحـد**، المنتشـر فـي كـلْ مكـان، الـذي هـو أنـت، وعنـدما تشـعر أنـك موجـود فـي جميـع الأشيـاء ولسـت منفصلاً عنهـا، عندئـذ يحـق لـك أن تقـول أنـك فـي طريقـك للتخلـص مـن الأنـا.

يـأتي وقـت يصبـح فيـه مسـتحيلاً أن تقـول عـن أي شـيء: "هـذا ليـس أنـا"، وحتـى مجـرد قولـك أن كـل الأشيـاء هـي أنـت، وأنـك الكـل، أو أنـك الواحـد-الكـل، دليـل علـى أن جـزءاً مـن "الأنـا" مـا زال فيـك.

هنـاك لحظـة عابـرة مـن لمـح البصـر أقصـر تشـعر فيهـا أن **الكـل** هـو الـذي يفكـر، أن **الكـل** هـو الـذي يعلـم، أن **الكـل** هـو الـذي يشـعر، وأن **الكـل** هـو الـذي يعيـش... ويكـون شـعورك خاليـاً مـن أي تفاخـر بأنـك قـد بلغـت مرحلـة متقدمـة فـي الـوعي.. عندئـذ فقـط تكـون قـد تخلصـت مـن الأنـا. ولكـن إلـى أن تـأتي هـذه اللحظـة، يكـون هنـاك بـاقٍ صغيـر مـن الأنـا فيـك، ألا وهـو هـذا الجـزء فيـك الـذي ينظـر ويراقـب ويشـهد..

A different Outlook – نـظـرة جديــدة

So do not assert that you have no more ego. It is not accurate. Say you are on the way towards having no more ego, that is the only correct thing to say.
May 2, 1958

Spiritual Ego

There is a spiritual ego even as there is a physical, vital* and mental ego. There is a spiritual ego. There are people who have made a great effort to overcome all their egoism and all their limitations, and attained a spiritual consciousness; and there, they have all the vanity and the sense of their importance and contempt for those who are not in the same condition as they. Indeed, all that is ridiculous and bad in the ego, they find there once again. There are many, many like that. They have overcome what was there in the physical or vital consciousness but the very effort they have made to master themselves and this victory they have gained give them the sense of their extreme importance. So they become puffed up and assert their authority. This happens so frequently that it is not even noticed.

Still, the spiritual ego is better than the ordinary ego, isn't it?
… It is much more dangerous than the ordinary one! For one is not aware that it is the ego. Outwardly, when one is egoistic, not only does one know it oneself but others make you realise it still more, and circumstances prove it to you every moment. But there, as unfortunately you meet people who respect you highly, you are not even aware that you are terribly egoistic.

Very dangerous. Spiritual vanity is much more serious than physical vanity.
December 9, 1953

لـذلك لا تَـدَّعي أنـك تحـررت مـن الأنـا. لـو فعلت ذلك، تحيد عن الصـواب والدقة. تستطيع، لـو شئت، أن تقول أنـك فـي الطريـق نحـو الـتخلص مـن الأنـا؛ هذا هو الشـيء الوحيـد الصـحيح الـذي يحـق لـك أن تقوله.

2 مايو 1958

الأنا الروحي

الأنـا يسـتطيع أن يتخـذ صـبغة روحيـة تمامـاً مثـل مـا يتخـذ صـبغة بدنيـة أو حيويـة* أو ذهنيـة. الأنـا الروحـي حقيقـة واقعـة. هنـاك قوم بـذلوا جهـداً كبيراً للتغلب علـى الأنانيـة فـي أنفسـهم ولتخطـي حـدودهم وحققـوا بـذلك وعيـاً روحيـاً؛ ولكـنهم مـا يزالـون، فـي المجـال الروحـي ، يتصـفون بـالخيلاء ويشـعرون بـأهميتهم البالغـة وبـازدراء تجـاه الـذين لـم يحققـوا مـا حققـوه، أي أنهـم يتصـفون فـي المجـال الروحـي بكـل السـخف والسـوء الـذي يتميـز بـه الأنـا فـي المجـالات الأخـرى. هؤلاء القوم ليسوا قليلين، بـل هنـاك العديد مـنهم. لقـد نجحـوا فـي التغلـب علـى مـا كـان فيهـم مـن أنـا علـى المسـتوى البـدني والمسـتوى الحيوي، والعجيب أن الجهد الـذي بـذلوه في ذلك هو بالتحديد مـا يعطيهم الإحسـاس المفرط بـأهميتهم. وإذا بهم يغترون ويؤمنون بحقهم في فرض سلطتهم على الغير.

ولكن الأنا الروحي لا بد أن يكون على الأقل أفضل من الأنا العادي، أليس الأمر كذلك؟

... بـل هو أخطر بكثير مـن الأنـا العـادي! لأنـك لا تلحـظ وجـوده. عنـدما تكون أنانيـاً بـالمفهوم العـادي، تكـون علـى علـم بـذلك، فـالآخرين ينبهونـك إليـه، والظـروف كلهـا تثبتـه لـك فـي كـل لحظـة. ولكنـك للأسـف [عنـدما تعـاني مـن الأنـا الروحـي كثيراً مـا] يبدي النـاس لـك كـل احتـرام، ويحجبـون عنـك باحترامهم حقيقة أنه ما زال موجوداً فيك.

الأنا الروحي خطير للغاية والغرور الروحي داء أخطر بكثير من الغرور البدني.

9 ديسمبر، 1953

A different Outlook – نــظـرة جديــدة

About Reality – عـن الحقيقة الواقعة

The Relativity of our Notions

If one enters into a somewhat philosophical, psychological and subjective consciousness, one can very easily become aware of a sort of "objective unreality" of things; and the one thing which is real, tangible, concrete, measurable, so to speak, for the ordinary consciousness becomes so fluid, almost unsubstantial, and has a reality only in the consciousness that perceives it – an absolutely variable reality and at times quite contradictory according to the perception of the consciousness. If we put before us the different explanations that have been given about the world, the different ways in which it has been expressed, we shall have a series of notions that are sometimes absolutely contradictory, which are nevertheless perceptions of one identical thing by different consciousnesses. In fact, with this last paragraph, we have an extreme point which is the affirmation that all that is, is the total and complete expression of the Divine Will – there is what could be called a certain school of thinkers who, on the basis of their personal experience, have asserted that everything is the expression of the Divine Will in a perfect way – and then, at the other extreme, the affirmation that the world is a sort of chaos without rhyme or reason, which has come into being one doesn't know how or why, which is going one doesn't know where, which has no logic, no reason, no coordination is just chance. It happens to be like this, one doesn't know why. Well, if you take these two extremes and put before you all that has been said, written, taught, thought about the world from one end to the other, and if you can see all that together, you will realise that, since it is all about the same world and yet the explanations are so totally different, this world exists, so to say, only in the consciousness of the one who sees it....There must indeed be "something" there, but that something must be beyond what men think about it – far beyond, very different. And so the whole feeling is of an elusive unreality.

And in fact, the reality of the world is entirely subjective for each person's consciousness. The world has no objective reality, for in one case it can be said that it is the result of the supremely conscious, supreme Will and that all is ruled by that, and in the other case, it may be said that it is something without any reason for existence except an elusive chance – and yet, these two notions apply to one and the same thing.

Have you never thought about that?

About Reality — عن الحقيقة الواقعة

نسبية مفاهيمنا

عندما نكـون في وعـي يميل إلى الفلسفة أو علـم الـنفس أو الذاتيـة، نستطيع بسهولة أن نـدرك أن [مـا نسميه] **الحقيقة** شيء نسبي للغايـة، وأن مـا قد يبـدو للـوعي العـادي واقعـاً ملموسـاً يمكن قياسـه، قـد يبـدو لـوعي أسمى لـدِناً وأثيريـاً، وأن مـا يسميه النـاس **الحقيقـة** حقيقي فقط بالنسبة للـوعي الـذي يدركـه، وأنـه يكـون أحيانـاً متغيـراً للغايـة، بـل ومحفوفـاً بالتنـاقض. لـو نظرنـا إلى التفسـيرات المختلفة التي قدمت لشـرح العـالم، وإلى الأسـاليب المختلفة التي استخدمت في التعبير عنها، نجد أنفسنا أمام مجموعـة مـن المفـاهيم تمثـل طرائـق مختلفة لرؤيـة شـيء واحـد وعـي مختلفـة، وأن هذه المفـاهيم قـد تتضـارب أحيانـاً. الفقرة الأخيـرة التـي قرأناهـا [مـن كتـاب "الحيـاة الإلهيـة"] لشـري أوروبينـدو] هـي تعبيـر جلـي عـن الـرأي الـذي ينـادي بـأن **الوجود** كلـه هـو التجسـيد الأقصى والأكمـل **لـلإرادة الإلهيـة.** هـذا رأي نـادى بـه نخبـة مـن المفكريـن الـذين استنتجوا مـن تجربتهم الشخصية أن جميـع الأشـياء والأمـور تعبـر بصـورة كاملـة وتامـة عـن **الإرادة الإلهيـة.** ولكـن هنـاك، في الطـرف الآخـر، مجموعـة أخـرى مـن المفكريـن نـادوا بـأن العـالم مـا هـو إلا فوضـى وتشـوش بـدون مبـرر أو تناسـق، وكانـت حجتهم في ذلـك أن لا أحـد يعلـم كيف ولمـاذا ظهـر هذا العـالم في حيز الوجـود، أو الوجهـة التـي يسـير فيهـا أو المنطـق أو النظـام الـذي يحكمـه، واستنتجوا مـن ذلـك أن العـالم وُجـد وتَكَـوَّن بطريـق الصـدفة، وأن البحـث في أسـباب وجـوده عبـث لا طائـل منـه. فـإذا مـا أحـذنا في الاعتبـار التضـاد الأقصـى بيـن هذيـن الـرأيين والاختـلاف الشـديد في كـل مـا قيـل وكُتِـب ودُرِّس عـن خلـق العـالم، وأنهـا كلهـا تـدور حـول عـالم واحـد تفسـره بطـرق غايـة في التقـارب... نجـد أنفسـنا مضطريـن لاستنتاج أن [مـا يسـميه المفكر منهم] "العـالم" لا وجـود لـه إلا في وعيـه الشخصي. العـالم حقيقـة واقعـة، لا شـك في ذلك، ولكنهـا حقيقـة تتخطى كـل مـا يفكـره النـاس عنهـا. وهذا هـو مـا يجعلنا نشـعر أحيانـاً أن العالم وَهم يراوغنا ويتملص منا.

العـالم حقيقـة ذاتيـة وشخصية بالنسـبة لـوعي الفـردي، وليس حقيقـة موضوعية [ثابتـة بالنسـبة إلى الجميـع]. مـن ناحيـة، يمكننـا القول أنـه نتيجـة وعي فـائق يسـود على أسـمى مسـتويات الـوعي ويـدبر كـل شـيء، ومـن ناحيـة أخـرى يمكننـا أيضـاً أن نقـول أنـه نتيجـة صدفة عشوائية تتملص مـن فهمنـا — ومـع ذلك هذان المفهومان المتضادان يدوران حول نفس شيء.

ألم تفكروا في ذلك من قبل؟

A different Outlook – نـظـرة جديـدة

Everyone has his own idea which is more or less clear, more or less organised, more or less precise, and this idea he calls the world. Everyone has his own way of seeing, his own way of feeling and his particular relationship with everything else, and this he calls the world. He naturally puts himself at the centre, and then everybody is organised around him, according to the way in which he sees it, feels it, understands and desires it, according to his own reaction, but since for each consciousness, individually, it is different, this means that what we call the world – the thing in itself – escapes our perception completely. It must be something else. And we must come out of our individual consciousness to be able to understand what it is; and this is what Sri Aurobindo calls the passage from the lower to the higher hemisphere. In the lower hemisphere there are as many universes as individuals, and in the higher hemisphere there is "something" – which is what it is – in which all consciousnesses must meet. This is what he calls the "Truth-Consciousness".

As the human consciousness progresses, it has a greater and greater sense of this relativity, and at the same time a sort of feeling, it could be said a vague impression that there is a Truth, which is not perceptible by ordinary means but must be perceptible in some way or other.
October 9, 1957

Knowledge by Identification

Is it not possible to know the universe in its reality as it is in itself, independently of the observer or thinker?

Yes, there is a way: it is by identification. But obviously it is a means which eludes absolutely all physical methods. I think that this weakness comes solely from the method used, because one has remained in an absolutely superficial consciousness; and the phenomenon which took place the first time takes place again a second time. If you push your investigation far enough, you suddenly come to a point where your physical methods are no longer of any worth.

نـظـرة جـديـدة – A different Outlook

لكـل فـرد مفهـوم خـاص وطريقـة خاصـة للرؤيـة وللشـعور ولـه ردود فعـل خاصـة علـى الأشـياء، كلهـا علـى درجـة مـا مـن الوضـوح والدقـة والتنسـيق فـي ذهنـه، وهـذا هـو مـا يسـميه هـذا الفـرد "العالم". هذا الشـخص يضـع نفسـه تلقائيـاً فـي مركـز هـذا العـالم وينسـق الأمـور حـول ذاتـه حسـب رؤيتـه وشـعوره وفهمـه ورغبتـه ورد فعلـه، ولكـن حيـث أن مفهـوم هـذا العـالم يختلـف تمامـاً مـن فـرد إلـى فـرد، نسـتنتج أن العـالم فـي حـد ذاتـه خـارج عـن نطـاق فهمنـا كليـاً ولا بـد أن يكـون ا شـيئاً آخـر غيـر كـل هـذه المفاهيم. لكـي نـتمكن مـن فهـم العـالم لا بـد أن نخـرج مـن وعينـا الـذاتي، وأن نرتفـع، علـى حـد تعبيـر شـري أوروبينـدو، مـن "نصـف الكـرة السـفلي" إلـى "نصـف الكـرة العلـوي". فـي نصـف الكـرة السـفلي لكـل فـرد عـالم خـاص بـه، أمـا فـي النصـف العلـوي، فهنـاك نقطـة تلتقـي فيهـا أشـكال الـوعي المختلفـة كلهـا. هذا الوعي هو ما يسميه شري أوروبيندو "وعي الحقيقة".

كلمـا تقـدم الـوعي البشـري، كلمـا زاد إدراكـه بنسـبية المفـاهيم البشـرية، وكلمـا قَـوِي حدسـه بـأن هنـاك **حقيقة واحدة**، لا يمكن فهمها بالوسائل العادية، ولكن يمكن فهمها بوسائل أخرى.
9 أكتوبر، 1957

المعرفة بالتطابق

هل يمكن معرفة حقيقة الكون في حد ذاته، أي حقيقته التي لا تتوقف على الملاحظ أو المفكر؟

نعـم، ذلـك ممكـن عـن طريـق التطابـق. مـن الواضـح أن هـذه الطريقـة تستعصـى علـى كـل المنـاهج الفيزيائيـة. ولكنـي اعتقـد أن هـذا القصـور يـأتي فقـط لأن البـاحثين يظلـون علـى مسـتوى وعـي سـطحي تمامـاً. لو واظبت على البحث، تكتشف ذات يوم أن المناهج الفيزيائية لا قيمة لها.

A different Outlook – نـظـرة جديـدة

And in fact one can know only what one is. So if you want to know the universe, you must become the universe. You cannot become the universe physically, you know; but perhaps there is a way of becoming the universe: it is in the consciousness. If you identify your consciousness with the universal consciousness, then you know what is happening. But that's the only way; there are no others. It is an absolute fact that one knows only what one is, and if one wants to know something, one must become that. So you see, there are many people who say, "It is impossible", but that's because they remain on a certain plane. It is obvious that if you remain only on the material plane or even on the mental plane, you cannot know the universe, because the mind is not universal; it is only a means of expression of the universe; and it is only by an essential identification that you can then know things, not from outside inwards but from inside outwards. This is not impossible. It is altogether possible. It has been done. But it can't be done with instruments, however perfected they may be. Here one must once again make something else intervene, other regions, other realities than purely material ones, including the mind which belongs to the physical life, the terrestrial life.

One can know everything, but one must know the way. And the way is not learnt through books, it cannot be written in numbers. It is only by practising... And here then, it demands an abnegation, a consecration, a perseverance and an obstinacy – still more considerable than what the sincerest, most honest, most unselfish scientists have ever shown. But I must say that the scientific method of work is a marvelous discipline; and what is curious is that the method recommended by the Buddha for getting rid of desires and the illusion of the world is also one of the most marvelous disciplines ever known on the earth. They are at the two ends, they are both excellent; those who follow one or the other in all sincerity truly prepare themselves for yoga. A small click, somewhere, is enough to make them leave their fairly narrow point of view on one side or the other so as to be able to enter into an integrality which will lead them to the supreme Truth and mastery.

I don't know whether ignorance is the greatest obstacle on the path of humanity... We said that it was an almost exclusively mental obstacle and that the human being is much more complex than a mental being, though he is supremely mental, for he is its new creation in the world. He represents the last possibility of Nature, and in that, naturally his mental life has taken immense proportions, because he has the pride of being the only one upon earth to have it. He does not always make a good use of it, still it is like this. But it's not here that he will find the solution. He must go beyond. October 5, 1955

A different Outlook – نـظرة جديـدة

الحقيقة هـي أن المـرء لا يستطيع أن يعلم إلا مـا هو موجود فـي ذاتـه بالفعل. ولـذلك لـو أردت أن تعلم الكـون، يجب أن تصيـر الكـون. بـالطبع لـن يمكنـك أن تصير الكـون مـاديـاً؛ ولكن ربمـا استطعت أن تفعل ذلك في وعيك. عندما تتطابق في وعيـك مـع الـوعي الكـوني، عندئذ تعلم مـاذا يدور فـي الكـون. هـذه هـي الطريقـة الوحيدة ولا توجـد طريقـة أخـرى. إنهـا حقيقـة مطلقـة أن المـرء لا يعلم إلا مـا فـي داخلـه، وأن المـرء إذا أراد أن يعلـم شيئـاً، يجب أن يصيـر هـذا الشيء. كثير مـن النـاس يعتبـرون هـذا التطـابق مستحيلاً، ومـا ذلك إلا لأنهـم يظلون علـى مستوى خفيض مـن الـوعي. واضـح أنـك لـو لـم تتخطـى مستوى الـوعي المـادي أو حتـى الـذهني، لـن يمكنـك أن تعلم حقيقـة الكـون، لأن الـذهن لـيس كونيـاً، وإنمـا هـو أداة للتعبيـر عـن الكـون. الطريقـة الوحيدة الحقـة للمعرفـة هـي التطـابق الجـوهري: أن تتطـابق مـع الأشياء فتعلم حقيقتهـا مـن الداخل إلى الخـارج ولـيس مـن الخـارج إلـى الـداخل. المعرفـة بالتطـابق ليست مستحيلـة، وقـد حققهـا البعض بالفعل. ولكن تحقيقهـا لا يحـدث باستخدام أدوات، حتى لـو كانـت أفضل الأدوات وأكثرهـا كمـالاً، بـل أنـه يستلزم الاستعانـة بقـوى تـأتي مـن مجـالات أخـرى وبحقائق غير الحقائق المادية البحتة، وغير العقل الذي ينتمي إلى الحياة الفيزيائية على الأرض.

معرفـة جميـع الأشياء متاحـة لنـا، علـى شـرط أن نعـرف طريقـة فعل ذلك. وهـذه معرفـة لا نحدهـا فـي الكتب أو فـي المعـادلات الرياضيـة... بـل إنهـا تـأتي بالممارسـة... وهـي تتطلب نكـران الـذات والتكريس ومثـابرة تفـوق كثيـراً مثـابرة أكثـر العلمـاء صـدقـاً وإخلاصـاً وتضحية بـالنفس. أنـا لا أنكـر أن مـنهج البحـث العلمي مـنهج رائـع، ولا أنكـر أيضـاً أن المـنهج الـذي أوصـى بـه بـوذا للتخلص مـن لشهـوات وأوهـام العـالم هـو أيضـاً مـن أروع المنـاهج التي ظهـرت علـى وجـه الأرض. كلاهما منهجـان رائعـان وإن كانـا يقاربـان الحقيقـة مـن اتجـاهين متضـادين. أيمـا شخص يمـارس أحـد هـذين المنهجين بكل إخلاص، يعد نفسـه إعـداداً جيداً لليوغـا. كـل مـا يحتاجـه بعد ذلك هو مجـرد خطـوة أخيـرة صغيرة تمكنه من تخطي نظره الضيقة إلى الشمول الذي يقوده إلى **الحقيقة الأسمى.**

لا أعلم إن كـان الجهـل هـو أكبر العقبـات فـي طريـق الإنسانية... سبق أن ذكرنـا أن الجهـل عقبـة ذهنيـة بحتـة، وأن الإنسان لـه جوانب أخـرى غير الجـانب العقلي، وإن كـان الجـانب العقلـي هـو مـا يميزه في تطـور الخليقـة عـن سـائر الكائنـات. الإنسان أحدث المخلوقـات [فـي سلم التطور] وهـو يمثل آخر مـا توصلـت إليـه **الطبيعة.** ومـع أن الإنسان لا يستخدم عقلـه دائمـاً الاستخدام الصـحيح، فإن العقـل يبقـى أقـوى نواحيـه. ولكـن علـى الـرغم مـن كل ذلك، لـن يجـد الإنسـان الحقيقـة بواسطة العقـل، بـل إنـه يجب أن يتخطى العقل إلى ما وراء العقل ليجدها.

5 أكتوبر، 1955

A different Outlook – نــظـرة جديــدة

Why all this Confusion in the World?

You have said that the world and the darkness were concomitant. What is the cause of this concomitance?

The cause... is the light which has become the darkness and the consciousness which has become the inconscience! How to speak about these things? You may call this an accident if you like, if that satisfies your mind. It was perhaps, after all, the best thing that could have happened, one can't tell. All depends upon the point of view one takes. There must certainly be a consciousness in which this was foreseen, and if it has not been avoided, it means that it forms part of the programme!... It is a human way of looking at the problem, for things do not happen quite like that in those regions. One may also relate a story which could make a subject, a magnificent drama, but it would be only a story, a way of saying things.

A story is of value only to the extent it can help you to understand things. Ah! Here is an interesting subject... A story, that is, a way of saying things, is of value only if it can make you understand the thing. A language (which is a kind of story) is of value only to the extent it is capable of putting you in contact with the Reality. Science is a language, Art is a language – all activity is a sort of language, that is, a way of expression. And the way of expression is of value only in as far as it puts you in contact with what it wants to express. It is a very interesting generalisation, for you can bring into it all the categories you want and you will see that it is true.

It is the same for everything. The way of approaching the universe and the universal truth is also a language and all depends upon the person who uses it, the person to whom the understanding is to be communicated. Whatever may be the way of telling, if you understand, that is all that is necessary. If you do not understand, even if it be the wonder of wonders, the truth of truths, it will have no value for you. This is an essentially pragmatic point of view of the universe; things have value only in so far as they realise that for which they have been made, and the most beautiful philosophies of the world are of no use to those who do not understand them. The most beautiful works of art in the world are quite useless to those whom they do not put on the path of the Truth. And the most perfect yoga in the world is useless to those whom it does not lead to the Realisation.

لماذا كل هذه الفوضى في العالم؟

لقد قلتِ أن العالم يعيش في الظلام. ما هو السبب في ذلك؟

السبب هو... النـور الـذي تحـول إلـى ظلمـة، والـوعي الـذي تحـول إلـى لاوعـي! كيـف يمكنـني أن أتحـدث عن هذه الأشياء. تستطيع أن تصـف مـا حـدث بأنـه كان حادثـة، إن كان ذلك سيرضـي ذهنك. ومن يعلم، ربما كـان مـا حـدث، فـي آخـر المطـاف، أفضـل شـيء كـان يمكـن أن يحـدث. كـل شـيء يتوقف على وجهـة النظـر التـي نتخـذها. هنـاك بالتأكيـد وعي كانـت فيه هـذه الحادثـة مقدَّرَة، وحيث أن الحادثـة حدثت بالفعل، لا بـد أنهـا كانت جزءاً مـن البرنـامج [الإلهـي]. [الأسف علـى حـدوث الحادثـة] هـو طريقـة البشـر فـي النظـر إلـى الأمـور، ولكـن الأشيـاء لا تحـدث تبعـاً لمفهـوم البشـر فـي تلـك المجـالات [العليـا]. نستطيع أن نفسر الحادثـة بواسطـة قصـة موضـوعها يصـلح لأن يكـون درامـا رائعـة، ولكنهـا ستكون مـع ذلك مجـرد قصـة وهيئـة واحـدة مـن هيئـات عديـدة يمكن أن نفسر بهـا مـا حدث.

أي قصـة لا قيمـة لهـا إلا إلـى المـدى الـذي تساعدنا بـه علـى فهـم الأمـور. هنـا نـدخل فـي موضـوع مشـوق حقـاً... أي لغـة (اللغـة مـا هـي إلا نـوع مـن القصص) لا أهميـة لهـا إلا إلـى حـد قدرتهـا علـى تبيـين الحقيقـة لنـا. العلم لغـة، كمـا أن الفـن لغـة ––– جميـع النشـاطات أنـواع مـن اللغـات مـن حيـث أنهـا وسائـل مـن وسائـل التعبير. وأي وسيلـة تعبير لا أهميـة لهـا إلا إلـى المـدى الـذي تجعلنا نـرى ونفهم مـا هـي تريـد أن تعبـر عنـه. هـذا تعميـم مشـوق للغايـة نستطيع أن نتحقـق مـن صحتـه عندما نطبقـه علـى كافة وسائل التعبير.

هـذه النظـرة تسـري علـى جميـع الأمـور. الطريقـة التـي ننظـر بهـا إلى الكـون لنتقصـى الحقيقـى الكونيـة هـي أيضـاً لغـة، وكـل شـيء يتوقف علـى الشخص الـذي يستعمل هـذه اللغـة، وعلـى الشخص اُمُخَاطَب الـذي يتلقاهـا. مهمـا كانـت طريقتك في الإبـلاغ، لـو كنـت تـدرك مـا تقول، هـذا هـو كـل مـا هـو مطلـوب منـك. لـو كنـت لا تـدري مـا تقول، لـن يكـون لمـا تقول، حتـى لـو شـمل أعظـم الحقـائق وأروعهـا، أي قيمـة. إذا نظرنـا إلـى الكـون مـن وجهـة نظـر براغماتيـة بحتـة نجـد أن الأشيـاء ليـس لهـا أي قيمـة إلا عندمـا تحقق الغـرض الـذي خلقـت مـن أجلـه، كمـا أن أروع الأعمـال الفلسفية لا قيمة لهـا إذا لـم تكـن مفهومـة وأجمـل الأعمـال الفنيـة لا نفـع منهـا إذا لـم ترشـد النـاظـر إلـى طريـق **الحقيقـة** وأكثـر أنـواع اليوغا كمـالاً عديمة القيمة إذا لم تؤدِ إلى التحقيق.

A different Outlook – نـظـرة جديـدة

And if you have this sense of relativity, you have finished with all dogmatism, all sectarianism, all that kind of absolutism which leads one always to think that all that has done us good is "the truth" – it is the truth for us, it is not necessarily the truth for our neighbour. And what our neighbour thinks is the truth for him, and when you say, "It is idiotic, it is quite useless", if it helps him to realise the truth, it is excellent, it is the best thing possible for him. And everything, everything on earth is like that. And if you do not want to be altogether narrow, to put on visors and not see farther than the tip of your nose, you must first of all understand this. You must understand that all things in the universe tend towards a goal and that it is to the extent they help to realise this goal that they have a value, and that this value is quite relative; and what is good for one may not be so for another, what is good at one moment may not be so at another and, consequently, every kind of dogmatism is an absurdity.

It is very easy to say, "That, that's true, now I know that it is true and I shall not think otherwise"; this is very easy, and in fact something has suddenly put you in touch with a light, you have had an experience, you have become conscious of yourself, conscious of something which transcends you and is the reality of your being, so for you it is perfect. But do not imagine that you must go from door to door, from city to city, country to country, telling people, "I proclaim the Truth", because what is true for you may not be at all good for another. What you have seen has its truth in itself – everything has its truth in itself – but the true raison d'être of this truth is that it has helped you to find yourself, to find the truth of your being, and it may quite possibly not help your neighbour, unless you have a considerable power of persuasion and oblige him to see things as you have seen them yourself, but this is not tremendously valuable.

When you have understood this, you will no longer say, "Why is there such a diversity in the world, why all this multiplicity, why all this confusion, why... ?" It is a confusion simply because you don't understand and things are not in their place. If things were in their place, there would be no confusion. And we come to this, that you cannot take away one atom from this world without dislocating the universe. All that is, was necessary – if it had not been necessary, it would not have been. The whole totality of things is indispensable for realising the Divine. If you took away one of these things, there would be a hole in the realisation. And I am not speaking only of material things, material points, I am speaking of all the depths. So when you say as many do, "Ah! If that were not there in the world, how fine the world would be", you are displaying your ignorance.
April 5, 1951

A different Outlook – نـظـرة جديـدة

عندما تكتسب هذا الإحساس بنسبية الأمور، تكون قد تخطيت كل أنواع الدوغماتية والطائفية والأحكام المطلقة التي تنادي بأن كل ما هو في مصلحتنا ونافع لنا هو "الحقيقة" — ربما كان الحقيقة بالنسبة لنا، ولكنه ليس بالضرورة الحقيقة بالنسبة لجارنا. ما يعتقده جارنا، هو الحقيقة بالنسبة له، حتى لو بدى لنا حماقة ولغواً، وحيث أنه يساعده على التحقيق، فهو أفضل شيء في الإمكان بالنسبة له. نستطيع أن نعمم هذه النظرة بحيث تشمل كل شيء آخر على ظهر الأرض. لو أردت أن تتجنب ضيق الأفق وأن ترفع الحجاب الذي يمنعك من أن ترى أبعد من طرف أنفك، ينبغي أن تفهم ما أقوله هنا. يجب أن تفهم أن كل الأمور في الكون لها هدف، وأن قيمة الأشياء تتوقف على المدى الذي تساهم به هذه الأشياء في تحقيق أهدافها، وأن هذه القيمة نسبية إلى حد بعيد، وأن ما هو خير بالنسبة لعمرو قد لا يكون خيراً بالنسبة لزيد، وأن ما هو صالح في لحظة ما، قد لا يصلح في لحظة أخرى، وأن جميع أنواع الدوغماتية سخف وحماقة.

أحياناً تمر بتجربة متنورة، تخبر فيها شيئاً يتخطى كيانك ويلائم حقيقتك ويجعلك تقول: "لقد وَجَدت الحقيقة، وأنا لا أريد أي حقيقة سواها". ولكن لا تتصور في تلك الحالة، أنك مُطالَب بأن تطوف من باب إلى باب، ومن مدينة إلى مدينة، ومن بلد إلى بلد قائلاً للناس "لقد جئتكم بالحقيقة"، لأن الحقيقة التي صلحت لك قد لا تصلح للآخرين. تجربتك، مثل كل شيء آخر، تحمل حقيقتها في نفسها، والهدف الأول من حدوثها لك هو أن تساعدك على اكتشاف نفسك وحقيقة كيانك، ولكن أغلب الظن أنها لن تنفع جارك — إلا لو كنت تملك قدرة عظيمة على الإقناع و أجبرت هذا الجار على أن ينظر إلى الأمور بنفس نظرتك، وهي حالة افتراضية ضئيلة القيمة على أي حال.

عندما تفهم كل ذلك، تكف عن التساؤل: "لماذا كل هذا التنوع في العالم؟ لماذا كل هذا التعدد؟ وما هو السبب في كل هذه الفوضى؟" إنها فوضى لأنك، من ناحية، لا تفهمها، ولأن الأشياء ليست في مكانها الصحيح، من ناحية أخرى. عندما تكون الأشياء في مكانها الصحيح، لا تكون هناك فوضى. ولو تابعنا هذا المنطق نتوصل في النهاية إلى فهم أننا لا نستطيع أن نقتطع من الكون ذرة واحدة بدون أن نُخلِّ بالكون كله، وأن كل ما في الكون ضروري، وإنه لو لم يكن ضرورياً، لما وُجد أساساً. الأشياء والأمور كلها ضرورية لتحقيق **الواحد-الكل***. ولو استبعدت شيئاً واحداً من كل هذه الأشياء، فإنك تنتقص من هذا التحقيق. وأنا لا أتكلم عن الأشياء المادية والبعْت المادي فحسب، بل أتكلم عن جميع الأبعاد. ولذلك فإنك عندما تقول، كما يفعل الكثيرون: "آه، لو زال هذا الشيء من العالم، كم يكون العالم رائعاً"، يكون ذلك دليلاً على جهلك.
5 أبريل، 1951

A different Outlook – نـظـرة جـديـدة

About Science – عـن العلوم الفيزيائية

The really important scientific discovery

The only really important thing modern science has discovered is that from the purely outer and physical point of view things are not what they seem to be. When you look at a body, a human being, an object, a landscape, you perceive these things with the help of your eyes, your touch, hearing and, for the details, smell and taste; well, science tells you: "All that is illusory, you don't see things at all as they are, you don't touch them as they really are, you don't smell them as they really are, you don't taste them as they really are. It is the structure of your organs which puts you in contact with these things in a particular way which is entirely superficial, external, illusory and unreal."

From the point of view of science, you are a mass of – not even of atoms – of something infinitely more imperceptible than an atom, which is in perpetual movement. There is absolutely nothing which is like a face, a nose eyes, a mouth; it is only just an appearance. And scientists come to this conclusion – like the uncompromising spiritualists of the past – that the world is an illusion. That is a great discovery, very great....One step more and they will enter into the Truth. So, when somebody comes and says, "But I see this, I touch it, I feel it, I am sure of it", from the scientific point of view it's nonsense. This could be said only by someone who has never made a scientific study of things as they are. So, by diametrically opposite roads they have come to the same result: the world as you see it is an illusion.

Now what is the truth behind this? People who have sought spiritual knowledge tell you, "We have experienced it", but of course it is a purely subjective experience; there are as yet no grounds on which one can say absolutely that the experience is beyond question for everybody. Everyone's experience is beyond question for him. And if one takes it a little further...

In fact, the value of an experience or a discovery could perhaps be proved by the power it gives, the power to change these appearances and transform things, circumstances and the world as it appears to us, in accordance with the will that manifests through that experience.

عـن العلوم الفيزيائية — About Science

أهم اكتشاف علمي

مـن الناحيـة الفيزيائيـة والظاهريـة، أهـم اكتشـاف أتـت بـه العلـوم الحديثـة هـو أن الأشـياء ليسـت بالضـرورة مـا هـي تبـدو عليـه. عندما تعتبر المحسوسـات أو البشـر أو المناظـر الطبيعيـة، فإنـك تـدرك هـذه الأشـياء عـن طريـق البصـر واللمـس والسـمع، وأحيانـاً تكتسـب بعـض التفاصيـل عـن طريـق الشـم والمـذاق. العلـم الحديـث يخبرنـا أن مـا نـراه أو نلمسـه أو نشـمه أو نذوقـه مـن الأشـياء لـيس بالـضرورة حقيقتهـا، بـل أن تركيـب حواسـنا هـو الـذي يجعلنـا نراهـا ونلمسـها ونشـمها ونذوقهـا علـى هـذا النحـو السطحي والخارجي والوهمي والبعيد عن الحقيقة.

مـن وجهـة نظـر العلـم الحديـث، الأجسـام ليسـت إلا كتلـة مـن الـذرات، بـل مـن مكونـات متناهيـة فـي الصـغر لهـذه الـذرات، كلهـا فـي حركـة دائمـة. أي أن مـا نـراه وجهـاً أو أنفـاً أو عينيـن أو فمـ ليـس إلا مظهـراً [يتـوقف علـى حواسـنا]. وبذلـك يكـون العلمـاء قـد توصلـوا إلـى نفـس الحقيقـة التـي نـادى بهـا العديـد مـن الـروحيين فيمـا سـبق: ألا وهـي أن العـالم وهـم. [والعجيـب أن] علمـاء الفيزيـاء وعلمـاء الـروح توصلـوا إلـى نفـس الحقيقـة علـى طـريقين متضـادين تمامـاً. هـذا اكتشـاف عظيـم...عظيـم حقـاً. ولـو تقدم العلـم خطـوة أخـرى، ربمـا يتوصـل إلـى **الحقيقـة المطلقـة**. ولذلـك لـو ادعـى إنسـان بثقـة تامـة أنـه يعلـم الحقيقـة اسـتناداً علـى مـا يـراه ويلمسـه و يشـعر بـه، يكـون ذلـك لغـواً ودليـلاً علـى أنـه لـم يـدرس حقائق الأشياء دراسة علمية.

مـا هـي الحقيقـة إذاً وراء كـل ذلـك؟ بعـض البـاحثين عـن المعرفـة الروحيـة يقولـون لنـا أنهـم قـد خبـروا الحقيقـة، ولكـن تجربتهـم كانـت بالطبـع تجربـة شخصيـة بحتـة؛ ولا يوجـد، حتـى يومنـا هـذ، أسـاس يسـمح لنـا بـأن نقـول أن تجربتهـم تصلـح للجميـع؛ كـل مـا نسـتطيع أن نقولـه هـو أن كـل تجربـة فرديـة تصلـح للفـرد الـذي خبرهـا. ولـو اسـتطردنا قليـلاً علـى هـذه المنـوال.... [الأم قطعت حديثها هنا ولكنها عادت إلى هذه النقطة في أحد الفقرات التالية].

فـي الواقـع لا يمكـن الحكـم علـى قيمـة تجربـة أو اكتشـاف إلا بالنظـر إلـى القـدرة التـي يكتسـبها مجـرب التجربـة مـن تجربتـه أو مكتشـف الاكتشـاف مـن اكتشـافه، وهـل هـو قـادر باسـتخدام هـذه القـدرة علـى تغيير المظاهر وتحويل الأشياء والظروف.

A different Outlook – نـظـرة جديـدة

It seems to me that the most universal proof of the validity of an individual or collective experience would be its power to make things – these appearances that we call the world – different from what they are. From the subjective point of view, the effect of the experience on an individual consciousness is an undeniable proof; for one who attains bliss, sovereign peace, unchanging delight, the profound knowledge of things, it is more than proved. The effects on the outer form depend on many other things besides the experience itself – depend perhaps on the first cause of these experiences – but out of all this, one thing seems to be a proof which is accessible to other people as well as to the one who has the experience; it is the power over other people and things – which for the ordinary consciousness is "objective". For instance, if a person who has attained the state of consciousness I am speaking about, had the power of communicating it to others, it would be partially – only partially – a proof of the reality of his experiences; but further, if the state of consciousness in which he is – for instance, a state of perfect harmony – could create this harmony in the outer world, in what apparently is not harmony, it would be, I think, the proof most readily accepted, even by the materialist scientific mind. If these illusory appearances could be changed into something more beautiful, more harmonious, happier than the world we live in now, this would perhaps be an undeniable proof.

And if we take it a little farther, if, as Sri Aurobindo promises us, the supramental force, consciousness and light transform this world and create a new race, then, just as the apes and animals – if they could speak – could not deny the existence of man, so too man would not be able to deny the existence of these new beings – provided that they are different enough from the human race for this difference to be perceptible even to the deceptive organs of man.
18 December 1957

A different Outlook – نـظرة جديـدة

يبدو لـي أن أكثر البراهين عمومية على صـلاحية تجربة فردية أو جماعية هـو قدرة هذه التجربة على تغييـر الأشياء. مـن وجهة النظـر الشخصية، تـأثير التجربـة [الروحية] على وعـي الفرد الـذي عـاش هـذه التجربة واضـح ولا يحتـاج إلـى برهـان؛ وعنـدما يحقـق فـرد الهنـاء الـدائم، على سـبيل المثـال، أو السـلام المهيمن أو المعرفـة العميقة، يكون ذلك، بالنسبة لـه، تحقيقـاً داخليـاً لا يحتـاج إلـى برهـان. أمـا تـأثير تجربـة على الهيئة الخارجية [وليس فقط على الحالة الداخلية للمجرب]؛ فإنه يعتمد على أشياء أخرى كثيرة بالإضافة إلى التجربة نفسها ― وربما يعتمد أيضاً على مصدر هذه التجربة. ولكن يبدو أن البرهـان على صـدق أي تجربة الـذي يقبله الجميع، وليس فقط صـاحب التجربـة نفسه، هـو القدرة على التأثير على النـاس والأشياء، على أن تكون قـدرة "موضـوعية" وليست فقط شخصية. على سبيل المثال، لو حقق شخص مـا حالة معينة من حالات الوعي، وأمكنه أن يبلغها إلـى الآخـرين، يكـون ذلـك برهانـاً جزئيـاً ― جزئيـاً فقـط، وليـس عامـاً ― علـى صـدق تجربته. أمـا لو توصل هـذا الشخص إلـى تغييـر العـالم الخارجي بحيث يُحِل التناسـق محـل الفوضـى ويصيـر هـذا العـالم أكثر جمالاً وسـعادة، يكـون ذلـك في رأيـي، برهانـاً [علـى صـدق تجربة هـذا الشخص] يقبله الجميع، حتى الماديون الذين لا يؤمنون إلا بالعلم.

ولـو استطردنا علـى هـذا المنـوال وافترضـنا، حسـب مـا وعـد بـه شـري أوروبينـدو، أن السـوبرامنتال سـيغير هـذا العـالم بواسـطة قوتـه ووعيـه ونـوره وسـيخلق جنسـاً جديداً مـن الكائنـات يختلـف بدرجـة كافيـة عـن الانسان الحـالي، يكـون ذلـك تحقيقـاً لا يسـتطيع البشـر إنكـاره، تمامـاً مثـل مـا حـدث فـي النشـوء والتطور عندما ظهـر الإنسـان، وأصبح مسـتحيلاً علـى القـردة وسـائر الحيوانـات أن تنكر وجوده ― هذا لو فرضنا أنها كانت قادرة على الكلام!

18 ديسمبر، 1957

About Miracles — عن المـعـجـزات

Miracles have their own logic

There are very few people who know that there exists in the universe an infinite number of gradations and that each one of these gradations has its own reality, its own life, its own law, its own determinism, and that the creation did not come about "like that", by an arbitrary will, in an arbitrary way but is a deploying of consciousness and each thing has evolved as a logical result of the preceding one.

I am telling you all this as simply as I can, you see, it is a very incomplete expression, but if I wanted to tell you the story exactly as it is, it would be a little difficult to make you understand. Only I would like you to know my conclusion (I have already spoken about it several times, more or less in detail), it is this: each one of these numberless regions has its own very logical determinism – everything proceeds from cause to effect; but these worlds, although differentiated, are not separate from each other and, by numerous processes which we may study, the inner or higher worlds are in constant contact with the lower or external worlds and act upon these, so that the determinism of one changes the determinism of the other.

If you take the purely material domain, for instance, and if you notice that the material laws, the purely material laws are altered by something all of a sudden, you ought to say that it was a "miracle", because there is a rupture of the determinism of one plane through the intervention of another, but usually we do not call this a miracle. For example, when the human will intervenes and changes something, that seems to you quite natural, because you have been accustomed to it from your childhood; you remember, don't you, the example I gave you the other day: a stone falls according to the law of its own determinism, but you wish to interrupt its fall and you stretch out your hand and catch it; well you ought to call this a "miracle", but you don't because you are used to it (but a rat or a dog would perhaps call it a miracle if they could speak).

And note that it is the same for what people call a "miracle"; they speak of a "miracle" because they are absolutely ignorant, unaware of the gradations between the will which wants to express itself and the plane on which it expresses itself. When they have a mental or a vital will, the thing seems quite natural to them, but when it is a question of the will of a higher world ... which all of a sudden upsets all your little organisation, that seems to you a miracle. But it is a miracle simply because you are unable to follow the gradations by which the phenomenon took place.

عن المعجزات — About Miracles

المعجزات لا تحدث اعتباطاً

قليل مـن النـاس يعلمـون أن الكـون يتكـون مـن طبقـات لا حصـر لهـا، وأن كـل طبقـة مـن هـذه الطبقـات لهـا حقيقتهـا الذاتيـة وحياتهـا الخاصـة وقـوانين خاصـة بهـا، وأن الخليقـة لـم تحـدث عفـواً أو تبعـاً لإرادة عشـوائية وبطريقـة اعتباطيـة، بـل إنهـا تعبيـر عـن وعـي دبـر الأمـور جميعـاً بحيـث يتطـور كـل شـيء مـن شـيء آخـر سبقه.

أقـول لكـم كـل ذلـك فـي صـورة مبسطة وناقصة، لأني لـو قصصـت عليكم القصة بكـل حـذافيرها كمـا هـي فـي الواقـع، سيصـعب عليكم الفهـم. يكفـي هنـا أن أطلعكم علـى الاسـتنتاج الـذي توصلـت إليـه (وسـبق أن تحـدثت عنـه تكـراراً بـبعض التفصيل): كـل مـن هـذه المنـاطق التـي لا حصـر لهـا يعمـل جبريـاً تبعـاً لمنطـق خـاص بـه، بحيـث يكـون لكـل مسبب أثـره، ولكـن هـذه العـوالم، علـى الـرغم مـن أنهـا متمـايزة، ليسـت معزولـة ومنفصلة بعضـها عـن بعـض، وإنمـا هـي فـي اتصـال دائـم بحيـث تـؤثر العـوالم الداخليـة العليـا علـى العـوالم الخارجيـة الـدنيا بحيـث تغيـر مجـرى الأمـور فيهـا [كـل هـذه الأشـياء يمكـن دراستها].

لـو اعتبرنـا، علـى سـبيل المثـال، المجـال المـادي وحـده، ولاحظنـا تغيـراً مفاجئـاً فـي قـوانين المـادة نتيجة لتـدخل مـن مجـال آخـر، ينبغـي أن نقـول أن مـا حـدث "معجـزة" ، ولكنـا فـي العـادة لا نفعـل ذلـك. إذ أننـا كثيـراً مـا نتـدخل ونغيـر مسـار الأحـداث ويبـدو لنـا هـذا طبيعيـاً للغايـة لأننـا تعودنـا علـى فعلـه منـذ طفولتنـا. لعلكم تـذكرون المثـال الـذي ضـربته لكـم سـابقاً: عندمـا نراقـب حجـراً أثنـاء وقوعـه تبعـاً لقـانون الجاذبيـة ونمـد يـدنا ونلتقـط الحجـر وننهـي عمليـة وقوعـه، مـن المفـروض أن نصـف هـذه الحادثـة بأنهـا معجـزة، ولكننـا لا نفعـل ذلـك لأننـا تعودنـا علـى أفعـال شـبيهة (فـي حيـن لـو شـاهد كلـب أو قـط هـذه الحادثـة فربمـا يسـميها "معجزة" لـو كان قـادراً علـى الكلام!)

النـاس يتكلمـون عـن "معجـزات" لأنهـم يجهلـون كليـاً وجـود طبقـات ودرجـات ويجهلـون أن إرادة فـي طبقـة معينـة تسـتطيع أن تحـدث تغييـراً فـي طبقـة أخـرى. أن تكـون لهـم إرادة ذهنيـة أو حيويـة، هـذا شـيء يبـدو لهـم طبيعيـاً للغايـة، ولكـن تـدخل إرادة مـن عـالم علـوي فـي النظـام الـذي تعودوا عليـه علـى الأرض يبـدو لهـم معجـزة. ومـا ذلـك إلا لأنهـم عـاجزون عـن تتبـع الخطـوات المتتابعـة التـي أحدثـت التغيير.

A different Outlook – نـظـرة جديـدة

Therefore, the Supreme Will, that which comes from the very highest region, if you saw it in its logical action, if you were aware of it continually, it would seem to you altogether natural. You can express this in two ways: either say, "It is quite natural, it is like this that things must happen, it is only an expression of the divine Will", or, each time you see on the material plane an intervention coming from another plane, you ought to say, "It is miraculous!"

So I may say with certainty that people who want to see miracles are people who cherish their ignorance! You understand my logic, don't you? These people love their ignorance, they insist upon seeing miracles and being astounded! And that is why people who have done yoga seriously consider it altogether fatal to encourage this tendency; hence it is forbidden. There is a "miracle" because you do not give people time to see the procedure by which you do things, you do not show them the stages.
February 8, 1951

A different Outlook – نـظـرة جديـدة

لـو كنـت واعيـاً باستمرار **بـالإرادة الأسـمى** التـي تـأتي مـن الآفـاق العليـا، سـتبدو لـك جميـع التغييـرات طبيعيـة للغايـة. لـذلك تسـتطيع أن تفسـر أي حـدث بطـريقتين: إمـا أن تقـول أنـه طبيعـي للغايـة وإنـه كـان لا بـد أن يحـدث بهـذه الطريقـة لأنـه تعبيـر عـن **الإرادة الإلهيـة**، أو تقـول فـي كـل مـرة تـرى فيهـا تَـدُخل مـن طبقـة فـي طبقـة أخـرى: "يا لهـا مـن معجـزة".

وبـذلك اسـتطيع أن أجـزم أن الـذين يريـدون رؤيـة المعجـزات، مـا هـم إلا جـاهلون مغرمـون بجهلهـم ويحبـون التعجـب والانـدهاش! أرجـو أن تكونـوا قـد فهمتـم منطقـي؟ هـذا هـو السـبب فـي أن ممارسـي اليوغـا الجـادين يعتبـرون الشـغف بـالمعجزات خطـراً مهلكـاً يجـب الامتنـاع عنـه. النـاس يعتبـرون حـوادث كثيـرة "معجـزات" لأننـا لا نتيـح لهـم الوقـت الكـافي للتعـرف علـى العمليـة والمراحـل المختلفـة التـي تمـر بهـا هـذه الحـوادث.

8 فبراير، 1951

About Evolution — عـن النشوء والتـطور

Progression of Forms

If you take terrestrial history, all the forms of life have appeared one after another in a general plan, a general programme, with the addition, always, of a new perfection and a greater consciousness. Take just animal forms – for that is easier to understand, they are the last before man – each animal that appeared had an additional perfection in its general nature – I don't mean in all the details – a greater perfection than the preceding ones, and the crowning point of the ascending march was the human form which, for the moment, from the point of view of consciousness, is the form most capable of manifesting consciousness; that is, the form at its height, at the height of its possibilities, is capable of more consciousness than all preceding animal forms.

This is *one* of Nature's ways of evolution.

Sri Aurobindo told us last week that this Nature was following an ascending progression in order to manifest more and more the divine consciousness contained in all forms. So, with each new form that it produces, Nature makes a form capable of expressing more completely the spirit which this form contains. But if it were like this, a form comes, develops, reaches its highest point and is followed by another form; the others do not disappear, but the individual does not progress. The individual dog or monkey, for instance, belongs to a species which has its own peculiar characteristics; when the monkey or the man arrives at the height of its possibilities, that is, when a human individual becomes the best type of humanity, it will be finished; the individual will not be able to progress any farther. He belongs to the human species, he will continue to belong to it. So, from the point of view of terrestrial history there is a progress, for each species represents a progress compared with the preceding species; but from the point of view of the individual, there is no progress: he is born, he follows his development, dies and disappears.

Therefore, to ensure the progress of the individual, it was necessary to find another means; this one was not adequate. But within the individual, contained in each form, there is an organisation of consciousness which is closer to and more directly under the influence of the inner divine Presence, and the form which is under this influence.–

عن النشوء والتطور — About Evolution

تطور الأجناس والأشكال

عندما ننظـر إلـى تـاريخ الأرض، نـرى صـور الحيـاة المختلفـة وقـد ظهـرت واحـدة تلـو الأخـرى تبعـاً لخطـة وبرنـامج شـاملين، بحيـث تمثـل كـل صـورة منهـا تقدمـاً فـي الكمـال والـوعي بالمقارنـة بالصـور التي سبقتها. دعنـا نعتبـر أشكال الحيـوان لأنهـا أسـهل فـي الفهم. الحيوانـات ظهـرت فـي المرحلـة التـي سبقت الإنسان مباشرة بحيـث كـان كـل صنف مـن أصنـافها أكمـل فـي طبيعتـه العامـة — ليـس فـي جميـع التفاصيـل — مـن الصـور السـابقة. وأخيـراً ظهـر الإنسـان وكـان ذلـك تتويجـاً لهـذا التطـور المطـرد. الهيئـة البشـرية، مـن وجهـة نظـر الـوعي، هـي أصلـح الهيئـات للتعبيـر عـن الـوعي، بمعنـى أنها، عندما تكون في أحسن صـورها وأقصـى إمكانياتها، تفوق كل الهيئات السابقة من هذه الناحية.

تطور الهيئات والأشكال هو أحد طريقتين تتطور بهما **الطبيعة**.

يقـول لنـا شـري أوروبينـدو، فـي النـص الـذي قرأنـاه الأسـبوع الماضـي، أن **الطبيعـة** تسـعى فـي تطورهـا المتصاعد للتعبير، بشـكل متنـامي، عـن الـوعي الإلهـي الكـامن فـي جميـع الكائنـات. **الطبيعـة** تجعـل كـل هيئـة جديـدة تنتجهـا أكثـر قـدرة علـى التعبيـر عـن الـروح الكـامن فيهـا. الهيئـة الجديـدة تـأتي وتتطـور وتبلـغ قمتهـا، فـي حيـن تبقى الهيئـات التـي سبقتها علـى مـا هـي عليـه. وبـذلك يكـون هنـاك تقدم عـام للجـنس أو الفصـيلة، ولكـن أفـراد الفصـيلة الواحـدة يتوقفـون عـن التطـور. كـل مـن الكلـب أو القـرد أو الإنسـان ينتمـي إلـى فصـيلة لهـا خصـائص معينـة، وإذا مـا توصـل إنسـان فـرد مثـلاً إلـى قمـة إمكانياتـه البشـرية، يتوقـف نمـوه كفـرد. وبـذلك يكـون هنـاك تقـدم مـن وجهـة نظـر الأرض عامـة، إذ أن كـل نـوع يمثل تقدماً بالمقارنة بالنوع السابق، أما الفرد فإنه يولد ويتبع مسار حياته ويموت ويختفي.

لضمان تقـدم الفرد، أصبـح مـن الضـروري إيجـاد وسـيلة أخـرى تكمـل الوسـيلة التـي شـرحناها أعـلاه. لـذلك نُظـّم الـوعي الفردي بحيـث يكـون فيـه جـزء أقـرب إلـى تـأثير **الحضـرة الإلهيـة** — عـن طريـق تركيز داخلي للطاقة — وبحيث تكون له حياة مستقلة لا تتوقف على الهيئة البدنية.

A different Outlook – نــظـرة جديــدة

This kind of inner concentration of energy – has a life independent of the physical form – this is what we generally call the "soul" or the "psychic* being" – and since it is organised around the divine centre it partakes of the divine nature which is immortal, eternal. The outer body falls away, and this remains throughout every experience that it has in each life, and there is a progress from life to life, and it is the progress of the *same* individual. And this movement complements the other, in the sense that instead of a species which progresses relative to other species, it is an individual who passes through all the stages of progress of these species and can continue to progress even when the species have reached the limit of their possibilities and...stay there or disappear – it depends on the case – but they cannot go any farther, whereas the individual, having a life independent of the purely material form, can pass from one form to another and continue his progress *indefinitely*. That makes a double movement which completes itself. And that is why each individual has the possibility of reaching the utmost realisation, independent of the form to which he momentarily belongs.

There are people – there used to be and there still are, I believe – who say they remember their past lives and recount what happened when they were dogs or elephants or monkeys, and tell you stories in great detail about what happened to them. I am not going to argue with them, but anyway this illustrates the fact that before being a man, one could have been a monkey – perhaps one doesn't have the power to remember it, that's another matter – but certainly, this inner divine spark has passed through successive forms in order to become more and more conscious of itself. And if it is proved that one can remember the form one had before becoming a psychic being as it is found in the human form, well, one might very well recollect climbing trees and eating coconuts and even playing all sorts of tricks on the traveller passing beneath!

In any case, the fact is there...it is this double movement of evolution intersecting and complementing itself which gives the utmost possibilities of realisation to the divine light within each being. This is what Sri Aurobindo has explained. (*Turning to the child*) This means that in your outer body you belong to the animal species in the course of becoming a supramental species – you are not that yet! but within you there's a psychic being which has already lived in many, many, countless species before and carries an experience of thousands of years within you, and which will continue while your human body remains human and finally decomposes.

A different Outlook – نـظـرة جـديـدة

نحن نسـمي هذا الجزء بصفة عامـة "الـروح" أو "الكيـان السيكي*"، وحيث أنـه يتمحـور حـول المركز الإلهـي فـي الكيـان، فإنـه يكتسب الطبيعـة الإلهيـة مـن حيث كونـه أبـدياً لا يموت. . بعد المـوت، يتحلـل البـدن، ولكـن الـروح لا تفنـى تبقـى لتمـر بتجـارب كثيـرة فـي كل حيـاة تعيشـها وتتقـدم مـن حيـاة إلى أخـرى، وبـذلك ينمـو الفـرد [كفـرد فـي حـد ذاتـه]. طريقـة التطـور هـذه تكمـل الطريقـة الأولى، وتسـمح للفرد بـالتطور حتى يبلـغ جنسه أو نوعـه أقصى مـداه مـن التطـور. بعـض الأجنـاس ينـدثر لأسبـاب سنذكرها فيمـا بعـد، ولكـن روح الفـرد، حيـث أن لهـا حيـاة مسـتقلة عـن الهيئـة المـاديـة البحتـة، تستطيع أن تمـر مـن نـوع إلـى نـوع آخـر وأن تتقـدم إلـى مـا لا نهايـة. التطـور إذاً مـزدوج ويتكـون مـن حـركتين تكمـل إحـداهما الأخـرى. هـذا تفسـير أن كـل فـرد يسـتطيع أن يبلـغ أقصـى التحقيقات، بصرف النظر عن الهيئة التي قد ينتمي إليها في أي وقت معين.

كـان هنـاك قـوم — وأعتقـد أنهـم مـا زالـوا موجـودين — يقولـون إنهـم يتـذكرون حيـواتهم السـابقة ويقصـون القصـص المفصلـة عمـا حـدث لهـم عندمـا كـانوا كلابـاً أو فيلـة أو قـردة. أنـا لا أنـوي على مجـادلتهم، ولكـن مـا يقولـون يشيـر إلـى حقيقـة أن المـرء ربمـا كـان قـرداً قبـل أن يبلـغ مرحلـة الإنسان — حتـى لـو كـان غيـر قـادر علـى تـذكر ذلك، ولكـن التـذكر موضـوع آخـر — مـا هو أكيـد هـو أن الشـرارة الإلهيـة الداخليـة [أي الـروح] تمـر بهيئات متتاليـة وتـزداد وعيـاً بـذاتها فـي كـل مـرة. وإذا أمكـن إثبـات أن الإنسان يسـتطيع أن يتذكـر هيئـة كـان عليهـا قبـل أن يصبـح كيانـاً سيكيـاً مكتمـلاً، ربمـا أمكـن أيضاً إثبـات أن الإنسان كـان سابقاً يتسلق الأشجار ويأكل جوز الهند ويتسلى بإلقائـه بـه على المـارين من تحته الشجرة!

على أي حـال، الحقيقـة ثابتـة... ألا وهـي أن حركـة التطـور المزدوجـة التـي شرحناها تعطـي أقصى إمكانيـات التحقيـق للنـور الـداخلي الموجـود فـي كـل كيـان. هـذا هـو مـا شـرحـه شري أوروبينـدو. (الأم مخاطبـة أحـد الأطفـال:) هـذا معنـاه إنـك فـي بـدنك الخـارجي تنتمـي إلـى جنس الحيوان ولكنـك فـي الطريـق إلـى بلـوغ السوبرامنتال* — أنت لـم تصـل بعـد هنـاك. ولكـن هنـاك بـداخلك كيـان سيكي* عـاش سابقـاً فـي هيئـات وأجنـاس لا حصـر لهـا ويحمـل فـي ذاتـه تجـارب آلاف السـنين، وسيستمر في جمع التجارب حتى لو بقي بدنك الآدمي عرضة في النهاية للموت والتحلل.

A different Outlook – نـظـرة جديـدة

We shall see later whether this psychic being has the possibility of transforming its body and itself creating an intermediate species between the animal man and superman – we shall study this later – but still, for the moment, it is an immortal soul which becomes more and more conscious of itself in the body of man....

Mother, in Nature we often see the disappearance of an entire species. What is that due to?

Probably Nature thought that it was not a success!...You see, she throws herself into action with abundance and a total lack of sense of economy. We can see this. She tries everything she can, in every way she can, with all sorts of inventions which are obviously very remarkable, but at times...it's like a blind alley. Pushing forward in that direction, instead of progressing, one would reach things that are absolutely unacceptable.... For Nature, you see, there is a limitless abundance. I believe she doesn't shrink from any kind of experiment. Only if something has a chance of leading to a successful issue does it continue. Certainly there have been intermediaries or parallel forms between the ape and man; traces of them have been found – perhaps with some wishful thinking! but anyway, traces have been found – well, those species have disappeared. So, if we like to speculate, we may wonder whether the species which is now to come and which is an intermediary between animal man and superman will remain or whether it will be considered uninteresting and rejected....That we shall see later. The next time we meet we shall speak about it again!

It is quite simply the activity of a limitless abundance. Nature has enough knowledge and consciousness to act like someone with innumerable and countless elements which can be mixed, separated again, reshaped, taken to pieces once more and...It is a huge cauldron: you stir it, and something comes out; it's no good, you throw it back in and take something else. Imagine the dimension...just take the earth: you understand, one or two forms or a hundred, for her this is of no importance at all, there are thousands and thousands and thousands of them; and then a few years, a hundred, a thousand, millions of years, it is of no importance at all, you have eternity before you!

Simply, when we look at things on the human scale, in space and time, oh! it seems enormous, but for Nature it is nothing. It is just a pastime. One may like it or not, this pastime, but still it is a pastime. It is quite obvious that Nature enjoys it and is in no hurry. If she is told to press on without stopping and to finish one part of her work or another quickly, the reply is always the same: "But what for, why? Doesn't it amuse you?"
October 30, 1957

نـظـرة جديـدة – A different Outlook

سنرى مستقبلاً إن كـان هـذا الكيـان السـيكي قـادراً على تحويـل نفسـه وبدنـه بحيـث يصبح جنسـاً وسطاً بـين الإنسـان الحيـواني والإنسـان الفـائق — سـوف نـدرس هـذا فيمـا بعـد — ولكـن يكفـي فـي الوقت الحالي أن نقول أن كيانك السيكي أبدي وأنه يزداد وعياً بذاته في بدن بشري...

*أمي، في **الطبيعة**، نلاحظ أحيانا أن فصائل بأكملها تندثر. ما هو سبب ذلك؟*

ربمـا تنثر هـذه الفصـائل لأن **الطبيعـة** تعتبرهـا فاشلـة!... عنـدما تخلـق **الطبيعـة**، تفعل ذلك بـوفرة وبـدون أي اعتبـار للناحيـة الاقتصـادية. هـذا شـيء تسـهل ملاحظتـه. وهـي تحـاول كـل مـا فـي وسـعها وبكـل الطـرق التـي فـي جعبتهـا وتتوصـل إلـى أنـواع لا حصـر لهـا مـن الابتكـارات المذهلـة... ولكـن بعـض هـذه الابتكـارات يكـون أحيانـاً مثل الطريق المسـدود، بحيـث أن لـو اسـتمرت **الطبيعـة** فـي هـذا الطريـق، تكـون النتـائج حتمـاً غيـر مقبولـة. امكانيـات **الطبيعـة** لا حـدود لهـا، وهـي لا تتـردد فـي القيـام بـأي تجربـة، ولكنهـا لا تسـتمر فـي تجربـة إلا لـو كـان لهـذه التجربـة فرصـة كافيـة للنجـاح. لقـد كـانت هنـاك حتمـاً فصـائل متوسـطة بـين القـرد والإنسـان، وقـد وجـدت آثـار لهـذه الفصـائل بالفعـل [وإن كـان كثيـر مـن الاكتشـافات التـي نسـمع عنهـا زعـم باطـل]... حسـناً هـذه الفصـائل المتوسـطة قـد اندثـرت. ولـذلك لـو أردنـا أن نخمـن ونتنبـأ، نسـتطيع أن نتسـاءل مـا إذا كـانت **الطبيعـة** سـتخلق الفصـيلة القادمـة التـي سـتتوسط بـين الإنسـان وبـين الإنسـان الفـائق أم سـترفضها. سـنرى ذلـك عنـدما نجتمـع المـرة القادمة.

إنها مجرد مسألة وفرة لا حدود لها. **الطبيعة** تملك تحت تصرفها معرفـة ووعيـاً كافيـاً وعنـاصر لا حصـر لهـا يمكنهـا أن تخلطهـا وتشكلها ثـم تفكهـا وتُفَتِّتُهـا مـرة أخـرى وتلقـي بهـا فـي بوتقـة عظيمـة تصهرهـا، ثـم تمـزج كـل ذلـك وتنتقـي منـه عينـة تفحصهـا، فـإن لـم ترضـى عنهـا تلقـي بهـا فـي البوتقـة مـرة أخـرى وتنتقـي عينـة أخـرى وهكـذا. بالنسـبة **للطبيعـة** شـكل واحـد أو شـكلان أو حتى مـائة شـكل مـن آلاف الأشـكال لا يهـم على الإطـلاق. كـذلك وقـت **الطبيعـة** غيـر محـدود، ومـائة أو ألـف أو حتى مليون عام لا أهمية لهم على الإطلاق.

عندما ننظـر بمقاييس الإنسـان، تبـدو الأمـور ضخمـة للغايـة، ولكنهـا تبـدو بالنسـبة إلـى **الطبيعـة** مجـرد توافـه وتسـالي. وسـواء أرضينـا أو لـم نرضـى، فـإن الطبيعـة تفعل مـا تريـد، ومـن الواضـح أنهـا ليسـت فـي عجلـة، وأنهـا راضيـة عـن أفعالهـا. وعنـدما نطلـب منهـا أن تسـرع وتقتصـد فـي الوقـت الـذي تحتاجـه لإتمـام أعمالهـا، يكـون جوابهـا باسـتمرار: "ولـم العجلـة والتسـرع؟ ألا تـرى أن كـل ذلـك مسـلي للغاية؟!"
30 أكتوبر، 1957

264

Some Experiences of the Mother — من تجارب الأم

Prayers and Meditations — صلوات وتأملات

November 3, 1912 — 1912 ،3 نوفمبر

Let Thy Light be in me like a Fire that makes all alive; let Thy divine Love penetrate me. I aspire with all my being for Thy reign as sovereign and master of my mind and heart and body; let them be Thy docile instruments and Thy faithful servitors.

November 19, 1912 — 1912 ،19 نوفمبر

I said yesterday to that young Englishman who is seeking for Thee with so sincere a desire, that I had definitively found Thee, that the Union was constant. Such is indeed the state of which I am conscious. All my thoughts go towards Thee, all my acts are consecrated to Thee; Thy Presence is for me an absolute, immutable, invariable fact, and Thy Peace dwells constantly in my heart. Yet I know that this state of union is poor and precarious compared with that which it will become possible for me to realise tomorrow, and I am as yet far, no doubt very far, from that identification in which I shall totally lose the notion of the "I", of that "I", which I still use in order to express myself, but which is each time a constraint, like a term unfit to express the thought that is seeking for expression. It seems to me indispensable for human communication, but all depends on what this "I" manifests; and how many times already, when I pronounce it, it is Thou who speakest in me, for I have lost the sense of separativity. But all this is still in embryo and will continue to grow towards perfection. What an appeasing assurance there is in this serene confidence in Thy All-Might! Thou art all, everywhere, and in all, and this body which acts is Thy own body, just as is the visible universe in its entirety; it is Thou who breathest, thinkest and lovest in this substance which, being Thyself, desires to be Thy willing servant.

Some Experiences of the Mother — من تجارب الأم

Prayers and Meditations — صلوات وتأملات

November 3, 1912 — 1912 ،3 نوفمبر

دع **نورك** يغشاني كالنار التي تحيي كل شيء. اسمح **لحبك الإلهي** بأن يتخللني. أتوق بكل كياني إلى أن تكون **مولاي والسيد المهيمن** على ذهني وقلبي وبدني، عسى أن أصير في جميع أجزائي أداتك الوديعة وخادمتك المخلصة.

November 19, 1912 —1912 ،19 نوفمبر

قلت البارحـة لـذلك الرجـل الإنجليزي الـذي يبحـث عنك ويسعى إليك بصدق تـام وإخـلاص شـديد إننـي قد وجدتك بكل تأكيد وأن اتحادي معك قد أصبح دائماً. هذه هي بالفعل الحال التي تراني عٰليها. كل أفكاري تتجـه نحوك، وكل أفعـالي مكرسـة لـك، و**حضـورك** معـي قـد صـار حقيقـة مطلقـة لا تتبـدل، وسكينتك أصبحت تقطـن في قلبي بصفة مستمرة. ولكني مـع كـل ذلك أعلم أن الوحدة الـذي حققتها معك بالفعل قاصرة وحرجـة بالمقارنـة مـع الوحدة الـذي سيكون في مقدوري تحقيقها مستقبلاً، وأعلم كـذلك أني مـا زلـت بعيدة كل البعد عن حالـة التطابق معك التي سأفقد فيهـا كليـاً مفهوم الـ "**أنا**"، تلك الكلمـة التي مـا زلـت استخدمها لأعبر عـن نفسي، على الـرغم من أنهـا تبدو لـي في كـلِ مـرة قيداً يحـدني، أو مصـطلحاً غير لائـق للتعبير عـن الفكرة في ذهني التي تحـاول التعبيـر عـن نفسـها. مصـطلح "**الأنا**" يبدو لـي ضرورياً في المـداولات البشـرية؛ ولكـن كـل شـيء يتوقـف كليـاً علـى مـدلول هذه الكلمـة. كـم مـن المـرات بـدا لـي فيهـا، عندما نطقت بهـذه الكلمة، أن المـتكلم هـو **أنـت**... إلـى هـذا الحد فقـدت الشعـور بـأني منفصلة عنـك. ولكـن كـل ذلك مـا زال مثـل جنـين صـغير ينمـو باستمرار نحـو الكمـال. كـم أشـعر بالطمأنينة والبهجـة في ثقتي بأنك **القدير** علـى كل شـيءٍ! أنت الكـل، في جميع الأمكنة وفي كـل الأشياء، وهذا البدن النشـط مـا هو إلا بدنك أنت، مثلـه في ذلك مثل كل شـيء آخر في هذا الكون المرئي؛ وأنـت هو من يتنفس ويفكر ويحب في هـذه المـادة، التي لكونهـا أنت نفسك، تتوق وترغب في أن تكون خادمتك.

266

Some Experiences of the Mother — من تجارب الأم

November 28, 1912 — 1912, ‏28 نوفمبر

The outer life, the activity of each day and each instant, is it not the indispensable complement of our hours of meditation and contemplation? And is not the proportion of time given to each the exact image of the proportion which exists between the amount of effort to be made for the preparation and realisation? For meditation, contemplation, Union is the result obtained, the flower that blooms; the daily activity is the anvil on which all the elements must pass and repass in order to be purified, refined, made supple and ripe for the illumination which contemplation gives to them. All these elements must be thus passed one after the other through the crucible before outer activity becomes needless for the integral development. Then is this activity turned into the means to manifest Thee so as to awaken the other centers of consciousness to the same dual work of the forge and the illumination. Therefore are pride and satisfaction with oneself the worst of all obstacles. Very modestly we must take advantage of all the minute opportunities offered to knead and purify some of the innumerable elements, to make them supple, to make them impersonal, to teach them forgetfulness of self and abnegation and devotion and kindness and gentleness; and when all these modes of being have become habitual to them, then are they ready to participate in the Contemplation, and to identify themselves with Thee in the supreme Concentration. That is why it seems to me that the work must be long and slow even for the best and that striking conversions cannot be integral. They change the orientation of the being, they put it definitively on the straight path; but truly to attain the goal none can escape the need of innumerable experiences of every kind and every instant.

. . . O Supreme Master who shinest in my being and each thing, let Thy Light be manifest and the reign of Thy Peace come for all.

Some Experiences of the Mother — من تجارب الأم

أليست الحياة الخارجية بكل ما تشمله من أعمال نقوم بها في كل لحظة وفي كل يوم، الجزء المُكَمِّل الذي لا غنى عنه [لحياتنا الداخلية] وللساعات التي نمضيها في التأمل والتبصر؟ و ألا يتناسب الوقت الذي نخصصه لكل منهما مع مقدار الجهد الذي ينبغي أن نبذله في الإعداد والتحضير [من ناحية] وفي التنفيذ والتحقيق [من الناحية الأخرى]؟ فالتأمل والتبصر والاتحاد امع الألوهية هم النتيجة والزهرة التي تتفتح، في حين أن الأنشطة اليومية هي السندان الذي تطرق عليه جميع أجزاؤنا، مرة بعد المرة، لتنقيتها وتكريرها ولجعلها مرنة وجديرة بالتنوير الذي يأتيها عن طريق التبصر والمشاهدة. كل أجزاؤنا يجب أن تمر، الواحد بعد الآخر، خلال بوتقة [الصهر والتكرير] قبل أن نتمكن من الاستغناء عن النشاط الخارجي كضرورة من ضرورات نمونا المتكامل. [فإذا ما تطهرت هذه الأجزاء] يتحول النشاط الخارجي إلى وسيلة لتحقيقك بهدف إيقاظ مراكز وعي أخرى لهذا العمل المزدوج: عمل الإعداد والتنوير. لذلك اعتبر الافتخار وانرضا اقبل الأوان عن النفس أسوء العقبات. يجب على العكس أن نستغل في تواضع جميع الفرص المتاحة لنا لكي نعجن وننقي عناصر كياننا العديدة ونجعلها لدنة، ومتخطية لحدود ذاتنا الصغيرة، وقادرة على نسيان الذات ووهب النفس والإخلاص واللطف والوداعة. عندما تعتاد عناصرنا هذه الأنماط [السامية] تصبح مستعدة للمساهمة في **التأمل الإلهي** وللتطابق **معك** في **التركيز الأقصى.** لذلك يبدو لي أن العمل لا بد أن يكون طويلاً وبطيئاً حتى بالنسبة إلى أقدر الناس، وأن التحولات [لمفاجئة] الباهرة لا يمكن أن تكون شاملة أو متكاملة. صحيح أن التحولات المفاجئة تغير وجهة الكيان وتقوده إلى الصراط المستقيم؛ ولكن لبلوغ الهدف بالفعل، لا مفر، في كل لحظة، من تجارب عديدة من كل الأنواع.

... أيها **المولى الأعظم،** يا من تسطع في كياني وفي جميع الأشياء، دع **نورك** يتجلى ودع **سلامك** يسود كل القلوب.

Some Experiences of the Mother — من تجارب الأم

December 5, 1912 — 1912, ديسمبر 5

In Peace and Silence the Eternal manifests; allow nothing to disturb you and the Eternal will manifest; have perfect equality in face of all and the Eternal will be there.

. . . Yes, we should not put too much intensity, too much effort into our seeking for Thee; the effort and intensity become a veil in front of Thee; we must not desire to see Thee, for that is still a mental agitation which obscures Thy Eternal Presence; it is in the most complete Peace, Serenity and Equality that all is Thou even as Thou art all, and the least vibration in this perfectly pure and calm atmosphere is an obstacle to Thy manifestation.

No haste, no inquietude, no tension, Thou, nothing but Thou, without any analysis or any objectivising, and Thou art there without a possible doubt, for all becomes a Holy Peace and a Sacred Silence.

And that is better than all the meditations in the world.

Some Experiences of the Mother — من تجارب الأم

في **السلام والصمت** يتجلى **الأبدي**؛ لا تسمح لأي شيء بأن يزعجك، وسوف يتجلى **الأزلي**؛ كن متساوياً تماماً في وجه جميع الأمور، وسوف تخبر حضرة **الأبدي**.

... نعم، ينبغي ألا نفرط في بذل الجهد أو في السعي في بحثنا عنك؛ لنتجنب أن يصير الجهد الزائد نقاباً يخفيك عنا؛ كما يجب ألا نشتهي رؤيتك، لأن هذا الاشتهاء نفسه يكون بمثابة هيجان ذهني يعتم **حضورك الأزلي**. فقط في جو من **السلام** التام و**السكينة** الشاملة و**التساوي** الكامل تصبح جميع الأشياء **أنت** وتصير **أنت** كل شيء، وأقل هزة في هذا الجو الطاهر الهادئ تكون عقبة تعوق **تجليتك**.

بعداً للعجلة، بعداً للبلبلة، بعداً للتوتر، **أنت** ولا شيء سواك، بدون أي تحليل أو موضوعية، عندئذ ستكون معنا بكل تأكيد، ويغمر **السلام والصمت القدسيان** كل شيء.

وذلك يكون أفضل من كل التأملات في العالم.

Some Experiences of the Mother — من تجارب الأم

At the bottom of the Inconscience

Last evening in the class [Mother's weekly "Wednesday class", held at the Ashram Playground] I noticed that the children, who had a whole week to prepare questions on the text we are reading, did not find a single one. A terrible somnolence! A total lack of interest! When I had finished my reading, I said to myself, "But what is there in these brains that does not take interest in anything but their small personal affairs? After all, what is happening inside there, behind these forms?"

Then during the meditation, I began going down into the mental atmosphere of the people around me, in order to find there the small light, the thing that responds. And I was literally dragged down to the bottom, as if into a hole.

In this hole I saw what I am still seeing. I went down into a fissure, as it were, between two steep rocks, rocks made of something harder than basalt, black, metallic at the same time, with edges so sharp that you had the impression that were you simply to touch them, you would be flayed. It was something that seemed to have no bottom and no end, and it became narrower and narrower like a funnel, so narrow that there was almost no room left even for the consciousness to pass. The bottom was invisible, a black hole, and that went down and down and down, without air, without light, only a kind of glimmer, like a reflection at the peak of the rocks, a glimmer that came from beyond, from something that could be the heavens, but something invisible. I continued to slide down the fissure and I saw the edges, the black rocks, cut with scissors, as it were, shining like a fresh cut, the edges so sharp that they were like knives. Here was one, there another, there another, everywhere, all around. And I was dragged, dragged, dragged down, – I went down, down, down and there was no end to it, it became more and more oppressive, stifling, suffocating.

Physically, the body followed, it participated in the experience. The hand that was on the arm of the chair slipped down, then the other hand, then the head bent down in an irresistible movement. Then I said to myself, "But this must stop, for if it continues, my head will be down on the ground!" (The consciousness was elsewhere, but I was looking at my body from outside.) And I asked myself, "But what is there at the bottom of this hole?"

Some Experiences of the Mother — من تجارب الأم

في قاع اللاوعي

لاحظت مساء الأمس أثناء الدرس [درس أسبوعي كانت الأم تعقده للتلاميذ والمريدين في ملعب الأشرام] أن التلاميذ لم يُعِدُّوا سؤالاً واحداً بخصوص النص الذي ندرسه، على الرغم من أنه قد مضى على الدرس السابق أسبوع كامل. يا له من تكاسل بشع! و يا له من افتقار تام في التشوق للدراسة! تساءلت عندما أنهيت قراءتي متعجبة: "ما هذا الذي يدور في تلك الأذهان ويجعلها لا تهتم إلا بشئونها الخاصة التافهة؟ ماذا يحدث بداخل هذه الكائنات البشرية المغلقة؟"

بعدها بدأت، أثناء حلقة التأمل الجماعي، في الغوص في أعماق الجو الذهني الذي يعيش فيه الناس المحيطون بي، بأمل أن اكتشف فيهم ضوءاً صغيراً أو شيئاً قادراً على التجاوب. وإذا بي أجد نفسي َ منجذبة إلى الحضيض كما لو كنت وقعت، بكل معنى الكلمة، في حفرة عميقة.

على الرغم من عتمة الهوة، كنت ما زلت قادرة على الرؤية. رأيت إني أهبط في صدع بين صخرتين شديدتي الانحدار تتكونان من مادة معدنية سوداء، أكثر صلابة من البازلت، ذات حواف حادة مجرد لمسها يؤدي إلى السلخ. بدت الهوة كأنها لا قرار لها ولا نهاية وأصبحت أضيق وأضيق مثل قمع يتعذر حتى على الوعي نفسه النفاذ من طرفه! لم أكن أرى القاع، وبدت لي الهوة كثقب أسود يمتد ويمتد بدون هواء وبدون نور. لم يكن هناك إلا بصيص من نور يأتي من وراء، ربما من السماء، من شيء لم أكن قادرة على رؤيته. استمر انزلاقي وكنت أرى حواف الصخر الأسود تحيط بي من جميع النواحي، حادة كحواف المقص، تلمع كالسكاكين بلمعة المعادن التي قطعت حديثاً ولم تصدأ بعد. استمر الجذب نحو الأسفل وزاد شعوري بالضغط والعسر والاختناق أكثر وأكثر.

كنت جالسة [وسط التلاميذ] في مقعدي أتأمل، ثم بدأ بدني يشترك في تجربتي الداخلية ويتبعها. انزلقت يدي التي كانت على مسند المقعد أولاً، ثم تبعتها يدي الأخرى، وأخيراً عجز رأسي عن حمل ثقله ومال على صدري، فقلت لنفسي: "لا بد أن يتوقف كل ذلك وإلا سأجد نفسي في نهاية المطاف ممددة على الأرض!" (كان وعيي في مكان آخر وكنت أنظر إلى بدني من الخارج). سألت نفسي: "ماذا يوجد في قاع هذه الحفرة؟"

Some Experiences of the Mother — من تجارب الأم

Hardly had I formulated the question when it was as if I had touched a spring that was there at the very bottom of the hole, a spring I had not noticed yet, which acted at once with a tremendous force and at one bound shot me up straight into the air; I was cast out of the fissure into a limitless, formless vast which was infinitely comfortable – not exactly warm, but it gave a comfortable impression of inner warmth. After this painful enough descent, it was a kind of super-comfort, an ease, an ease at its maximum. And my body immediately followed the movement, the head at once became straight again. And I lived all this without objectifying it at all; I was not taking stock of what it was, I did not look for any explanation of what was happening; it was what it was, I lived it and that was all. The experience was absolutely spontaneous.

… After a moment I asked myself, "What is this, to what does it correspond?" Naturally I found out afterwards, and finally this morning I told myself, "Well, it is just to give me my message for the coming year." Then I transcribed it – naturally, you cannot make a description, it is indescribable. It was a psychological phenomenon and the forms were nothing but a way of describing the psychological state to oneself. And this is what I noted, obviously in a mental way. I have described nothing, I have only stated a fact:

At the very bottom of the inconscience most hard and rigid and narrow and stifling I struck upon an almighty spring that cast me up forthwith into a formless limitless Vast vibrating with the seeds of a new world."

There was in fact this entire impression of power, of warmth and of gold. It was not fluid, but like a powdery mist. And each one of these things (they cannot be called particles or fragments or even points, unless point is taken in the mathematical sense, a point that does not occupy any place in space) was like living gold, a powdery mist of warm gold – one cannot call it bright, nor can one call it dark; neither was it light: a multitude of small points of gold, nothing but that. One could say that they touched my eyes, my face… and with a tremendous force! At the same time, there was the feeling of a plenitude, of an all – powerful peace – it was rich, it was full. It was movement at its maximum, infinitely more swift than anything that one can imagine, and at the same time it was absolute peace, perfect stillness.

Some Experiences of the Mother — من تجارب الأم

ما أن صغت هذا السؤال فكأني لمست زنبركاً في أقصى أعماق القاع لم أكن لاحظته من قبل، وإذا بهذا الزنبرك ينطلق بقوة هائلة ويدفعني دفعة واحدة في الهواء خارج الصدع إلى فضاء شاسع بلا حدود أو هيئة — فضاء مريح إلى أقصى درجة ومع أنه لم يكن دافئاً تماماً إلا أنه كان يوحي بالدفء الداخلي. بعد كل الألم الذي كنت عانيته أثناء وقوعي، شعرت براحة عظمى واسترخاء تام. تابع بدني الحركة، وانتصب رأسي على الفور. عشت كل ذلك بدون أن أحاول أن أفهم ما كان يحدث أو أن أسجله؛ كنت أقبله على علاته دون أن أتقصى الأمر أبعد من ذلك. كان كل ذلك قد حدث تلقائياً وبدون أي تدخل من الذهن.

تساءلت بعد لحظة عن مغزى هذه التجربة وتوصلت إلى هذا المغزى فيما بعد... ثم "ترجمت" التجربة إلى كلمات... وهذا هو ما كتبته، بدون أن أحاول الوصف، بل اكتفيت بسرد ما حدث فعلاً:

"في أقصى قاع اللاوعي المتصلب، الصلد، الضيق، الخانق وجدت زنبركاً جباراً قذف بي في فضاء شاسع لا حدود له و لا هيئة، فضاء يرتعش ببذور عالم جديد".

... أحسست في هذا الفضاء بالقوة والدفء في كل مكان، وكنت محاطة برذاذ من مسحوق الذهب. كان مسحوقاً دقيقاً مكوناته كأنها نقاط رياضية لا حجم لها ولا تحتل أي مكان في الفضاء. كان المسحوق حياً ودافئاً، يصعب تحديده لونه، فهو لم يكن فاتحاً، ولم يكن غامقاً ولم يكن مضيئاً... وكان الرذاذ الدافئ يلمس عيني ووجهي بقوة عظيمة! وفي الوقت ذاته كنت أشعر بالوفرة والسلام المهيمن والكثرة والرخاء. كنت أشعر أيضا إنني أتحرك بسرعة أي تصور، ومع ذلك كانت حركتي في سلام مطلق وسكينة تامة.

Some Experiences of the Mother — من تجارب الأم

And this almighty spring was a perfect image of what happens, is bound to happen and will happen *for everybody*: all at once you shoot up into the vast.

The experience that I have just described was followed by another which was also noted down at the time. [This experience is given below under the title: "Reversal of Consciousness"].

5 November 1958

Reversal of Consciousness

To tell the truth, you are never freed from hostile [anti-divine] forces until you come out for good into the Light, above the lower hemisphere. And there the phrase "hostile forces" loses its meaning; only the forces of progress are there in order to compel you to progress. But you must come out of the lower hemisphere in order to see things in that way; because below, they are very real in their opposition to the divine plan.

It was said in the old traditions that one could not live more than twenty days in that higher state without leaving one's body and returning to the supreme origin. Now that is no longer true.

It is precisely this state of perfect harmony, beyond all attacks, that will become possible with the supramental realisation. It is that which will be realised for all who are destined for the supramental transformation. The adverse forces know quite well that in the supramental world they will automatically disappear: having no more use, they will be dissolved without the need to do anything, simply through the presence of the supramental force. That is why they rush about in a rage, negating everything, everything.

... The experience of November fifth was a new step in the construction of the link between the two worlds. I was indeed projected into the very origin of the supramental creation: all that warm gold, that living tremendous power, that sovereign peace. I saw once again that the values which govern in this supramental world have nothing to do with our values here below, even the values of the wisest, even those values which we consider most divine at the time we live constantly in the divine Presence. It is altogether different.

هذا الزنبرك الجبار هو رمز لما يحدث وما سوف يحدث لنا جميعاً عندما ننطلق يوماً ما كقذيفة ترتفع في الفضاء.

هذه التجربة التي وصفتها للتو تبعتها تجربة أخرى دونتها بعد حدوثها. [نص هذه التجربة يلي أسفله تحت عنوان : "انقلاب الوعي".]
5 نوفمبر 1958

انقلاب الوعي

في الحقيقة لن نتخلص نهائياً من القوى المعادية [المضادة لكل ما هو إلهي] حتى نكون قد ارتفعنا لنعيش بصفة دائمة في نور نصف-الكرة الأعلى [الذي يشمل مستويات الوعى التي تفوق الذهن]. هناك يفقد مصطلح "القوى المعادية" معناه، ويصبح من الأنسب أن ننظر إلى هذه القوى كدوافع ترغمنا على التقدم. ولكن لكي نتمكن من أن نرى الأمور من هذا المنظور، يجب أن نكون قد ارتفعنا من نصف-الكرة الأسفل [الذي يشمل مستويات الذهن والحياة والمادة واللاوعي] حيث تكون مقاومة هذه القوى للخطة الإلهية حقيقة واقعة وملموسة.

نادت التعاليم والتقاليد القديمة بأن الإنسان لا يطيق البقاء أطول من عشرين يوم في نصف-الكرة الأعلى، يموت بعدها ويعود إلى الأصل الأسمى. ولكن ذلك لم يعد صحيحاً في يومنا هذا.

لكي نعيش في مأمن تام من هجمات القوى المعادية وفي حالة تناسق كامل يجب أن نرتفع إلى وعي السوبرامنتال* وأن نجتاز عملية التحول الضرورية لبلوغ هذا الوعي. القوى المعاكسة تعلم جيداً أنها ستزول تلقائياً في عالم السوبرامنتال حيث تفقد وظيفتها ويبطل نفعها، وتعلم أن قوى السوبرامنتال قادرة على أن إبادتها ببساطة وبدون بذل أي جهد. هذا هو السبب في أن هذه القوى تصول وتجول حالياً في حالة هيجان عارم [محاولة تحقيق أقصى ما يمكنها من الضرر أينما أمكنها ذلك].

.... تجربة الخامس من نوفمبر [انظر أعلاه تجربة "في قاع اللاوعي"] كانت خطوة جديدة في بناء الوصلة بين عالمنا وعالم السوبرامنتال. فقد قذفني فيها هذا الزنبرك إلى صميم الخلق في عالم السوبرامنتال بكل ما فيه من ذهب دافئ وقدرة نابضة هائلة وسلام مهيمن. هذه التجربة أرتني مرة أخرى كيف أن القيم السائدة في السوبرامنتال ليس لها أي علاقة لها بقيم عالمنا، حتى بالقيم التي نعتبرها هنا خلاصة الحكمة وحتى بقيمنا عندما نعيش بصورة مستمرة في الحضرة الإلهية. الفارق بين القيم هناك وهنا عظيم حقاً.

Some Experiences of the Mother — من تجارب الأم

… The quality or the kind of relation that I had with the Supreme at that moment was quite different from that which we have here, and even the identification had a different quality. With regard to the lower movements one understands very well that they are different, but that was the summit of our experience here, that identification by which it is the Supreme who rules and lives. Well! He rules and lives quite differently when we are in this lower hemisphere and when we are in the supramental life. And at that moment what gave intensity to the experience was that I came to perceive, vaguely, these two states of consciousness at the same time. It is almost as if the Supreme himself is different, that is to say, the experience we have of him. And yet in both cases there was contact with the Supreme. Well, probably what differs is what we perceive of him or the way in which we translate it; but the quality of the experience is different.

There is in the other hemisphere an intensity and a plenitude which expresses itself through a power different from the one here. How to explain it? You cannot. The quality of the consciousness itself seems to change. It is not something higher than the summit to which we can rise here, it is not one step more: here, we are at the end, at the summit. It is the quality that is different, the quality, in the sense that there is a plenitude, a richness, a power. This is a translation, in our manner, but there is something that escapes us – it is truly a new reversal of consciousness.

When we begin to live the spiritual life, 'a reversal of consciousness' takes place which is for us the proof that we have entered the spiritual life; well, another reversal of consciousness occurs when one enters the supramental world. Besides, perhaps each time that a new world opens up, there will again be a new reversal of this kind. Thus even our spiritual life – which is such a total reversal in relation to ordinary life – is and appears to be, in relation to the supramental consciousness, the supramental realisation, something so totally different that the values of the two are almost opposite.

One can put it in this way (but this is very imprecise, more than diminished – deformed): it is as if our entire spiritual life were made of silver whereas the supramental is made of gold… This whole spiritual life of our psychic being and our present consciousness, which appears so warm, so full, so wonderful, so sparkling to the ordinary consciousness, well, all this splendour appears poor in relation to the splendour of the new world.

... علاقتي مع **الكائن الأسمى** في تلك التجربة اختلفت كثيراً في نوعيتها عن علاقتي معه هنا، وحتى تماثلي معه كان مختلفاً. هذا الاختلاف مفهوم تماماً عندما نتكلم عن الحركات الأدنى [كالغضب والجشع مثلاً]، ولكن ما يدعو إلى العجب هو أن تكون العلاقة مختلفة حتى بالنسبة لقمة الوعي التي نحققها هنا والتي نتماثل فيها مع **الكائن الأسمى** الحي الذي يُسَيِّر كل الأمور. فهو يسيرها بطريقة تختلف في نصف-الكرة الأسفل عنها في عالم السوبرامنتال. في تلك التجربة أدركت حالتي الوعي كلتاهما في نفس الوقت، وذلك هو ما أضفى على التجربة شدته وقوتها. فكأني خبرت **الكائن الأسمى** نفسه بطريقتين مختلفتين على الرغم من أنني كنت متصلة به في كلتا الحالتين. الاختلاف يأتي، على ما أظن، من نوعية الإدراك، وذلك هو ما أضفى على التجربة نوعية مختلفة.

هناك في نصف-الكرة الأعلى حماس ووفرة يعطيان إحساساً بالقدرة يختلف عما نحس به هنا. كيف يمكن شرح ذلك؟ إنه يستعصي على الشرح. يبدو أن نوعية الوعي نفسها تختلف. الوعي هناك ليس أعلى من قمة الوعي التي نبلغها هنا، وليس أكثر تقدماً... ولكنه يختلف في نوعيته من حيث الوفرة والسعة والقدرة. ما أقوله هنا هو مجرد ترجمة ناقصة، إذ أن هناك شيء يفلت ويتعذر على التعبير... ولكن في الحقيقة هذه التجربة تمثل انقلاباً جديداً في الوعي.

عندما نبدأ حياتنا الروحية نجتاز "انقلاباً في الوعي" يكون دليلاً على أننا بدأنا نعيش الحياة الروحية بالفعل. وبالمثل عندما نرتفع من الحياة الروحية إلى عالم السوبرامنتال نمر بانقلاب جديد في الوعي. من المحتمل أنه في كل مرة ينفتح أمامنا عالم جديد، سيكون هناك انقلاب جديد من هذا النوع. وهكذا نجد أن حياتنا الروحية التي تنقلب فيها قيم الحياة العادية رأساً على عقب تبدو بدورها انعكاساً تاماً لقيم عالم السوبرامنتال.

نستطيع أن نصف هذه الظاهرة بصورة تقريبية للغاية ونقول أنه لو كانت الحياة الروحية مصنوعة من الفضة، فحياة السوبرامنتال مصنوعة من الذهب... هذه الحياة الروحية التي يعيشها كياننا السيكي* والتي تمثل وعينا الحالي وتبدو دافئة ورائعة ومتألقة بالنسبة للوعي العادي، كل تلك الروعة تبدو ضئيلة بالمقارنة بروعة عالم السوبرامنتال.

Some Experiences of the Mother — من تجارب الأم

But as long as this realisation is not an accomplished fact, it will still be a progression – a progression, an ascension: you gain, you gain ground, you climb up and up; as long as it is not the new reversal, it is as if everything needed to be done over again. It is the repetition of the experience here below – it is reproduced up there. And each time, you have the impression that you have lived on the surface of things. It is an impression that is repeated and repeated. At each new conquest you have the impression: "Until now I had lived only on the surface of things – on the surface of things – on the surface of realisation, the surface of surrender, the surface of power – it was merely the surface of things, the surface of experience." Behind the surface there is a depth, and it is only when you enter into the depth that you touch the true thing.

And each time it is the same experience: what appeared as a depth becomes a surface, a surface with all that it means, something inaccurate, artificial, an artificial transcription, something that gives one the impression that it is not truly living: it is a copy, an imitation – it is an image, a reflection, not the thing itself. You pass into another zone and you have the impression that you have discovered the Source and the Power, the Truth of things; and then, this source, this power and this truth become in their turn an appearance, an imitation, a transcription in relation to the new realisation.

Meanwhile, we must indeed recognise that we have not got the key yet, it is not within our hands. Or rather we know quite well where it is, and we have only one thing to do: the perfect surrender of which Sri Aurobindo speaks, the total self-giving to the Divine Will, whatever happens, even in the midst of the night.

There is the night and there is the sun, the night and the sun, again the night, many nights; but one must cling to this will to surrender, cling to it as in a tempest, and give up everything into the hands of the Supreme Lord, until the day when the Sun will come for ever, the total victory.
15 November 1958

Some Experiences of the Mother — من تجارب الأم

ولكـن طالمـا أن هـذا الـوعي لـم يصبح حقيقـة ملموسـة، سيكون هنـاك تقـدم وتصـاعد تـدريجي — نرتفـع ونتقـدم خطـوة بعد خطـوة، وطالمـا أن انقـلاب الـوعي لـم يتم كليـاً، نشـعر أننـا مضصرون لأن نعيد كل مـا سبق أن حققنـاه مرة أخـرى، يتكـرر علـى المستويات الأعلـى. وفـي كـل مـرة يكـون انطباعك أنـك قـد عشـت علـى السطح الخـارجي فقـط، وهـذا انطبـاع يتكـرر ويتكـرر. وفي كـل مـرة تتغلب فيهـا علـى عقبـة يكـون انطباعك: "لقـد عشـت حتى الآن علـى القشـرة: تحقيقـاتي كانـت سطحية، تسليمي كـان سطحيـاً، قـدراتي كانـت سطحية وتجـاربي كانـت سطحية." ولكـن وراء السطح هنـاك أعمـاق، ولـن يمكننـا أن نمـس الشـيء الحقيقـي طالمـا لـم نـدخل هـذه الأعمـاق.

وفـي كـل مـرة نتقـدم فيهـا خطـوة، نشعـر أن مـا كـان عمقـاً قـد صـار سطحـاً بكـل مـا تعنيـه هـذه الكلمـة، أي أنـه أصبح شيئـاً مفتعـلاً يفتقـد الدقـة ويجعلنـا نشعـر أننـا لـم نعـش حقيقـة، وأن الحيـاة التـي عشنـاها مجـرد نسـخة مـن الحقيقـة أو محاكـاة او صـورة أو انعكـاس لهـا، وليس الشـيء الحقيقـي نفسـه. وكـل مـرة نتقـدم فيهـا إلـى مجـال جديد ونظن أننـا أخيـراً قـد اكتشـفنا **المنبـع ومصـدر القـدرة والحقيقـة**، إذا بهـذا المنبـع وهـذه القـدرة وهـذه الحقيقـة يصيـرون بـدورهم مجـرد مظهـر أو محاكـاة أو ترجمـة بـالمقارنـة بـالتحقيق الذي يسطع أمامنا.

فـي الأثنـاء، يجب أن نقبل ونعتـرف بأننـا لا نملك المفتـاح بعـد. أو بـالأحرى، أننـا نعلم جيـداً أيـن هـو هـذا المفتـاح، والشـيء الوحيـد المطلـوب منـا هـو التسـليم التـام الـذي يتحـدث عنـه شـري أورويـندو: أن نهـب أنفسنـا لـلإرادة الإلهيـة وهبـاً تامـاً، بـدون اعتبـار لمـا قـد يحـدث، وأن نـواظب علـى ذلـك، حتـى عندما يطبق علينا الظلام الحالك.

فـي تقدمنـا سيتوالـى علينـا الليـل والنهـار، الظـلام والنـور، ثـم الليـل مـرة أخـرى وليالي أخـرى كثيـرة؛ ولكـن يجب أن نتشـبث برغبتنـا فـي التسـليم، نتشـبث بهـا كمـا لـو كانـت سندنا الوحيـد فـي عاصفـة هوجـاء، ونسـلم كـل شـيء في يـد **المـولى الأعظـم**، إلـى أن يـأتي يـوم لا تغيب فيـه الشـمس، ويتحقـق فيـه النصر التـام.

15 نوفمبر 1958

280

Towards the Future, a Play — نحو المستقبل، مسرحية

Towards the Future

A one-act play in prose that can be staged in any country, with small changes in the details of the presentation which local custom may require.

Persons of the drama:
She
The Poet
The Clairvoyant:
The Painter
The Schoolfriend

As the curtain rises, She and the School friend are sitting side by side on the sofa.

She: How nice of you to come and see me after such a long time... I thought you had forgotten me.

Schoolfriend: Certainly not. But I had lost trace of you and did not know where to find you. And now that I have found you, what a surprise! You, married!... how strange! I can't believe it.

She: I too find it hard to believe.

Schoolfriend: I understand... I remember how ironically you used to refer to marriage as "a co-operative venture in consumption and production", and how distasteful you used to find everything that displayed human animality, the beast in man. And how you used to say, "Let us not be mammals..."

She: Yes, I have always enjoyed making fun of current ideas and social conventions. But in all fairness you must admit that I have never said anything against true love, the love that comes from a deep affinity and is marked by an identity of views and aspirations. I always dreamt of a great love that would be shared, free from all animal activity, something that could physically represent the great love which is at the origin of the worlds. This dream accounts for my marriage. But the experience has not been a very happy one. I have loved deeply, with great sincerity and intensity, but my love has not met with the response it hoped f or...

نحو المستقبل، مسرحية — Towards the Future, a Play

Towards the Future, a Play — نحو المستقبل، مسرحية

نحو المستقبل

مسرحية من فصل واحد، تصلح للتقديم في أي بلد بمجرد تعديلات بسيطة في التفاصيل تتنسب مع العرف المحلي.

أشخاص المسرحية:

هــي
الشاعر
المستبصرة
الرسام
زميلة الدراسة

عندما يرتفع الستار، نرى **هـي** وزميلة الدراسة جالستين على أريكة جنباً إلى جنب.

هــي: كم هو ظريف منك أن تحضري لزيارتي بعد هذه الغيبة الطويلة... ظننتك نسيتيني.

زميلــة الدراســة: بالتأكيـد لـم أنسكِ. ولكنـي كنـت، منـذ أن انقطعت صـلتنا، أجهـل مقـرك الجديـد. والآن وقد وجدتك، أفاجأ بأن أراك متزوجة! هذا عجيب فعلاً وأنا لا أكاد أصدق نفسي!

هـي: أنا نفسي أجد صعوبة في تصديق ذلك.

زميلــة الدراســة: أذكـر جيـداً كيـف كنـت تسخرين مـن الـزواج وتصـفيه بأنـه "جمعيـة تعاونيـة للاستهلاك والانتـاج" وتظهرين استقباحك لكـل مـا يُظهـر الناحيـة الحيوانيـة في الانسـان. كنت كثيراً ما تقولين: "لا داعي لأن نعيش مثل الثدييات...".

هـي: نعـم، كنـت أجد متعـة دائمـاً في السخريـة مـن الآراء الجاريـة والعـرف المتـداول. ولكـن كُـوني عادلـة واعترفـي بـأني لـم أسخر قط مـن الحب الحقيقي، الحب الـذي ينبـع مـن ألفـة عميقـة وتقـارب تـام في الآراء والطموحـات الروحيـة. كنـت دائمـاً أتمنى وأحلم بـأن أوفـق إلـى حبٍ متبـادل عظيـمٍ لا يكون فيـه أي نشـاط حيـواني، إلـى حبٍ يُجَسِـد علـى المسـتوى المـادي الحـب الشـامل في أصـل الخليقـة. هـذا الحلم هو الـذي دفعنـي إلـى الـزواج. ولكـن مـا كنـت آملـه لـم يتحقق. لقـد أحببت بكـل عـواطفي وبعمـق وإخلاص شديدين، ولكن حبي لم يلق رد الفعل المأمول...

Towards the Future, a Play — نحو المستقبل، مسرحية

Schoolfriend: My poor friend!

She: Oh, I am not telling you this to arouse your pity. I am not to be pitied. My dream is practically unrealisable in the world as it is. Human nature would have to change so much for this to become possible. Besides, my husband and I are very good friends, although that does not prevent us both from feeling very isolated. Esteem and mutual concessions create a harmony that makes life more than merely bearable. But is that happiness?

Schoolfriend: For many people that might be happiness.

She: True, but sometimes I feel such an emptiness in my life! It may have been to fill this emptiness that I gave myself entirely and in all sincerity to that marvelous cause which is so dear to me: to relieve suffering humanity, to awaken it to its capacities and its true goal and ultimate transformation.

Schoolfriend: I can see that something great, something out of the ordinary rules your life. But as I do not know what it is, it seems rather mysterious to me.

She: Of course, I owe you an explanation. I must tell you about it in detail, but that will take some time. Would you like me to come and visit you?

Schoolfriend: What an excellent idea! Nothing could please me more. When will you come? Would you like to come today?

She: Yes, I would be very glad to do so. I always find a deep joy in speaking of the marvelous teaching that guides our life and directs our wills. Just now, I have a few things to arrange so that when my husband returns from his walk he will find everything ready. And as soon as he has started his work, I can go out and I shall come and see you.

Schoolfriend: Very well, then. Goodbye, I shall see you soon. (*She accompanies her friend to the door behind the screen. Then She returns to the writing table to arrange some papers and books and writing materials. She places some flowers in a vase on the table and looks around her to see that everything is in order. At that moment a key is heard turning in the lock.*)

She: Ah, there he is. (*The Poet enters. She approaches him affectionately.*) Did you have a pleasant walk?

Towards the Future, a Play — نحو المستقبل، مسرحية

زميلة الدراسة: أيتها المسكينة العزيزة!

هـي: أنـا لـم أخبـرك بـذلك استـدراراً لشفقتك، فالشفقة لا تليـق بـي. بـل إن حلمـي هـو الـذي يصعـب تحقيقه في عالمنا على حالته الراهنة. لا بـد مـن أن تتغيـر الطبيعـة البشرية كثيراً لكي يتحقق مثل هذا الحلم. أضف إلـى ذلـك أن علاقتـي بزوجـي تنبنـي علـى صداقـة وطيـدة، علـى الـرغم مـن أن كـل منا يحس بعزلـة شـديدة. صحيـح أن التقديـر المتبـادل بيننـا وبعـض التنـازلات مـن الطرفين يخلقان جواً من الانسجام يجعل الحياة مقبولة، ولكن هل تلك سعادة؟

زميلة الدراسة: بالنسبة إلى الكثيرين، ما تصفين سعادة كافية.

هـي: صحيـح، ولكن هـذا لا يمنـع مـن أنـي أحيانـا أشعـر بفراغ كبير في حياتي. وربما كانت حاجتي إلـى مَلء هـذا الفـراغ هـي التـي دفعتنـي إلـى وهـب نفسـي الهـدف العظيـم أصبـح كـل حيـاتي، هـدف تخفيـف عنـاء البشـر، وتـوعيتهم بالطاقـات الكامنـة فيهم وبالغايـة الحقـة التـي ينبغـي أن يسعـوا إليـه وبالتحول العظيم الذي سيطرأ عليهم في نهاية المطاف.

زميلـة الدراسة: أستطيع أن أرى بوضـوح أن شـيئاً عظيمـاً وغيـر معتـاد قد صـار يمـلأ حياتـك. ولكنـي لا أعلمه، وكل ما تقولين يبدو غامضاً لي.

هـي: لا عجـب، وأنـا مدينـة لـك بالتوضيـح. ولكـن لكـي أوضـح لـك يجـب أن أطلعـك علـى كثيـر مـن التفاصيل، وذلك سوف يحتاج إلى بعض الوقت. هل يلائمك أن آتي لزيارتك؟

زميلة الدراسة: فكرة رائعة! لا أتمنى شيئاً خيراً من ذلك. متى تودين القدوم؟ هل اليوم يلائمك؟

هـي: نعم، ذلك سوف يسعدني كثيراً. أجد دائمـاً متعـة كبيرة في التحـدث عـن التعاليـم الرائعـة التـي ترشـد حيـاتي والتـي توجـه إراداتـي. ولكـن أود أولاً إنجـاز بعـض الترتيبـات بحيـث يجـد زوجـي عنـد عودته من جولته كل ما يحتاجه معداً. ومتى بدأ هو عمله، سأكون مستعدة لزيارتك.

زميلة الدراسة: اتفقنـا إذاً. وداعـاً الآن وإلـى لقـاء قريـب (**هـي** تصاحـب صديقتها إلـى البـاب المتـواري وراء سـتار ثـم تعـود إلـى المكتـب لترتـب بعـض الأوراق وأدوات الكتابـة. تضـع إنـاء فيـه بعـض الزهـور علـى المكتـب وتنظـر حولهـا للتأكـد مـن أن كـل شـيء فـي مكانـه الصحيـح. فـي هـذه اللحظـة يُسمع دوران مفتاح في قفل الباب).

هـي: ها هو قد أقبل! (يدخل الشاعر. تقتـرب منه بحنان.) هل استمتعت بالتمشي؟

Towards the Future, a Play — نحو المستقبل، مسرحية

Poet (*absent-mindedly*): Yes, thank you. (*He puts his hat down on a chair.*) I have found an ending for my poem. It came while I was walking. A little activity in the open air really does help the inspiration. Yes, I think this will be good: I end with a song of triumph, a hymn of victory in praise of the evolved man who has discovered, together with the consciousness of his origin, the knowledge of all that he is capable of doing and the power to realise it. I describe him advancing in the happy splendour of union towards the conquest of earthly immortality. It will be beautiful and truly universal, don't you think? It is high time that art should stop being a justification for ugliness and defeat... What a happy day it will be when poetry, painting and music express only beauty, victory and joy, leading the way towards the realisation of the future, towards the advent of a world in which falsehood and suffering, ugliness and death will be no more... But meanwhile, how much misery still for man, how much pain and anguish and bitter solitude... It is terrible! Each one has his burden to bear, come what may, whether he wants it or not. (*He stands deep in thought.*)

She (*approaching him affectionately and putting her hand on his arm*): Come, set to work, you know that is the best cure for sadness. I am going to leave you to your inspiration. I promised my friend that I would go and spend the afternoon with her and tell her something about the marvellous teaching that guides our life. We shall probably read together some of those pages that are so full of profound truth. To meditate on these things is a great joy to both of us. That would upset the ideas of many men, wouldn't it? They are convinced that women cannot do anything except talk about clothes. On the whole, they are not entirely wrong. Most women are terribly frivolous, or at least they seem to be. For very often this lightness on the surface hides a heavy heart and veils an unfulfilled life. Poor creatures! I know so many of them who deserve to be pitied.

Poet: You are right. Women really deserve to be pitied. Almost all of them lack the protection they need and are like frail craft with no harbour to shelter them from the storm. For most of them do not receive the education that would teach them to protect themselves.

She: That is true. Besides, even in the strongest of women, there is a deep need for affection and protection, for an all-powerful strength that leans over her and enfolds her in comforting sweetness. This is what she seeks in love, and when she has the good fortune to find it, it gives her confidence in life and opens up for her the door to every hope. Without that, life for her is like a barren desert that burns and shrivels up the heart.

Towards the Future, a Play — نحو المستقبل، مسرحية

الشاعر (*غائب البال*): نعم، شكراً، شكراً. (*يضع قبعته على كرسي.*) أخيراً وجدتُ خاتمة لقصيدتي— أتاني وحيها أثناء المشي. حقاً إن الرياضة في الهواء الطلق تُيَسِّر نزول الإلهام. أعتقد إنها ستكون خاتمة جيدة للقصيدة: فهي نشيد نصر وترنيمة ثناء على الإنسان المتطور، الذي ارتقى في وعيه إلى الوعي الأصيل [الذي لا زيف فيه]، واكتشف كل ما في نفسه من طاقات، واكتسب القدرة على التحكم فيها. أصِفُ هذا الإنسان في تقدمه وابتهاجه بهذا الشعور الرائع بالوحدة الشاملة الذي سيصحبه في سعيه نحو الخلود الأرضي. ستكون قصيدة جميلة وكونية في شمولها، ألا تظنين ذلك؟ لقد آن الأوان لكي يَكُفَّ الفن عن تبرير القبح والهزيمة، ولكي يزول الموت من الوجود... كم سيكون سعيداً اليوم الذي تقتصر فيه فنون الشعر والرسم والموسيقى على التعبير عن الجمال والنصر والبهجة، مُمَهِّدة بذلك الطريق لتحقيقات المستقبل، وحلول عالم لا مكان فيه للزور والمعاناة والقبح والموت... ولكن كم من الشقاء والألم والكرب والعُزلة المُرَّة سيكونوا ضروريين إلى أن يحقق الإنسان ذلك المستقبل الباهر... إنه لشيء بشع! كل إنسان ملزَم بعبئه الثقيل أينما ولى وجهه سواء أراد أم لم يرد. (*يقف غارقاً في تفكير عميق.*)

هي: (*تقترب منه بحنان وتضع يدها على ذراعه*) كل شيء مُعَدٌّ لك لكي تبدأ العمل: فكما تعلم العمل هو خير علاج للحزن. سأتركك لإلهامك. وَعَدت صديقتي بأن أمضي سائر اليوم معها في قراءة تلك الصفحات الزاخرة بكل ما هو حق وعميق ولأطلعها على قبس من التعاليم الرائعة الكامنة فيها. سيكون تَأمُّل هذه التعاليم بهجة عظيمة لكل منا. ربما يكون تسامرنا على هذا النحو شيئاً لا يتوقعه الكثير من الرجال، فهم مقتنعون بأن النساء لا يقدرن على أي شيء سوى الحديث عن الأزياء. على وجه العموم، هؤلاء الرجال ليسوا بعيدين عن الصواب كل البعد. فالنساء على الأغلبية طائشات، أو على الأقل هن يعطين هذا الانطباع. ولكن كثيرا ما يُخفي هذا العبث الظاهري قلباً ثقيلاً وحياة فراغ لم تتحقق. يا للتعاسة! أنا أعرف كثيرات من هاته النساء الجديرات بالإشفاق.

الشاعر: أنت محقة. النساء جديرات بالشفقة فعلاً. فهن على الأغلب لا يجدن الحماية التي يحتجن إليها مثل السفن التي لا تجد ميناء يقيها من العواصف فغالبيتهن لا يتلقين التربية التي تعلمهن كيف يحمين أنفسهن.

هي: هذا صحيح. وبالإضافة، فإن المرأة، حتى لو كانت أكثر النساء قوة، لها حاجة شديدة إلى عواطف الود والحماية، إلى قوة تسندها وتشملها بالهناء والراحة. هذا هو ما تبحث عنه المرأة في الحب، وعندما يسعدها الحظ ويوفر لها حاجتها، تزداد ثقة بالحياة وتتفتح لها أبواب الآمال. أما بدون ذلك الحب، فإن الحياة تصبح بالنسبة لها مثل صحراء ملتهبة تجفف القلوب.

Towards the Future, a Play — نحو المستقبل، مسرحية

Poet: Oh, how well you say these things! You say them like one who has experienced them very deeply. I shall make a note of them for my next book, which will deal with the education of women. Well then, I shall start my work.

She: That's right; I am going. Goodbye, work well. (*She takes a book and goes out.*)

Poet: (*sitting down at his desk and seeing everything ready for his work*) Always the same kind and affectionate attentions. She never fails in her care and her sweetness. When I look at her, it is like seeing a light: her intelligence and kindness shine so brightly around her, spreading to all who are near her, whom she guides towards nobler horizons. I admire her, I feel a deep respect for her... But all that is not love... Love! What a dream! Will it ever become a reality? (*A melody sung by a magnificent voice is heard. The poet jumps to his feet and goes to the open window.*) What a wonderful voice! (*He listens in silence until the melody dies away. Sighing, he is about to return to his table when there is a knock at the door.*) Hello, who's there? (*He opens the door. The Painter enters.*)

Poet: It's you! Hello, old friend, what good wind brings you here?

Painter: I had something to tell you. I met your wife and she told me you were in your "sanctum". So I am here.

Poet: You did the right thing... So come into the "sanctum" as you call it, and speak. Don't keep me in suspense. Is it about painting?

Painter: No, my painting is going well. But I shall tell you about that another time. It is about music. (*The Poet shows interest.*) Yesterday evening, when visiting some friends, I heard a true singer who, I am told, is your neighbour. (*The Poet makes a gesture of surprise and interest.*) Do you know her?

Poet: No, but I often hear her singing from here. She has a superb voice, a voice that stirs all the fibres of my being. The very first time it struck my ears, it sounded familiar to me, like an echo from very ancient times. For nearly six months I have been hearing this voice, which forms a kind of pleasant accompaniment to my work. I have very often wished to become acquainted with the owner of such a beautiful voice.

Towards the Future, a Play — نحو المستقبل، مسرحية

الشاعر: كم تحسنين قول هذه الأمور كما لو كنت تتكلمين عن تجربة وخبرة! سأدوّن ما قلتيه للتو واستعمله في كتابي المقبل الذي سيدور حول تربية المرأة. حسناً إذاً، سأبدأ في العمل.

هـي: خيراً تفعل! إلى اللقاء، أتمنى لك ساعات عمل ممتعة. (تأخذ كتاباً وتخرج)

الشاعر: (*يجلس إلى مكتبه ويرى كل شيء معداً لعمله*) **هي** دائماً تغمرني برعايتها العطوفة ولا تُقَصّر إطلاقاً في عنايتها العذبة. كلما نظرت إليها، أرى ضوءاً ساطعاً يشع من ذكائها وحنانها وينتشر إلى جميع من حولها ويرشدهم إلى آفاق أكثر نبلاً. كم أشعر نحوها بالإعجاب والاحترام العميق.. ولكن كل هذا التقدير لا يبلغ مرتبة الحب... الحب! يا له من حلم! هل سيتحقق في يوم من الأيام؟ (*يسمع صوتاً خلاباً يترنم ببعض الأنغام ويهبّ قائماً ويذهب إلى النافذة المفتوحة.*) يا له من صوت ساحر! (*ينصت في صمت حتى تخمد النغمة. يتنهد ويوشك على الرجوع إلى مكتبه عندما يسمع طرقة على الباب. يدخل الرسام*)

الشاعر: ها أنت ذا! مرحباً، صديق الأيام الخالية، ترى أي الرياح الطيبة يأتي بك إلينا؟

الرسام: كنت أريد أن أخبرك بشيء. وعندما قابلت زوجتك قبل دقائق وأخبرتني إنك في صومعتك، قررت زيارتك.

الشاعر: خيراً فعلت... تفضل إذاً إلى ما تسميه "صومعتي" وافصح ولا تتركني أتلظى على نار التشوق. هل الأمر يتعلق بالرسم؟

الرسام: كلا، "الرسم" على ما يرام في حالتي، وسوف أخبرك عنه في مرة مقبلة. الأمر يتعلق بالموسيقى هذه المرة. (*الشاعر يبدي تشوقه ليعلم المزيد*). سمعت مساء أمس في زيارة لبعض الأصدقاء مُغَنِّية تحسن فهم روح الغناء قيل لي إنها جارتك. (*الشاعر يبدي دهشته وتشوقه*). هل تعرفها شخصياً؟

الشاعر: كلا، ولكني كثيراً ما أسمعها تغني أثناء وجودي هنا في المنزل. صوتها بالفعل رائع لدرجة إنه يحرك كل خلجات نفسي. منذ أول مرة سمعتها، بدا لي صوتها مألوفاً وكأنه صدى من أزمان سحيقة. في الأشهر الستة الأخيرة كنت أستمع إلى هذا الصوت وأجد فيه رفيقاً ساراً لعملي. كم تمنيت أن أتعرف على صاحبته.

288

Towards the Future, a Play — نحو المستقبل، مسرحية

Painter: What a wonderful coincidence! Yesterday evening I was introduced to this young lady and she seems to be very charming indeed. We had a long chat together and in the course of the conversation she expressed her admiration for your poetry, which she seems to read with enthusiasm. She also told me that she is all alone in life, that she has to fend for herself and that sometimes she finds it difficult to pull through, and so on. She dreams of becoming a concert-singer. I immediately thought of you and all your connections. Everyone knows how obliging you are. So I volunteered to speak to you about her and to ask well-known musicians or composers. That is why I have come.

Poet: You did just the right thing. It will be a great pleasure for me to do something for her. So what did the two of you decide?

Painter: It was arranged that, if you agreed, I would go and fetch her immediately —it is not very far—and bring her to you so that you may get to know each other.

Poet: Perfect. Go and fetch her. I shall wait for you. (*The Painter goes out.*)

Poet: (*striding restlessly back and forth*) How strange, how strange... There is no such thing as chance; everything is the effect of causes that are simply beyond our control. The power of affinity—who knows? I am curious to know whether the singer is as beautiful as her voice. Here they are. (*The door, which was only pulled, is pushed open from outside.*) Oh, how pretty she is! (*The Clairvoyant enters, smiling, followed by the Painter.*)

Painter: Mademoiselle, may I introduce my friend, the well-known poet whom you admire so much.

Poet: I am very happy to meet you, mademoiselle, and to be able to tell you how much I admire your beautiful voice, which you use with such artistry.

Clairvoyant: You are very kind, monsieur, and I thank you. You will excuse me, won't you, for coming with so little ceremony. But we are such near neighbours. I knew you even before I was introduced to you. I noticed that you often came to your window to listen to me singing and even, at first, I was not very pleased when you applauded me. I thought you were making fun of me.

Poet: How wrong you were! I simply wanted to express my admiration and to thank you for all the aesthetic pleasure you give me.

Towards the Future, a Play — نحو المستقبل، مسرحية

الرسام: يا لـه مـن تـزامن بـديع. فقدم قدَّمَني بعض الأصدقاء مسـاء أمـس إلـى هـذه السيدة الشـابة وقـد وجـدتهـا سـاحرة بالفعـل. تحادثنـا طـويـلاً وفـي أثنـاء الحـديـث ذكـرت لـي إعجابهـا بشـعرك، ويـبـدو أنهـا تقـرأه بحمـاس. وقـد أخبرتنـي أيضـاً أنهـا وحيـدة تمامـاً فـي حياتهـا، وأن عليهـا أن تعـول نفسـها وهـي تجـد صعـوبة أحيانـاً فـي ذلـك، إلـى آخـره. حلمهـا أن تصبـح مغنية كونسـرت. عندئـذ تذكـرتك وكـل مـا لـك مـن صـلات فـي عـالم الفـن. ولأني أعلم حبك لمسـاعـدة الغيـر عرضـت عليهـا أن أتحـدث بشـأنها معك وكذلك مع بعض الموسيقيين والملحنين المشهورين. هذا هو سبب قدومي.

الشاعر: أحسنت. سيسرني كثيراً أن أسعى في مصلحتها. هل اتفقتما على شيء؟

الرسـام: اتفقنـا علـى أن أجلبهـا إليـك، ولـو كنت لا تمـانـع — أستطيع أن أحضـرهـا إلـى هنـا علـى الفـور، فهي تسكن هنا بجوارك — وأعرفكما أحدكما على الآخر.

الشاعر: عظيم! اذهب واحضرها. سأكون في انتظاركما. (*الرسام يخرج*)

الشاعر: (*يمشـي ذهابـاً وإيابـاً دون أن يستقـر فـي مكـان واحـد*) يا للعجب، يا للعجـب... لا توجـد صُـدُفات؛ وإنمـا ببسـاطة جميـع الأشيـاء هـي نتـائج أسباب خارجـة عـن إرادتنـا. هل هـي قـوة الألفـة والتشـابه — ربمـا؟ أنـا متشـوق لمعرفـة مـا إذا كـان مظهرهـا يعـادل صـوتهـا فـي جمالـه. هـ' همـا قـد أقدمـا. (*تدخل المستبصرة مبتسمة، يتبعها الرسام.*)

الرسام: أتسمحين يا آنسة بأن أقدم لك صديقي الشاعر المشهور الذي نال شعره اعجابك الشديد؟

الشاعر: كـم أنـا سعيد بمقابلتـك، يـا آنسـة، وكم أود أن أعَبِّر لـك عـن اعجابي الشـديد بصوتك الجميل وبالطريقة التي تستخدمين بها هذا الصوت في غنائك.

المستبصـرة: هذا مـن كرمـك وفضلـك يـا سيدي وأنـا أشكرك. أرجو المعـذرة لقدومـي بـدون أي تكلـف. ولكننـا جيـران قـربة. لقد عرفتك حتى مـن قبل تقديمي إليك اليوم إذ لاحظت كيف أنك كنت كثيراً مـا تقتـرب مـن النافـذة لتستمـع إلـي وأنـا أغـني، والعجيب إنـي أحسست بالاستياء قليـلاً فـي البـدء عندما كنت تصفق لي إذ ظننت أنك تسخر مني.

الشاعر: كـم كنـت مخطئـة! لـم أكـن أريد إلا أن أعبـر عـن اعجابي وأن أشكـرك علـى كـل المتـع الجمالية التي كنت أتلقاها منك.

Towards the Future, a Play — نـحـو المـستقبل، مسرحية

Painter: Now that I have done my duty, I shall leave you. I have an appointment with my art-dealer. Ah, the blackguard! He wants to make me paint absurdities because, he says, it is the current taste. But I am resisting...

Poet: Yes, resist, resist valiantly. Do not encourage this degeneracy of modern taste, this lapse into falsehood which seems to have seeped into the consciousness of all our contemporaries, in every field of human creativity.

Painter: Very well, my friend, I go, fired with a new courage, to do battle for the truth. Goodbye.

Poet and Clairvoyant: Goodbye.

Poet (*indicating the sofa*): Please sit down, mademoiselle.

Clairvoyant: (*sitting*) So you are willing to introduce me to a few people and let them hear me?

Poet: Certainly. One of our foremost conductors is a friend of mine and with a talent like yours all doors will easily open to you.

Clairvoyant: It will be a great help to me. Thank you so much.

Poet: No, no, do not thank me. (*He sits by her side.*) If you knew all the joy you have given me... If you knew what a pleasant accompaniment the harmony of your rich voice has been to my daily work. I owe you many good and happy hours; yes, it is I who should be grateful to you.

Clairvoyant: It is very kind of you to tell me all this. (*She looks around her, then turns to the Poet with a smile.*) It is strange how familiar everything seems to me here, perhaps not so much the objects themselves as the air, the atmosphere which envelops them. Excuse my boldness, but I feel as if I were at home, I feel as if I had been coming here always. And I have the feeling that all sorts of wonderful things are going to happen to me now.

Poet: I shall be the first person to be glad of it.

Towards the Future, a Play — نحو المستقبل، مسرحية

الرسـام: الآن وقد أديت مهمتي، سـأغادركما. أنـا على موعـد مـع تـاجر الأعمـال الفنيـة الـذي أتعامـل معه. هذا الوغد يتوقع مني أن أرسم حماقات لمجرد إنها تتفق مع الذوق الشائع. ولكني أقاوم...

الشاعر: نِعمَ مـا تفعل، قاوم، قاوم ببطولـة. لا تشـجع هذا التدهور الـذي طرأ حديثاً على الـذوق الفني، هذا الانتكاس إلى الزور الذي تسلل إلى وعي جميع المعاصرين في كل مجالات الخلق والإبداع.

الرسام: حسناً إذاً أيها الصديق العزيز، سأذهب وقد تجدد عزمي على النضال في سبيل الحق.

الشاعر والمستبصرة: تصحبك السلامة.

الشاعر: (مشيراً *إلى الأريكة*) تفضلي بالجلوس يا آنسة.

المستبصرة: (وهي *تجلس*) أنت إذا تريد تقديمي إلى بعض القوم ليستمعوا إليّ؟

الشـاعر: بكـل تأكيـد. أحـد أصدقائي يعتبـر مـن أفضـل قائـدي الأوركسـترا اليـوم، وموهبة مثـل موهبتك لا بد أن تفتح لك كل الأبواب بسهولة.

المستبصرة: سيكون ذلك عوناً كبيراً لي. لك جزيل الشكر.

الشـاعر: عفـواً، عفـواً، لا داعـي للشـكر. (يجـلـس *بجوارهـا*). لـو كنـت تعلمـين البهجـة التـي كنـت استمدها من غنائك... ولو عرفت كم كـان إيقاع صـوتك المؤثر خير رفيـق لي في عملي اليـومي. أنـا مدين لك بكثير من الساعات السعيدة والشكر واجب عليَ لا عليك.

المستبصرة: إنـه لعطـف كبيـر منـك يـا سـيدي أن تخبرنـي بكـل ذلـك. (*تنظـر إلـى الغرفـة حولهـا ثـم تتلفت مـرة أخـرى إلـى الشـاعر مبتسمة*.) عجيـب كيـف يبـدو لـي كـل شـيء هنـا مألوفـاً، لا أعنـي بذلك الأشـياء الماديـة، ولكـن الجـو الـذي يحيـط بهـا. أرجـو أن تغفـر جرأتـي، ولكنـي أشـعر هنـا كمـا لـو كنـت في منزلـي، وكمـا لـو كنـت اعتـدت الحضـور إلـى هنـا مـن قبـل. يخالجنـي شـعور بـأن أشـياء رائعـة سـوف تحدث لي من هنا منذ الآن.

الشاعر: سماع ذلك يجعلني أسعد الناس!

Towards the Future, a Play — نحو المستقبل، مسرحية

Clairvoyant: (*after a short silence*) I must tell you a strange thing. When I came to settle in this town about six months ago, after my mother's death, in the hope of earning my living, I had a choice of several small apartments, each one with its advantages and inconveniences. The one that I rented here in this house is no better than any other, but I was impelled to take it by a kind of intuition that I would be happy here, that good things were in store for me here... It is strange, isn't it?

Poet: (*thoughtfully*) Strange, yes, very strange... (*Aside*) Is this affinity? Who knows? (*To the Clairvoyant:*) You know, this is strange too, I have felt much calmer and more contented since I have been hearing your voice each day, and I had a very great desire to know you.

Clairvoyant: And I knew you only as a writer whose talent I greatly admired and whom I hardly dared to hope to meet one day. There are such extraordinary and mysterious things in life... mysterious perhaps only because we do not know their causes, otherwise everything would be very simple and natural. And look, at this moment, I too feel a sensation of calm and well-being, and it gives me great strength. If only you knew how much I need strength and encouragement... Life is hard for a helpless and unprotected orphan who is forced to earn her living all alone and who knows nobody to support her in her struggle. But now that I have met you, I feel that all my difficulties will melt away.

Poet: Rest assured that I shall do everything in my power to help you. It is a duty and a very great pleasure to be of use to an artist and a woman like you.

Clairvoyant: (*taking his hand in a spontaneous movement*) Thank you. I feel as if we have always been sitting like this, side by side, and that we are friends, old friends... We are friends, aren't we?

Poet: (*solemnly*) Yes, from the depths of our hearts.

Clairvoyant: I feel so much at ease here, that I am forgetting all conventions. And now to crown my impoliteness, I am overcome by an imperative need to sleep. I have been sleeping so badly at home for such a long time. I feel uneasy, spied on by invisible enemies who wish me harm. I am unable to achieve the calm which would give me a much-needed rest. Whereas here, I have the feeling that something warm and strong enfolds me like a living cloak and little by little I am being overwhelmed by sleep.

Towards the Future, a Play — نحو المستقبل، مسرحية

المستبصرة: (بعد صمت قصير) يجب أن أخبرك بشيء غريب. قبل ستة أشهر، قدمت إلى هذه البلدة لأستقر فيها بعد وفاة والدتي، بأمل أن اكتسب فيها قوتي. كان أمامي الخيار بين عدة شقق صغيرة للسكن، لكل منها مميزاتها ومآخذها. شقتي الحالية بجوارك ليست أفضل من الشقق الأخرى، ولكني انسقت الى اختيارها بنوع من الحدس بأني سأكون سعيدة فيها، وبأن أموراً طيبة تنتظرني في هذا المكان.... أليس ذلك غريباً؟

الشاعر: (بعد تفكير) غريب، نعم إنه غريب فعلاً... (محدثاً نفسه) هل هذا دليل على تآلف الأرواح وتشابهها؟ كيف لنا أن نعلم؟ (مخاطباً المستبصرة) من الغريب أيضاً أنني ازددت هدوءً ورضى منذ أن تعودت على سماع صوتك كل يوم، هكذا نَمَت في نفسي رغبة شديدة في التعرف عليك.

المستبصرة: وأنا لم أكن أعرفك إلا ككاتب موهوب أكن له كل إعجاب بدون أن أتجرأ حتى على الأمل في لقائه في يوم من الأيام. هناك أشياء غير اعتيادية وغامضة في الحياة... ربما يكون السبب الوحيد لغموضها هو أننا لا نعرف أسبابها، ولو عرفناها، لوجدناها بسيطة وطبيعية للغاية. انظر: في هذه اللحظة أنا بدوري أحِسّ بالهدوء والهناء، وذلك الإحساس يعطيني قوة عظيمة. لو كنت تعلم مدى احتياجي إلى القوة والتشجيع... الحياة قاسية على يتيمة لا حول لها ولا حماية، تعتمد على نفسها فقط في اكتساب معيشتها ولا تعرف أحداً يسندها في كفاحها. أما الآن، وبعد أن وجدتك، فإني أشعر بأن كل صعوباتي ستتلاشى...

الشاعر: كوني واثقة إني سأفعل كل ما في وسعي لمساعدتك. إنه لواجب محبب إلى قلبي أن أكون نافعاً لفنانة وسيدة مثلك.

المستبصرة: (تأخذ يده بحركة تلقائية) أشكرك. أشعر كما لو كنا قد جلسنا كثيراً مثل جلستنا هذه، جنباً إلى جنب، وأشعر إننا أصدقاء، أصدقاء عِشرة طويلة.... نحن أصدقاء، أليس كذلك؟

الشاعر: نعم، بكل خوالج قلبينا.

المستبصرة: شعوري العميق بالراحة هنا يجعلني أنسى كل قواعد العرف. والآن، كتتويج لقلة ذوقي، أحس بحاجة طاغية للنوم، فأنا لم أنم جيداً منذ وقت طويل. أشعر بالتوتر وبأن أعداء لا أراهم يتجسسون علي ويريدون الإضرار بي، وذلك يمنعني من الوصول إلى السكينة والراحة اللتين أنا في أشد الحاجة لهما. ولكني هنا أحس بشيء دافئ وقوي يحيط بي كمعطف حي وأشعر بالنوم يتملكني تدريجياً.

Towards the Future, a Play — نحو المستقبل، مسرحية

Poet: (*looking at her tenderly*) Lie down here, on these cushions. Make yourself comfortable; don't let anything bother you. And above all do not think even for a moment of customs and conventions; they are fetters of no real value which seem to have been forged by man for his own misery.

Clairvoyant: I am in great need of sleep. I have a persistent pain in my head which makes me suffer a great deal. I have worked so hard to achieve a result as quickly as possible and my brain is terribly tired.

Poet (*eagerly*) Will you allow me?... I think I can easily give you some relief. (*He passes his hand several times across her forehead, then lays it on her head for a moment. The Clairvoyant, who is lying on the cushions, falls asleep with an expression of joy and well-being.*)

Clairvoyant: (*half asleep*) It is all right now, there is no more pain... And I feel so happy.

Poet: (*arranging the cushions so that she may lie comfortably and sitting by her side, holding her hand in his; to himself*) Poor child, so pretty and yet so lonely.

Clairvoyant: (*speaking in her sleep*) Oh, how beautiful!

Poet: (*softly*) What is beautiful?

Clairvoyant: (*still asleep*) There, all around you, that violet light... It is like a living and luminous amethyst. It is all around me too, it is giving me strength. It is a protection, a sure protection... Nothing harmful can come near me now. (*Enraptured*) How beautiful is the violet light a round you!

Poet: Since you are comfortable, sleep quietly now, without seeing anything.

Clairvoyant: (*in a far-away voice*) I am falling asleep, falling asleep. Oh, what calm, what ease.

Towards the Future, a Play — نحو المستقبل، مسرحية

الشاعر: (ينظر إليها برقة) ارقدي هنا على هذه الوسائد. خذي راحتك ولا تزعجي نفسك بأي شيء. والأهم من كل ذلك، لا تشغلي بالك ولو للحظة واحدة بالعرف والتقاليد، فهي قيود لا وزن لها يبدو أن الإنسان خلقها لتكون سبباً في تعاسته.

المستبصرة: أنا في أشد الحاجة إلى النوم. أشكو من ألم مستمر في رأسي يسبب لي الكثير من المعاناة. لقد بذلت مجهوداً جباراً لأحقق النجاح بأسرع ما يمكن، والآن دماغي مرهق تماماً.

الشاعر: (بتلهف) أتسمحين؟... أعتقد إني أستطيع أن أخفف عنك قليلاً. (يمر بيده على جبينها مرات عديدة ثم يضعها على رأسها. المستبصرة تستسلم للنوم مستلقية على الوسائد وقد بت على وجهها علامات الحبور والهناء.)

المستبصرة: (وهي تغالب النوم) زال الألم وأصبح كل شيء على ما يرام الآن... أشعر بسعادة غامرة.

الشاعر: (يرتب الوسائد ليمكنها من الرقود في راحة ويجلس بجوارها ممسكاً بيدها ويهمهم لنفسه:) كم هي ظريفة هذه المسكينة ومع ذلك فهي تعاني من الوحدة.

المستبصرة: (تتكلم وهي تغالب النوم) كل هذا الجمال!

الشاعر: (بصوت خافت) ماذا تجدين جميلاً؟

المستبصرة: (على وشك الاستسلام للنوم) هذا الضوء البنفسجي الذي يحيط بك.... إنه مثل حجر جمشت حي ومضيء. هذا الضوء يشملني أنا أيضاً ويحيط بي ويمنحني القوة والشعور بالأمان والحماية... بفضل هذا الضوء لن يستطيع أي شيء ضار أن يقترب مني. (بنشوة وابتهاج) كم هو جميل هذا الضوء البنفسجي حولك!

الشاعر: الآن وقد وجدت راحتك، نامي هادئة ولا تحاولي التفكير في أي شيء.

المستبصرة: (صوتها يأتي الآن من بعيد) النوم يغلبني ويستحوذ علي. يا لها من سكينة و يا لها من راحة.

Towards the Future, a Play — نحو المستقبل، مسرحية

Poet: (*looking at her tenderly*) Yes, sleep, child—a healing sleep. Life has been hard for you and you have great need of rest. (*After a moment's silence*) What is the use of trying to deceive myself? I have to admit it: just as her voice thrilled my whole being, so too her presence fills me with a calm and profound happiness. And now she has fallen asleep, under my protection, her first conscious sleep. Her very trust gives me a responsibility, a responsibility which would be very sweet to me. But my wife! I know that she is strong and brave, I know that long ago she realised that what I feel for her is nothing more than friendly affection. She herself cannot be satisfied with that; the depths of her love remain untouched. Yet I have responsibilities towards her too. How can I tell her that my whole being is concentrated upon another? And yet I cannot conceal my feelings; falsehood is the only evil. Besides, it would be quite useless: a woman like her cannot be deceived. Oh, life is often so cruel!

Clairvoyant: (*still sleeping, turning round and laying her hand on his*) I am happy... happy... (*She rests her head on the Poet's lap in a movement of childlike confidence.*)

Poet: Dear child! What can I do? (*He gazes at her, deep in his thoughts. The Clairvoyant: sighs, stretches, and wakes.*)

Clairvoyant: (*looking around her with some surprise*) I have slept... How well I have slept, never in my life have I slept so well.

Poet: I am so glad.

Clairvoyant: (*looking at him affectionately*) You see, the light that encircled you and covered me too was at once a nourishment and a protection; it was so beautiful, so comforting. Even now that I am awake I can feel it around me.

Poet: Yes, it is still around you. Is this the first time you have seen coloured lights like this?

Clairvoyant: I remember having seen lights or a coloured mist around certain people. But I have never seen any as beautiful as yours or any to which I have felt so close. Often, around others, it is like a turbid, unwholesome fog. What is it?

Towards the Future, a Play — نحو المستقبل، مسرحية

الشاعر: (*يتأملها بحنان*) نامي أيتها الطفلة العزيزة نوماً شافياً. لقد قست الحياة عليك وأصبحت في أشد الحاجة إلى الراحة. (*بعد صمت قصير*) ما النفع في أن أحاول أن أخدع نفسي؟ يجب أن أعترف بأن صوتها قد فتن كياني كله، وأن وجودها يملأني بالسكينة والسعادة العميقة. ها هي تنام، تحت رعايتي، في أول مرة تراني فيها، في وعي وسكينة وطمأنينة. ثقتها في تُحَمِّلُني مسئولية، كبيرة وكم اعتز بهذه المسئولية. ولكن زوجتي ما تزال هناك! أعلم أنها قوية وشجاعة، وأعلم أيضاً إنها تعرف منذ وقت طويل أن شعوري نحوها ليس أكثر من شعور الود بين صديقين. ومع هذا لا بد أن يكون غير كافٍ بالنسبة لها؛ فإن حبها لي لا يتبدل على الإطلاق. كيف يمكنني أن أخبرها بأن كياني كله قد أصبح يتمحور حول امرأة أخرى؟ ولكن، من ناحية أخرى، لا يصح أن أكتم مشاعري، فالكذب والزور هما أصل كل شر. أضف إلى ذلك أن الخداع لن ينطلي على امرأة على مستواها. كم تقسو علينا الحياة في كثير من الأحيان!

المستبصرة: (*تضع يدها وهي نائمة على يده*) أنا سعيدة... سعيدة... (*ثم تنقل يدها إلى حجر الشاعر ببساطة الطفل الذي لا يرتاب*)

الشاعر: طفلتي العزيزة: ماذا أستطيع أن أفعل لك؟! (*يتأملها غارقاً في أفكاره. المستبصرة تتنهد ثم تتمدد وتستيقظ.*)

المستبصرة: (*تنظر حولها ببعض الاندهاش*) لقد نمت، وأي نوم هانئ نمت، لم أنم في حياتي قط مثل نومي هذا.

الشاعر: كم يسعدني سماع ذلك.

المستبصرة: (*تنظر إليه بحنان*) هذا الضوء الذي أحاط بك والذي امتد إلي وشملني كان غذاء ووقاية، وكان جميلاً ومطمئناً لدرجة إنني الآن وبعد أن استيقظت ما زلت أشعر به من حولي.

الشاعر: نعم، إنه ما زال حولك. هل هذه أول مرة ترين فيها أضواء ملونة كما رأيت للتو؟

المستبصرة: أتذكر إني رأيت أضواء ملونة أو بالأصح غيم ملون حول بعض الناس. ولْكني لم أر قط ضوءًا أكثر جمالاً أو أقرب إلى نفسي من ضوئك. كثيراً ما أرى حول آخرين ما يشبه الضباب العكر ما هذا الضباب؟

Towards the Future, a Play — نحو المستقبل، مسرحية

Poet: It would take rather long to give a clear reply. But I shall try to explain it to you as best I can in a few words. Stop me if I bore you. We are made up of different states which can be compared to earth, water, air and fire Do you follow?

Clairvoyant: Yes, it is most interesting.

Poet A less dense state penetrates and flows through a denser one, as water evaporates through a porous vessel, with the difference that no loss follows. In the same way, what is more subtle in us forms a kind of sheath around our bodies and we call this subtle sheath the aura.

Clairvoyant: I understand, it is very clear. So then it can be very useful to see auras in this way?

Poet: You are right, it is most useful. You can easily understand that the aura is the exact reflection of what is within us, of our feelings and our thoughts. If the thoughts and feelings are calm and harmonious, the aura too will be calm and harmonious; if the feelings are tumultuous and the thoughts disturbed, the aura will express this tumult and disturbance. It will be like the mist which you say you have seen around certain people.

Clairvoyant: Yes, I understand. So these auras are very revealing.

Poet: Yes, for those who see auras, deception can no longer exist. For example, however much a man of bad will may try to look like an angel of light, it will be in vain. His aura will reveal that his thoughts and motives are dark.

Clairvoyant: (*admiringly*) Magnificent! What effects this knowledge might have in the world! But where did you learn such beautiful things? For I do not think that many people are aware of them.

Poet: No, especially in modern times, in an age like ours in which success and the material satisfactions it brings are the only things that matter. And yet an ever-growing number of dissatisfied people are trying to find the purpose and goal of life. On the other hand, there are those who know and strive to help suffering humanity; they are guardians of the supreme knowledge which has been handed down from generation to generation and which serves as the basis of a method of self-development whose aim is to awaken man to the consciousness of what he truly is and what he can do.

Towards the Future, a Play — نحو المستقبل، مسرحية

الشاعر: شرح ذلك شرحاً وافياً يقتضي وقتاً طويلاً. ولكني سأحاول أن أشرح بأحسن ما في وسعي في كلمات قليلة. أوقفيني لو أملتك. الإنسان مكون من حالات يمكن أن نشبهها بالأرض والماء والهواء والنار. هل تستطيعين متابعتي؟

المستبصرة: نعم، نعم، هذا مشوق للغاية.

الشاعر: العنصر الأقل كثافة يتخلل وينتشر في العنصر الأكثر كثافة، كما يتبخر الماء من خلال إناء ذي مسام دون أن يكون هناك تبديد للمادة. وبالمثل فإن ما هو أكثر رهافة ورقة ينتشر إلى خارجنا ويكون طبقة تحيط ببدننا؛ هذه الطبقة تسمى بالطبقة الرقيقة أو الأورا.

المستبصرة: أنا أرى ذلك، وهو واضح تماماً. رؤية الأورا بهذه الطريقة لا بد أن تكون مفيدة جداً.

الشاعر: أنت محقة، هي نافعة للغاية. تستطيعين بسهولة أن تفهمي أن الأورا ما هي إلا انعكاس دقيق لما هو بداخلنا، أي لمشاعرنا وأفكارنا. لو كانت المشاعر والأفكار هادئة ومنسجمة، تكون الأورا أيضاً هادئة ومنسجمة، أما إذا كانت المشاعر عنيفة ومتضاربة والأفكار مشوشة، فإن الأورا تكون تعبيراً عن هذا العنف والتشوش وتصير مثل ذاك الضباب الذي ذكرتي إنك قد رأيت حول بعض الناس.

المستبصرة: نعم، هذا واضح. هذه الأورا تكشف عن الكثير بالفعل.

الشاعر: حقيقة، هؤلاء الذين يرون الأورا لا يمكن أن يُخدَعُوا. على سبيل المثال، لو أراد رجل سيء النية أن يبدو كملاك نوراني، فإنه لن ينجح في ذلك، لأن الأورا المحيطة به ستكشف أفكاره ودوافعه المظلمة.

المستبصرة: (بإعجاب) رائع! هذه المعرفة قد يكون لها نتائج عظيمة في العالم. ولكن أين تعلمت هذه الأشياء الجميلة؟ فأنا لا أظن أن كثيرين على دراية بها.

الشاعر: لا، خاصة في الأزمان الحديثة، وفي عصر مثل عصرنا لا يهتم الناس فيه إلا بالنجاح والمتع المادية التي تأتي في ركابه. ومع ذلك نجد أن عدد الناس الذين يحاولون اكتشاف هدف الحياة يتزايد باستمرار. ولكن هناك أيضاً ذوو المعرفة الذين يسعون إلى تخفيف عناء البشر؛ هؤلاء هم الحافظون للمعرفة الأسمى التي توارثها الناس جيلاً بعد جيل والتي تصلح لأن تكون أساساً لمنهج تطور ونمو يهدف إلى إيقاظ الإنسان وتوعيته بحقيقة كيانه وبما هو قادر على فعله.

Towards the Future, a Play — نحو المستقبل، مسرحية

Clairvoyant: How beautiful this teaching must be! You will reveal it to me little by little, won't you? For we are going to see each other often, aren't we? I wish we never had to part again.... While I was asleep I felt that you were everything for me and that I belong to you forever. And I felt that from now on your protection will always enfold me. And I who was so full of fear, who felt exposed to so many enemies, I am now quiet, calm, confident, for I can tell all who want to harm me: "I fear you no longer, I am effectively protected, by a protection that will never fail me." I am right, am I not?

Poet: Yes, yes, you are right.

Clairvoyant: I am so happy to have met you at last. I have waited for you so long! And you, are you happy?

Poet: Yes... Just now, while you were asleep, I felt a calm and a quiet happiness which I had never experienced before. (*Thoughtfully*) Yes, this is the true love, which is a force; it is the union that enables new possibilities to be realised... But...

Clairvoyant: But what? Since we are so happy together, what could prevent us...?

Poet: (*rising suddenly*) Oh, you do not know! (*He stops short at the sight of She, who has been standing behind the screen for some time already.*) Oh! (*She comes forward smiling and very calm.*)

Clairvoyant: (*amazed*) I did not know that you were married!

Towards the Future, a Play — نحو المستقبل، مسرحية

المستبصرة: لا بد أن يكون هذا منهجاً رائعاً، وأنا آمل أن أتعلمه منك بالتدريج؛ هل توافق على ذلك؟ فنحن سوف نلتقي كثيراً في المستقبل، أليس كذلك؟ أتمنى ألا نفترق أبداً بعد اليوم.. شعرت أثناء نومي بأنك قد أصبحت كل شيء في حياتي وبأنني سوف أنتمي إليك إلى الأبد. وشعرت أيضاً أنني سأكون دائماً في حمايتك. وبعد أن كنت فريسة للخوف ومُعرَّضَة لأعداء كثيرين، أشعر الآن بالهدوء والسكينة والاطمئنان وأني أستطيع أن أقول لمن يريد بي الضر: "لم أعد أخافك. أنا الآن في الحماية، وهذه الحماية لن تتخلى عني أبداً." أنا محقة، أليس كذلك؟

الشاعر: نعم، نعم، أنت على حق.

المستبصرة: أنا سعيدة لأني وجدتك أخيراً، فقد انتظرتك طويلاً! وأنت، هل أنت سعيد؟

الشاعر: نعم... قبل دقائق، أثناء نومك، شعرت بسكينة وبسعادة هادئة لم أشعر بها من قبل. (متعمقاً في التفكير) نعم، هذا هو الحب الصادق، وهو قوة، إنه اتحاد يفتح مجالات جديدة للتحقيق... ولكن..

المستبصرة: ماذا تعني بـ"ولكن"؟ ما دمنا كلانا سعداء معا، ماذا يقدر أن يمنعنا...؟

الشاعر: (يقوم فجأة) آه، أنت لا تعلمين! (يلمح زوجته التي كانت تقف وراء الستار منذ بعض الوقت ويكف عن الكلام) آه! (**هي** تأتي إلى الأمام مبتسمة وفي غاية الهدوء.)

المستبصرة: (في تعجب ودهشة) لم أكن أعلم إنك متزوج!

Towards the Future, a Play — نحو المستقبل، مسرحية

She (*to the Clairvoyant:*) Do not be upset. (*Turning to the Poet*) Nor you. Yes, I heard the end of your conversation. I returned just as Mademoiselle was waking up. I did not want to disturb you and was about to withdraw, but I thought it would be more useful for all of us if I heard. So I stayed. For I was sure, my dear, that you would find yourself in a cruel predicament. I know your straightforwardness, your loyalty, and I knew that you would be painfully divided between two opposite paths. You know what is said in the teaching which for us is the truth: love is the only legitimate bond of union. The absence of love is enough to invalidate any union. Certainly, there are unions without love, based on esteem and mutual concessions, which can be quite tolerable, but consider that when love comes, everything else should give way to it. My friend, you remember our pact: we promised each other full freedom the moment love would awaken in either of us. That is why I listened, and now I have come to tell you: you are free, be happy.

Poet: (*deeply moved*) But you, you? I know you always live at the summit of your consciousness, in a pure and serene light. But solitude is sometimes hard and the hours can be monotonous and sad.

She: Oh, I shall not be alone, for I shall go and join those through whom we have found the path, those who possess the eternal wisdom and who have, from a distance, guided our steps until now. Surely they will shelter me. (*She turns towards the Clairvoyant: and takes her by the hand.*) Come, do not be upset. Women who are sensitive and sincere have the right to freely choose the person who will be their protector and guide in life. You have acted according to the natural law and all is well. Our way of looking at things and our behaviour may surprise you; they are new to you and you do not know the reasons for them. (*Pointing to the Poet*) He will explain them to you. I am going away, but before I go let me join your hands. (*She places the hand of the Clairvoyant: in the hand of the Poet.*) No blessing can ever be equal to the blessing of love. And yet I shall give you mine, knowing that it will be dear to you. And if you permit, I shall add some advice which is almost a request. Do not allow your union to serve as an excuse for the satisfaction of animal appetites or sensual desires. On the contrary, make it a means of mutual support so that you may transcend yourselves in a constant aspiration and an effort for progress towards the growing perfection of your being. May your association be both noble and generous, noble in quality, generous in action. Be an example to the world and show all men of goodwill the true aim of human life.

Towards the Future, a Play — نحو المستقبل، مسرحية

هـي: (موجهة الحديث إلى المستبصرة) لا تنزعجي. (تلتفت إلى الشاعر) ولا داعي لأن تنزعج أنت أيضاً. سمعت الجزء الأخير من محادثتكما، فقد دخلت من الخارج في اللحظة التي ستيقظت فيها الآنسة. لم أرد أن أزعجكما وأوشكت على الانسحاب ولكني لم أفعل لأني أدركت إنـه ربما يكون من الأفضل للجميع لو بقيت واستمعت. فقد كنت متأكدة أيها العزيز أنك ستجد نفسك في ورطة قاسية. ولأني أعلم استقامتك وإخلاصك، أدركت أنك ستعاني من انجذابك المؤلم في اتجاهين متضادين. انت تعلم أنه تبعاً للمذهب، الذي أصبح يمثل الحقيقة بالنسبة لنا، الحب هو الرباط الوحيد الذي له شرعية في أي اتحاد، وغياب الحب كافٍ لنقض هذا الاتحاد. بالتأكيد يمكن أن يكون هناك اتحاد مبني على التقدير والتنازلات المتبادلة، ومثل هذه العلاقات قد تكون مقبولة إلى حد بعيد، ولكني أرى أن كل اعتبار آخر يجب أن يتنحى أمام الحب. أنت تذكر يا صديقي ما تعاهدنا عليه إذ وعد كل منا الآخر بأن يمنحه الحرية التامة لو استيقظ في قلبه الحب. هذا هو السبب في أني استمعت، والآن أقول لكما: أنتما أحرار، كونا سعيدين.

الشاعر: (بتأثر عميق) ولكن أنت، أنت؟ أعلم أنك تعيشين دائماً على قمة وعيك في ضوء صافٍ ومشرق، ولكن الوحدة قد تكون قاسية، والساعات قد تمر رتيبة تعيسة أحياناً.

هـي: لن أكون وحيدة، فسوف أذهب وانضم إلى أولئك الذين أرشدونا إلى الطريق، أصحاب الحكمة الخالدة الذين كانوا حتى الآن يسددون خطانا من بعيد. بالتأكيد سأجد عندهم مأوى يأويني. (تلتفت إلى المستبصرة وتأخذ يدها:) تعالي، لا تحملي أي هم. أرى أنه من حق المرأة، عندما تكون صادقة وذات شعور مرهف، أن تختار في حرية تامة الرفيق الذي يوفر لها الحماية ويرشدها في الحياة. لقد تصرفتِ تبعاً لقانون الطبيعة، ولم تفعلي ما يستحق اللوم أو العتاب. قد تدهشك طريقتنا في النظر إلى الأمور وتصرفاتنا، فهي جديدة بالنسبة لك وأنت لا تعلمين أسبابها. (مشيرة إلى الشاعر) ولكنه سوف يشرحها لك. الآن أغادركما، اسمحي لي بوصل يديكما. (تضع يد المستبصرة في يد الشاعر.) بركة الحب هي أعظم البركت. وأنا أباركما عالمة أن مباركتي ستكون عزيزة إلى قلبيكما. ولكني استأذنكما في أن أضيف نصيحة تكاد أن تكون رجاءً: لا تسمحا لاتحادكما أن يكون مبرراً لإرضاء شهوات الجنس الحيوانية. بل، على العكس، اجعلا هذه الوحدة وسيلة لتبادل العون على تخطي النفس في اجتهاد وتشوق روحي مستمر للكمال المطرد. ليكن رباطكما مُتَّسماً بالنبل والكرم: نبيلاً في صفاته وكريماً في سعيه وأفعاله. كونا في العالم مثالاً يظهر لكل ذوي النوايا الطيبة الهدف الحقيقي للحياة.

Towards the Future, a Play — نحو المستقبل، مسرحية

Clairvoyant: (*deeply moved*) You can be sure that we shall do our utmost to deserve the trust you have shown us and be worthy of your esteem. But I would like to hear from your own lips that my coming to this house and the event that has followed do not mean an irreparable misfortune to you.

She: Have no fear. I now know for certain that only one love can satisfy my being: it is the love for the Divine, the divine love, for that alone never fails. Perhaps one day I shall find the favourable conditions and the necessary help for the achievement of the supreme realisation, the transformation and divinisation of the physical being which will change the world into a blessed place full of harmony and light, peace and beauty. (*The Clairvoyant:, more and more deeply moved, remains silent, her hands clasped as if in prayer. The Poet bows respectfully to Her, takes her hand and lays his forehead on it as the curtain falls.*)

Collected Works of the Mother, Vol. 12, On Education, Part 3, Dramas

Towards the Future, a Play — نحو المستقبل، مسرحية

المستبصرة: (في تأثر شديد) كوني متأكدة إننا سنفعل كل ما في وسعنا لنستحق الثقة التي تضعين فينا ولنكون جديرين بحسن تقديرك. ولكني أود أن أسمع من شفتيك تحديداً أن قدومي إلى هذا البيت وما تبعه من أحداث لن يكون كارثة كبرى في حياتك.

هي: لا تخافي. أعلم الآن تأكيداً أنه لا يوجد إلا حب واحد يمكن أن يرضيني: ألا وهو **الحب الإلهي**، فهو وحده لا يخذل ولا يخيب. عسى أن أجد يوماً الظروف الملائمة والعون الضروري لأنجز أعظم التحقيقات، ألا وهو تحويل الكيان البدني وتطويره بحيث يصبح البدن نفسه إلهياً، فذلك التحقيق هو الذي سيجعل من العالم مكاناً مباركاً مليئاً بالتناسق والنور والسلام والجمال. (المستبصرة تبقى صامتة، وقد اشتد تأثرها أكثر وأكثر، ضامةً يديها كما لو كانت تصلي الشاعر ينحني في تبجيل أمام **هي** ويأخذ يدها وينحني واضعاً جبهته عليها في حين ينسدل الستار.)

الأعمال المجمعة للأم، مجلد 12، عن التربية، الجزء الثالث، مسرحيات

قاموس المصطلحات

الأنا: Ego

الواحد-الكل: The Divine

كما يتضح من الفصل الأول في هذا الكتاب، يستخدم شري أوروبيندو والأم هذا المصطلح بمفهوم مرن وشامل إلى أقصى درجات المرونة والشمول: إما للتعبير عن الذات الإلهية أو عن الصفات الإلهية.

أوبانيشاد: Upanished

مجموعة من النصوص القديمة تُكوّن جزءا أساسيا من الديانات الهندوسية لها تأثير كبير على معظم الفلسفات الهندية وهي مصدر مستديم للحكمة.

أوروفيل: Auroville

بلدة صغيرة ناشئة في جنوب الهند أسستها الأم عام 1968 "لكل من يطمح في أن يكون خادماً طوعياً للوعي الإلهي".

براهمان: Brahman

"حقيقة الأشياء التي تملأ وتسند فكرتها وهيئتها"

شري أوروبيندو، مكتبة الميلاد المئوي لشري أوروبيندو [17:166]

تحت-الواعي: subconscient

انظر لوعي التحتي

تحوّل: transformation

التغير الجذري في طبيعة الإنسان الباطنة والظاهرة الذي يتحقق تدريجيا في اليوغا المتكاملة بواسطة قوى تنتمي إلى مستويات متصاعدة في الوعي تصل إلى السوبرمايند*. وهو من الأهداف الأساسية في يوغا شري أوروبيندو والأم.

تخليق: synthesis

بعكس التحليل Analysis، التخليق هو مزج عناصر مختلفة في مكون واحد. التخليق في الكيمياء مثلا هو خلق مواد جديدة أكثر تعقيدا من مواد بسيطة.

تشكيل فكري mental formation

للذهن قدرة تشكيلية لا يستهان بها، وترى الأم أننا لو أتقنا عمل تشكيل فكري، مثلاً بأن نركز على شيء نرغبه بشدة، فإن ذلك التشكيل الفكري يخرج منا في كيان مستقل ويسعى لتحقيق هذه الرغبة حتى بعد أن نكون قد نسيناها. ولذلك كانت الأم تنصح دائما بتجنب الأفكار السيئة والضارة وبالاقتصار في تشكيلنا الفكري على ما هو إيجابي ونافع ومفيد.

قاموس المصطلحات

تعادل: equality

مواجهة جميع الأمور بذهن وكيان حيوي لا يهتزان. ينبني على معرفة أن الألوهية واحدة وموجودة في كل مكان وفي جميع الأشياء.

تطلع: aspiration

الصلاة ودعاء **الألوهية** ومناداتها والتوق إلى كل ما هو سامي وينتمي إلى الوعي الإلهي. وهو مزيج من الإرادة الخالصة من الطموح الشخصي والرغبة الخالصة من شوائب الشهوات. من أكثر الوسائل فعالية للتحقيق في اليوغا المتكاملة.

توق: aspiration

انظر التطلع أعلاه

جيتا: Gita

من أهم النصوص المقدسة في الهندوسية.

حب العبادة: bhakti

العبادة عن طريق الحب. أن يحب المرء ما هو أسمى وأرفع حب عبادة ويهب ذاته للألوهية.

حيوي: vital انظر أيضا كائن حيوي: vital being

ينتمي إلى قوة الحياة. جزء الطبيعة البشرية الذي يصل العقل بالبدن. وظيفته الأساسية هي التمتع والتملك. طاقاته ضرورية لكمال الحياة الأرضية، ولكنه كثيرا ما يسبب اضطرابات من جميع الأنواع إلى أن تتم تنقيته بواسطة اليوغا.

حيوي/بدني: vital-physical

جزء قوة الحياة المتداخل في حالات وأنشطة البدن.

الذات الجوهرية: Self

الوجود الجوهري الواعي في جميع الكائنات وجميع الأشياء.

الروح: Spirit

الوعي فوق العقل في اتحاد دائم مع الذات الإلهية. [عادة تترجم الكلمة الإنجليزية soul إلى العربية أيضا بـ: روح، ولكن لتلافي الخلط، سنترجمها بـ: الكيان السيكي* استنادا إلى التعريف التالي لشري أوروبيندو: "الروح والكيان السيكي هما، من الناحية العملية، نفس الشيء".

سوبرامنتل: supramental، انظر: سوبرمايند

308

قاموس المصطلحات

سوبرمايند: supermind

وعي لحقيقة. الاسم الذي أطلقه شري أوروبيندو على الوعي الذي يتخطى مستويات العقل كلها طبيعته معرفة الوحدة اللانهائية التي تعبر عن نفسها في تعدد لا نهائي. وهو وعي الحقيقة الذي يتطور الإنسان نحوه في مسار التطور الطبيعي والذي لابد أنه بالغه في المدى البعيد. يوغا شري أوروبيندو في أعلى مراحله تسعى لتثبيت السوبرمايند في المجال الأرضي.

سيكي: psychic انظر الكيان السيكي.

شاكتي: Shakti

القوة والقدرة الإلهية، قوة الأم الإلهية، وعي وقوة الألوهية، طاقة الأم الكونية

شري راماكريشنا: Sri Ramakrishna

من أعظم الشخصيات الروحية الهندية [عاش في القرن التاسع عشر].

انظر: http://en.wikipedia.org/wiki/Ramakrishna

شانكارا: مصلح هندوسي من القرن الثامن الميلادي

انظر: http://en.wikipedia.org/wiki/Shankaracharya

عقل: mind

شري أوروبيندو يعطي مصطلحات العقل دلالات خاصة في كتاباته:

"كلمات "عقل" و "عقلي" في لغة هذه اليوغا تستخدم خاصة للدلالة على جزء الطبيعة الذي يتعامل مع الإدراك والذكاء، مع الأفكار، مع المفاهيم الذهنية والفكرية، مع ردود فعل الفكر على الأشياء، مع الحركات والتراكيب الذهنية الخالصة والرؤية الذهنية والإرادة... إلى آخره، التي هي جزء من ذكائـــــه."
— "العقل هو أداة تحليل وتخليق*، ولكنه ليس أداة للمعرفة الجوهرية.

العقل الفيزيائي: Physical Mind

جزء لعقل الذي لا يهتم إلا بالأشياء المادية والتي تدرك بالحواس أو بالأحداث الخارجية، ويأخذ معلوماته ومدلولاته منها فقط، ولا يفقه أي حقيقة أسمى منها ما لم يتم تنويره من أعلى. جزء الوعي الفيزيائي* الذي يضفي على التجارب البدنية صيغة عقلية.

العقل التحتي: subconscient mind انظر الوعي التحتي*

العقل الحيوي: vital mind

جزء الوعي الذي يعطي صورة ذهنية للحركات الحيوية مثل الشهوات والدفعات والعواطف.

غنوصي: gnostic

ينتمي إلى الغنوصية أو المعرفة الروحية التي تتخطى الذهن.

قاموس المصطلحات

غورو: Guru
مرشــد روحي، مرشــد فــي اليوغــا؛ شــخص توصــل إلــى الحقيقــة فــي نفســه ويستطيع أن يُبَلِّغ نورهـا وتجربتها.

الفلسفة الوضعية: Positivism
إحـدى فلسـفات العلـوم التـي تسـتند إلـى رأي يقـول أنـه فـي مجـال العلـوم الاجتماعيـة، كمـا فـي العلـوم الطبيعيـة، فـإن المعرفـة الحقيقيـة هـي المعرفـة والبيانـات المسـتمدة مـن التجربـة الحسـية، والعلاجـات المنطقيـة والرياضيـة لمثـل هـذه البيانـات والتـي تعتمـد علـى الظواهـر الطبيعيـة الحسـية وخصائصـها والعلاقـات بينهم والتي يمكن التحقق منها من خلال الأبحاث والأدلة التجريبية.

فيفيك أناندا: Vivikananda
انظر: http://en.wikipedia.org/wiki/Swami_Vivekananda

الكيان الحيوي: vital being , the vital - انظر "حيوي" أعلاه
قـوة الحيـاة، وهـي تتجلـى فـي الـدوافع والعواطـف والمشـاعر والرغبـات والشـهوات والمطـامح. جـزء الكيـان الإنسـاني الـذي يصـل العقـل بالبـدن. وظيفتـه الأساسـية هـي الاسـتمتاع والتملـك. طاقاتـه ضـرورية للتحقيـق ولكمـال الوجـود الأرضـي، ولكنـه مـا لـم يُنَقَّى ويُحَوَّل باليوغـا، كثيـرا مـا يكـون مصـدرا لكثيـر مـن الاضطرابات والمعاناة.

الكيان الحيوي الأدنى: lower vital
حركـات رغبـة الحيـاة الـدنيا مثـل شـهوة الطعـام والرغبـة الجنسـية والاستحسـان والبغـض والغريـر وحـب الثناء والغضب ورغبات وردود فعل صغيرة من كل الأنواع.

الكيان السيكي: The Psychic
روح الإنسـان المقتبس من الروح الإلهي. وهو عادة ما يكون في الإنسـان العـادي مغمـور تحـت حجاب كثيف من العقل والكيان الحيوي والبدن. تَقَدُّم الكيان السيكي إلى الأمام ليمسك بزمام الكيـان الفـردي هـو التحقيـق الحاسـم والضـروري فـي اليوغـا المتكاملة. يَسنِد التطـور مـن حيـاة إلـى حيـاة وهـو مفتـاح التحول والارتقاء.

لا شعوري: subconscient , subconscious – انظر "الوعي التحتي".

المادة الدقيقة: Subtle Phsical
المـادة الغليظـة هـي المـادة كمـا نـدركها بالحـواس الخمسـة، ولكـن هنـاك أيضـاً مـادة دقيقـة يمكـن أن نـدركها بالحواس الدقيقة والبدن الدقيق يمتد قليلاً خارج البدن وله وعي خاص يدرك به الأشياء.

مزج تخليقي: synthesis
في الكيمياء وغيرها مزج مادتين لتركيب مادة ذات خصائص جديدة

نيرفانا: Nirvana
التحـرر مـن الجهـل والـتخلص مـن التعلـق والرغبـة و الأنـا والعمـل الأنانـي والعقليـة الأنانيـة." حالـة السلام اللانهائي التي يسعى إليها كل بوذي.

310

قاموس المصطلحات

الوعي التحتي : The Subconscient

الجزء المغمور من الكيان تحت مستوى الذهن والمشاعر الواعية، حيث لا يوجد نظام أو تنسيق في الأفكار والإرادة وردود الفعل وحيث يتم تخزين انطباعات الأشياء. منه تنبعث الحوافز في الأحلام (وفي اليقظة كذلك) وهو مسئول عن الكثير من العادات التي تسيطر على الانسان. انظر أيضا الفصل الخامس من الجزء الأول من هذا الكتاب.

وعي البدن: body consciousness

وعي لخلايا الذي يختص بوظائف الجسم. لا شعوري في معظمه، ولكنه يملك معرفة غريزية. يؤثر على الجسم بدون حاجة إلى إرادة ذهنية، بل أحيانا على الرغم من هذه الإرادة. لاحظ أن شري أوروبيندو يميز بين وعي البدن وبين وعي أشمل يسميه: الوعي الفيزيائي* أي أن وعي البدن جزء من الوعي الفيزيائي. انظر الوعي الفيزيائي* أسفله.

الوعي الفائق   The Superconscient

مجال الوعي فوق الرأس الذي يحتوي المجالات الذهنية العليا. من الوعي الفائق ينزل الوعي الأعلى إلى البدن.

الوعي الفيزيائي: physical consciousness

فيزيائي هنا تعني طبيعي/مادي. يشمل عقل البدن*، والكيان البدني/حيوي physical vital وكذلك وعي البدن*.

اليوغا: Yoga

حرفيا الاتحاد. وصفها شري أوروبيندو بأنها "ما هي إلا علم نفس عملي"، وأنها الوسيلة لتحقيق الصلة والاتحاد مع الألوهية. تشمل مناهج مختلفة لتخطي الحدود المعتادة للطبيعة البشرية والدخول في وعي أعلى وحقيقة أسمى. كلمة يوغا تشير في هذا الكتاب في معظم الأحيان إلى اليوغا المتكاملة* التي طورها شري أوروبيندو والأم.

يوغا الأعمال: Karma yoga

التدرب على العمل لتحقيق أهداف سامية بدون رغبة أو إصرار على منفعة شخصية.

اليوغا المتكاملة: Integral Yoga

منهج لليوغا الذي طوراه شري أوروبيندو والأم. وهو يسعى إلى تحقيق الروح في الحياة وفي المادة عن طريق تحويل جميع نواحي الطبيعة البشرية إلى صورة أقرب إلى الأصل الروحي.

يوغي: yogi

الواصل في اليوغا الذي بلغ التحكم في النفس والتحقيق الروحي الذي تسعى إليه اليوغا.

Glossary

Adhar: vessel; the physical, vital and mental system as a vehicle of the consciousness and force of the Spirit.

Adverse forces: forces of the vital world that oppose the higher movement of evolution and are agents of disharmony in human life at its present stage; also referred to as hostile or anti-divine forces.

Ananda: bliss; the unvarying delight which is at the core of all things.

Body-consciousness: the consciousness that belongs to the body and is concerned with its functionings. It is a part of the physical consciousness, below the level of the physical mind and largely subconscient, but possessing an instinctive knowledge.

Brahmic consciousness: awareness of the eternal Reality (Brahman) that is expressed in the universe.

Formation: see Mental Formation

Gnostic: pertaining to the gnosis or spiritual knowledge beyond mind, especially on the plane of Supermind.

Guru: a spiritual guide; a teacher of any branch of ancient knowledge in the Indian tradition.

Inconscience, the inconscient: the negation of consciousness from which evolution in this world began. Until it is transformed by Supermind, it persists as the cause of the inability of matter to embody the truth and immortality of the Spirit.

Integral Yoga: a form of Yoga that seeks to manifest the Spirit in life and matter by effectuating a transformation in all parts of our nature.

Mental: pertaining to mind, the faculty of thought and intelligence, which is the instrument of a kind of cognition where the subject is separate from the object; an intermediate range of the spectrum of consciousness which has found expression in the human stage of evolution.

Mental Formation: The mind has a considerable power of formation so that, according to the Mother, when we concentrate intensely on a certain desire, this

Glossary

"formation" can acquire a separate identity and leave us on its own and goes in the world seeking to fulfill this desire, even though we may ourselves have forgotten all about it!

Mental world: a supra-physical plane of existence governed by the mental principle.

Physical consciousness: the consciousness in the body (sometimes including the subtle body*).

Physical mind: the part of the physical consciousness that gives mental form to physical experience.

Positivism: the philosophy of science that information derived from logical and mathematical treatments and reports of sensory experience is the exclusive source of all authoritative knowledge.

Psychic: pertaining to the soul; the inmost being which is normally hidden from us in the depths of our subliminal consciousness. It supports our evolution from life to life and is the key to the possibility of transformation.

Sadhak: one who seeks spiritual realisation by Sadhana*.

Sadhana: spiritual discipline; practice of Yoga.

Shakti: the self-existent, self-cognitive, self-effective Power of the Lord (Purusha)

Shankara — an 8th century CE reformer of Hinduism. See: http://en.wikipedia.org/wiki/Shankaracharya

Spirit: the one Self of all, whose nature is immortal existence, consciousness, force and bliss. Although it has concealed itself behind the appearances of the material world, it is the source of all things and is present everywhere. It can be experienced through Yoga and embodied in life through an integral transformation.

Sri Ramakrishna: see: http://en.wikipedia.org/wiki/Ramakrishna

Subconscient, subconscious: below the level of normal conscious awareness; an obscure and incoherent part of the being which borders on inconscience and exerts a powerful influence on the body.

Glossary

Subtle body: a body made of subtle physical substance, forming part of the subliminal being and supporting the gross (physical) body.

Subtle physical: belonging to the lowest of the immaterial planes of existence, that which resembles most closely the physical world in which we live, but goes beyond the range of the outward senses.

Superconscient: The plane of consciousness above the head that includes the higher mental planes, and from which the higher consciousness comes down into the body.

Supermind: the plane of consciousness on which the limits of mind (including the spiritual mind-planes from Higher Mind to Overmind) are entirely transcended; its nature is a knowledge of infinite unity expressing itself in an infinite multiplicity.

Supramental: belonging to the Supermind.

Tapasya: the concentration of the will to get the results of the sadhana* and to conquer the lower nature.

Transformation: radical change in the inner and outer nature in all its parts, brought about progressively in Integral Yoga by the action of forces belonging to higher and higher planes of consciousness up to Supermind.

Upanishad: any of a class of ancient Sanskrit texts regarded which form the theoretical basis of the Hindu religion.

Vital: pertaining to the life-force; the part of our nature that links the mental and the physical. Its essential function is enjoyment and possession; its energies are necessary for the fullness of our embodied existence, but can be the cause of many disturbances until they are purified and transformed by Yoga.

Vital mind: the part of the consciousness that gives mental form to vital movements such as impulses, desires and emotions.

Vital-physical: pertaining to the part of the life-force that is involved in the states and activities of the body (sometimes including the subtle body*).

Vital world: a supra-physical plane of existence governed by the vital principle.

Vivekananda: See: http://en.wikipedia.org/wiki/Swami_Vivekananda

Glossary

Yoga: literally, union; any of various methods of transcending the normal limits of human nature and entering into contact and union with a higher.